Clashing Views on Controversial

Issues in Sex and Gender

SECOND EDITION

Clashing Views on Controversial

Issues in Sex and Gender
SECOND EDITION

Selected, Edited, and with Introductions by

Elizabeth L. Paul
College of New Jersey

McGraw-Hill/Dushkin
A Division of The McGraw-Hill Companies

To the baby who gazed up at me adoringly
while I wrote this book

Photo Acknowledgment
Cover image: © 2002 by PhotoDisc, Inc.

Cover Art Acknowledgment
Charles Vitelli

Manufactured in the United States of America

Second Edition

123456789BAHBAH4321

Library of Congress Cataloging-in-Publication Data
Main entry under title:
Taking sides: clashing views on controversial issues in sex and gender/selected, edited, and with
introductions by Elizabeth L. Paul.—2nd ed.
Includes bibliographical references and index.
1. Sex (Psychology). 2. Sex differences. I. Paul, Elizabeth L., *comp.*
306.7
0-07-248925-1
ISSN: 1526-4548

Printed on Recycled Paper

Preface

Issues having to do with males and females, "maleness" and "femaleness," are omnipresent in Western culture and around the world. Our lives revolve around presumed distinctions between males' and females' attitudes, characteristics, emotions, behaviors, preferences, abilities, and responsibilities. We have clear definitions of what males and females can and should do differently from one another. In some cultures, there are third and fourth gender categories, complete with their own expectations and proscriptions. What has triggered such a deep gender divide? Is it rooted in our biology? Is it a cultural creation that gets reproduced through socialization practices and interpersonal interaction? What is the future of gender? Controversy abounds.

Taking Sides: Clashing Views on Controversial Issues in Sex and Gender is a tool for stimulating critical thought about males and females, maleness and femaleness, and beyond. Consideration of the complexity of sex and gender necessitates a multidisciplinary perspective. Thus, you will learn about definitions and views of sex and gender from such fields as sociology, ethnic studies, women's studies, men's studies, gay and lesbian studies, queer studies, gender studies, transgender studies, education, language, political science, global studies, religion, history, medicine, law, psychology, and biology. The multidisciplinarity of inquiry on sex and gender has created a rich, exciting, and emotionally and politically charged body of theory, research, and practice. The study of sex and gender is so dynamic that it is one of the most fast-paced areas of inquiry, characterized by great fervor and rapid growth. It is also one of the most contentious areas of thought, distinguished by deep theoretical and philosophical differences. Such division also marks public discourse on sex and gender.

This book contains 19 issues, organized into 6 parts, that are being hotly debated in contemporary scholarly and public discourse on sex and gender. They are phrased as yes/no questions so that two distinct perspectives are delineated and contrasted. Each issue is prefaced by an *issue introduction* containing background material contextualizing the dual positions. Additional perspectives are presented in a *postscript* following each issue to enrich and enliven debate and discussion. No issue is truly binary, adequately represented by only two points of view. Considering other perspectives will broaden your understanding of the complexity of each issue, enabling you to develop an informed ideology. The *suggestions for further reading* that appear in each issue postscript should help you find resources to continue your study of the subject. At the back of the book is a listing of all the *contributors to this volume,* which will give you information on the various writers whose views are debated here. Also, on the *On the Internet* page that accompanies each part opener, you will find Internet site addresses (URLs) that are relevant to the issues in that part. These Web sites should prove useful as starting points for further research.

You begin this quest with an existing personal gender ideology of which you may not even be aware. It serves as a filter through which you process information about males and females, maleness and femaleness. It draws your attention to some information and points of view and allows you to disregard other more dissonant perspectives. Your challenge is to probe your personal gender ideology (and intersecting ideologies such as ethnicity, sexual orientation, social class) so that you can open your mind to other perspectives and information and develop a more informed ideology. To do so takes courage and active thought. As you work through this book, note your reactions to different points and perspectives. Exchange reactions and relevant experiences with your peers. "Try on" different perspectives by trying to represent a view with which you initially disagree. Explore *suggestions for further reading* and Web sites provided for each part or issue. Challenge yourself to explore all angles so that your own theories or views become more reasoned and representative.

No matter what field of study, career path, and/or other personal choices you pursue, issues of sex and gender will be pervasive. Great sociohistorical change in sex and gender marked the twentieth century, catalyzing even greater momentum for the twenty-first century. The goal of this book is to help you develop an ideological toolchest that will enable you to intelligently and responsibly navigate the changing gender landscape. Collectively, you will chart the course of the future of gender.

Changes to this edition   There are four new issues in this edition: *Does the John/Joan Case Prove That Gender Identity Is Innate?* (Issue 2); *Is Gender the Most Critical Factor in the Recent Spate of School Shootings?* (Issue 12); *Is Domestic Violence Best Treated as a Gender Crime?* (Issue 13); and *Are Welfare Reforms Ineffective Because Welfare Mothers Are Irresponsible and Lazy?* (Issue 16). In Issue 5 (*Are Sex Differences in the Brain Primarily Responsible for Males' and Females' Differing Cognitive Abilities?*) the YES selection has been replaced with a more recent selection. In all, there are 9 new selections. Part openers, issue introductions, and issue postscripts have been revised as necessary.

A word to the instructor   An *Instructor's Manual With Test Questions* (multiple-choice and essay) is available through the publisher for the instructor using *Taking Sides* in the classroom. A general guidebook, *Using Taking Sides in the Classroom,* which discusses methods and techniques for integrating the pro-con approach into any classroom setting, is also available. An online version of *Using Taking Sides in the Classroom* and a corrrespondence service for *Taking Sides* adopters can be found at http://www.dushkin.com/usingts/.

Taking Sides: Clashing Views on Controversial Issues in Sex and Gender is only one title in the Taking Sides series. If you are interested in seeing the table of contents for any of the other titles, please visit the Taking Sides Web site at http://www.dushkin.com/takingsides/.

Acknowledgements   A rich network of colleagues supported the creation of this book; I gratefully acknowledge their contributions. Anne Law (Rider University), Mechthild Nagel (SUNY-Cortland), Jackie James (The Henry A. Murray Research Center, Radcliffe College), Erica Polakoff (Bloomfield College), Molly Dragiewicz (George Mason University), and the College of New Jersey colleagues Mark Kiselica, Melinda Roberts, MaryAnn Baenninger, Juda Bennett, Diane Kobrynowicz, Janet Gray, and Robin Truth Goodman were generous with their expertise, enthusiasm, and support. Karen Hartman and Melissa Hofmann of the Roscoe L. West Library at the College of New Jersey used their professionalism and creativity to provide valuable assistance. Kristen Pipes was a persistent and skilled library assistant. Ted Knight and the staff at McGraw-Hill/Dushkin have provided me with all the necessary expertise, support, and encouragement for preparing this book at warp speed! My deepest gratitude goes to my husband and colleague, William Ball, who is always most generous in supporting my work and family goals. He contributed his expertise in political argumentation to the creation of this book and offered insightful critical commentary on every written word. Also laudable is his deep commitment to being an equal partner with me in caring for and fostering the development of our family. To our daughters, Martha and Sophie, thank you for your love, pride, and promise. Because of you, a beautiful rainbow symbolizes my future vision of gender.

Elizabeth L. Paul
College of New Jersey

Contents In Brief

Contents

Demographer J. Richard Udry asserts that human gender patterns are
limited to the two categories of male and female by the sex-dimorphic biological processes applicable to all vertebrates. Anthropologist Will Roscoe
presents Native American berdache status as evidence of multiple genders, arguing that physical sex and gender are socially constructed.

Sex researcher Milton Diamond and psychiatrist H. Keith Sigmundson
argue that the John/Joan case provides proof that gender identity is innate. Associate professor of English Bernice L. Hausman examines the
narratives or stories told about the John/Joan case to reveal biases and
oversights about nonbiological contributions to John/Joan's experiences.

Psychoanalyst John B. McDevitt uses American Psychiatric Association diagnostic criteria in presenting the case of a gender identity disorder in a four-year-old boy. Katherine K. Wilson of the Gender Identity Center of Colorado, Inc. critically analyzes biases in the diagnosis of gender identity disorder, charging that the diagnostic criteria rely upon subjective assumptions about "normal" sex and gender and underestimate the effects of distress associated with societal prejudice.

Psychologist David M. Buss applies evolutionary theory to explain psychological differences between human males and females. Biologist Anne Fausto-Sterling questions Buss's theory and calls for the application of stricter standards to evolutionary accounts of human behavior.

Clinical neurologist Doreen Kimura states that early effects of sex hormones on brain organization establish differences between males' and females' cognitive abilities. Psychologists MaryAnn Baenninger and Nora Newcombe assert that social and environmental factors contribute greatly to sex-related differences in spatial and mathematical ability.

Author Philip Yancey maintains that men and women have different conversational styles. Psychologist Mary Crawford critically evaluates the assertion that men and women have different conversational styles, arguing that it is invalid and inflammatory.

Third-wave feminist and author Rebecca Walker describes her sexuality as free, pleasurable, and affirming. Author Athena Devlin recounts the devastating influences of a traditional sexual script on her sexuality.

PART 4   SEX, GENDER, AND YOUTH   205

Author Gail Vines argues that sex selection of unborn fetuses and efforts to "create" fetuses of a particular sex may have unforeseen consequences for parenting, societal gender relations, and the use and abuse of technology. In this editorial the editors of *Lancet* review acceptable reasons for sex selection, refuting arguments about societal dangers of such practices.

Sociologist Michael Kimmel observes that most of the perpetrators in recent school killings have been white boys. He argues that we must examine the social construction of white masculinity to better address such social problems. Clinical professor of psychiatry Alvin Poussaint describes youth violence as the result of festering anger and aggression fueled by family violence and violence portrayed in the media.

PART 5   ALL IN THE FAMILY   225

Lori Heise, codirector of the Center for Health and Gender Equity (CHANGE), Mary Ellsberg, senior associate at CHANGE, and Megan Gottemoeller, program associate at CHANGE, describe domestic violence as endemic to broader cultural issues, such as gender norms, expectations, and pressures, thereby arguing that it is only "treatable" through social change. A. E. Eyler, clinical associate professor of family medicine, and social worker Marian Cohen provide guidelines for treating domestic violence as an interpersonal problem in couple relationships.

Psychologist Sandra Lipsitz Bem describes the "feminist" child-rearing practices she and Daryl Bem used to raise their two children. Their underlying argument stems from gender schema theory, asserting that gender-neutral child-rearing practices can be effective in developing gender-aschematic thinking in children. Sociologists Denise A. Segura and Jennifer L. Pierce use sociologist Nancy Chodorow's psychoanalytic theory to understand the acquisition of heterosexual gender identity in Chicana/o families.

Author and artist Jennifer Diane Reitz describes her plight in becoming a postoperative transsexual woman. Her poignant story documents the role of sex and gender in her experience of transsexualism. Transgender scholars Richard Ekins and Dave King discuss the limitations of the medical categories of transvestism, transsexualism, and gender dysphoria and promote a process of blending gender and even of living "beyond gender" altogether.

Sherry Turkle, a professor in MIT's Program in Science, Technology, and Society, explores "virtual genderswapping" in Multi-User Domains (MUDs), showing that they allow individuals to try out new identities and potentially to redefine their many selves. Assistant professor of sociology Lori Kendall concludes from her experience on MUDs that gender stereotypes and expectations are even more constraining in cyberspace than in face-to-face socializing.

Introduction

Sex and Gender: Knowing Is Believing, but Is Believing Knowing?

Elizabeth L. Paul

Within any species of living organisms, there is variety. What are the primary ways in which individual organisms vary? In Western thought, a primary individual difference is sex. What do we "know" about the ways in which individuals differ by sex? Of course, an obvious response is that individuals are either male or female. In the human species, you are probably quite certain that all individuals are either male or female—we treat it as fact. What else do you *know* about human variation by sex? Are there other *facts* about human males and females? Perhaps you will state such facts as males' greater physical strength than females, males' taller stature than females, and females' unique capacity for childbearing. Make a list of what else you *know* about human variation by sex.

Most of us hold a vast network of knowledge about human variation by sex. Many of the claims stem from knowledge of the differential biology of males and females and extend to variation in human emotion, thought, and behavior. In fact, some individuals maintain that males and females are so different that they are from different planets! For most of us, this is an interconnected network of "givens" about the far-reaching effects of maleness and femaleness. In that this knowledge stems from what we consider to be an undeniable fact of human sex variation, we rarely question these claims and see them instead as essential truths or facts—unquestionable, unchangeable, and inevitable. The goal of this book is to guide your critical evaluation of this network of knowledge. What you may discover as you critically consider the controversial issues in this book is that many of the things we believe to be factually true and objectively provable about human sex variation are instead unsupported beliefs.

How do we know that a piece of information is a fact rather than a belief? Do we base our classification on evidence? What kind of evidence do we require? What constitutes enough evidence to classify a claim as a fact rather than a belief? Starting with what we *know* to be the most basic fact about human variation by sex, that humans are either male or female, how do you know that? Did someone tell you (e.g., a parent, a teacher)? Did you observe differences between yourself and others or among others? How did this information or observation get generalized from a few individuals to all humans? Is this kind of generalization warrantable, based on human variation? Are there any exceptions (i.e., individuals that do not fit neatly into the categories of male or female)? Would such exceptions lead you to question this *fact* of sex as male or female? For something to be fact, must it be universally true of all individuals within a given species? Have you ever thought critically about this before?

What is the difference (if any) between facts and beliefs? Do we treat knowledge differently if we classify it as fact versus belief or opinion? Are facts more important to us than beliefs? Do we question the veracity of facts as much as that of beliefs? Why not? What are the ramifications of not submitting facts to critical questioning? Rethink the facts you listed about human variation by sex. How do you know these are facts? What is your evidence? Does your evidence indisputably support the claim as fact? Do you detect defensiveness about or resistance to critically questioning facts? Why?

Knowledge and Beliefs in the Study of Sex and Gender

For decades, in public discourse and in numerous academic disciplines, there has been widespread debate and discussion of the extent of human variation by sex. In addition, there is extensive consideration of the cultural meaning and significance attached to maleness and femaleness. The terms *sex* and *gender* are used to refer to these various phenomena. Although sex and gender are commonly thought to be synonyms, many scholars have assigned different meanings to these terms. Sex is often used to refer to the biological distinction between males and females. Gender refers to the social and cultural meaning attached to notions of maleness and femaleness. Depending on one's theory of how sex and gender are related, there are varying degrees of overlap or interconnection between these two terms.

Sex and gender are complex concepts. They are both comprised of many elements and phenomena. Biological features of sex include genetic factors of male and female chromosomes, hormones and the endocrine system, internal and external sexual and reproductive organs (appearance and functionality), and central nervous system sex differentiation. The assumption or the defined norm is that there is consistency among these different biological factors, differentiating individuals into males and females.

The concept of gender has been construed in many ways, spawning a highly complex field of inquiry. Some scholars perceive gender as an attribute of individuals or something we "have." Others see gender as something we "do" or perform; gender is seen as a product of interpersonal interaction. Gender has also been construed as a mode of social organization, structuring status and power dynamics in cultural institutions. Some see gender as universal; others believe gender to be historically—and culturally—specific. The latter perspective has yielded a proliferation of investigations into how, why, when, where, and for whom gender "works."

Gender has been employed in theory and research in various ways and toward various goals. The study of gender has been used to assess the validity of claims of human sex differences. It has also been used to challenge assertions of biological roots of gendered behavior by testing alternate causal theories (e.g., environmental, learning, cognitive theories). Some studies of gender aim to analyze the social organization of male/female relations, elucidating gendered power dynamics and patterns of dominance and subordination. Gender studies have also been used to show how burdens and benefits are inequitably distributed among males and females in society. Other scholars have used conceptions of gender to explain the structure of the human psyche, individuals' sense of self, identity, and aspiration.

How are elements of gender produced? Biological essentialists believe that biological sex differences directly lead to behavioral, cognitive, and emotional differences (i.e., gender affects) between males and females. In other words, there are *essential* differences between males and females that stem from biology and pervade human psychology and sociality. Evolutionary theorists believe that ancestral responses to environmental challenges created physiological differences between males and females that underlie contemporary behavioral differences. In contrast, social constructionists believe gender to be a social or cultural creation. Infants and children are socialized and disciplined so as to develop sex-appropriate gender attributes and skills. As individuals mature, they develop a gender identity or a sense of self as male or female. They internalize the dominant cultural gender ideology, develop expectations for self and other, and assume sex-congruent gender roles, behaving in gender-appropriate ways. Symbolic interactionists point to the power of pervasive cultural gender symbolism in the production and reproduction of gender in cultures. They show how gender metaphors are assigned to cultural artifacts and how language structures gender meanings and dynamics creating to a dominant cultural meaning system. Standpoint theorists show us how our position in the social hierarchy impacts our perspective on and involvement in cultural gender dynamics.

As you can see from this brief review of many of the ways in which gender has been construed and studied, there are differences and even contradictions among the various perspectives and approaches. Some individuals champion gender as stimulating complementarity and interdependence among humans; others see gender as a powerful source of segregation and exclusion. Some scholars emphasize differences between males and females; others allow for greater individual variation that crosses sex and gender boundaries or they even emphasize similarity between males and females. Some people think of gender as invariant and fixed; others think of gender as malleable and flexible. Some scholars see gender as politically irrelevant; others see gender as the root of all social and political inequities. Some view "gender-inappropriate" behavior with disdain and fear, labeling it problematic and pathological and in need of correction; others see gender variance as natural and cause for celebration. Some individuals believe "traditional" differentiated sex roles should be preserved; others believe that these conventional notions of gender should be redefined or even transcended. Some individuals view gender processes and dynamics as personally relevant; others have little conception of the role of gender in their lived experience. How do we deal with this controversy? How can we evaluate and weigh different assertions and arguments?

Tools for Argument Analysis

Each pair of selections in this volume present opposing arguments about sex and gender. How do you decide which argument is "right" or, at least, which argument is better? Argument analysis is a field with many approaches and standards. Here a few major components and criteria are briefly presented to help you in making judgments about the quality of the arguments advanced in the book.

To assess an argument's quality it is helpful to break it down into seven components, including its *claim, definitions, statements of fact, statements of value, language and reasoning, use of authority,* and *audience.* However, first we must touch on the issue of *explicit versus implicit elements* within an argument. Real-world arguments contain many implicit (unstated) elements. For example, they may use unstated definitions of key terms or rely on value judgments that are not made clear within the body of the argument itself. Occasionally these elements are left out because the author wants to hide the weaknesses of her or his argument by omitting them. However it is probably more often the case that they are omitted because the author assumes the audience for their work knows about the missing elements and already accepts them as true. The job of the argument analyst begins with identifying implicit elements in an argument and making them explicit. Since we usually do not have direct access to the argument's author, making implicit elements explicit requires a good deal of interpretation on our part. However, few arguments would stand up to analysis for long if we did not try our best to fill in the implicit content. Specific examples of making implicit elements explicit are provided in what follows.

Claim

The first component one should look for in an argument is its claim. What, specifically, are the authors trying to convince us of? The notion of a claim in an argument is essentially the same as that of a thesis in a term paper. In almost all cases it is possible to identify a single overarching claim that the authors are trying to get their audience to accept. For example, in Issue 15, David Popenoe claims that mothers and fathers should play different roles in childrearing. Once the claim of an argument is identified, the analyst can begin to look for and evaluate supporting components. If no claim can be identified, then we do not have an argument that is well formed enough to evaluate fairly.

Definitions

At first thought, an argument's definitions might not seem a very interesting target for analysis. However, definitions are often highly controversial, implicit, and suspect in terms of their quality. This is especially the case in the study of sex and gender. How are the key terms in an argument's claim and supporting reasons defined, if at all? Does the author rely on dictionary definitions, stipulative definitions (offering an original definition of the term), definition by negation (saying what the term does not mean), or definition by example?

Dictionary definitions are relatively uncontroversial but rare and of limited application. Stipulative definitions are conveniently explicit but often the subject of controversy. Other types of definitions can be both implicit and not widely accepted. Once you have identified definitions of the key terms in an argument's claim and supporting reasons, ask yourself if you find these definitions to be acceptable. Then ask if the argument's opponent is using these same definitions or is advocating a different set. Opposing arguments cannot be resolved on their merits until the two sides agree on key definitions. Indeed many long-term debates in public policy never seem to get resolved because the two sides define the underlying problem in very different ways.

Statements of Fact

Claims have two fundamentally different types of supporting reasons. The first type is statements of fact. A fact is a description of something that we can presumably verify to be true. Thus the first question to be answered about an argument's factual statements is how do we know they are true? Authors may report original empirical research of their own. With an argument that is reporting on original research, the best means of checking the truth of their facts would be to repeat, or replicate, their research. This is almost never realistically possible, so we then must rely on an assessment of the methods they used, either our own assessment or that of an authority we trust. Authors may be relying on facts that they did not discover on their own, but instead obtained from some authoritative source.

Aside from the question of the truth of facts is the question of their sufficiency. Authors may offer a few facts to support their claim or many. They may offer individual cases or very broad factual generalizations. How many facts are enough? Since most arguments are evaluated in the context of their opponents, it is tempting to tally up the factual statements of both arguments and declare the one with the most facts the winner. This is seldom adequate, although an argument with a wealth of well-substantiated factual statements in support of its claim is certainly preferable to one with few statements of fact that are of questionable quality. In persuasive arguments it is very common to see many anecdotes and examples of individual cases. These are used to encourage the audience to identify with the subject of the cases. However, in analyzing these arguments we must always ask if an individual case really represents a systematic trend. In other words, do the facts offered generalize to the whole or are they just persuasive but isolated exceptions? On the other hand, it is also common to see the use of statistics to identify general characteristics of a population. The analyst should always ask if these statistics were collected in a scientific manner and without bias, if they really show significant distinct characteristics, and how much variation there is around the central characteristics identified.

A final question about statements of fact concerns their relevancy. We sometimes discover factual statements in an argument that may be true, and even interesting reading, but that just don't have anything to do with the claim being advanced. Be sure that the forest is not missed for the trees in evaluating statements of fact—in other words, that verifying and tallying of factual statements does not preempt the question of how well an author supports the primary claim.

Statements of Value

The philosopher David Hume is famous for his observation that a series of factual statements (that something "is" the case) will never lead to the conclusion that something "ought" to be done. The missing component necessary to move from "is" to "ought," to move from statements of fact to accepting an argument's claim, are statements of value. Statements of value declare something to be right or wrong, good or bad, desirable or undesirable, beautiful or ugly. For example, "It is wrong for boys to play with dolls."

Although many people behave as if debates can be resolved by proving one side or the other's factual statements to be true, statements of value are just as critical to the quality of an argument as are statements of fact. Moreover, because value statements have their roots in moral and religious beliefs, we tend to shy away from analyzing them too deeply in public discourse. Instead, people tend to be *absolutist,* rejecting outright values that they do not share, or *relativist,* declaring that all values are equally valid. As a result, statements of value are not as widely studied in argument analysis and standards of evaluation are not as well developed for them as for factual statements.

At the very least, the argument analyst can expect the value statements of an argument to be part of what has been referred to as a "rational ideology." A rational ideology is one in which value statements are *cogent* and *coherent* parts of a *justifiable* system of beliefs. A cogent value statement is one that is relevant and clear. Coherent value statements fit together; they are consistent with one another and help support an argument's claim. A system of beliefs is justifiable if its advocate can provide supporting reasons (both facts and values) for holding beliefs. A morality that makes value judgments but refuses to offer reasons for these judgments would strike us as neither very rational nor very persuasive. Although we rarely have the opportunity to engage in a debate with authors to test their ability to justify their value statements, we can expect an argument's value statements to be explicit, cogent, coherent, and supported by additional statements of fact and value as justification. As in the case of definitions, it is also fruitful to compare the value statements of one argument with those of the opposing view to see how much the authors agree or disagree in the (usually) implicit ideology that lies behind their value statements.

Language and Reasoning

There are a vast number of specific issues in the use of language and reasoning within arguments. Any introductory book on rhetoric or argumentative logic will provide a discussion of these issues. Here just a sample of the most common ones will be touched on. The analyst gives less weight to arguments that use language that is overly emotional. Emotional language relies on connotation (word meanings aside from formal definition), bias or slanting in word choice, exaggeration, slogan, and cliché. Emotional language is sometimes appropriate when describing personal experience but it is not persuasive when used to support a general claim about what should be believed or done in society.

The analysis of reasoning has to do with the logical structure of an argument's components and usually focuses on the search for logical fallacies (errors in logic). A common fallacy has already been discussed under statements of fact: hasty generalization. In hasty generalizations claims are made without a sufficient amount of factual evidence to support them. When authors argue that one event followed another and this proves the first event caused the second, they are committing the *post hoc* fallacy (it may just be a coincidence that the events happened in that order). Two fallacies often spotted in arguments directed at opponents are *ad hominem* and straw man. The first involves attacking the person advocating the opposing view, which is generally irrelevant to the quality of their statements. The second is unfairly describing an opponent's argument in an overly simplified way that is easy to defeat. Fallacies directed at the argument's audience include false dilemma, slippery slope, and *ad populum*. Authors commit the fallacy of false dilemma when they argue that only two alternatives exist when, in fact, there are more than two. Slippery slope is an unsupportable prediction that if a small first step is taken it will inevitably lead to more change. An appeal to public opinion to support a claim is an *ad populum* argument if there is reason to believe that the public is prejudiced or plain wrong in its views, or if what the public believes is simply not relevant to the issue. In general, the argument analyst must not only look at the individual statements of an argument but must also ask how well they are put together in an argument that is logical and not overly emotional.

Use of Authority

The issue of authority is relevant in argument analysis in two places. The first has to do with the authority of the argument's author. Analysts should use whatever information they can gather to assess the expertise and possible biases of authors. Are authors reporting on an issue that they have only recently begun to study, or have they studied the issue area in considerable depth? Do they occupy a professional position that indicates recognition by others as authorities in the field? Do you have reason to believe that their work is objective and not subject to systematic biases because of who pays for or publishes their work? Be careful not to commit *ad hominem* on this one yourself. The brief biographies of contributors to this volume give you a bit of information about the authors of the arguments that follow.

The second place authority enters into analysis is the citation of authorities within the body of the argument itself. To a greater or lesser degree, all arguments rely on citation of outside authorities to support their statements. We should ask the same questions of these authorities as we ask of authors. In general, we want authorities that are widely accepted as experts and that do not have systematic biases. Even if we do not have the time or resources to check out the authorities cited in an argument, it is reasonable to expect that an argument makes very clear whom it is citing as an authority.

Audience

The final component of argument analysis is consideration of an argument's intended audience. Clues to the intended audience can be found in the type of publication or forum where the argument is presented, in the professional standing of its author, and in the type of language that the author uses in the argument itself. Knowledge of audience is critical in evaluating an argument fairly. Authors writing an argument for an audience that shares their core values and general knowledge of the subject tend to leave definitions and statements implicit and use language that is highly technical, dense, and symbolic. This applies equally well to scientists writing for a journal in their field and politicians addressing their supporters. Authors writing for an audience that is very different from them tend to make the various components of their arguments much more explicit. However if an author believes the audience disagrees with them on, for example, an important value statement, they tend to make statements that are both explicit and yet are still very general or ambiguous (this is a skill that is highly developed in politicians). It is difficult to make a fair judgment across these two basic types of author-audience relationships, since the former requires much more interpretation by the evaluator than the latter.

Analyzing arguments by evaluating their quality in terms of the seven components listed above is by no means guaranteed to give you a clear answer as to which argument is better for several reasons. The relevant criteria applicable to each component are neither completely articulated nor without controversy themselves. In the process of making implicit elements explicit, analysts introduce their own subjectivity into the process. It should also be clear by this point that argument analysis is a very open-ended process—checking the truth of statements of fact, the justifiability of statements of values, the qualifications of authorities—could go on indefinitely. Thus the logic of argument analysis is underdetermined—following each step exactly is still no guarantee of a correct conclusion. However, if you apply the analytical techniques outlined above to the essays in this volume you will quickly spot implicit definitions, hasty generalizations, unsupported value statements, and questionable authorities as well as examples of well-crafted, logical, and persuasive argumentation. You will be in a much stronger position to defend *your* views about the arguments you find in this book.

Issues in This Volume

The critical examination of sex and gender in this text is segmented into six parts. In Part I, fundamental assumptions about sex and gender are considered, revealing that "simple" definitions of sex as male or female and gender as directly derivative from biology are shortsighted. Moreover, debate over these fundamental assumptions has yielded some of the most contentious controversy in this field. In Part II, the "difference model," the primary paradigm for conceptualizing and studying sex and gender is critically analyzed. Sex and gender are usually construed as binary oppositions: male versus female, masculine versus feminine. Thus, a primary way in which sex and gender are studied is the comparison of groups of males and females (i.e., sex comparison or sex difference). In this section, you will grapple with underlying theoretical rationales for excavating such differences (including biological, evolutionary, and learning theories), and you will critically evaluate the difference model in terms of methodology, social meaning and significance, and political impact. Is the search for differences between males and females a useful approach to elucidating gender or is it meaningless and even politically dangerous?

In Part III, gender as a cultural creation is examined in the context of three issues. In some issues, you are challenged to confront American cultural dictates about gender. How do cultural definitions of gender limit opportunity for individuals of a certain sex? Are these limitations warranted? What is the function of these limitations? Some issues examine how American cultural gender prescriptions intersect and interact with other cultural dimensions of difference (e.g., sexual orientation, race). In one issue, a multicultural examination of gender challenges you to be sensitive to your own cultural gender ideology and to think about how it informs and should inform your evaluation of gender in other cultures.

Parts IV and V examine gender in a critical developmental domain—childhood, and a critical social domain—family, respectively. Gender is influential before conception, in making decisions to carry a fetus to term, and in the life expectancy of male and female children. Sex selection is a common practice in many cultures, including Western cultures. Why is higher value placed on male versus female offspring? From some theoretical perspectives, gender begins with early socialization and intensifies with further development. National concern has intensified recently about boys' vulnerability to distress and social problems. Our response to these important social issues depends in large part upon our construal of the role of gender in these behaviors and problems.

One of the most gendered social institutions is the family. Traditional Western family ideology is heterosexist (regarding the heterosexual union as the only acceptable family context) and sexist (prescribing different roles for husbands and wives). In Part V these fundamental values and assumptions are examined. What is the role of power differentials between men and women and gendered relational dynamics in domestic violence? Gender ideology also riddles the construction of parenthood. Does gender influence men's and women's capacities for and approaches to parenting? What are the ramifications of this question for poor people, especially women? How does socioeconomic class intersect with gender? As reproductive technologies advance and family structures proliferate, how are traditional family gender ideologies challenged?

What is the future of gender? In Part VI, possibilities for redefining and even transcending gender are examined. Must the socialization of children result in gendered thoughts, feelings, and behaviors? Must definitions of sexuality and sexual identity be limited to fixed and linked notions of sex and gender? Must our experiences be limited by our identity as a male or as a female? If gender can be redefined or even transcended, by what mechanisms could this occur?

Conclusion

Equipped with your new toolchest complete with tools for analyzing arguments, begin your exploration of knowledge and belief in the study of sex and gender. Remain open to considering and reconsidering beliefs and knowledge in ways that you never imagined. Your "gender quest" begins now; where you will end up, no one knows!

Intersex Society of North America

The Intersex Society of North America (ISNA) is a peer support, education, and advocacy group for intersexuals. This Web site includes annotated bibliographies on intersexuality, scholarly and popular press resources on intersexuality, and numerous links to related sites.

http://www.isna.org

The Zuni Man-Woman

The Zuni Man-Woman page includes discussion of and excerpts from Will Roscoe's book entitled *The Zuni Man-Woman—In Life Where There Are Only Differences, "Good"/"Bad" Are Merely Ideas* (University of New Mexico Press, 1991). This book describes the Zuni berdache.

http://www.ratical.org/many_worlds/
onlyDifferent.html

The True Story of John/Joan

This Info-Circumcision Web site by the Circumcision Information Resource Centre includes John Colapinto's original article entitled, "The True Story of John/Joan," *Rolling Stone* (December 11, 1997). This article reveals details of the John/Joan case.

http://www.infocirc.org/rollston.htm

John Colapinto on GenderTalk Web Radio

This GenderTalk Web Radio site allows visitors to listen to John Colapinto, author of *As Nature Made Him: The Boy Who Was Raised as a Girl* (HarperTrade, 2001), discuss the John/Joan case.

http://www.gendertalk.com/real/gt247.shtml

The Gender Identity Center of Colorado, Inc.

This educational Web site by The Gender Identity Center of Colorado, Inc., is about gender identity nontraditionality. It includes an interesting discussion of gender dysphoria and additional writings by Katherine K. Wilson.

http://www.transgender.org/gic/

PART 1

Definitions and Boundaries:
A Moving Target

*W*hat is sex? What is gender? What is the association between sex and gender? What determines sex? What determines gender? These are controversial questions with a diversity of answers. In fact, the vast array of contradictory "answers" loosens the boundaries of these concepts to the point of losing any sense of certain definition. Definitions often reveal important theoretical standpoints underlying much of the controversy in the study of sex and gender. Moreover, they raise the question of cultural relativity of definitions of sex and gender. Can these concepts be objectively defined or is the most objective and scientific definition still a product of culture? This section will explore the limits and limitlessness of definitions and boundaries of sex and gender within biology, psyche, and culture.

- Are Humans Naturally Either Male or Female?

- Does the John/Joan Case Prove That Gender Identity Is Innate?

- Is Gender Variation a Psychological Illness?

ISSUE 1

Are Humans Naturally
Either Male or Female?

YES: J. Richard Udry, from "The Nature of Gender," *Demography* (November 1994)

NO: Will Roscoe, from "How to Become a Berdache: Toward a Unified Analysis of Gender Diversity," in Gilbert Herdt, ed., *Third Sex, Third Gender: Beyond Sexual Dimorphism in Culture and History* (Zone Books, 1994)

ISSUE SUMMARY

YES: Demographer J. Richard Udry asserts that human gender patterns are limited to the two categories of male and female by the sex-dimorphic biological processes applicable to all vertebrates.

NO: Anthropologist Will Roscoe presents Native American berdache status as evidence of multiple genders, arguing that physical sex and gender are socially constructed.

Sex is often defined as an absolute biological classification as male or female. Biological theories of sex differentiation have promoted the importance of hormones in utero and during puberty in creating primary and secondary sex characteristics. Given ethical constraints, the research base for these claims is animal research. J. Richard Udry argues that the action of hormones on sex dimorphism (the process of sex differentiation) is characteristic of all vertebrates. Thus, results from animal research are extrapolated to understand the effects of sex dimorphism on human neural systems, brains, and behavior. While some biological essentialists might view sex and gender as synonymous, many social scientists differentiate gender as the constellation of behaviors, attitudes, and feelings socially constructed on the basis of cultural associations of male and female.

Sex defined as a natural dichotomy, rooted in biology and evolution, is typically unquestioned and viewed as fixed. Sex is the purview of science and thus its study is viewed as objective and free from bias. In contrast, gender as a human social invention and social scientific construct is viewed as "slippery" or "fuzzy," and its study is perceived as marked by cultural bias.

Critics have begun to question the immunity of biological constructs from cultural analysis, urging that we must recognize that the practice of science occurs within a sociopolitical context. Therefore, biological notions of sex are cultural, social, and political creations.

The dominant Western definition of sex delineates two "normal" categories: male and female. Notions of gender follow suit, typically contrasting masculine and feminine behavior patterns. Is this dichotomy universal? Anthropologists have uncovered compelling evidence that dichotomous definitions of sex are not universal, arguing instead that many cultures have multiple genders. They argue that when looking for binaries, we observe a dichotomous reality. But what remains unseen—gender diversity—is also an important reality. Will Roscoe argues that gender diversity is a natural, worldwide phenomenon.

Some revisionists have begun to "reinvent sex" by replacing dichotomous conceptions of sex with arrays reflecting the complexities of sexual variability naturally characteristic of humans. For example, concepts such as "gender-crossing" have been coined. The problem with such concepts is that they still rely on the fixed binary of male/female, and they problematize deviations. In contrast, construing diversity as multiple genders enables the transcendence of this binary and notions of deviance associated with nonmale and nonfemale genders.

In the following selections, a biological theory of sexual dimorphism is contrasted with an anthropological account of multiple genders. The authors' definitions of sex and gender reflect important theoretical distinctions. Udry defines gender as the relationship between biological sex and behavior. In place of gender, he explains that biologists use the term *sex dimorphism* to refer to sex-differentiated behavior determined by hormones characteristic of all vertebrates. Roscoe views gender as primarily determined by social and cultural factors and minimally associated with physical sex characteristics. Physical sex characteristics are viewed as fluid and unfixed and cannot in isolation establish gender; therefore, they attain meaning only through cultural interpretation. As you read these selections, consider the implications of each theoretical position for social change.

J. Richard Udry

 **YES**

The Nature of Gender

The Primate Gender Theory

Let us take a closer look at a primate model of sex-dimorphic behavior and its possible application to humans. With this theory I can explain why males and females behave differently, why these differences have cross-cultural generality, why some males are more masculine than others, and why some females are more feminine than others. I cannot explain secular change; by agreement we stipulate that secular change is to be explained by social science theories alone. The primate model can explain only variance in a cohort. Our theory says that some particular behaviors are sensitive to hormonal influence, and others are not. It is not a historical accident or a random outcome that some behaviors are gendered, and others are not. We know which behaviors to examine for the hormone effects: gendered behaviors.

By 1970 a rather clear picture of the hormonal foundation for sex-dimorphic behavior had already been worked out for primates and other mammals (Goy 1970). For primates, the process operates in two stages. The first stage takes place in mid-pregnancy: male fetuses' testicles begin producing large amounts of testosterone early in the second trimester. This not only masculinizes their genitalia, but also masculinizes their brains by affecting the neural structure. By the third trimester, males have a different brain structure from females. This difference in brain structures predisposes males and females to different behavior, given the same environmental stimulus. Females receive very little testosterone fetally; what they receive comes from their mothers' blood, passing through the placenta. In the absence of testosterone, nature makes female genitalia and a female brain. Because the effects of the fetal testosterone reorganize the brain permanently, these are called organizational effects.

The second phase is the development at puberty of further anatomical sex dimorphism, caused by the sex hormones of adulthood. These adult hormones not only cause anatomical changes but also act on the neural structures laid down during the prenatal period to produce adult sex-dimorphic behavior. The degree to which the adult hormones affect sex-dimorphic behavior is contingent on the degree of prenatal exposure to androgens (or male hormones),

From J. Richard Udry, "The Nature of Gender," *Demography*, vol. 31, no. 4 (November 1994), pp. 568-573. Copyright © 1994 by The Population Association of America. Reprinted by permission of the publisher and the author. Notes omitted.

specifically to testosterone. The primary adult sex hormones of interest are also androgens—testosterone and androstenedione.

Applying Primate Models to Humans

A body of research on humans tests separate pieces of this theory; most of this work concerns clinical syndromes of hormonal anomaly. To greatly simplify this literature, it shows the following:

1. Human females exposed fetally to abnormally high levels of androgens show distinctly masculinized behavior beginning in childhood and extending through adolescence into adulthood (Ehrhardt and Meyer-Bahlburg 1981; Reinisch et al. 1991).
2. Girls who, because of a genetic anomaly, lack all sex hormones (even female sex hormones) grow up to be unusually feminine (Money and Ehrhardt 1972).
3. Females exposed as fetuses to physician-administered androgenic hormones for the mother's therapy show masculinized behavior in childhood, even though they show no masculinization of anatomy (Reinisch 1977).
4. Women with high adult androgen levels show masculine-skewed behavior, as compared to women with low androgen levels (Purifoy and Koopmans 1979).

My Study

I want to describe a project I conducted (with NICHD [National Institute of Child Health and Human Development] support), applying the primate hormonal model to predict within-sex patterns of gendered behavior among women.

To test this theory, I needed a sample of adult women for whom I had multiple measures of prenatal hormone exposure, a socialization history in childhood and adolescence, a measure of adult hormone levels, and measures of adult gendered behavior.... In the early 1960s, prenatal patients at Kaiser Plan facilities were recruited into the study. Each woman provided blood samples during each trimester of pregnancy. These samples were stored, and later were made available to researchers. For those giving birth from 1960 through 1963, the children and mothers were followed up with measurement and interviews at children's ages 5, 9–11, and 15–17....

We reinterviewed about 350 female offspring when they were 27 to 30 years old. From 250 we took blood samples during a controlled period of their menstrual cycles and at a controlled time of day. During this interview, the women completed a self-administered questionnaire in which we obtained measures of their adult gendered behavior. This procedure gave us all the required elements of the needed research design.

Measurement of Gendered Behavior

We measured many different gendered behaviors on our respondents; we tried to tap various domains of life and behavior manifestations. Our measurement technique was to identify a gendered behavior, identify the direction of difference between males and females, and call feminine high. Table 1 lists the measures of gendered behavior we obtained. . . .

Table 1

Gendered Behavior Components

Ever married to a man

Number of live births

Index of Sex Role Orientation

Importance of career

Importance of children

Domestic division of labor

Sex-typed activities scale

Importance of marriage

Feminine appearance factor

Strong Vocational Interest Inventory

Likes baby care

Proportion female in current occupation

Featherman socioeconomic index

Proportion female in work unit

Bem Sex Role Inventory, feminine score

Bem Sex Role Inventory, masculine score

Adjective Check List

Personality Research Form, masculine score

Personality Research Form, feminine score

We have 19 measures of gendered behavior. . . . All gender components load on a common superfactor. . . . This finding is important, because it says that there is some overall consistency in the way individual behavior is gendered.

Results of My Study

. . . [F]indings are highly consistent with what we would expect from the theoretical foundations we started with. . . . We found gendered behavior correlations only to second-trimester androgens, not to first- and third-trimester androgens, just as predicted by the theory. . . . [W]e were able to confirm several very specific hypotheses concerning the specific hormones involved prenatally, the trimester of effects of prenatal hormones, the specific hormones involved in adulthood, and the interaction of adult with prenatal hormones. . . . We measured some other, hypothetically irrelevant hormones (such as estrogen) and found them to be irrelevant. . . .

Implications of Biological Gender Theory

To see what the theory means for social demographers and other social scientists, we invoke the corollary proposition: Those processes which affect within-sex variance in gendered behaviors are the same processes as cause between-sex differences. With increasing confidence we can now say that individual women differ in their biological propensity to sex-typed behavior. We can also infer that males and females differ from one another in their average biological propensity to the same behaviors. . . .

Once these propositions are admitted, social science gender theories are in big trouble. Gender has biological foundations. We have become so immersed in our own social science theories of gender that we haven't thought seriously about confronting alternative theories. The closest we come to confrontation is to say that it is impossible for a behavior to have biological foundations while experiencing secular change at the same time. Most demographers are accustomed to thinking that the variables which predict individual variance also predict secular change. No such logical deduction can be made, however. . . .

What does an admission of a biological basis for individual variance in gendered behavior *not* mean? It does not mean that social forces do not also contribute to individual variance. Social scientists, of all people, often think that if certain behaviors have biological foundations, then those behaviors are foreordained, and there is nothing that society can do about influencing them. . . .

Lay society has always taken it for granted that much undesirable behavior has biological foundations, but society has never believed that there was nothing to be done about it. The whole force of social institutions is designed to "trump" these "biological instincts." Parents have always believed that "natural instincts" produced adolescent sexual behavior, but they never accepted its inevitability. Likewise, laymen have always believed that behavior differences in the sexes were part of the natural order of things.

So now, given a sound understanding of the way in which both biological and social forces affect variance in gender, and given that only social forces may affect secular change in gender, we can ask about the fit between social forces and biological propensities.

When social scientists still believed in human nature, a hot topic was the fit between human nature and social structure. Our hypothetical gender structures are a way of talking about that fit. If our biosocial model is correct, then there is a human nature, and it is gendered. The permissive society allows a perfect fit to human nature. The traditional society provides a poor fit: it starts with a biological base and constrains humans to fit it. The unisex society starts with an ideology and constrains humans to fit it.

Let me be clear about my views. The future of gender in our society can, should, and will be determined by ideology. If we believe that one type of social structure is evil and another is good, then we must try to achieve the good one. On the other hand, if our theory of gender is not correct, then we will not know how to achieve our goals.

I don't know how far society can differ from nature without encountering difficult problems of social control, but I never said that the goal of society was to make people comfortable. My goal is not to create happiness, but to fulfill our most worthy ideals for humanity. Human dignity may be achieved at the price of happiness. I emphasize that society has never hesitated to encourage behavior it thought unnatural (for example, celibacy), even at the cost of making people miserable. We have not always been happy with our success in controlling what we considered biologically natural but bad, but we have always considered the effort worthwhile, even if it was only partially successful.

Two general types of implications can be drawn from my propositions. The first is for programs of social change; the second, for demographic and social science research on gender.

First, in regard to programs of social change, we can identify two alternative agendas. First, society should provide gender-neutral opportunity structures. Naturally occurring variation in gender predispositions will determine how people take advantage of these opportunities. This is the permissive society that encourages the unfettered flowering of natural endowments and propensities. The second alternative is the degendering of society (Bem 1994). Those in favor of such degendering assume that gender-neutral opportunity structures would degender society, but degendered socialization is impossible because males and females respond differently to the same socialization. Gender-neutral opportunity structures will produce gendered responses and therefore gendered societies. Degendering society will require compensatory gendered socialization and compensatory gendered opportunity structures.

The second type of implications from my propositions affects research. Demographers and social scientists continue to ascribe all gender findings to gendered socialization and gendered opportunity structures. Although this might be attributed to their desire to be politically correct, such attribution is an injustice to social scientists. They merely have an inadequate theory.

With an improved theory, the demographer and social scientist can see gender in new ways.

First, the existence of gendered social structure is not evidence for gendered behavior norms.

Second, gender norms may be consequences, not causes, of sex differences.

Third, the existence of gendered social structure is not evidence of sex discrimination.

Fourth, parental socialization may bear little responsibility for differences in gendered behavior.

Fifth, if demographers and social scientists don't want to tangle with biological predispositions in their models, they can focus on explaining social change and macrocomparative studies.

Now, I should add the warnings. Work on the biology of gender and how it can be integrated with the demography and social science of gender has just begun. My work is only another step. It needs to be replicated; it needs to be remodeled and tested on males; other implications need to be examined. Demographers are not the most likely people to carry out this work. The empirical support or modification will accumulate only gradually. As we examine the issues further, they will always turn out to be more complicated than our simple models. Even so, we should not be surprised that our own human pattern of gender shares fundamental causes with the sex dimorphism of our animal relatives. The interesting questions will turn out to be not *whether,* but *how much,* and *in what ways.* There is nothing embarrassing about being a primate.

References

Bem, S. L. 1987. "Androgyny and Gender Schema Theory: A Conceptual and Empirical Integration." Pp. 179–226 in *Nebraska Symposium on Motivation: Psychology and Gender,* edited by R. A. Nienstbier and T. B. Donderroger. Lincoln: University of Nebraska Press.

———. 1994. *The Lenses of Gender: Transforming the Debate on Sexual Inequality.* New Haven: Yale University Press.

Ehrhardt, A. A. and H. F. L. Meyer-Bahlburg. 1981. "Effects of Prenatal Sex Hormones on Gender-Related Behavior." *Science* 211 (4488): 1312–18.

Goy, R. W. 1970. "Experimental Control of Psychosexuality." *Philosophical Transactions of the Royal Society of London* 259 (828): 149–62.

Money, J. and A. A. Ehrhardt. 1972. *Man and Woman, Boy and Girl: The Differentiation and Dimorphism of Gender Identity from Conception to Maturity.* Baltimore: Johns Hopkins University Press.

Purifoy, F. E. and L. H. Koopmans. 1979. "Androstenedione, Testosterone, and Free Testosterone Concentrations in Women of Various Occupations." *Social Biology* 26 (3): 179–88.

Reinisch, J. M. 1977. "Prenatal Exposure of Human Foetuses to Synthetic Progestin and Oestrogen Affects Personality." *Nature* 266 (5602): 561–62.

Reinisch, J. M., N. Ziemba-Davis, and S. A. Sanders. 1991. "Hormonal Contributions to Sexually Dimorphic Behavioral Development in Humans." *Psychoneuroendocrinology* 16 (1–3): 213–78.

Will Roscoe

← **NO**

How to Become a Berdache: Toward a Unified Analysis of Gender Diversity

What has been written about berdaches reflects more the influence of existing Western discourses on gender [and] sexuality... than what observers actually witnessed.

Typically described, in the words of Matilda Stevenson, as men who "adopt woman's dress and do woman's work," male berdaches have been documented in nearly 150 North American societies. In nearly half of these groups, a social status also has been documented for females who undertook a man's life-style, who were sometimes referred to in the native language with the same term applied to male berdaches and sometimes with a distinct term. Although the existence of berdaches has long been known to specialists in North American anthropology, the subject has been consigned to footnotes and marginal references. In the past twenty years, however, berdaches have become a subject of growing interest. An expanding base of empirical data concerning the social, cultural and historical dimensions of berdache status has become available....

❧

Until quite recently, serious investigation of berdaches has been confined to the most basic problems of description and definition. Throughout five centuries of contact, a bewildering variety of terms has been employed by Europeans and Americans to name this status, with new ones introduced in almost every generation. Such practices have created doubt not only about the nature of berdache roles but also concerning their very presence in cases in which confusing terminology makes it difficult to know whether different writers were referring to the same phenomena. The difficulty is that Euro-American cultures lack social and linguistic categories that can translate the pattern of beliefs, behaviors and customs represented by North American berdaches. Instead, writers have chosen between mutually exclusive terms that emphasize either gender variation or sexual variation—"hermaphrodite" and "sodomite," for example, or, more recently, "transsexual" (gender) and "homosexual" (sexuality). *Berdache* was originally an Arabic and Persian term for the younger partner in a male homosexual relationship, synonymous with "catamite" or "Ganymede." Used in North America since the seventeenth century, the term was not generally adopted until the nineteenth century, and only then by American anthropologists....

Although the principle of cultural relativity has been central to twentieth-century anthropology, its application to differences in gender and sexuality has been slow. Perhaps this is because most discourse on sexuality and gender in Euro-American societies during this period has been dominated by psychology and sexology. Perceiving the relativity of sexuality and gender patterns requires the simultaneous perception of the cultural basis of the knowledge produced by these disciplines. Not recognizing the importance of culture in constructing the desires, roles, identities and practices that constitute gender and sexuality, anthropologists and other observers have paid little attention to local beliefs, focusing instead on a much grander story, one that holds enduring fascination for the Western imagination—how culture confronts nature (and the individual confronts society) and all the possible outcomes that these givens can produce.

Above all, it took the emergence of feminist theory and its critique of biological determinism to make a serious reevaluation of the berdache role possible. This can be traced back to the work of Elsie Clews Parsons and Ruth Benedict, whose insightful, if brief, discussions of berdaches in the early twentieth century were informed by a feminist understanding of the social construction of gender roles. Between the 1920s and the 1960s, a similar perspective can be traced in references to berdaches by Ruth Landes, Ruth Underhill, Gladys Reichard, Nancy Lurie, Omer Stewart, Harry Hay and Sue-Ellen Jacobs. A less direct but just as significant influence has come from the field of literary criticism and the methods of discourse analysis. The degree to which poststructuralist theory has sensitized scholars to the relativity of the categories and taxonomies they use cannot be underestimated. In the field of anthropology, analyzing the "rules of discourse" that shape the texts readers rely on, whether anthropological, historical, literary or native, has become a key tool of cultural analysis.

In the 1970s, these intellectual developments combined with a social climate in which gender and sexual differences had become topics of broad public interest to produce a fluorescence in berdache studies....

As a result of these diverse contributions, a consensus on several points has begun to develop. The key features of male and female berdache roles were, in order of importance, *productive specialization* (crafts and domestic work for male berdaches and warfare, hunting and leadership roles in the case of female berdaches), *supernatural sanction* (in the form of an authorization and/or bestowal of powers from extrasocietal sources) and *gender variation* (in relation to normative cultural expectations for male and female genders). In the case of gender variation, cross-dressing was the most common and visible marker, but it has proven a more variable and less reliable indicator of berdache status than previously assumed.... [I]n some tribes male berdaches dressed distinctly from both men and women. In other cases, berdaches did not cross-dress at all, or only partly. In the case of female berdaches, cross-dressing was even more variable. Often, female berdaches wore men's clothes only when hunting or participating in warfare.

The sexual behavior of male and female berdaches was also variable. Where data exist, they indicate that the partners of berdaches were usually nonberdache members of the same sex—that is, berdaches were homosexual, if we define that term narrowly in terms of behavior and anatomy. Some berdaches, however, appear to have been bisexual and heterosexual. This was most often the case when adult men entered berdache status primarily on the basis of visions or dreams.... Berdaches participated in both casual encounters (reported for male berdaches) and long-term relationships (reported for both male and female berdaches)....

In sum, the most reliable indicators of berdache status were its economic and religious attributes and not gender or sexual difference alone. Further, the variation of berdaches in terms of occupational and religious pursuits *surpassed* rather than fell short of social norms. Again and again one finds berdaches attributed with exceptional productivity, talent and originality....

A second point of agreement is that berdaches were accepted and inte-grated members of their communities, as their economic and religious repu-tations indeed suggest. In many cases, berdaches enjoyed special respect and honors. In a few cases they were feared because of the supernatural power they were believed to possess. If berdaches were scorned, hated or ridiculed by their tribespeople, however, it was likely for individual reasons and not a function of their status as berdaches. In yet other cases, Indian joking relationships have been mistakenly interpreted as evidence of nonacceptance. In fact, in many tribes, individuals were subjected to teasing precisely *because* they enjoyed high status or prestige. Finally, many reports attributing American natives with hos-tility toward berdaches have been shown to reflect the Euro-American author's values and not native judgments. Indeed, what is missing at this point is an analysis of a confirmed case of a tribe *lacking* such a role or genuinely hostile to it.

A third area of consensus involves the abandonment of deterministic hypotheses concerning the "cause" of berdache behavior. Viewing berdaches as wholly determined products of social forces has a long history.... [A]nthro-pological ... etiological theories ... account for berdaches in terms of external forces alone—for example, the suggestion that the berdache role was a social status imposed on men too weak or cowardly to measure up to stringent tribal standards of masculinity. This suggestion has been convincingly disproved by evidence of males uninterested or unsuccessful in warfare who, nonetheless, do not become berdaches and by the actual participation of berdaches in warfare. Indeed, a good part of the prestige of berdaches was due to the belief that they enjoyed the same kind of supernatural sanction as successful hunters and warriors. Consequently, most recent work on berdaches acknowledges the role of individual motivations, desires and talents in determining who be-came a berdache. Berdaches are finally being recognized as historical subjects —individuals who actually desired to be berdaches because of the rewards that life-style offered.

A fourth area of emerging consensus addresses the problem of translation referred to above. Whereas berdaches have been traditionally conceptualized as crossing or exchanging genders, as the terms *transvestite* or *transsexual* imply (or exchanging object choice, as *homosexual* suggests), several investigators (including myself) have begun to argue that berdaches in fact occupied a third gender role, or, in the case of tribes with both male and female berdaches and distinct terms for each, third and fourth genders. A multiple-gender paradigm was first proposed by M. Kay Martin and Barbara Voorhies, whose 1975 book, *Female of the Species,* included a chapter titled "Supernumerary Sexes." They noted that "physical sex differences need not necessarily be perceived as bipolar. It seems possible that human reproductive bisexuality establishes a minimal number of socially recognized physical sexes, but these need not be limited to two." In her 1983 commentary on [Charles] Callender and [Lee] Kochems, Jacobs referred to berdache status as a third gender, a characterization she considers more inductive than the Western paradigm of gender-crossing. The first definitive argument for a multiple-gender paradigm was put forward by [Evelyn] Blackwood, who proposed the "rigorous identification and labeling of the berdache role as a separate gender." "The berdache gender...," she concluded, "is not a deviant role, nor a mixture of two genders, nor less a jumping from one gender to its opposite. Nor is it an alternative role behavior for nontraditional individuals who are still considered men or women. Rather, it comprises a separate gender within a multiple gender system."

Both positive and negative evidence supports the argument that berdache status constituted a culturally acknowledged gender category. On the one hand, it can easily be shown that a dual-gender model fails to account for many of the behaviors and attributes reported for berdaches—for example, berdaches who did not cross-dress or attempt to mimic the behavior of the "opposite" sex or those who engaged in a combination of female, male and berdache-specific pursuits. On the other hand, the consistent use of distinct terms to refer to berdaches, a practice that prevented their conceptual assimilation to an "opposite" sex, is positive evidence that berdache status was viewed as a separate category. Such native terms have various translations, from the obvious "man-woman" (e.g., Shoshoni *tanowaip)* to "old woman–old man" (e.g., Tewa *kwidó*) to terms that bear no relation to the words for "man" or "woman" or simply cannot be etymologized (e.g., Zuni *lhamana*).

In many tribes, the distinction of berdaches from men and women was reinforced by sartorial practices and the use of symbols, such as the distinct color of feathers worn by Floridian berdaches.... In other cases, as I have shown in *The Zuni Man-Woman,* the religious functions of berdaches and the life-cycle rites they underwent were specific to their status while paralleling the kind of functions and rites pertinent to men and women. Similarly, among such tribes as the Zunis, Navajos, Crows and others, myths accounting for the origin of berdache status placed that event in the same context in which male and female gender categories were defined (stating, in so many words, "when the spirit people made men and women, they also made berdaches").

Although the points made so far apply equally to male and female berdaches, it is clear that female roles were not simply mirror opposites of male berdache roles. Unfortunately, the study of female berdaches lags behind that of male berdaches, and several features of this status await clarification. Medicine concluded that "warrior women," like male berdaches, occupied "socially sanctioned role alternatives." These were "normative statuses which permitted individuals to strive for self-actualization, excellence, and social recognition in areas outside their customary sex role assignments." Some researchers, however, have concluded that female berdache roles were less viable and female berdaches less tolerated than were their male counterparts, and others have argued that the term *berdache* should not be applied to women at all. Callender and Kochems found documentation of female berdaches in only thirty tribes. [Harriet] Whitehead concluded that "when women did the equivalent of what men did to become berdaches, nothing happened." On the other hand, Blackwood has argued that the female berdache role was socially and ontologically on par with male berdache status in the sense of being a distinct alternative identity. At Zuni, I found that the female berdache role was less visibly marked than the male role (i.e., there are no reports of cross-dressing by women) and may have been more variable from individual to individual, but linguistic and religious practices still countenanced a distinct status for women who combined male and female pursuits, as evidenced by the use of the same term, *lhamana,* to refer to both male and female berdaches.

Where Do Berdaches Come From?: The Theoretical Challenge

Derived from the Latin *genus*—meaning "kind, sort, class"—"gender" has come to be used by researchers in several fields to distinguish socially constructed roles and cultural representations from biological sex. Indeed, throughout Western history, popular belief and official discourse alike have acknowledged the role of social learning in sex-specific behavior, but biological sex has always been considered both the point of origin and natural limit of sex roles. What we call gender, in this view, *should* conform to sex, a belief that is rationalized alternately on moral and naturalistic grounds. The study of non-Western cultures, however, reveals not only variability in the sociocultural features of sex roles but also ... wide variation in beliefs concerning the body and what constitutes sex.

If gender can be multiple, and potentially autonomous from sex, it becomes crucial to clarify exactly what it denotes. (In fact, definitions of *gender* are rare in the literature of "gender studies.") For the purposes of cross-cultural analysis, therefore, I define *gender* as a multidimensional category of personhood encompassing a distinct pattern of social and cultural differences. Gender categories often draw on perceptions of anatomical and physiological differences between bodies, but these perceptions are always mediated by cultural categories and meanings. Nor can we assume the relative importance of these perceptions in the overall definition of personhood in a given social context, or that these differences will be interpreted as dichotomous and fixed, or that they will be viewed as behavioral or social determinants (as opposed to, for example, a belief that behavior might determine anatomy). Gender categories are not only "models of" difference (to borrow Clifford Geertz's terminology) but also "models for" difference. They convey gender-specific social expectations for behavior and temperament, sexuality, kinship and interpersonal roles, occupation, religious roles and other social patterns. Gender categories are "total social phenomena," in Marcel Mauss's terms; a wide range of institutions and beliefs find simultaneous expression through them, a characteristic that distinguishes gender from other social statuses. In terms of this definition, the presence of multiple genders does not require belief in the existence of three or more physical sexes but, minimally, a view of physical differences as unfixed, or insufficient on their own to establish gender, or simply less important than individual and social factors, such as occupational preference, behavior and temperament, religious experiences and so forth.

Since the work of Ruth Benedict and Margaret Mead, anthropological studies of sex roles have focused on the relationship between sex and gender—a relationship that has been described as both motivated and arbitrary. A multiple-gender paradigm, however, leads us to analyze the relationship between the body and sex as well. Although morphological differences in infants may motivate a marking process, in a multiple-gender paradigm the markers of sex are viewed as no less arbitrary than the sociocultural elaborations of sex in the form of gender identities and roles. North American data, for example, make it clear that not all cultures recognize the same anatomical markers and not all recognize anatomical markers as "natural" and, therefore, counterposed to a distinct domain of the "cultural."

In traditional Zuni belief, for example, a series of interventions were considered necessary to ensure that a child has a "sex" at all. This began before birth, when the parents made offerings at various shrines to influence the sex of the developing fetus. In fact, the infant's sex was still not fixed at the time of birth. If a woman took a nap during labor, for example, the Zunis believed the sex of her child might change. After birth, interventions intended to influence physical sex continued. The midwife massaged and manipulated the infant's face, nose, eyes and genitals. If the infant was male, she poured cold water over its penis to prevent overdevelopment. If the child was female, the midwife split a new gourd in half and rubbed it over the vulva to enlarge it. In this context, knowing the kind of genitals an individual possesses is less important than knowing how bodies are culturally constructed and what particular features and processes (physiological and/or social) are believed to endow them with sex....

As Whitehead argues, "A social gender dichotomy is present in all known societies in the sense that everywhere anatomic sexual differences observable at birth are used to start tracking the newborn into one or the other of two social role complexes. This minimal pegging of social roles and relationships to observable anatomic sex differences is what creates what we call a 'gender' dichotomy in the first place." Callender and Kochems echo this when they state that gender "is less directly tied to this anatomical basis, although ultimately limited by it." Unpacking these formulations reveals two propositions: social gender is based on the "natural facts" of sex, and, since there are only two sexes, there are only two genders. It follows that, if an individual is not one, then she must be the other. The only variation possible is an exchange of one gender for its "opposite" or some form of gender-mixing; but there are no possible variations that cannot be defined by reference to male or female. It also follows that in such a system there can be only one sexual orientation, namely, heterosexual.

The assumptions of a dual-gender system have been criticized in recent years on both empirical and theoretical grounds. It may, indeed, be arguable that all societies have *at least* two genders and, as suggested above, that these two genders are linked to perceptions of physiological differences. What constitutes anatomical sex, however—which organs (or fluids or physiological processes) are considered the signs of maleness and femaleness—has been shown by scholars in several fields to be as much a social construction as what has been termed *gender.*

Deconstructing the sex/gender binary reveals a hierarchical relationship between the two terms. That is, anatomy has primacy over gender, and gender is not an ontologically distinct category but merely a reiteration of sex. This is apparent in Whitehead's comments on female berdaches. "For someone whose anatomic starting point was female," she argues, "the infusion of an official opposite sex component into her identity was by no means so easily effected," because, "throughout the continent, the anatomic-physiological component of gender was more significant in the case of the female than in the case of the male, and was thus less easily counter-balanced by the occupational component." But this raises the question: If gender differences are to be viewed as anchored to an "anatomic-physiological component," then on what grounds can we argue that gender roles are not, in fact, "natural" (i.e., mirroring and/or determined by biology)? And if we accept the contention that having a female body makes it more difficult to become a berdache, then have we not conceded that the difference that defines women also makes them inferior?

In sum, if berdaches are to be understood as simply exchanging one gender for another, then they can indeed be interpreted as upholding a heterosexist gender system. If they are to be understood as entering a distinct gender status, however, neither male nor female, then something more complex is occurring. A multiple-gender paradigm makes it possible to see berdache status not as a compromise between nature and culture or a niche to accommodate "natural" variation but as an integral and predictable element of certain sociocultural systems, not a contradiction in Native American beliefs but a status fully consistent with them. . . .

Conclusion

Berdache status was not a niche for occasional (and presumably "natural") variation in sexuality and gender, nor was it an accidental by-product of unresolved social contradictions. In the native view, berdaches occupied a distinct and autonomous social status on par with the status of men and women. Like male and female genders, the berdache gender entailed a pattern of differences encompassing behavior, temperament, social and economic roles and religious specialization—all the dimensions of a gender category, as I defined that term earlier, with the exception of the attribution of physical differences (the Navajos may be one exception . . .). But physical differences were constructed in various ways in Native American perception, and they were not accorded the same weight that they are in Western belief. Social learning and personal experiences (including ritual and supernatural experiences) were considered just as important in defining individual social identity as anatomy. Viewing female and male berdache roles as third and fourth genders, therefore, offers the best translation of native categories and the best fit with the range of behaviors and social traits reported for berdaches. Conversely, characterizations of berdaches as crossing genders or mixing genders, as men or women who "assume the role of the 'opposite' sex," are reductionist and inaccurate. . . .

There are no definitive variables for predicting the presence of multiple genders, but I believe we can specify a set of minimal conditions for the possibility of such statuses. First is a division of labor and prestige system organized in terms of gender categories, so that the potential exists for female specialization in production and distribution of food or exchange goods. Second is a belief system in which gender is not viewed as determined by anatomical sex or in which anatomical sex is believed to be unstable, fluid and nondichotomous, and, therefore, an autonomous third category is viable. Third are the occurrence of historical events and individuals motivated to take advantage of them in creating and shaping gender identities. If these conditions are present, then multiple gender roles can develop—and it becomes possible to become a berdache. Conversely, I would hypothesize that, for a given society in which multiple genders were present, it would take not only the elimination of the economic dimension of such statuses but a lapse in the belief systems rationalizing them and the introduction of a dual-sex ideology to effect a full collapse of such roles.

The next step in berdache studies will be the recognition that gender diversity is not an isolated feature of North American societies but a worldwide phenomenon, represented in most culture areas as well as in certain historical periods of Western societies. Gender diversity will become one more part of the story of human culture and history that is anthropology's job to tell.

POSTSCRIPT

Are Humans Naturally Either Male or Female?

Nature versus nurture? Biology versus social determinism? Just as some anthropologists argue that we need to move beyond gender binaries to better understand human complexity, we must also move beyond neat either/or propositions about the causes of sex and gender. Traditional thought dictates that biology affects or determines behavior. But behavior can also alter physiology. Recent advances explore the complex interaction between biology (genes, hormones, brain structure) and environment. We have learned that it is impossible to determine how much of our behavior is biologically based and how much is environmental. Moreover, definitions of gendered behavior are temporally and culturally relative. Yet why do researchers continue to try to isolate biological from environmental factors?

Advancements in the study of biological bases of sex and critiques of applications of biological theory to human behavior challenge some of Udry's assertions. Is sex dimorphism universal? Biologists recognize species diversity in hormone-brain-behavior relationships, which makes the general application of theories based on animal physiology and behavior to humans problematic. Moreover, species diversity challenges male/female binaries. The validity of the presence/absence model of sex dimorphism has been challenged. In embryonic development, do females "just happen" by default in the absence of testosterone? No, all individuals actively develop through various genetic processes. Moreover, the sexes are similar in the presence and need of both androgens and estrogens; in fact, the chemical structures and derivation of estrogen and testosterone are interconnected.

Suggested Readings

A. Fausto-Sterling, *Body Building: How Biologists Construct Sexuality* (Basic Books, 1999).

G. Herdt, *Third Sex, Third Gender* (Zone Books, 1994).

T. Laqueur, *Making Sex: Body and Gender From the Greeks to Freud* (Harvard University Press, 1990).

W. Roscoe, *The Zuni Man-Woman* (University of New Mexico Press, 1991).

S. V. Rosser, *Biology and Feminism: A Dynamic Interaction* (Twayne Publishers, 1992).

C. Tavris, *The Mismeasure of Woman* (Simon & Schuster, 1992).

ISSUE 2

Does the John/Joan Case Prove That Gender Identity Is Innate?

YES: Milton Diamond and H. Keith Sigmundson, from "Sex Reassignment at Birth: Long-term Review and Clinical Implications," *Archives of Pediatrics and Adolescent Medicine* (March 1997)

NO: Bernice L. Hausman, from "Do Boys Have to Be Boys? Gender, Narrativity, and the John/Joan Case," *NWSA Journal* (September 30, 2000)

ISSUE SUMMARY

YES: Sex researcher Milton Diamond and psychiatrist H. Keith Sigmundson argue that the John/Joan case provides proof that gender identity is innate.

NO: Associate professor of English Bernice L. Hausman examines the narratives or stories told about the John/Joan case to reveal biases and oversights about nonbiological contributions to John/Joan's experiences.

I magine you or your partner is giving birth. When the baby is delivered, you anxiously await the doctor's declaration of the baby's sex. The doctor excitedly begins to say, "It's a ..." then stops, her or his demeanor changing to one of feigned unconcern. Both female and male genitalia are observed in the baby and thus your child is diagnosed with a form of intersexuality. The next morning the hospital clerk comes in for the completion of the birth certificate. The designation of the child's sex, male or female, is required by law. In the afternoon, your neighbor excitedly calls to hear the details of the baby's birth. The first question she asks is, "What did you have?" The only acceptable answers are male or female. Later that evening, the volunteer nurses' aid comes in to offer you a handknit cap for your infant—pink or blue?

The term *intersex* has been used in medical literature to refer to three major subgroups of individuals with both male and female biological characteristics: (1) true hermaphrodites have one ovary and one testis, (2) female pseudo-hermaphrodites have ovaries and partial male genitalia (except testes), and (3) male pseudohermaphrodites have partial female genitalia (except ovaries) and testes.

Physicians now diagnose most intersexuals at birth, immediately entering them into a program of surgical and hormonal management. The goal is to "restore" one's "true" sex—to return the body to what it naturally ought to have been had normative sexual differentiation taken its course. The leading researcher of intersexual infant case management is John Money, whose theory of gender continues to dominate medical case management practices. He advocates assigning sex as early as possible (at the latest by 18 months when gender identity is no longer malleable) so that gender identity (sense of self as belonging to a female or male category) can develop successfully. Surgical correction should also be undertaken as soon as possible so that genitalia conforming to the chosen (i.e., "true") sex can be created. After all, the theory goes, the genitals will determine the way parents will interact with the child.

There is considerable controversy over Money's theory that gender identity is socially constructed, not innate. Money's theory is generally uncontested by medical professionals but challenged by psychologists studying the effects of prenatal hormones on brain structure, gender identity, and gendered behavior. Money has spent his career conducting psychological research on children who were born intersexual and were surgically "corrected" soon after birth. His aim was to document the successful accommodation of the child and family to sex assignment resulting in a secure gender identity—a gender identity that may not match chromosomal sex. Recent critical analyses of this research, however, alert us to research design flaws that call for a reconsideration of the biological underpinnings of gender identity.

A pivotal case is that of John/Joan, a boy (with a twin brother) who at eight months of age was injured in a botched circumcision and subsequently reared as a girl. This case was revealed by Milton Diamond and H. Keith Sigmundson and told in great detail by John Colapinto in *As Nature Made Him: The Boy Who Was Raised as a Girl* (HarperCollins, 2000). Money became involved in the child's psychological treatment, seizing this rare opportunity to study "naturalistically" whether or not gender identity could be socially constructed, hoping to offer strong evidence once and for all against the innateness of gender identity. But at the age of 14, upon learning the facts of his birth and sex reassignment, the child rejected his reassigned sex and is now living as a man.

In the following selections, Diamond and Sigmundson argue that Money's "botched experiment" provides evidence of the innateness of gender identity. Bernice L. Hausman examines the narratives or stories told about the John/Joan case to reveal biases and oversights about nonbiological contributions to John/Joan's experiences. She also observes that the specialized and heightened medical attention and differential parental treatment of children born as intersexuals (of which parents may not be consciously aware) may profoundly impact gender identity outcomes.

Milton Diamond and
H. Keith Sigmundson

 **YES**

Sex Reassignment at Birth

Among the more difficult decisions physicians have to make involve cases of ambiguous genitalia or markedly traumatized genitalia. The decision as to how to proceed typically follows this contemporary advice: "The decision to raise the child as a male centers around the potential for the phallus to function adequately in later sexual relations"[1(p580)] and "Because it is simpler to construct a vagina than a satisfactory penis, only the infant with a phallus of adequate size should be considered for a male gender assignment."[2(p1955)] These management proposals depend on a theory that says it is easier to make a good vagina than a good penis and because the identity of the child will reflect upbringing and the absence of an adequate penis would be psychosexually devastating, fashion the perineum into a normal looking vulva and vagina, and raise the individual as a girl. Such clinical advice, concerned primarily with surgical potentials, is relatively standard in medical texts[3–6] and reflects the current thinking of many physicians.[7]

This management philosophy is based on 2 beliefs held strongly enough by pediatricians and other physicians to be considered postulates: (1) individuals are psychosexually neutral at birth and (2) healthy psychosexual development is dependent on the appearance of the genitals. These ideas arise most strongly from the original work of Money and colleagues.[8–11(pp46–51),12] ...

Report of a Patient

The case involved a set of normal XY twins, one of whom, at 8 months of age, had his penis accidentally burned to ablation during phimosis repair by cautery.[11] After a great deal of debate, the child was seen for consultation at The Johns Hopkins Hospital, Baltimore, Md, and, following the beliefs mentioned earlier, the recommendation was made to raise the child as a girl. The pseudonym John will be used when referring to this individual when living as a male and the pseudonym Joan when living as a female. Orchiectomy and preliminary surgery followed within the year to facilitate feminization. Further surgery to fashion a full vagina was to wait until Joan was older. This management was monitored and reinforced with yearly visits to The Johns Hopkins

Hospital. The treatment was described as developing successfully with John accepting life as Joan.[11]

> Although the girl is not yet a woman, her record to date offers convincing evidence that the gender identity gate is open at birth for a normal child no less than for one born with unfinished sex organs or one who was prenatally over or underexposed to androgen, and that it stays open at least for something over a year after birth.[12(p98)]

A follow-up stated: "The girl's subsequent history proves how well all three of them (parents and child) succeeded in adjusting to that decision."[12]

The effects of such reports were widespread. Sociology, psychology, and women's study texts were rewritten to argue that, as *Time* magazine (January 8, 1973) reported,

> This dramatic case ... provides strong support ... that conventional patterns of masculine and feminine behavior can be altered. It also casts doubt on the theory that major sex differences, psychological as well as anatomical, are immutably set by the genes at conception.

Lay and social science writings still echo this case as do medical texts.[3–6,14] ... Our current article challenges those reports and advice. It is based on a review of the medical clinical notes and impressions of therapists originally involved with the case and on contemporary interviews. One of us (H. K. S.) was head of the psychiatric management team to which the case was referred in the patient's home area. Although the patient was assigned to the immediate care of female psychiatrists to foster female identification and role modeling, H. K. S. maintained direct supervisory control of the case. The unique character of this case attracted the attention of the British Broadcasting Co and they invited M. D. as a consultant.[15] In 1994 and 1995, we collaboratively reinterviewed and recorded John, his mother, and his wife to provide updated accounts of his progress. Findings are listed in chronological order under the appropriate postulate for pediatric sexual assignment. John himself, while desiring to remain anonymous, strongly desires his case history be made available to the medical community to reduce the likelihood of others suffering his psychic trauma.

Postulate 1: Individuals Are Psychosexually Neutral at Birth

Mother recalls:

> As soon as he had the surgery, the doctor said I should now start treating him as a girl, doing girl things, and putting him in girl's clothes. But that was a disaster. I put this beautiful little dress on him ... and he [immediately tried] to rip it off; I think he knew it was a dress and that it was for girls and he wasn't a girl.

On the other hand, Joan could act quite feminine when she wanted to and at approximately 6 years old was described as doing so, eg, his mother was quoted as saying: "One thing that really amazes me is that she is so feminine. I've never seen a little girl so neat and tidy as she can be when she wants to be...."[11(p119)] More often, however, Joan rejected such behavior. More commonly she, much more so than the twin brother, would mimic the father. One incident the mother related was typical. When the twins were 4 or 5 years old, they were watching their parents. Father was shaving and mother was applying makeup. Joan applied shaving cream and pretended to shave. When Joan was corrected and told to put on lipstick and makeup like mother, Joan said: "No, I don't want no makeup, I want to shave."

Girl's toys, clothes, and activities were repeatedly proffered to Joan and most often rejected. Throughout childhood Joan preferred boy's activities and games; she had little interest in dolls, sewing, or girl's activities. Ignoring the toys she was given, she would play with her brother's toys. She preferred to tinker with gadgets and tools, dress up in men's clothing, and take things apart to see what made them tick. She was regarded as a tomboy with an interest in playing soldier. Joan did not shun rough and tumble sports or avoid fights....

Joan's realization that she was not a girl jelled between ages 9 and 11 years. John relates:

> There were little things from early on. I began to see how different I felt and was, from what I was supposed to be. But I didn't know what it meant. I thought I was a freak or something.... I looked at myself and said I don't like this type of clothing, I don't like the types of toys I was always being given. I like hanging around with the guys and climbing trees and stuff like that and girls don't like any of that stuff. I looked in the mirror and [saw] my shoulders [were] so wide, I mean there [was] nothing feminine about me. I [was] skinny, but other than that, nothing. But that [was] how I figured it out. [I figured I was a guy] but I didn't want to admit it. I figured I didn't want to wind up opening a can of worms.

Joan knew she already had thoughts of suicide caused by this sort of cognitive dissonance and did not want additional stress.

Joan fought the boys and girls who were always "razzing" her about her boy looks and her girl clothes. She had no friends; no one would play with her. "Every day I was picked on, every day I was teased, every day I was threatened. I said enough is enough...." Mother relates that Joan was good looking as a girl. But, "When he started moving or talking, that gave him away, and the awkwardness and incongruities became apparent." ...

Despite the absence of a penis, Joan often tried to stand to urinate. This made a mess as it was difficult to direct the urine stream. Although she learned to sit and void, she nevertheless continued to occasionally stand and urinate. Despite admonitions against the behavior and its untidiness, Joan persisted. At school, at age 14 years, she was caught standing to urinate in the girl's bathroom so often that the other girls refused to allow her entrance. Mother recalls the other girls threatening to "kill" her if she persisted. Joan would also sometimes go to the boy's lavatory to urinate.

Joan was put on an estrogen regimen at the age of 12 years but rebelled against taking the hormones. They made her "feel funny" and she did not want to feminize. She would often dispose of her daily dose. She was unhappy at developing breasts and would not wear a bra. Things came to a critical point at age 14 years. In discussing her breast development with her endocrinologist she confessed, "I suspected I was a boy since the second grade." The physician, who personally believed Joan should continue her medication and proceed as a girl, used that opening to explore the possible male and female paths available and what either one would mean. The local psychiatric team had noticed Joan's preference for boy's activities and refusal to accept female status so they already had discussed among themselves the possibility of accepting Joan's change back to a male. The endocrinologist explored Joan's options with her. Shortly thereafter, at age 14 years, Joan decided to switch to living as a male.

Joan was the daily butt of her peers' jibes and the local therapists, having knowledge of her previous suicidal thoughts, went along with the idea of sex re-reassignment. In a tearful episode following John's prodding, his father told him of the history of what had transpired when he was an infant and why. John recalls: "All of a sudden everything clicked. For the first time things made sense and I understood who and what I was."

John requested male hormone shots and gladly took these. He also requested a mastectomy and phalloplasty. The mastectomy was completed at the age of 14 years; surgical procedures for phallus construction were at ages 15 and 16 years. After the surgical procedures, John adjusted well. As a boy he was relatively well accepted and popular with boys and girls. At 16 years, to attract girls, John obtained a windowless van with a bed and bar. Girls, who as a group had been teasing Joan, now began to have a crush on John. When occasions for sexual encounters arose, however, he was reluctant to move erotically. When he told 1 girlfriend why he was hesitant, that he was insecure about his penis, she gossiped at school and this hurt John very much. Nevertheless, his peers quickly rallied around him and he was accepted and the girl rejected.

John's life subsequently was not unlike that of other boys with an occult physical handicap. After his return to male living he felt his attitudes, behaviors, and body were in concert in a way they had not been when living as a girl. At age 25 years he married a woman several years his senior and adopted her children.

Postulate 2: Healthy Psychosexual Development Is Intimately Related to the Appearance of the Genitals

First in Baltimore and then with the local therapists prior to the sex re-reassignment, Joan's expressed feelings of not being a girl would draw ridicule. She would be told something such as: "All girls think such things when they're growing up." John recalls thinking: "You can't argue with a bunch of doctors in white coats; you're just a little kid and their minds are already made up. They didn't want to listen." To ease pressures to act as a girl, Joan would often not argue or fight the assignment and would "go along."

Beginning at age 7 years, Joan began to rebel against going for the consultations at The Johns Hopkins Hospital. Her reasons were discomfort and embarrassment with forced exposure of her genitals and constant attempts, particularly after the age of 8 years, to convince her to behave more like a girl and accept further vaginal repair. This was always strongly resisted and led to recurrent confrontations. To temper Joan's reluctance to travel to the consultants, her parents combined such visits with vacation trips.

In Baltimore the consultants enlisted male-to-female transsexuals to convince Joan of the advantages of being female and having a vagina constructed. She was so disturbed by this that in one instance Joan, at age 13 years, ran away from the hospital. She was found hiding on the roof of a nearby building. After age 14 years, Joan adamantly refused to return to the hospital. Joan then came fully under the care of local clinicians. This group consisted of several pediatricians, 2 pediatric surgeons, an endocrinologist, and a team of psychiatrists.

John recalls thinking, from preschool through elementary school, that physicians were more concerned with the appearance of Joan's genitals than was Joan. Her genitals were inspected at each visit to The Johns Hopkins Hospital. She thought they were making a big issue out of nothing and they gave her no reason to think otherwise. John recalls thinking: "Leave me be and then I'll be fine. . . . It's bizarre. My genitals are not bothering me; I don't know why it is bothering you guys so much."

When asked what Joan thought of her genitals as a youngster, John replied, "I didn't really have anything to compare myself against other than my brother when we were taking a bath." Mother confirmed that as a devout family in a very conservative religious community there would have been few opportunities for the twins to have seen anyone else's genitals. Nudity was never acceptable. At their yearly visit to The Johns Hopkins Hospital, the twins were made to stand naked for inspection by groups of clinicians and to inspect each other's genitalia. This experience, in itself, was recalled with strong negative emotions. John's brother, decades later, recalls the experience with tears.

John recalls frustration, which remains, at not having his feelings and desires recognized. Without consideration of genitals, despite the obvious absence of a penis, Joan nevertheless knew she was not a girl. When she tried to express such thoughts the physicians would change the subject. "[They] didn't want to hear what I had to say but wanted to tell me how I should feel." Clinical notes from the time report Joan saying she felt "like a trapped animal." . . .

At first, as suggested by the consultants from The Johns Hopkins Hospital, the local physicians and her parents continued to treat Joan as a girl, preparing her for vaginal reconstructive surgery and life as a female. Psychotherapy, primarily by female therapists, was aimed at reinforcing her female identity and redirecting her male ideation. This course of action became increasingly difficult because of Joan's growing conviction that she was not right as a girl and anger at being treated like one. Joan's reactions were not unlike those in post-traumatic stress disorder, where the cause of the stress is not remembered. John recalls, "They kept making me feel as if I was a freak."

John knew what the clinicians wanted and recognized it was not what he wanted. Beginning at age 14 years, against the recommendations of the clinicians and family and without yet knowing of the original XY status, Joan refused to live as a girl. Jeans and shirts, because of their gender-neutral status, became her preferred manner of dress; boy's games and pursuits her usual activities. Joan's daytime fantasies and night dreams during elementary school involved seeing herself "as this big guy, lots of muscles and a slick car and have[ing] all kinds of friends." She aspired to be a mechanic. She rejected requests to look at pictures of nude females, which she was supposed to emulate. Rorschach and Thematic Apperception Tests at the time elicited responses more typical of a boy than a girl. Her adamant rejection of female living and her improved demeanor and disposition when acting as a boy convinced the local therapists of the correctness of sexual re-reassignment. . . .

John recalls thinking it was small-minded of others to think all his personality was summed up in the presence or absence of a penis. He expressed it thus:

> Doctor . . . said, 'it's gonna be tough, you're going to be picked on, you're gonna be very alone, you're not gonna find anybody [unless you have vaginal surgery and live as a female].' And I thought to myself, you know I wasn't very old at the time, but it dawned on me that these people gotta be pretty shallow if that's the only thing they think I've got going for me; that the only reason why people get married and have children and have a productive life is because of what they have between their legs. . . . If that's all they think of me, that they justify my worth by what I have between my legs, then I gotta be a complete loser. . . .

Comment

Long-term follow-up of case reports are unusual but often crucial. This update to a case originally accepted as a "classic" in fields ranging from medicine to the humanities completely reverses the conclusions and theory behind the original reports. Cases of infant sex reassignment require inspection and review after puberty; 5- and 10-year postsex reassignment follow-ups are still insufficient. . . .

Comments from John's parents reveal another important consideration. With a sex reassignment they were asked to make a dramatic psychological adjustment in rearing an otherwise normal child. Mother herself required psychiatric treatment to help manage her feelings. The penile ablation aside, the parents were more comfortable dealing with their child's original sex and the accident than with the reassigned sex. Although they had tried to make a success of the sex reassignment, they were supportive, while guilt ridden, when Joan decided to become John.

The last decade has offered much support for a biological substrate for sexual behavior. In addition to the genetic research mentioned, there are many neurological and other reports that point in this direction.[19,20,21-36] The evidence seems overwhelming that normal humans are not psychosexually neutral at birth but are, in keeping with their mammalian heritage, predisposed and biased to interact with environmental, familial, and social forces in either a male or female mode. This classic case demonstrates this. And the fact that this predisposition was particularly expressed at puberty, a critical period, is logical and has been predicted.[18,24]

Although this article deals with a classic case of sex reassignment often cited in the literature, follow-up to related cases are available. Reilly and Woodhouse[37] described 20 patients with micropenises who were reared as boys. None of them had any doubt as to the correctness of the assignment as males. Other reports describe males originally reassigned as females who switched back and successfully lived as males, despite the absence of a normal penis.[17,20,38–42] Several of these cases offer findings similar to ours, including the ages at which various milestones were passed, feelings developed, and the reassignment challenged.[39,40] ...

These cases of successful gender change, as well as the present one, also challenge the belief that such a switch after the age of 2 years will be devastating. Indeed, in these cases it was salutary.

It must be acknowledged that cases of males accepting life as females after the destruction of their penises has been reported.[44] These reports, however, do not detail the individuals' sexual or personal lives.

Conclusions

Considering this case follow-up, and as far as an extensive literature review can attest, there is no known case where a 46-chromosome, XY male, unequivocally so at birth, has ever easily and fully accepted an imposed life as an androphilic female regardless of physical and medical intervention. True, surgical reconstruction of traumatized male or ambiguous genitalia to those of a female is mechanically easier than constructing a penis. But the attendant sex reassignment might be an unacceptable psychic price to pay. Concomitantly, no support exists for the postulates that individuals are psychosexually neutral at birth or that healthy psychosexual development is dependent on the appearance of the genitals. Certainly long-term follow-up on other cases is needed.

In the interim, however, we offer new guidelines. We believe that any 46-chromosome, XY individual born normal and with a normal nervous system, in keeping with the psychosexual bias thus prenatally imposed, should be raised as a male. Surgery to repair any genital problem, although difficult, should be conducted in keeping with this paradigm. This decision is not a simple one to make[7,13,16,43,45–47] and analysis should continue.

As parents will still want their children to be and look normal as soon after birth or injury as possible, physicians will have to provide the best advice and care consistent with current knowledge. We suggest referring the parents and child to appropriate and periodic long-term counseling rather than to immediate surgery and sex reassignment, which seems a simple and immediate solution to a complicated problem. With this management, a male's predisposition to act as a boy and his actual behavior will be reinforced in daily interactions and on all sexual levels and his fertility will be preserved. Social difficulties may reveal themselves as puberty is experienced. However, there is no evidence that with proper counseling and surgical repair when best indicated, adjustment will not be managed as well as teenagers manage other severe handicaps. Future reports will determine if we are correct.

References

1. Duckett JW, Baskin LS. Genitoplasty for intersex anomalies. *Eur J Pediatr.* 1993; 152(suppl 2): 580–584.
2. Perlmutter AD, Reitelman C. Surgical management of intersexuality. In: Walsh PC, Retik AB, Stamey TA, Vaughan JR, eds. *Campbell's Urology.* 6th ed. Philadelphia, Pa: WB Saunders Co; 1992: 1951–1966.
3. Behrman RE, Kliegman RM. *Nelson Essentials of Pediatrics.* 2nd ed. Philadelphia, Pa: WB Saunders Co; 1994: 636–637.
4. Blethen SL, Weldon W. Disorders of external genitalia differentiation. In: Kelly VC, ed. *Practice of Pediatrics.* Philadelphia, Pa; Harper & Row Publication Inc; 1985: 1–23.
5. Catlin EA, Crawford JD. Neonatal endocrinology. In: Oski FA, ed. *Principles and Practices of Pediatrics.* Philadelphia, Pa: JB Lippincott; 1990; 420–429.
6. Ratzan SK. Endocrine & metabolic disorders. In: Dworkin PH, ed. *Pediatrics.* 3rd ed. Baltimore, Md: Williams & Wilkins; 1996: 523–565.
7. Kessler SJ. The medical construction of gender: case management of intersexed infants. *Signs: J Women Culture Soc.* 1990; 16: 3–26.
8. Money J, Hampson JG, Hampson JL. An examination of some basic sexual concepts: the evidence of human hermaphroditism. *Bull Johns Hopkins Hosp.* 1955; 97: 301–319.
9. Money J. Sex hormones and other variables in human eroticism. In: Young WC, ed. *Sex and Internal Secretions,* 3rd ed. Baltimore, Md: Williams & Wilkins; 1961: 1383–1400.
10. Money J. Cytogenetic and psychosexual incongruities with a note on spaceform blindness. *Am J Psychiatry.* 1963; 119: 820–827.
11. Money J, Ehrhardt AA. *Man and Woman/Boy and Girl.* Baltimore, Md: Johns Hopkins University Press; 1972.
12. Money J, Tucker P. *Sexual Signatures: On Being a Man or Woman.* Boston, Mass: Little Brown & Co Inc; 1975: 95–98.
13. Money J. *Sex Errors of the Body and Related Syndromes: A Guide to Counseling Children, Adolescents, and Their Families.* 2nd ed. Baltimore, Md: Paul H. Brookes Publishing Co: 1994: 132.
14. Burg FD, Merrill RE, Winter RJ, Schaible DH. *Treatment of Infants, Children and Adolescents.* Philadelphia, Pa: WB Saunders Co; 1990: 8–9.
15. Diamond M. Sexual identity, monozygotic twins reared in discordant sex roles and a BBC follow-up. *Arch Sex Behav.* 1982; 11: 181–185.
16. Diamond M. Sexual Identity and Sexual Orientation in Children With Traumatized or Ambiguous Genitalia. *J Sex Res.* In press.
17. Cappon D, Ezrin C, Lynes P. Psychosexual identification (psychogender) in the intersexed. *Can Psychiatry J.* 1959; 4: 90–106.
18. Diamond M. A critical evaluation of the ontogeny of human sexual behavior. *Q Rev Biol.* 1965; 40: 147–175.
19. Diamond M. Some genetic considerations in the development of sexual orientation. In: Haug M., Whalen RE, Aron C, Olsen KL, eds. *The Development of Sex Differences and Similarities in Behavior.* Dordrecht, the Netherlands: Kluwer Academic Publishers; 1993: 291–309.
20. Diamond M. Biological aspects of sexual orientation and identity. In: Diamant L, McAnulty R, eds. *The Psychology of Sexual Orientation, Behavior and Identity: A Handbook.* Westport, Conn: Greenwood Press Inc; 1995: 45–80.

21. Allen LS, Hines M, Shryne JE, Gorski RA. Two sexually dimorphic cell groups in the human brain. *J Neurosci.* 1989; 9: 497–506.
22. Allen LS, Gorski RA. Sexual orientation and the size of the anterior commissure in the human brain. *Proc Natl Acad Sci USA.* 1992; 89: 7199–7202.
23. Diamond M. Genetic-endocrine interactions and human psychosexuality. In: Diamond M, ed. *Perspectives in Reproduction and Sexual Behavior.* Bloomington, Ind: University of Indiana Press; 1968: 417–443.
24. Diamond M. Sexual identity and sex roles. In: Bullough V, ed. *The Frontiers of Sex Research.* Buffalo, NY: Prometheus Books; 1979: 33–56.
25. Diamond M. Bisexualität aus biologischer sicht. In: Haeberle EJ, Gindorf R, eds. *Bisexualitäten: Ideologie und Praxis des Sexualkontaktes mit beiden Geschlectern.* Stuttgart, Germany: Gustav/Fischer Verlag; 1994; 41–48.
26. Gorski RA, Gordon JH, Shrayne JE, Southam AM. Evidence for a morphological sex difference within the medial preoptic area for the rat brain. *Brain Res.* 1978; 148: 333–346.
27. Gorski RA. Hormone-induced sex differences in hypothalamic structure. *Bull Tokyo Metrop Inst Neurosci.* 1988; 16: 67–90.
28. Hines M. Gonadal hormones and human cognitive development. In: Balthazart J, ed. *Hormones, Brain and Behaviour in Vertabrates: 1. Sexual Differentiation, Neuroanatomical Aspects, Neurotransmitters and Neuropeptides.* Farmington, Conn: S Karger AG; 1990: 51–63.
29. ines M. Hormonal and neural correlates of sex-typed behavioral in human beings. In: Haug M, Whalen RE, Aron C. Olsen KL, eds. *The Development of Sex Differences and Similarities in Behavior.* Dordrecht, the Netherlands: Kluwer Academic Publishers; 1993: 131–149.
30. LeVay S. A Difference in hypothalamic structure between heterosexual and homosexual men. *Science.* 1991; 253: 1034–1037.
31. LeVay S. *The Sexual Brain.* Cambridge, Mass: MIT Press; 1993.
32. LeVay S, Hamer DH. Evidence for a biological influence in male homosexuality. *Sci Am.* 1994; May: 44–49.
33. Swaab DF, Fliers, E. A sexually dimorphic nucleus in the human brain. *Science.* 1985; 228: 1112–1115.
34. Swaab DF, Hofman MA. Sexual differentiation of the human hypothalamus: ontogeny of the sexually dimorphic nucleus of the preoptic area. *Dev Brain Res.* 1988; 44: 314–318.
35. Swaab DF, Hofman MA. An enlarged suprachiasmatic nucleus in homosexual men. *Brain Res.* 1990; 537; 141–148.
36. Swaab DF, Gooren LJG, Hofman MA. Brain research, gender and sexual orientation. *J Homosex.* 1995; 28: 283–301.
37. Reilly, JM, Woodhouse CRJ. Small penis and the male sexual role. *J Urol.* 1989; 142: 569–572.
38. Burns E, Segaloff A, Carrera GM. Reassignment of sex: report of 3 cases. *J Urol.* 1960; 84: 126.
39. Dicks GH, Childers AT. The social transformation of a boy who had lived his first fourteen years as a girl: a case history. *Am J Orthopsychiatry.* 1934; 4: 508–517.
40. Ghabrial F, Girgis SM. Reorientation of sex: report of two cases. *Int J Fertil.* 1962; 7: 249–258.
41. Hoenig J. The origins of gender identity. In: Steiner WB, ed. *Gender Dysphoria: Development, Research, Management.* New York, NY: Plenum Press; 1985: 11–32.
42. Khupisco V. The tragic boy who refused to be turned into a girl. In: *Sunday Times Johannesburg.* May 21, 1995.
43. Reiner WG. Case study: sex reassignment in a teenage girl. *J Am Acad Child Adolesc Psychiatry.* 1996; 35: 799–803.
44. Gearhart JP. Total ablation of the penis after circumcision with electrocautery: a method of management and long-term followup. *J Urol.* 1989; 142: 799–801.

45. Fausto-Sterling A. The five sexes: why male and female are not enough. *Science.* 1993; 1993: 20–25.
46. Meyer-Bahlburg HFL. Gender identity development in intersex patients. *Child Adolesc Psychiatry Clin North Am.* 1993; 2: 501–511.
47. Zucker KJ, Bradley SJ. *Gender Identity Disorder and Psychosexual Problems in Children and Adolescents.* New York, NY: Guilford Press; 1995: 265–282.

Bernice L. Hausman  **NO**

Do Boys Have to Be Boys?

Introduction

Standard medical theory and practice for sex reassignment during childhood maintains that gender identity (the sense of oneself as one sex or the other) develops postnatally and is not established definitively until the child reaches about 2 years of age, that vaginas are more easily made than penises, that gender identity reflects sex assignment and rearing more than chromosomal and other physical factors, and that to be male without a penis is unthinkable in psychological or social terms. Thus, chromosomally (and often gonadally) male infants born with deformed or unspecific genitals are almost always reared as girls; throughout their childhood and adolescence, they are subject to medical and surgical treatments to bring their anatomy into conformity with typical female morphology. This protocol was first initiated by John Money and colleagues in the 1950s at Johns Hopkins Hospital and then solidified as standard practice in the 1960s and 1970s (Dreger 1998; Fausto-Sterling 2000; Hausman 1995; Kessler 1990, 1998).

According to Alice Dreger, 96 percent of intersex infants are "made into girls" (Dreger 1999). One in 1500 infants are born with genitalia so unusual that sex assignment into the standard categories of male and female is difficult, although one in 200 or 300 infants are referred to surgery because of "somewhat problematic" genital configurations, such as hypospadias, a condition in which the urethra does not exit from the tip of the penis (Dreger 1999). One particularly interesting aspect of the treatment protocols for intersex infants, however, is that they are based on an "index case" where the initial sex assignment of the child was not in question. (An index case is one that establishes treatments for a particular condition.) In the late 1990s, the status and meaning of the outcomes of the index case for intersexuality came into question.

In the spring of 1997, a number of articles in the popular press announced that the medical community was now rethinking the standard treatment protocols concerning sex reassignment during childhood as the result of a follow-up study of an early, momentous case of identical twin boys, one of whose sex was reassigned following traumatic loss of his penis during his first year of life ("Medical Community Questions Theory on Sex Reassignment" 1997; "Can an

From Bernice L. Hausman, "Do Boys Have to Be Boys? Gender, Narrativity, and the John/Joan Case," *NWSA Journal*, vol. 12, no. 3 (September 30, 2000). Copyright © 2000 by *NWSA Journal*. Reprinted by permission of Indiana University Press. Notes omitted.

Infant's Sex Be Changed?" 1997). The case became known as the "John/Joan" case, in reference to the pseudonyms used for the subject at different stages of his/her life, and in its original form was the recognized "index case" for treatment of intersexuality in infants. John Money was a principle figure in that original case, which was itself written up in *Time* magazine in the 1970s ("Biological Imperatives" 1973). In the recent medical account, published in *Archives of Pediatrics and Adolescent Medicine,* Milton Diamond and H. Keith Sigmundson revisit the case and show that the little boy whose sex was reassigned from male to female is now living as a man. In a lengthy discussion of the experiences of this "boy" reassigned as "girl," and then assigned again as a boy, Diamond and Sigmundson claim that "The evidence seems overwhelming that normal humans are not psychosexually neutral at birth but are, in keeping with their mammalian heritage, predisposed and biased to interact with environment, familial, and social forces in either a male or female mode" (1997, 303). Thus the authors claim that this case, in its complete form, demonstrates that gender identity is not malleable before a specific age, as Money had originally asserted, but that it is innate and based on chromosomal and hormonal sex factors.

Diamond and Sigmundson's conclusion only makes sense, however, if one accepts the dichotomy that structures it: *either* gender identity is socially constructed through the individual's responses to environmental stimuli before the age of 2, *or* gender identity is innate and determined by genetics, prenatal hormones, or some other physiological force (or combination of forces) in fetal development. Yet while Money's original discussions of the case purport to demonstrate one theory, and Diamond and Sigmundson claim to show the other, the case in all its guises demonstrates that gender identity is the result of a process of self naming that is embedded within the cultural milieu and influenced by its gender stories. . . .

Gender and Narrativity

What does it mean to claim that gender (as identity, as positionality) is, at least in part, a product of narrativity? I want to suggest that even a basic consideration of the significance of story-telling to the creation of identity and gender can reorient our thinking about what gender is and how a gender identity comes about.

Peter Brooks opens his book, *Reading for the Plot: Design and Intention in Narrative,* with the following description of narrative:

> Our lives are ceaselessly intertwined with narrative, with the stories that we tell and hear told, those we dream or imagine or would like to tell, all of which are reworked in that story of our own lives that we narrate to ourselves in an episodic, sometimes semi-conscious, but virtually uninterrupted monologue. We live immersed in narrative, recounting and reassessing the meaning of our past actions, anticipating the outcome of our future projects, situating ourselves at the intersection of several stories not yet completed. (1992, 3)

... An interesting discussion of narratology by Mieke Bal divides narratives into three components: the *fabula,* events causally or logically related (the "real" of what happened); the *story,* aspects of the fabula presented in an organized fashion (in other words, the plot); and *text,* what has been written down ("finite structured whole composed of linguistic signs") (1985). This structural typology of narrative is helpful in discussing the narrativity of conflicting medical accounts, as it allows us to see precisely where the accounts differ—for example, at the level of "story/plot" or of "fabula/events"—and thus the points at which the medical interpretations of the case diverge.

Further, a narrative understanding of gender reorients what we think gender is, as well as what it does. The scientific accounts of the John/Joan case depend upon routine or systematic techniques of narration that can be typified with the categories just delineated. They also depend upon a static understanding of "gender," which is most often used to signify stereotypical social behavior. Considering "gender" in relation to the idea of narrative, it becomes a dynamic category of subjectivity, rather than a static referent of known contents. This analysis also makes it possible for us to see how the concept of gender is engaged to shore up the meanings of basic scientific and medical arguments about "sex." ...

If "we have not seriously grappled with the fact that we afflict ourselves with a need to locate a bodily basis for assertions about gender," as Suzanne Kessler puts it in *Lessons from the Intersexed,* it may be because we have been concentrating on the wrong question (1998, 132). This question—whether gender identity is innate (and the result of biology) or nurtured (and thus socially constructed)—seems legitimate but it keeps us focused on the opposition between the categories, and thus the maintenance or destruction of that opposition. Nature *versus* nurture doesn't work because both sides of the argument depend upon a loose, untheorized, and highly stereotyped category of human behavior: gender. Once we rethink gender in terms of narrativity, the important issue is how it (gender) functions as a culturally salient category of experience. And then all of the categories—gender, gender identity, and sex (etc.)—need to be treated as ideas rather than as facts. If it seems that we have left aside the nature side of the debate and entered into culture, it is because typical discussions assume simplistic and undertheorized conceptions of gender, all the while claiming to know its origins and its meanings. To subject both nature and nurture arguments to feminist and narrative analysis will not explode or do away with the binary, but will allow us to consider how its very structure has limited our thinking on the topic.

... Gender narratives are stories that organize life events into socially coherent plots about sex.

In the context of an epistemological approach to gender, one question that arises is whether researchers can put aside their beliefs in gender as an ontology to get at what we think of as biology at all. Investigating the twin sex reassignment case as a series of stories about gender shows that the theory of innate, biological sex identity put forth by Diamond and Sigmundson can be unsettled by attention to its own, unrecognized narrativity, and demonstrates that gendered identities are both process and product of elaborate attempts to make sense of the relationship between the body and experience (1997). As such, gender can never be just an effect of biological processes, but is always part of a dialectical engagement of interpretation and story-making—that is, of narrativity—by specific subjects in concrete biosocial circumstances.

John/Joan

Comparing accounts of the John/Joan case necessitates distinguishing the events of the fabula, some of which differ between the stories, as well as the plotted interpretations of these events, interpretations which produce the accounts we read as medical case studies. In Money's original discussions of the case, which appeared in two books, *Man and Woman, Boy and Girl* and *Sexual Signatures* (the first coauthored with Anke Ehrhardt, the second with Patricia Tucker), the case is presented with the kind of personal detail appropriate to books oriented toward lay audiences: the parents of the twins are from farm backgrounds, with little education; the mother is very observant of gender appropriate behavior, the father less so (Money and Ehrhardt 1972, 123–31; Money and Tucker 1975, 91–8). The routine report offered by Diamond and Sigmundson is very brief and lacks this level of detail concerning the family's background and ideas about gender (1997). It provides, however, other significant details, discussed below.

In all of the recountings of the case, the story goes something like this: at seven months of age, identical twin boys were taken to a local hospital for an apparently routine circumcision. The surgeon caused irreparable damage to the first twin's penis because he used excess electrical current in the cauterizing scalpel. The organ was completely ablated. The parents, understandably distraught, sought help and were eventually directed to the psychohormonal unit at Johns Hopkins Hospital, where the doctors encouraged the parents to raise the penisless twin as a girl, with appropriate medical and surgical intervention. The parents agreed, after some intervening months of indecision. When the twins were 17 months of age, the child without the penis underwent the first phase of surgical repair: orchiectomy (removal of the testes) and feminization of the external genitalia (shaping the empty scrotum to look like labia). After this, the child was dressed exclusively in girls' clothing, given a girl's name, and brought up with gender-specific behaviors and expectations. Yearly visits to the Johns Hopkins clinic monitored the development of both children.

In Money's original presentations of this case, the discussion always ends on a positive note, as if to suggest that "all's well that ends well." However, Money's early presentations of the case were published while the children were still very young, about 9 years old. Diamond and Sigmundson's work suggests that Money's original conclusions were not only wrong, but inattentive. Their later interviews with the family (in 1994 and 1995) state that even before the age of 6 the little "girl" rejected her female role (Diamond and Sigmundson 1997, 299). Of course, these later interviews may have been influenced by hindsight, since by this time the subject was living as a male and wanting to demonstrate a consistent narrative history as a male subject. Nevertheless, the story of the child's gender identity that Diamond and Sigmundson present is not of successful gender reassignment, which is the one Money told, but of the child's consistent resistance to feminization. In this organization of the fabula, at the age of 14 the child stopped living as a girl and succeeded in convincing a local team of physicians and psychiatrists (now in charge of the case) to be allowed to return to male status.

Diamond and Sigmundson's presentation and discussion of the case is illuminating, bringing out details that are embedded but somewhat obscure in the earlier publications. For example, they write that the Hopkins clinicians "enlisted male-to-female transsexuals to convince Joan [their pseudonym for the child as a girl] of the advantages of being female and having a vagina constructed" (Diamond and Sigmundson 1997, 300). This apparently bothered the child greatly, causing her to run away from the hospital on one occasion. This aspect of the treatment program is never mentioned in the original presentations of the case, although transsexuals do appear in a slightly different context. In *Sexual Signatures,* Money and Tucker write that the child's parents, originally reluctant to allow their child to be reassigned to the female sex, inadvertently saw a television program "about the work with transexuals [sic] at Johns Hopkins. On the screen was an adult male-to-female transexual who, they could see for themselves, looked and talked like a normal, attractive woman. After that they worked their way to the decision to reassign their son as a girl" (1975, 92).

Diamond and Sigmundson add further elements of the fabula in their presentation of the story, however: "At their yearly visit to Johns Hopkins Hospital, the twins were made to stand naked for inspection by groups of clinicians and to inspect each other's genitalia.... John's brother, decades later, recalls the experience with tears" (1997, 301). In addition, as a teenager the reassigned child "rejected requests to look at pictures of nude females, which she was supposed to emulate" (301). These aspects of the case are confirmed and expanded in greater detail by Colapinto (1997).

Diamond and Sigmundson's account of the case sheds new light on the earlier, triumphant narrative of the social construction of gender identity (and hence the malleability of gender up to a certain age). Diamond and Sigmundson, of course, assert that their follow-up on the case shows that the child's *original* and *normal male* identity eventually won the day. ... Diamond and Sigmundson assume that gender both precedes and follows from sex—the male's predisposition is to "act like a boy"—but it and the "actual behavior" of the boy need reinforcement "in daily interactions." In this use of gender-as-explanation, Diamond and Sigmundson maintain their claim about gender's innateness at the same time that they acknowledge gender as the result of social forces. This demonstrates their adherence to the natural attitude toward gender, which establishes gender as an ontology that is both origin and goal of development.

While one could hardly quibble with the preference for long-term counseling over the medical and surgical quick fix of sex reassignment, there are ways to interpret (and renarrativize) elements of the John/Joan fabula other than to conclude that males are necessarily predisposed to act as boys. My initial and continuing response to Diamond and Sigmundson's follow-up is that the child's return to a masculine identity was heavily influenced by the coercive attempts at feminization. That is, Joan resisted the heavy-handed plot to make her into a girl. In all of the accounts, appropriate behaviors (for the child) were clearly demarcated (by the adults) according to traditional gender codes: "At five, the little girl already preferred dresses to pants, enjoyed wearing her hair ribbons, bracelets and frilly blouses, and loved being her daddy's little sweetheart" (Money and Tucker 1975, 97). "Rehearsals of future roles can also be seen in girls' and boys' toy preferences. The girl in this case wanted and received for Christmas dolls, a doll house, and a doll carriage, clearly related to the maternal aspect of the female adult role, while the boy [the twin brother] wanted and obtained a garage with cars and gas pumps and tools, part of the rehearsal of the male role. His father, like many men, was very interested in cars and mechanical activities" (Money and Ehrhardt 1972, 127]. "When the twins were 4 or 5 years old, they were watching their parents. Father was shaving and mother was applying makeup. Joan applied shaving cream and pretended to shave. *When Joan was corrected* and told to put on lipstick and makeup like mother, Joan said: 'No, I don't want no makeup, I want to shave'" (Diamond and Sigmundson 1997, 299; emphasis added). Indeed, it was through such gender role training that the treatment protocol of reassignment was expected to succeed psychologically. Add to this rigid set of expectations the yearly clinical experience, where the child was made to display her body to the physicians at the hospital, submit to psychological testing, and agree to the desirability of vaginal construction (a proposal reinforced through conversations with transsexual women she did not know and had little understanding of), and we can begin to see this alternative narrative more clearly. Joan's desire to be John may simply have been a desire to be free of this coercive femininity, to be able to produce her own identity in opposition to the one that everyone else in her life seemed to want her to take on.

She may also have been responding to unconscious tension in the family. In a long and well-developed article for *Rolling Stone,* John Colapinto does the best job of revealing the familial anxiety about Joan's gender identity, an important element that goes largely unexamined in all of the accounts (even his own, where its existence is palpable but not analyzed) (1997). Before deciding upon sex reassignment, the parents "sank into a state of mute depression" (58). By the time they decided on their course of action, "they had eradicated any doubts they might have had about the efficacy of the treatment," but when the mother first put a dress on Joan,

> "She was ripping at it, trying to tear it off" [the mother said] ... "I remember thinking, 'Oh my God, she knows she's a boy and she doesn't want girls' clothing. She doesn't want to be a girl.' But then I thought, 'Well, maybe I can *teach* her to want to be a girl. Maybe I can train her so that she wants to be a girl.'" (64)

The twin brother recalled, as an adult, that "I recognized Joan as my sister ... but she never, ever acted the part. She'd get a skipping rope for a gift, and the only thing we'd use *that* for was to tie people up, whip people with" (68). With every action and every thing in her life carrying such heavy associations, no wonder Joan had a desire to rebel, which for a girl often means acting like a boy. Colapinto writes that the parents

> were troubled by Joan's masculine behavior. But they had been told by Dr. Money that they must not entertain any doubts about their daughter, and they felt that to do so would only increase the problem. Instead, [they] seized on those moments when Joan's behavior *could* be construed as stereotypically feminine. "And she could be sort of feminine, sometimes," [the mother] says, "when she wanted to please me. She'd be less rough, keep herself clean and tidy, and help a little bit in the kitchen." (1997, 66)

In transsexuals' autobiographies, the problem of producing an identity in the face of coercive gender conditioning is a common theme.... This same natural attitude toward gender is evident in the statements of John's family; for them, helping in the kitchen and staying clean is not only appropriate behavior for a girl, but evidence of an appropriately gendered identity within....

The transsexual autobiographies also demonstrate that becoming a man or a woman is a process of learning how to represent that identity publicly; in Judith Butler's terms, it means producing that identity though the repeated iterations of representing it as if it already existed (Butler 1990). If one can become a man by acting like one (as "Joan" was to become a girl at least in part by acting like one), then becoming a man can be understood as an antidote for coercive, enforced femininity. Becoming a man means establishing a definitive gender identity in the face of familial and medical uncertainty, as well as acquiring the cultural perks that go along with that privileged position: higher status, encouragement of active play, an allowance to get dirty while playing, greater sexual freedom, and toy trucks. Both Martino and "Joan" had brothers, and thus could observe first hand the comparative benefits of being a boy....

The "natural attitude" toward gender assumes heterosexuality, thus all those who are not heterosexual are suspected of being gender transgressors as well. This aspect of gender's ontology also works the other way: to be heterosexual is to guarantee other people's assumption that one has a "normal" (and thus socially appropriate, innate) gender identity. This is why Diamond and Sigmundson can be so secure in their claim that "John" has found his true "natural" gender as a man, because he is married and has adopted his wife's children. John's narrative has a happy and logical ending; the plot worked out the right way.

In this narrative, "John's" response to his particular situation was to repudiate the identity picked out for him and go for the one his twin got. Thus, "After his return to male living he felt his attitudes, behaviors, and body were in concert in a way they had not been when living as a girl" (Diamond and Sigmundson 1997, 300). He ends up, then, as a completely "normal" man (his wife remarks that "There is no doubt who wears the pants in this family" [302]), which is understandable, of course, after the experiences of his childhood. As Colapinto writes,

> [John] speaks of his pride in his role as husband, father and sole breadwinner in the family that he never believed he would be lucky enough to have. "From what I've been taught by my father," he says, "what makes you a man

is: You treat your wife well. You put a roof over your family's head. You're a good father. Things like that add up much more to being a man than just *bang bang bang*—sex." (1997, 97)

John's own words demonstrate that "being a man" is a completely *social* designation, given that what it takes to be one must be learned. Yet for Diamond and Sigmundson, John's status as male breadwinner, head of household, family disciplinarian, husband, and father, demonstrate that his original biological make-up as a male made him the man he eventually became.

Money's original assertions were wrong, of course, but not necessarily wrong-headed, since they suggested the essential narrativity of gender. He claimed that, given the optimal window of opportunity, you can make any individual into a woman. He argued that the stories about sex identity that one tells oneself and that are told to one are crucial to the development of identity. But this case might have taught him that gender narratives don't always work in the most expected ways, and that coercive narratives can incite creative, rebellious responses. (Publications of the Intersex Society of North America, such as the newsletter *Hermaphrodites with Attitude,* are bringing to visibility precisely such stories.) While the clinicians utilized gender narratives in their attempts to feminize the penisless twin, the child fought back with his/her own arsenal of stories. If a person's gender identity is a product of story-making, then what's to stop an individual from making him or herself up?

This begs the question, of course, of how coercive the imposition of gender is for those whose anatomy presents what are considered the normal signs of sex (what Alice Dreger [1999] calls "the standard parts"), and why most individuals do not seem to resist the rather forceful feminization and masculinization endemic to culture. One reason is that most people adhere to the natural attitude toward gender, they agree with and uphold culturally accepted gender ontologies (Kessler and McKenna [1978] 1985). For those subjects whose body does not seem to verify gender "naturally," or those who refuse the social requirements to make body and behavior match as binary gender coordinates, the coercive nature of its imposition is more salient, and thus subject to resistance in a more obvious way.

The follow-up on the twin sex reassignment case does not demonstrate that gender identity is innate, as Diamond and Sigmundson claim. Their discussion, which curiously ignores the psychological impact of the early attempts to enforce "Joan's" femininity—except insofar as "John" feels angry at the attempted enforcement—demonstrates their inability to see outside of the nature versus nurture debate concerning the origins of gender identity. In their view, feeling uncomfortable with an enforced and exhibitionistic femininity is evidence of an innate masculinity, and not a sign that the imposition of such an identity can be a problem even for genetically female women. Opening up the John/Joan case to the multiple possibilities that understanding gender as a narrative allows—and interrogating the ontology implied by that narrative—suggests another reading, in which "John's" conviction of his innate masculinity and the authors' obvious acceptance of this conviction *as fact* show how readily some will believe that, after all, boys will be boys, especially if they won't be girls.

Conclusion

... The John/Joan case—with its outlandish sex stereotyping, its heavy-handed interpretive gender schema, its anguished parents and distraught children—will never prove that gender identity is the result of an innate biological force, be it prenatal hormones, genetic influence, or something else. All it can prove is that the attempt to make John into Joan didn't work, and that plausible social reasons why this was the case can be argued. The oppressive plot of female gender identity presented in all printed versions of this case is enough to make anyone run screaming from the room. We need to be asking why this narrative about gender's relation to the body is so readily accepted as a seeming antidote to the "horror" of the idea that gender is a social construct. And we ought to wonder about how such simplistic views of gender were allowed to proliferate (and still do) in discourses meant to study and treat complex human behavior.

The John/Joan case resembles, but is not identical to, the intersexual cases that currently receive treatment and sex reassignment soon after birth. In both scenarios, there is a desire to "fix" the anatomical "error," as well as to "fix" the child into one sex or another. Diamond and Sigmundson recognize this when they comment that "[a]s parents will still want their children to be and look normal as soon after birth or injury as possible, physicians will have to provide the best advice and care consistent with current knowledge" (1997, 303). The current medical protocols for intersex infants certainly reveal a cultural discomfort with individuals whose bodily existence challenges categories we hold dear. These protocols also show that, at least in the realm of sexual behavior and identity, most of us suffer from a lack of imagination. Instead of enabling the creation of new narratives, both to aid these individuals in developing their identities as sexed persons and to free other people's rigid identity constructions as well, medical theory and practice enforces upon all of us tired and oppressive stories about who wears the pants, who gets to shave, and who plays with dolls, because it assumes that these stories constitute the necessary foundation for a "normal" life. But if, as the intersex activists suggest, we can resist the either/or dichotomous opposition of current gender scenarios—if we can, in other words, "unfix" identity from its current mooring in traditional, bipolar gender narratives—rereading the biological signifiers of sex can offer us the starting point for truly alternative stories of sexed identity.

The question then becomes, do there have to be boys (or girls, for that matter)?

References

Bal, Mieke. 1985. *Narratology: Introduction to the Theory of Narrative.* Toronto, Canada: University of Toronto Press.

"Biological Imperatives." 1973. *Time,* 8 January, 34.

Brooks, Peter. 1992. *Reading for the Plot: Design and Intention in Narrative.* Cambridge, MA: Harvard University Press.

Butler, Judith. 1990. *Gender Trouble: Feminism and the Subversion of Identity.* New York: Routledge.

"Can an Infant's Sex Be Changed?" 1997. *The Washington Post,* 18 March, Health Section, 7, 19.

Colapinto, John. 1997. "The True Story of John Joan." *Rolling Stone,* 11 December, 54–72, 92, 94–7.

Diamond, Milton, and Keith Sigmundson. 1997. "Sex Reassignment at Birth: Long-Term Review and Clinical Implications." *Archives of Pediatrics and Adolescent Medicine* 151: 298–304.

Dreger, Alice Domurat. 1998. *Hermaphrodites and the Medical Invention of Sex.* Cambridge, MA: Harvard University Press.

———. 1999. "In Love with a Ruler: Phallometers and the Surgical 'Treatment' of Intersexuality." Paper presented at the annual meeting of the Society for Social Studies of Science, 29 October, San Diego, California.

Fausto-Sterling, Anne. 2000. *Sexing the Body: Gender Politics and the Construction of Sexuality.* New York: Basic Books.

Hausman, Bernice L. 1995. *Changing Sex: Transsexualism, Technology, and the Idea of Gender.* Durham, NC: Duke University Press.

Kessler, Suzanne J. 1990. "The Medical Construction of Gender: Case Management of Intersexed Infants." *Signs* 16: 3–26.

———. 1998. *Lessons from the Intersexed.* New Brunswick, NJ: Rutgers University Press.

Kessler, Suzanne J., and Wendy McKenna. (1978) 1985. *Gender: An Ethnomethodological Approach.* Reprint. Chicago, IL: University of Chicago Press.

"Medical Community Questions Theory on Sex Reassignment." 1997. *American Medical News,* 24–31 March, 48.

Money, John, and Anke Ehrhardt. 1972. *Man and Woman, Boy and Girl.* New York: New American Library—Mentor.

Money, John, and Patricia Tucker. 1975. *Sexual Signatures: On Being a Man or a Woman.* Boston: Little, Brown.

POSTSCRIPT

Does the John/Joan Case Prove That Gender Identity Is Innate?

What are the implications of intersexuality for psychological health? Open investigation of this question has been skirted in the medical community by the near-automatic action to surgically and hormonally repair intersexuality. Many medical professionals reason that if "normal" sexuality is restored, we will not have to be concerned about psychological consequences. Important insights are provided by case studies of unaltered intersexuals completed in the mid-1900s before the norm of surgical intervention was established. Reports document the remarkable psychological adaptability of these individuals, leading to healthy psychological and social outcomes. Just as there are few more contemporary case studies of intersexuals, there are also few follow-up studies of "corrected" intersexuals. Anecdotal accounts such as the case of John/Joan reveal emotional pain, discomfort from frequent genital examinations and invasive treatments, and destruction of sexual pleasure.

Suzanne Kessler analyzed the medical construction of sex by interviewing six medical specialists in pediatric intersexuality about the medical decision-making process. She explains that in Western culture, chromosomal and hormonal makeup determines what is defined as the real, natural, biological sex. Yet in the medical management of intersexuality, cultural factors are considered —often preempting biological factors—when assigning the sex of the infant. For example, the key consideration for the assignment of a child as a boy is the appearance of an appropriately sized penis. In fact, in her interviews, Kessler reveals great latitude in assigning sex and concludes that appearance of external genitalia, not chromosomal makeup, is often the driving force.

Should genitalia be given primacy in determining gender? Every day, we make gender attributions without genital inspection based on outward performances that culturally define gender. To catch a revealing glimpse of this gender attribution process, ask a two- or three-year-old to determine the sex of individuals or fictitious characters; and have them indicate what makes the individual male or female. Indeed, preschool curricula often include direct instruction on gender attributions, and developmental diagnostic criteria often include the ability to make such gender attributions.

Medical professionals claim that the humanitarian aim of eliminating the child's intersexuality is to enable intersexuals to "fit in" as "normal" heterosexual males or females, avoiding feelings of deviance or freakishness. Anne Fausto-Sterling identifies the assumptions behind this goal as (1) there are only two sexes, (2) heterosexuality alone is normal, and (3) there is one true model of psychological health. Kessler asks whether or not this effort is in fact to free culture from having to deal with gender ambiguity. Alternately, medical professionals may not be practicing surgical and hormonal management to consciously reinforce the current social order but rather, as part of that social order, their perceptions of viable options are limited.

Fausto-Sterling argues that broadening definitions of sexuality beyond a binary to consider multiple sexualities will challenge cultural gender dictates. In contrast, Kessler suggests that challenging traditional notions of gender may serve to diminish the defining and delimiting power of biological sex characteristics.

Fausto-Sterling challenges us to imagine a culture that had overcome sexual division. What would it be like to raise children as "unabashed intersexuals"? If surgery is undertaken less often, and intersexuality acknowledged more openly, will our cultural notions of sex and gender change? What is involved in protesting a cultural norm?

Suggested Readings

J. Colapinto, *As Nature Made Him: The Boy Who Was Raised as a Girl* (HarperCollins, 2000).

A. D. Dreger, " 'Ambiguous Sex'—or Ambivalent Medicine?" *The Hastings Center Report* (May/June 1998).

A. Fausto-Sterling, "The Five Sexes: Why Male and Female Are Not Enough," *The Sciences* (March/April 1993).

M. Hendricks, "Is It a Boy or a Girl?" *John Hopkins Magazine* (November 1993).

S. Kessler, *Lessons From the Intersexed* (Rutgers University Press, 1998).

S. Kessler, "Meanings of Genital Variability," *Chrysalis: The Journal of Transgressive Gender Identities* (1997).

S. Kessler, "The Medical Construction of Gender: Case Management of Intersexed Infants," *Signs: Journal of Women in Culture and Society* (Autumn 1990).

F. M. E. Slijper, S. L. S. Drop, J. C. Molenaar, and R. J. Scholtmeijer, "Neonates With Abnormal Genital Development Assigned the Female Sex: Parent Counseling," *Journal of Sex Education and Therapy* (1994).

ISSUE 3

Is Gender Variation a Psychological Illness?

YES: John B. McDevitt, from "A Childhood Gender Identity Disorder: Analysis, Preoedipal Determinants, and Therapy in Adolescence," in Albert J. Solnit et al., eds., *The Psychoanalytic Study of the Child, vol. 50* (Yale University Press, 1995)

NO: Katherine K. Wilson, from "Gender as Illness: Issues of Psychiatric Classification," Paper presented at the Sixth Annual ICTLEP Transgender Law and Employment Policy Conference (July 1997)

ISSUE SUMMARY

YES: Psychoanalyst John B. McDevitt uses American Psychiatric Association diagnostic criteria in presenting the case of a gender identity disorder in a four-year-old boy.

NO: Katherine K. Wilson of the Gender Identity Center of Colorado, Inc. critically analyzes biases in the diagnosis of gender identity disorder, charging that the diagnostic criteria rely upon subjective assumptions about "normal" sex and gender and underestimate the effects of distress associated with societal prejudice.

Since the 1960s and 1970s, psychosexuality, or psychological behaviors and phenomena presumably associated with biological sex, has typically been defined as having three components: gender identity, gender role, and sexual orientation.

Gender identity is one's sense of self as belonging to one sex: male or female. Cognitive developmentalists such as Lawrence Kohlberg add the criterion of gender constancy. Gender constancy starts with the ability of a child to accurately discriminate males from females and to accurately identify her or his own status correctly, and develops into the knowledge that gender is invariant. The acquisition of gender identity is often affectively loaded and sometimes marked by negative emotion, otherwise known as gender dysphoria.

The term *gender role* refers to attitudes, behaviors, and personality characteristics that are designated by society (in particular sociohistorical contexts) as appropriately masculine or feminine (i.e., typical of the male or female role, respectively). Thus, assessments of gender role behavior in children have included toy preferences, interest in physical activities, fantasy role and dress-up play, and affiliative preference for same-sex versus opposite-sex peers.

Are gender roles solely cultural productions? There is considerable controversy about this issue. Many social scientists view gender roles as primarily social in origin. In contrast, some researchers have shown that in lower animals some gender role behaviors, such as rough-and-tumble play, are influenced by prenatal sex hormones. Perhaps, they suggest, phenotypically related behaviors in humans also have a biological component.

Gender Identity Disorder (GID) is defined as a strong psychological identification with the opposite sex and is signaled by the display of opposite sex-typed behaviors and avoidance or rejection of sex-typed behaviors characteristic of one's own sex. Distress or discomfort about one's status as a boy or a girl frequently accompanies these behaviors. The age of onset is 2 to 4 years. Some children self-label as the opposite sex, some self-label correctly but wish to become a member of the opposite sex. Other children do not express cross-sex desires but exhibit cross-sex-typed behavior. Some children cross-dress, sometimes insistently. Less characteristic are cross sex-typed mannerisms (e.g., body movements, voice pitch). Cross-sex peer affiliation preferences, poor peer relations, and alienation are typical. Although not extensively studied, genital dysphoria (distress about genitalia) is sometimes present. Children with GID are not typically biologically intersexed.

Child referrals for GID have increased in the last two decades. Speculations about the cause of this increase include the heightened sensitivity to gender identity issues among schools, doctors, parents, and others. Boys are about six times as likely as girls to be referred for GID. Three explanations have been offered: (1) perhaps boys have greater biological vulnerability to anomalous development, (2) social factors reflect less tolerance of cross-gender behavior in boys, thereby creating greater dysphoria, or (3) different base rates of cross-gender behavior (i.e., boys are less likely to display feminine behavior than are girls to display masculine behavior) make boys' cross-gender behavior more noticeable.

Treatment objectives include: (1) treatment of underlying individual and family psychopathology (including lack of parental discouragement of cross-gender behavior), (2) extinction or punishment of specific cross-gender behaviors, (3) reduction of social ostracism (primarily peer rejection), and (4) prevention of adult homosexuality or transsexualism (experience of the self as a member of the opposite sex and desire to be so recognized by others to the extent of seeking out hormonal and surgical sex reassignment).

In the following selections, John B. McDevitt presents a case of GID, following *Diagnostic and Statistical Manual, 4th. ed., (DSM-IV)* diagnostic criteria. Katherine K. Wilson critically analyzes the classification of GID as a disorder.

John B. McDevitt  **YES**

A Childhood Gender Identity Disorder

In this [selection] I present and discuss data from an analysis of a four-year-old boy who wanted to be a girl, the preoedipal determinants of this wish, and his therapy in adolescence.

Billy's mother consulted me when he was aged four because she was concerned that his wish to be a girl and his preference for playing with girls indicated that he was not happy with himself as a boy. He wanted to use her makeup, wear her clothes, and put his own hair as well as hers in a ponytail. He insisted that girls were stronger than boys, could do more, and had more —jewelry, clothes, hair. She added that he had always been quiet, shy, passive, and compliant. He had avoided boyish activities from the time he was two, had shown an interest in jewelry and girls' clothes from two and a half, and had liked to dress up as a girl from the age of three.

When I first met Billy, he told me that he would like a magic fairy to turn him into a girl and that playing with boys gave him a headache because they made too much noise. He then chose to play with two Barbie dolls. He was particularly interested in their dress, hair, and high-heeled shoes.

The History

Billy's mother, an attractive, reserved, articulate young woman, hid her femininity. She preferred slacks and jeans to skirts and dresses. Looking at herself in a mirror or going to a beauty shop to make herself attractive made her uncomfortable. She had always felt shy, insecure, and insignificant, and she had always felt the need to please others and depreciate herself. Asserting herself made her feel uneasy, and she was frightened by her own anger.

In her weekly meetings with me she cried when she talked about Billy's wish to be a girl. She abhorred homosexuality and felt extremely guilty thinking that she had damaged him, as if he had cancer. For this reason, in the second year of Billy's analysis, I recommended that she begin analysis herself. She was dedicated to Billy's analysis, driving miles from the suburbs to appointments.

Her own mother had been similarly restrained and reserved but also cold and distant, which she was not. By contrast, her father, who became ill with cancer when she was eleven and died when she was fourteen, was warm, loving,

From John B. McDevitt, "A Childhood Gender Identity Disorder: Analysis, Preoedipal Determinants, and Therapy in Adolescence," in Albert J. Solnit et al., eds., *The Psychoanalytic Study of the Child*, vol. 50 (Yale University Press, 1995). Copyright © 1995 by Albert J. Solnit, Peter B. Neubauer, Samuel Abrams, and A. Scott Dowling. Reprinted by permission of Yale University Press. Notes and references omitted.

and ebullient but had a temper that frightened her. Both parents, as they already had a daughter, had wanted her to be a boy.

As a child, the mother, like Billy, was shy, self-sufficient, and happy to play alone for hours in her room. During latency, she was a tomboy, which pleased her father, but no matter how much she tried to gain his love, she was always disappointed and enraged by his strong attachment to her pretty and popular sister, six years older. Her father and sister were in constant battle, but the father always gave in to his daughter's demands. The sister was preoccupied with her dress and appearance, especially her breasts, and frequently preened in front of the mirror. Dominating and temperamental, she belittled Billy's mother, humiliated and demeaned her. Yet Billy's mother thought her sister was beautiful, particularly admired her breasts, and envied and idealized her. She was also jealous and afraid of her.

For many years Billy's mother was subordinate and submissive to his father. At first, she thought that her husband was as strong, capable, and reliable as her father had been, but subsequently she was disappointed and angry because he was not. For all her shyness, she eventually became the dominant partner in the marriage, the disciplinarian in the family, and a successful businesswoman.

Although the father hoped to have a better relationship with Billy than he had had with his own father, he did not. Like his father he traveled frequently and was emotionally distant and unavailable during Billy's first three to four years.... [W]hen the boy was four, he was overly permissive rather than critical and dictatorial. He related to Billy more like a pal or brother than a father, often providing gifts and treats. He was more tolerant and permissive with Billy than his wife, who was more serious and the disciplinarian...,

The father... told me that he was not concerned about nor did he feel any responsibility for Billy's femininity, recalling that he himself had often dressed in his mother's clothes as a child—once in his mother's fur coat, when his parents were away on a trip when he was three. He added that if Billy became a homosexual he would still love him. Soon after Billy began his analysis, the father stopped his own therapy. Before Billy was six the father began to take him to sexually stimulating movies. I saw Billy's father every month or two.

... [When Billy was born] the mother would have preferred a girl. Although she felt happy and excited during her pregnancy, she was also apprehensive, afraid that she wasn't prepared to raise a child, particularly a boy, who would become too wild and sexually aggressive (as his father had been in adolescence) and who would stimulate her own sexual impulses. But she was delighted with Billy, a sweet, sensitive, happy infant, much like herself when she was a child. Until he was six months old she dressed him in a niece's pink clothes....

The mother never thought of her child as baby boy or baby girl, just as baby. She did not recall difficulties, conflicts, or confusion in her mind between herself and Billy during the first year and a half. From her description I could infer that Billy had been appropriately attached and responsive to her; it seemed that his separation and stranger reactions had been mild to moderate; and the practicing subphase, although subdued, seemed to have been otherwise normal.

Billy was described as a graceful, sensitive, cooperative, good-natured infant—a joy to be with. . . .

The mother . . . ignored and devalued Billy's masculinity and phallic urges, and, as a consequence, Billy seems to have similarly ignored and devalued the masculinity and sexuality that he was just becoming aware of. . . .

When Billy was two years old, the mother noticed that he did not like to play with cars and trucks as boys usually do. She attributed this to his "artistic" nature. Billy did not like the Superman outfit that he received as a gift for his second birthday, nor did he like football T-shirts. It soon became apparent that Billy preferred to play with girls and liked jewelry, the colors pink and purple, and the feel of such fabrics as velvet. She recalled buying him a pink bracelet and a "pull-string egg-beater" toy, and she thought it cute that he liked to play with an old straw handbag of hers. . . .

Billy did have an "artistic" nature. According to the mother he had always been sensitive to noise, color, texture, and visual nuances. On psychological testing at age six, he showed an extraordinary perception of visual nuances of shading, texture, and shape. The mother not only identified with Billy, she had a very special relationship with him, and he with her. She had an "uncanny" ability, she thought, to know what Billy was feeling or thinking, an unusual sensitivity to nonverbal cues. . . .

By four Billy was more outgoing and friendly in his manner. As he became more feminine he became less shy, enjoying acting out TV roles for parents and guests. At home he played happily for long periods of time in his room. He also became more assertive, battling with his mother over TV and schedules. She found his "greediness" for things difficult to take; his father his "whinyness." Each of them on occasion referred to Billy as "she." He sometimes called his mother "Daddy."

Although Billy got along well on play dates, he was excessively agreeable and submissive, needing, like his parents, to please, and he took physical abuse from a close girl friend, less from a boy friend. Billy had a unique ability to imitate and to play different roles with different children. He hid his femininity sufficiently so that no one other than his parents and I knew about his gender disorder.

The Analysis

At four years Billy was a good-looking, likable, considerate, well-behaved boy with feminine speech and gestures, his hands drooping in an exaggerated manner, a caricature of femininity, quite the opposite of his mother. From the beginning of treatment, separating from her was too easy for a child of his age. In fact, he always looked forward to becoming grown up and independent, to extricating himself from his close tie to her.

Billy's four-year-long analysis consisted largely of fantasies expressed in doll play. In the first year there were two main characters: Barbie and Ken. Billy's main interest was in playing the role of the Barbie doll, who, after several months, became a sexy adolescent girl. He put her hair in a ponytail, her feet in high-heeled shoes, and soon introduced Ken, a handsome adolescent boy to whom Barbie displayed her beauty and her remarkable abilities to perform. Barbie was portrayed as an all-powerful female who humiliated Ken. Nonetheless, Ken and other male dolls admired and experienced Barbie as captivating, and they envied her clothes, the attention she got, and the fact that she was so superior to them. Billy had me play the role of the Ken doll, who was portrayed as weak and helpless.

Billy's doll play seemed to give him great pleasure; it also had a driven quality, was repetitive, and occupied most of his sessions. He completely avoided boyish play or activities because they frightened him; they made him noticeably anxious. In the first two years, although fond of me, he maintained a physical and emotional distance, not engaging me directly in play or other activities. He did, however, speak to me as he played—as an accompaniment, a communication, or an explanation—and he shared his feelings with me. Billy spoke for all the dolls, although I sometimes asked questions or made comments in the role of the Ken doll, which he did not object to. Billy did not share with me the scary dreams, fears of ghosts and monsters, and fears of injury his parents reported. In fact, he was always in a good mood and rarely complained.

In play, Billy attributed to Barbie everything that he envied, admired, or found pleasurable, and to Ken everything unsatisfactory and unpleasurable. Barbie expressed Billy's exhibitionistic, narcissistic, possessive, aggressive, and sexual impulses as well as his wish to be grown up and independent. Ken expressed Billy's envy of Barbie's beauty, her breasts, and her power to attract men; of her strength and ability to dominate them; and of such of her possessions as dresses and cosmetics. And Ken expressed everything Billy disliked about himself—his doubts, anxieties, and inhibitions. At home and at school Billy, like Ken, showed no curiosity or interest in his own body or genitals and was unable to assert himself.

One theme in Billy's play in the first year was the fear of object loss. Barbie not only repeatedly ignored Ken, she also frequently left him. For example, when Barbie was taking off in an airplane on a trip similar to a trip recently taken by Billy's mother, Ken strenuously objected and tried to grab Barbie, particularly her breasts, in order to keep her from leaving. When Ken failed, Billy had a magic fairy change him into another Barbie doll, undoing the separation. On another occasion when Barbie was away, Ken became so enamored of the clothes in her room that Billy turned him into another Barbie, making up for his envy and loneliness.

In the second year Billy began to touch his penis and to have erections at home and in the office for the first time. Experiencing pleasurable sensations in the penis and beginning to value it caused Billy to view the male role more favorably, or perhaps was the result of this view. After Ken injured his penis in play and Billy reassuringly replaced it with a plastic tube, he reported a scary dream. A purple-people-eater monster grabbed Billy's penis, pulled it and bit it off, and put a plastic tube where the penis had been so that Billy could urinate. Billy then stole the penis from the monster and put it back on himself....

In the first year Billy had wanted to be the phallic Barbie, not a boy with a penis. Now, in the second year, he was uncertain about who he wanted to be. He said he had both a penis and a vagina, that he was half-boy, half-girl. This was the same expression his mother had used a year earlier when she told me how sad she felt looking at a photograph of Billy when he still had long hair.

Soon after Billy began to value his penis, he introduced competition between the Ken doll and the Bionic Man doll for Barbie's hand in marriage. This oedipal theme, along with the question of whether to be Barbie or to marry Barbie, whether to be a woman or a man, were Billy's major concerns for the remainder of the analysis. And it was not only a question of whether to be a woman or a man; it was also a question of how to be a man. Billy said he knew how to be a woman, but he did not know how to be a man or how to compete with a man.

The Ken doll, now played by Billy, was repeatedly beaten up by the Bionic man, a role Billy had assigned to me; or, almost as frequently, the Ken doll won out over the Bionic Man and stole his heart, power, and penis so that he could marry Barbie, just as a year earlier Barbie had stolen Ken's penis and power. Another Ken doll, also speaking for Billy, said that he would prefer to be a girl rather than marry Barbie.

Soon after the onset of the oedipal competition between Ken and the Bionic Man, sadomasochistic qualities became more prominent in Billy's play. Barbie made believe that she loved the Bionic Man and seduced him, with the purpose of teasing, belittling, and rejecting Ken. This hurt Ken and made him angry. He dramatically and excitedly put Barbie to sleep by pricking her finger, threatened her with monsters, threw her off cliffs into water full of sharks, and stuck her in the heart with thousands of needles so she would die. Although Barbie had repeatedly belittled Ken in the first year of treatment, Billy had not experienced sexual excitement and erections until now. The Bionic Man was not included in these scenes, but, at the same time that Ken was forcibly wooing, subduing, and torturing Barbie in order to get control over her and marry her, he was also fighting the Bionic Man for her hand in marriage, with one or the other winning out at different times. . . .

In the first year of treatment Barbie had been active, sadistic, and phallic but not maternal. Ken had been passive and masochistic, but neither castrated nor feminine. In the second year Barbie became masochistic, Ken sadistic. The roles were reversed. Ken had become more masculine and was able to stand up to and challenge Barbie, and the Bionic Man as well. This picture could change quickly, however, with Barbie once again gaining the upper hand and belittling Ken. On one occasion Ken's only recourse was to turn himself into another, stronger Barbie who shot a bullet from her breast and hit the breast of the Barbie who had belittled him. On occasion Billy played a more subdued family game in which a girl doll who represented Billy sat quietly and happily beside her father, who was driving a car.

Toward the end of the second year Billy invited me to play with the construction toy Lego. He was quite skilled at this and did not seem at all feminine while playing. This play was an acceptable boyish activity, compared with play with cars and trucks or superhero figures, which made him visibly anxious. This boyish behavior must have been what he showed to others in his everyday life—at school, for example. A few sessions later, however, he acted both the female and male roles in a show he performed for me. He danced like a seductive girl and also played that he was her lover, using a masculine voice and manner.

At the end of the second year Billy told me that, even though he still wanted to be a girl, he did not want to lose his penis; that he was not able to understand why, despite his best efforts at learning how to be a boy, he unintentionally continued to make movements like a girl; that he did want to know how to be a boy, to know what love is, and to learn how to love and marry a woman.

At the beginning of the third year, Billy talked more about his fears—of death, robbers, monsters—and he worried that his parents would die in a plane crash or that a stranger would shoot and kill his father. He explained that he could protect himself from being shot by robbers by dressing as an old woman with a long skirt. Even so, he was not safe because the robbers might see his pants underneath his skirt. After saying this he immediately began to play that he was a coy, seductive, charming, and beautiful girl who would captivate the robbers. When asked if the purpose of the disguise and the play was to avoid being shot, he said that it definitely was.

Billy then proceeded to put on many dramatic, romantic plays in which a seductive lady was treated badly by men. The plays were exciting, exhibitionistic, sadomasochistic, repetitive, and often accompanied by erections. Billy said that he enacted such frightening plays in order to get over the fears he had at night. Throughout the analysis, whenever Billy experienced castration anxiety he played that he was a girl. In the plays Barbie masochistically loved men who rejected, hurt, raped, and killed her, or, alternatively, she seduced and tricked men, throwing them in the water to be eaten by sharks, just as Ken had done to her the previous year. . . .

In the fourth year Ken and the Bionic Man continued to fight for Barbie's love, with Ken often winning. This could readily change, however. For example, when the Bionic Man returned from a trip he forced his love on Barbie, after she had put up a half-hearted resistance. She was not totally unresponsive even though she said she preferred Ken. Billy explained that the Bionic Man was Barbie's father, who, in disguise, had come to make love to her and to tell her that her mother had died in an accident. Barbie's father, in this session, died soon after of a heart attack. When his own father traveled, Billy missed him, feared that he might die, and began to express affection for his mother more openly.

Toward the end of treatment, as Billy entered latency, his play became more subdued, and he began to assume the male role almost exclusively. For a while he spoke appropriately for each role, but he then spoke only as a male. He spent less time in imaginative play and talked with me about such interests as traveling, reading, and movies. He hoped to be an airline pilot, an actor, or a lawyer when he grew up. He enjoyed swimming and bicycling and was chosen captain of his class soccer team.

Billy was able to hide his continuing feminine identification by weaving it into acceptable masculine play and behavior. He combined ballet or modern dancing with gymnastics, so that he looked masculine. In playing with Star War figures, he appeared to behave like a boy, but to him it was more important to dress the figures in fancy ways—for example, in purple pants—than to have the good guys beat the bad guys. His mother always saw through this disguise, his father never did.

When Billy was almost eight, he told me that he wanted to be a boy but often thought of himself as a girl. As an example, he explained that while on vacation he felt like a girl for two days, but the rest of the time he felt like a boy. He illustrated the difference with slightly different movements in a gym routine, one female and the other male. A few months later, he said that he no longer wished to be or thought of being a girl. The only thing that bothered him were occasional dreams of being badly treated, such as being attacked or shot by bad guys. After he heard on the news that a man had slashed a number of people with a knife, he woke with the fear that a robber would attack him with a knife. He associated the knife to a machete that his father used in the country.

During his analysis Billy became more aware of his anger toward his father and his mother. He was not, however, able to acknowledge feelings of longing or love for his father or his analyst. The changes that had occurred in Billy were the result of entering latency, his mother's firm opposition to his femininity, his acceptance as a boy in school, his social and academic success, and his analysis. His parents were pleased that he appeared to be more boyish.

Billy continued to be remarkably adaptable in his ability to enjoy a variety of play activities and roles with close friends. On the one hand, this adaptability was the result of his wit, charm, and intelligence; on the other, it was due to his unique ability to imitate and to assume and play a variety of roles. The parents reported that he imitated actors and performers on TV and that these imitations were often the "essence" of Billy. His acting was not limited to putting on plays, however; in a sense he was always acting. He needed "instant gratification"—for example, by imagining that he was a star on Broadway. On a few occasions his mother questioned the depth of his attachments and emotional commitments. She thought that his expression of his feelings was shallow and that they did not last long enough. The father believed that not until he was eight was Billy finally able to "integrate" what he had taken in from others so that his own personality could begin to emerge.

Discussion

When Billy began analysis at age four, he was in the phallic-narcissistic phase; his object relations were dyadic. It is likely that he regressed to this phase from the early oedipal phase. His wish to be a girl, portrayed by Barbie, was a compromise formation that provided the best available solution to his conflicts. It protected his mother against his phallic, destructive wishes while, at the same time, permitting him to use his femininity to express his hostility toward her. It gained her approval and maintained his close tie to her but was not incestuous. It warded off separation and castration anxiety, made up for his dissatisfaction at being a boy, and allowed him to gratify narcissistic and sadomasochistic wishes, including the wish to seduce the father he loved. Its repetitive and driven expression in play was an effort to master trauma. What he had endured passively he initiated actively, saying at the same time, "Don't worry, it's not real," thereby reassuring himself that the female genitals were not real and that he had not been castrated. Additional mechanisms operative were inhibition, reaction formation, submission, and masochism.

Early in the second year of treatment, when Billy reentered the oedipal phase, the compromise formation changed from the wish to be a girl to the wish to be both a girl and a boy—a bisexual solution. This new bisexual compromise formation—expressed in the endless battles for Barbie between Ken and the Bionic Man, and in the sadomasochistic sexual relations each of them had with her—consisted of a striking reshuffling of the developmental opposites of active-passive, sadistic-masochistic, phallic-castrated, and masculine-feminine, which had earlier been so out of kilter. Barbie, who had previously been active, sadistic, and phallic in her relation to Ken, became passive, masochistic, and castrated in relation to Ken and to the Bionic Man. Ken became active and sadistic with Barbie and competitive with the Bionic Man. In other words, Billy, who in the phallic phase had envied and identified with the phallic Barbie, now, in the oedipal phase, identified either with the masochistic Barbie, experiencing pleasure and excitement when she was mistreated by Ken or by the Bionic Man, or with Ken, who competed with the Bionic Man for Barbie and who treated her sadistically, which also excited him sexually. The oscillating shifts in these roles accounted for the bisexuality, with each of the three roles—phallic-narcissistic, negative and positive oedipal—serving as a defense against the others.

Although in the first year of the analysis Billy had turned Ken into another Barbie when Barbie left him, separation anxiety—the result of intense hostility toward the mother—was not a major issue in his analysis. His major concern was castration anxiety. Whenever it increased, it inevitably triggered his compromise formation: Billy became Barbie. And, conversely, Billy's compromise formation and its endless repetition in play minimized his castration anxiety. Early in the analysis the mother was the castrator; later, it was the father. Billy was afraid that his father would be killed when he traveled, and the robber in his nightmares was his father.

Although Billy's compromise formation at the time of his analysis was determined by the anxieties and conflicts of the phallic-narcissistic and oedipal phases, it had its roots in the entire preoedipal phase (see McDevitt, 1967, 1971). Since his wish to be a girl and his equally important fear of being a boy started when he was two years old, there must have been important preoedipal determinants for both the wish and the fear. The first such preoedipal factor was Billy's constitutional endowment—his passivity and compliance; his heightened visual, tactile, and auditory sensitivity, particularly to noise; and his appearance as an infant as a "mellow" baby with a "sweet" disposition. These qualities not only had a direct effect on Billy's development but also influenced the mother's attitude toward him. Had Billy been more assertive, his mother would have found it more difficult to mold him in a feminine direction.

The second determinant was the mother's unconscious need to shape Billy in a feminine manner. Her neurotic personality disorder and uncertain gender identity seriously interfered with Billy's masculine sexual development. The mother cared very much for Billy. She was loving, available, and reliable, and she was a consistent and efficient caretaker. Although she was empathic, her empathy was skewed in the direction of seeing her own wishes and needs in Billy. He was an extension of herself, of her own phallic-narcissistic wishes. In the first year and a half she was too controlling of Billy. In the next year and a half, during the anal and phallic phases, she found it difficult to be firm, fearing she would damage him. Later she became a strict disciplinarian, the "heavy."

The mother's preference for a girl, her fear of being sexually attracted to a boy child's developing phallic sexuality, and her hostile, competitive impulses toward men and toward Billy—all of which were very subtly expressed in her behavior—caused her to selectively respond to, mirror, and attune herself to those aspects of Billy's behavior that would later contribute to femininity. Her ambivalence and feminine shaping intensified in Billy's second and third year because her anxiety was intensified by Billy's emerging expression of his masculinity. She once said that if Billy were more masculine she would be tempted to seduce him. As a consequence of the conflict between his mother's preference and the onset of his awareness of his masculinity, Billy had to choose a feminine identity in order to assure himself of her love.

It was not only the external shaping that laid down a pathway for Billy's identification with his mother; internal forces also contributed: his temperament, his extraordinary visual and tactile sensitivity, his attunement with and closeness to his mother, and his remarkable imitative ability all fostered identification with her. An essential aspect of this closeness was the unconscious communication between the two, in which the mother saw herself [in] Billy, confusing herself with him, and Billy saw himself in her, confusing himself with her. The closeness, however, made him uncomfortable and caused him to struggle to free himself.

Another related internal force may have been a disturbance in self-object differentiation in the first two years of life. The first motive for identification with the mother seen in Billy's analysis was the fear of object loss. Ken became another Barbie in order to undo the separation brought on by Barbie's airplane trip. A disturbance in self-object differentiation would have created an uncertain, unstable mental representation of the mother and of the self. Identification with the mother may have taken place to relieve this uncertainty and may have prepared the ground for the subsequent use of identification with the mother as his main defense mechanism. Billy was said to have been shy between ages one and three and to have clung to his mother. As he became more feminine in behavior, he also became more certain of himself and less shy, and more certain of his mother, clinging to her less. In fact, he became a "ham," acting TV roles for his parents and guests and putting on plays in nursery school.

By age two to three years another powerful internal force—intrapsychic conflict—caused Billy to shape himself in a feminine direction in order to protect himself from the dangers of object loss and castration brought on by his hostility toward his mother. This was the first version of the compromise formation that was present when Billy entered analysis.

A third determining factor was trauma and overstimulation. On the one hand, the mother was prudish, anxious, and intolerant of sex in herself and Billy, and she devalued and depreciated his developing phallic sexuality. On the other, she overstimulated him by exposing herself to him, by exposing him to the primal scene, and by arranging for his operations [which included an adenoidectomy and a myringotomy]. Billy reacted with excitement and fright, frustration and rage, especially since he was so sensitive to sights and sounds. He turned away from and devalued the masculine body, genitals, and the phallic urges he was just becoming aware of; he repressed and inhibited sexual curiosity, interest, and excitement, as well as aggression.

A fourth determining force was constituted by the father's absence, unavailability, and indifference; his sibling relationship and rivalry with Billy; his permissiveness, especially his sexual permissiveness; and, significantly, his own unconscious gender confusion. When Billy was four his father began to spend more time with him and encouraged Billy to prefer him to his mother. He not only competed with Billy for his wife's attention, he also competed with his wife for Billy's attention. As mentioned earlier, when Billy was five to six years old his father began to take him to sexually stimulating movies. In addition to being seductive in his behavior, the father was not a reliable masculine figure with whom Billy could identify. And Billy's marked fear of anything masculine, which he equated with aggression, made it impossible for him to identify with his father.

In fact, instead of identifying with his father, as boys ordinarily do, Billy identified with the mother. But in contrast to the little girl, who usually identifies with the maternal qualities of the mother, Billy identified with his mother's phallic qualities. This diminished his concern over losing his penis. These qualities stood for the penis, just as an inanimate object or clothes stand for the penis in the fetishist and the transvestite, respectively. In his analysis Billy temporarily became a transvestite, displaying his erect penis underneath a make-believe skirt.

A fifth determinant was Billy's fear and intolerance of his hostility. This fear caused him to forgo phallic and masculine activity and to be willing to give up his penis because he evidently experienced it as a destructive weapon. In his analysis he was visibly frightened by boyish activities or toys—superheroes, cars, weapons—which he avoided. He took extreme measures to contain hostility by modifying it sadomasochistically and by attributing it to Barbie, and then alternately to Barbie, Ken, and the Bionic Man. In his everyday life he was unassertive and submissive.

Billy's intense, sadistic hostility was directed toward his mother, not his father, just as Ken's hostility was directed toward Barbie, not the Bionic Man, although he fought and competed with him. Billy was enraged with his mother for hampering his autonomous strivings, for squelching his masculinity, for preferring his father, and for the operative procedures, which left him feeling castrated. His view of her as an extremely strict, uncaring, and ungiving woman, as unfaithful as Barbie, was not correct. It was the result of his projection....

Billy identified with Barbie, rather than with the actual mother, who was shy and inhibited. I think it reasonable to infer that one of the mother's unconscious sexual fantasies was portrayed by the powerful, exhibitionistic, seductive, and captivating Barbie doll. These were the qualities that Billy envied. I assume that another sexual fantasy of the mother that Billy identified with was portrayed by the passive and masochistic Barbie.

Barbie's seductive exhibitionism, which Billy envied, resembled his mother's description of her sister. She particularly liked to exhibit her breasts, which the mother envied. Just as Billy was caught dressing in his mother's clothes and using her cosmetics while in her bathroom, the mother had been fearful as a child that she would be caught in her sister's bathroom using her cosmetics.

In exposing herself to Billy the mother may have done to him what her sister did to her and unknowingly may have imposed her fantasies on him. Barbie's breasts were important to Billy. When he staged plays he taped paper over his own breasts in order to draw attention to them. Furthermore, there was a similarity between Barbie's demeaning attitude toward Ken in Billy's play and his aunt's humiliating behavior vis-à-vis Billy's mother and also with Billy's mother's occasionally demeaning attitude toward Billy when she was angry with him....

Subsequent Treatment

... [By his late teenage years] Billy felt horrible and disgusted about himself. Although he liked his penis, and his body in general, he spoke of himself as a negative boy. One of his solutions to his dilemma was the fantasy of getting married and having children but secretly picking up men in gay bars. In many ways he was unclear about who he was or wanted to be, just as he did not have a clear sense of the nature of his relationships with other people. His real self came out most clearly when he tearfully expressed his wish to be sexually normal, to have a lasting, loving relationship with a woman, and to have a consistent, stable sense of himself.

NO

Gender as Illness: Issues of Psychiatric Classification

In this [selection], ambiguous and conflicting language in the DSM-IV [Fourth Edition of the Diagnostic and Statistical Manual of Mental Disorders] and its supporting literature which serves to endorse harmful stereotypes of transgendered individuals is examined. This [selection] does not attempt to address the broader question of the appropriateness of classification of any gender role diversity as mental disorder.

Transvestic Fetishism, 302.3

The diagnostic criteria for transvestic fetishism (APA, 1994), formerly transvestism, are as follows:

- A. Over a period of at least 6 months, in a heterosexual male, recurrent, intense sexually arousing fantasies, sexual urges, or behaviors involving cross-dressing.
- B. The fantasies, sexual urges, or behaviors cause clinically significant distress or impairment in social, occupational, or other important areas of functioning.
- Specify if: With Gender Dysphoria: if the person has persistent discomfort with gender role or identity.

Gender Identity Disorder of Adults, 302.85

The diagnostic criteria for gender identity disorder [GID] for adults and adolescents (APA, 1994), formerly transsexualism, are:

- A. A strong and persistent cross-gender identification (not merely a desire for any perceived cultural advantages of being the other sex). In adolescents and adults, the disturbance is manifested by symptoms such as a stated desire to be the other sex, frequent passing as the other sex, desire to live or be treated as the other sex, or the conviction that he or she has the typical feelings and reactions of the other sex.

From Katherine K. Wilson, "Gender as Illness: Issues of Psychiatric Classification," Paper presented at the Sixth Annual ICTLEP Transgender Law and Employment Policy Conference (July 1997). Copyright © 1997 by The Gender Identity Center of Colorado, Inc. Reprinted by permission of the Board of Directors for The Gender Identity Center of Colorado, Inc. Notes omitted.

- B. Persistent discomfort with his or her sex or sense of inappropri-
  ateness in the gender role of that sex. In adolescents and adults, the
  disturbance is manifested by symptoms such as preoccupation with
  getting rid of primary and secondary sex characteristics (e.g., request
  for hormones, surgery, or other procedures to physically alter sexual
  characteristics to simulate the other sex) or belief that he or she was
  born the wrong sex.
- C. The disturbance is not concurrent with a physical intersex condition.
- D. The disturbance causes clinically significant distress or impairment
  in social, occupational, or other important areas of functioning.
- Specify if (for sexually mature individuals) Sexually Attracted to
  Males, . . . Females, . . . Both, . . . Neither.

Gender Identity Disorder of Children, 302.85

The diagnostic criteria for gender identity disorder for children (APA, 1994) are:

- A. In children, the disturbance is manifested by four (or more) of the
  following:

  1. repeatedly stated desire to be, or insistence that he or she is,
     the other sex
  2. in boys, preference for cross-dressing or simulating female at-
     tire; in girls, insistence on wearing only stereotypical mascu-
     line clothing
  3. strong and persistent preferences for cross-sex roles in make-
     believe play or persistent fantasies of being the other sex
  4. intense desire to participate in the stereotypical games and
     pastimes of the other sex
  5. strong preferences for playmates of the other sex

- B. In children, the disturbance is manifested by any of the following:

  in boys, assertion that his penis or testes are disgusting or
  will disappear or assertion that it would be better not to
  have a penis, or aversion toward rough-and-tumble play and
  rejection of male stereotypical toys, games and activities;

  in girls, rejection of urinating in a sitting position, assertion
  that she has or will grow a penis, or assertion that she does
  not want to grow breasts or menstruate, or marked aversion
  toward normative feminine clothing.

- C & D. Same as for adults.

Ambiguous Language

Many questions regarding the characterization of cross-gender identity and expression as mental disorders are unresolved in the mental health professions. In some instances, a lack of scientific consensus is reflected in increasingly ambiguous and conflicting language in recent revisions of the Diagnostic and Statistical Manual of Mental Disorders. The result is that a widening segment of gender non-conforming youth and adults are potentially subject to psychiatric diagnosis, severe stigma, and loss of civil liberty. . . .

A Question of Degree

. . . [T]he Introduction to the DSM-IV (APA, 1994, p. xxii) states:

> Neither deviant behavior . . . nor conflicts that are primarily between the individual and society are mental disorders unless the deviance or conflict is a symptom of dysfunction . . .

However, it is contradicted in the gender identity disorder section (p. 536):

> Gender Identity Disorder can be distinguished from simple nonconformity to stereo-typical sex role behavior by the extent and pervasiveness of the cross-gender wishes, interests, and activities.

The second statement implies that one may deviate from social expectation without a diagnostic label, but not too much. Conflicting language in the DSM serves the agendas of intolerant parents, relatives, and employers and their medical expert witnesses who seek to deny transgendered individuals their freedom, children and jobs.

Sexist Language

The transvestic fetishism and gender identity disorder categories contain sexist language that appears to presume the superiority or desirability of one gender role over another.

The Dress Code for Males

Criterion A of the transvestic fetishism disorder limits diagnosis to heterosexual males. Therefore, women are free to wear whatever they choose without a diagnosis of mental illness. This criterion serves to enforce a stricter standard of conformity for males than females. Its dual standard not only reflects the disparate positions that men and women hold in American society, but promotes them. The implication is that men hold more power and privilege than women, therefore biological males who emulate women are presumed irrational and mentally disordered while biological females who emulate males are not.

The Dress Code for Boys and Girls

In the case of gender non-conforming children and adolescents, the GID criteria are significantly broader in scope in the DSM-IV (APA, 1994, p. 537) than in earlier editions. Boys are once again held to a much stricter standard of conformity than girls. A preference for cross-dressing or simulating female attire meets the diagnostic criterion for boys but not for girls, who must insist on wearing only male clothing to merit diagnosis. References to "stereotypical" clothing, toys and activities of the other sex are imprecise in an American culture where much children's clothing is unisex and appropriate sex role is the subject of political debate.

Prejudicial Language

The gender disorders of the DSM-IV and its supporting publications contain wording that is insensitive to the prejudice that transgendered individuals face and, in one instance, particularly offensive.

The Label Fetish

The burden of social stigma suffered by transgendered people is worsened by medical classification (Bolin, 1988). Transvestic fetishism, in particular, is presented in a most demeaning manner. Transvestism in the DSM-III was re-named "transvestic fetishism" in the DSM-III-R (APA, 1987). This misleading label serves to sexualize a diagnosis that... does not clearly require a sexual context. Cross-dressing by males very often represents a social expression of an inner sense of identity. In fact, the clinical literature cites many cases, considered diagnosable under transvestic fetishism, which present no sexual motivation for cross-dressing and by no means represent fetishism....

Clinical Significance Confusion

The focus of psychiatric classification in the early 1970s shifted from cause to consequence. Thomas Sasz's (1961) broad criticism of psychiatric nosology had a profound influence on the deletion of homosexuality from the DSM and later changes in the definition of mental illness. Consequently, distress and impairment became central to the definition of mental disorder in the DSM-IV (APA, 1994, p. xxi). A clinical significance criterion was added to all Sexual and Gender Identity disorders, including transvestic fetishism and gender identity disorder:

> The fantasies, sexual urges, or behaviors cause clinically significant distress or impairment in social, occupational, or other important areas of functioning (APA, 1994, p. 531).

A Distressing Lack of Consensus

Distress and impairment are not specifically defined for transgendered people in the DSM-IV. They are left to the interpretation of the reader. Tolerant clinicians may infer that transgender identity or expression is not inherently impairing, but that societal intolerance and prejudice are to blame for the distress and internalized shame that transpeople often suffer. Intolerant clinicians may infer the opposite: that cross-gender identity or expression by definition constitutes an impairment regardless of the individual's happiness or well-being. . . .

Views of inherent impairment and distress in transvestism and transsexualism rest on two threads, deviance from presumptions of biological function and association with other psychopathology. These same arguments supported the pathologization of homosexuality before 1973, when they were rejected by the psychiatric community. They were based on studies of clinical subjects who did not constitute a representative gay, lesbian and bisexual population, and failed to explain the existence of healthy constructive gays, lesbians and bisexuals in society (APA, 1980).

Rebuttals to theories of inherent transgender distress and impairment closely parallel those in the case of sexual orientation. . . . [A]nthropological research has revealed a long list of supernumerary gender roles among many non-European cultures. These were accepted, often highly respected, societal roles difficult to characterize as pathological. The medical presumption of gender essentialism, exactly two natural sexes determined by genitalia, has been challenged by a growing body of socio-cultural literature that considers gender a social construction, not a biological imperative. Psychiatric studies of clinical populations, like those of clinical gay and lesbian subjects in previous decades, have failed to consider the incidence of functional, well adjusted transgendered people and couples in society. . . .

Blaming the Victim

Transgendered people do suffer distress and impairment from societal intolerance, discrimination, violence, undeserved shame, and denial of personal freedoms that ordinary men and women take for granted. The psychiatric interpretation of inherent transgender pathology serves to attribute the consequences of prejudice to its victims, neglecting the true cause of distress. It promotes treatment paradigms that are punitive rather than affirmative with the goal of conformity and not self-acceptance.

In stark contrast, the APA has articulated a growing compassion and understanding of the issues faced by gays, lesbians and bisexuals. An amicus brief filed by the American Psychiatric Association, the American Psychological Association, the National Association of Social Workers and the Colorado Psychological Association in the case of Romer vs. Evans (APA, et al., 1994) states the following:

> The harmful effects of prejudice, discrimination, and violence, however, are not limited to such bodily or pecuniary consequences . . . The effects can include depression, a persistent sense of vulnerability, and efforts to

rationalize the experience by viewing one's victimization as just punishment. Gay people, like members of other groups that are subject to social prejudice, also frequently come to internalize society's negative stereotypes.

Clearly, the American Psychiatric Association does not consider such distress symptomatic of mental disorder for gay and lesbian people as it does for transgendered people. Ironically, the same document acknowledges that gay and transgendered individuals face much the same discrimination: "Both gay men and lesbians are often associated with cross-sex characteristics."

A key point in the declassification of sexual orientation as a mental disorder was the distinction between distress or impairment caused by society and that believed inherent to homosexuality itself. It is unfortunate that, over two decades later, this distinction is left unresolved for the transgender disorders in the DSM-IV.

The Disordered Childhood

As stated previously, the diagnostic criteria for gender identity disorder of children were significantly broadened [in] the DSM-IV (APA, 1994, p. 537) to the concern of civil rights advocates. A child may now be diagnosed with gender identity disorder without ever having stated any desire to be, or insistence of being, the other sex. Boys are inexplicably held to a much stricter standard of conformity than girls in their choice of clothing and activities. More puzzling is a criterion which lists a "strong preference for playmates of the other sex" as symptomatic, and seems to equate mental health with sexual discrimination.

The Prehomosexual Agenda

Author Phyllis Burke (1996) describes cases of children as young as age three institutionalized or treated with a diagnosis of gender identity disorder for widely varying gender nonconformity. She presents evidence of increasing use of GID for children suspected of being "prehomosexual," and not necessarily transsexual. Diagnosis and treatment is often at the insistence of non-accepting parents with the intent of changing a perceived homosexual orientation. Burke quotes Kenneth Zucker, of the GID subcommittee, that parents bring children to gender clinics for the most part "because they don't want their kid to be gay" (p. 100).

Zucker and Bradley (1995, p. 53) noted that "homosexuality is the most common postpubertal psychosexual outcome for children [with GID]." They defended the treatment of gender nonconforming children on three points: reduction of social ostracism, treatment of underlying psychopathology, and prevention of GID in adulthood (pp. 266–7). The first appears to shift the blame for the distress of discrimination from its inflictors to its victims. The second presumes theories of psychodynamic etiology which lack evidence in nonclinical populations (Wilson, 1997). With respect to the third, the authors conceded that,

> there are simply no formal empirical studies demonstrating that therapeutic intervention in childhood alters the developmental path toward either transsexualism or homosexuality (p. 270).

This use of Gender Identity Disorder for children and youth was recently condemned by the National Gay and Lesbian Task Force (originally the National Gay Task Force, founded in 1973 to lobby against inclusion of homosexuality in the DSM-II, Lobel, 1996) and the San Francisco Human Rights Commission (1996). . . .

Far from promoting consistency in diagnosis and treatment, ambiguous and conflicting language in the DSM-IV has created much confusion and controversy. Interpretation of the Gender Identity Disorder and Transvestic Fetishism diagnostic criteria may range from a narrow definition of objective distress to an overinclusive loophole to the American Psychiatric Association decision to declassify homosexuality as a mental disorder.

Transsexualism Diluted

For sex reassignment procedures (SRS), the Standards of Care for the Hormonal and Surgical Sex Reassignment of Gender Dysphoric Persons, from the Harry Benjamin International Gender Dysphoria Association (1990), specifically require a diagnosis of transsexualism as listed in the DSM-III-R. The rationale is that cross-gender identity is legitimized by psychiatric classification as a condition worthy of evaluation and treatment (Pauly, 1992; Bolin, 1988). By implication, SRS procedures might cease to be offered to transsexuals without a diagnosis to validate their medical necessity and justify their risks.

This rationale is inconsistent with the APA's decision to merge the DSM-III-R categories of transsexualism and gender identity disorder of adolescence or adulthood, nontranssexual type (GIDAANT) in the DSM-IV:

> The desire to uncouple the clinical diagnosis of gender dysphoria from criteria for approving patients for SRS was one factor in the subcommittee's recommendation that these categories be merged under the single heading of Gender Identity Disorder. The subcommittee was also influenced by the perception of many clinicians that there are no distinct boundaries between gender dysphorics who request sex reassignment surgery and those whose cross-gender wishes are of lesser intensity or constancy. (Bradley, et al., 1991)

Curiously, the Harry Benjamin standards of care have not been revised since the publication of the DSM-IV or reconciled with its broader definition of gender identity disorder. If gender identity and not sexual orientation is defined as a mental illness for the purpose of legitimizing surgical and hormonal procedures, then two questions emerge: Why was GID expressly uncoupled from SRS approval criteria, and what is the purpose of diagnosing those who live in a cross-gendered role without surgery?

The Unmarked Exit

Transsexuals who openly face stigma and discrimination every day are poorly served by the DSM-IV. The label of psychiatric disorder burdens them to continually prove their mental competence. Fraught with murky and ambiguous language, gender identity disorder has failed to provide a compelling "medical necessity" for many hospitals and nearly all US insurers, who have dropped SRS procedures and coverage. Moreover, the current wording has no clear exit clause for post-operative transsexuals. It lists postsurgical complications as "associated physical examination findings" of individuals with GID (APA, 1994, p. 535).

Summary

American psychiatric perceptions of transgendered people are remarkably parallel to those for gay and lesbian people before the declassification of homosexuality as a mental disorder in 1973. The present diagnostic categories of gender identity disorder and transvestic fetishism, like homosexuality in past decades, may or may not meet current definitions of psychiatric disorder depending on subjective assumptions regarding "normal" sex and gender role and the distress of societal prejudice. Recent revisions of the Diagnostic and Statistical Manual of Mental Disorders have made these categories increasingly ambiguous and reflect a lack of consensus within the American Psychiatric Association. The result is that a widening segment of gender non-conforming youth and adults are potentially subject to diagnosis of psychosexual disorder, stigma and loss of civil liberty. Revising these diagnostic categories will not eliminate transgender stigma but may reduce its legitimacy, just as DSM reform did for homophobia in the 1970s. It is possible to define a diagnosis that specifically addresses the needs of transsexuals requiring medical sex reassignment, with criteria that are clearly and appropriately inclusive. It is time for the transgendered community to engage the psychiatric profession in a dialogue that promotes medical and public policies which, above all, do no harm to those they are intended to help.

References

American Psychological Association, American Psychiatric Association, National Association of Social Workers, Inc., Colorado Psychological Association (October, 1994), Amicus brief in case of Romer vs. Evans, et al., United States Supreme Court, No 94-1039. [Online] Available: www.apa.org/pi/romer.html.

American Psychiatric Association (1980). Diagnostic and Statistical Manual of Mental Disorders, Third Edition, Washington, D.C.: Author.

American Psychiatric Association (1987). Diagnostic and Statistical Manual of Mental Disorders, Third Edition, Revised, Washington, D.C.: Author.

American Psychiatric Association (1994). Diagnostic and Statistical Manual of Mental Disorders, Fourth Edition, Washington, D.C.: Author.

Bolin, A. (1988). In Search of Eve, South Hadley MA: Bergin & Garvey.

Burke, P. (1996). Gender Shock, Exploding the Myths of Male and Female, New York: Anchor Books.

Lobel, K. (1996). "NGLTF Statement on Gender Identity Disorder and Transgender People," Washington D.C.: National Gay and Lesbian Task Force. [Online] Available: http://www.gendertalk.com/GTransgr/ngltfl.htm.

San Francisco Human Rights Commission (1996). "Resolution Condemning the Use of Gender Identity Disorder Diagnosis Against Children and Youth," San Francisco: Author.

Szasz, T. (1961). The Myth of Mental Illness. New York: Hoeber-Harper.

Wilson, K. (1997, April). "The Disparate Classification of Gender and Sexual Orientation in American Psychiatry," Psychiatry On-Line, [Online] Available: http://www.publinet.it/users/ad88/psych/disparat.htm and http://www.publinet.it/users/ad88/psych.htm.

Zucker, K. and Bradley, S. (1995). Gender Identity Disorder and Psychosexual Problems in Children and Adolescents, New York: Guilford Press.

POSTSCRIPT

Is Gender Variation a Psychological Illness?

The etiology (cause) of GID is still more unknown than known. The biological perspective explores the effects of prenatal androgens and maternal prenatal distress on gender atypicality. This research is primarily conducted on lower animals or on intersexual humans (even though GID is not typical in intersexuals). Social scientists examine sex-related socialization practices, including parental attitudes, social reinforcement processes (consistently and without ambiguity rearing a child as a boy or a girl, including encouragement of same-gender behavior and discouragement of cross-gender behavior), and self-socialization. An interactionist perspective suggests that sexual biology makes some individuals more vulnerable to certain psychosocial rearing conditions.

Different ideologies about whether or not GID is a disorder seem to rest on this question: do we view sex, gender, and sexual orientation as distinct domains or as inextricably linked? Phyllis Burke notes in *Gender Shock: Exploding the Myths of Male and Female* (Anchor Books, 1996) that "when you look at what society pathologizes, you can get the clearest glimpse of what society demands of those who wish to be considered normal." It appears, then, that our society expects congruence among sex, gender, and sexual orientation and believes that to be the norm. But some critics caution that the biodiversity of nature is greater than our norms allow us to observe. Moreover, we have little understanding, beyond stereotype and presumption, of the association between this biodiversity and gender identity and behavior. For example, how many of us have biological evidence (beyond visible external genitalia) that we are the sex that we believe ourselves to be? There have been cases where female athletes were surprised to find that they have a Y chromosome, yet by other biological measures they are clearly female. What, then, is this individual's "appropriate" gender identity?

Suggested Readings

N. K. Sandnabba and C. Ahlberg, "Parents' Attitudes and Expectations About Children's Cross-Gender Behavior," *Sex Roles* (Feburary 1999).

D. Scholinski and J. M. Adams, *The Last Time I Wore a Dress* (Riverhead Books, 1997).

K. J. Zucker and S. J. Bradley, *Gender Identity Disorder and Psychosexual Problems in Children and Adolescents* (Guilford Press, 1995).

Cultural Psychology Meets Evolutionary Psychology

This Web site by the Nijmegen Cultural Psychology Group (NCPG) contains a paper by Paul Voestermans and Cor Baerveldt that was presented at the 8th conference of the International Society for Theoretical Psychology (ISTP) in Sydney, Australia. The paper is entitled "Cultural Psychology Meets Evolutionary Psychology: Toward a New Role of Biology in the Study of Culture and Experience," and is a rich overview of evolutionary psychological thought.

http://www.socsci.kun.nl/psy/cultuur/voestermans_baerveldt.html

Behavior, Biology, and the Brain

This Web site from the Department of Philosophy at Illinois State University contains an essay entitled "Behavior, Biology and the Brain: Addressing Feminist Worries About Research Into Sex Differences," by Robert Stufflebeam. This essay reviews and responds to feminist concerns about sex difference research.

http://www.cas.ilstu.edu/philosophy/stufflebeam/pages/papers/sex.html

Genderlect Styles of Deborah Tannen

This Web site on the genderlect styles of Deborah Tannen provides an overview of Deborah Tannen's popular work on gender and communication.

http://www.usm.maine.edu/com/genderlect/

Men, Women, and Sex Differences: The Attitudes of Three Feminists—Gloria Steinem, Gloria Allred, and Bella Abzug

A paper by Russell Eisenman entitled "Men, Women, and Sex Differences: The Attitudes of Three Feminists—Gloria Steinem, Gloria Allred, and Bella Abzug" is presented on this Web site. This paper is a case study of perspectives on sex differences of three prominent feminists.

http://www.theabsolute.net/misogyny/eisenman.html

PART 2

The Question of Difference

*W*hat *is the most fruitful approach for better understanding sex and gender? For decades, the dominant approach in social scientific research on sex and gender is studying sex differences, termed a* difference model. *The goal is to examine whether or not sex differences exist and to describe the differing group tendencies. In this research, sex differences are identified from a comparison of the average tendency of a group of males to the average tendency of a group of females. The result is typically expressed in the form of generalizations of ways in which males and females differ, presuming within-sex homogeneity (i.e., all females are alike). Although most of the research is descriptive, assumptions and theories of what causes these sex differences abound. The three aims of this section are to:*

(1) explore some ways in which the difference model has shaped our understanding of gender in various domains of human functioning,

(2) examine critically and compare explanations of what causes sex differences, and

(3) illustrate the lively debate about the value and viability of the difference model for the study of gender.

- Does Evolutionary Theory Explain Psychological Sex Differences in Humans?

- Are Sex Differences in the Brain Primarily Responsible for Males' and Females' Differing Cognitive Abilities?

- Do Women and Men Communicate Differently?

- Should We Continue to Study Sex Differences?

ISSUE 4

Does Evolutionary Theory Explain Psychological Sex Differences in Humans?

YES: David M. Buss, from "Psychological Sex Differences: Origins Through Sexual Selection," *American Psychologist* (March 1995)

NO: Anne Fausto-Sterling, from "Beyond Difference: A Biologist's Perspective," *Journal of Social Issues* (1997)

ISSUE SUMMARY

YES: Psychologist David M. Buss applies evolutionary theory to explain psychological differences between human males and females.

NO: Biologist Anne Fausto-Sterling questions Buss's theory and calls for the application of stricter standards to evolutionary accounts of human behavior.

In the last two decades, evolutionary psychology has advanced many theoretical propositions about why differences exist between males and females, arguing that these differences are rooted in our ancestral past. Evolutionary psychology represents the intersection of evolutionary biology and the psychological study of human behavior. The goal of evolutionary psychology is to gain understanding of the adaptive processes underlying cultural phenomena. Our ancestors (i.e., Pleistocene hunters and gatherers) faced problems to which they needed to adapt for the species to survive. Charles Darwin defined an "adaptive problem" as one for which the solution impacts reproduction. Our interaction with the natural environment sets up a feedback system (i.e., natural selection) whereby a psychological mechanism that is effective in solving an adaptive problem (i.e., facilitating reproduction) will be "naturally selected" to become universal. Therefore, psychological mechanisms are functional in that they developed in adaptation to problems. Psychological mechanisms include design features of physical components of the brain and information-processing systems that govern its operation. Specific design features of the mind include preferences, perceptual processes, memory systems, categorization schemes, and learning mechanisms, all of which cause specific behaviors.

Applications of evolutionary psychology to understanding sex and gender predict that psychological and behavioral differences between males and females will occur in domains where the sexes have faced different adaptive problems in ancestral times. Evolutionary psychologists argue that by examining contemporary manifestations of differences between the sexes, evolutionary theories can be tested.

Critics of evolutionary psychology assert that evolutionary psychologists state as fact the key ancestral adaptive problems and contemporary manifestations of the psychological solutions to these problems when they are actually assumptions based on scant evidence. Critics also charge that generalizing from one animal species to another is problematic. Humans are not the same as other animal species; moreover, there is great variety in the ancestral environmental surrounds of humans and therefore great human physical and cultural variation.

In response, evolutionists argue that behavioral, physiological, and psychological clues support the identification of ancestral adaptive problems. They also assert that universals underlie the surface diversity of humans. Some evolutionists state that a central premise of evolutionary psychology is that while there exists a universal human nature, this universality is primarily at the level of evolved psychological mechanisms rather than expressed cultural behaviors. Furthermore, evolved psychological mechanisms and behaviors are adaptations to ancestral environments and not necessarily to modern circumstances. Evolutionists conclude that the contemporary human mind evolved in response to a hunting and gathering way of life.

Feminist critics argue that research on sexual selection is androcentric, overemphasizing male behaviors while undervaluing female behaviors. In response, it has been suggested that feminist scholars reject evolutionary claims out of hand just because they don't like its political message. Feminists argue that biases riddle evolutionary psychology and question whether or not any science is value-free. They assert that they are using scientific, not just political, methods and in doing so have formulated alternate explanatory frameworks that have greater predictive power for understanding sex differences.

Another counterargument is that higher animals have more complex nervous systems that allow for more rapid adjustment to the environment. Thus, evolution may be less a process of alteration of genotype through natural selection than alteration of the brain by experience within an organism's life cycle.

In the following selections, David M. Buss argues for the efficacy of evolutionary psychology in explaining human sex differences, reviewing major propositions and supporting evidence. Anne Fausto-Sterling critiques evolutionary psychological theory and research on human sex differences from feminist and biological perspectives. She argues that such work has fallen short of offering a useful explanatory framework for understanding human sex differences and that future evolutionary theory and research need to follow more stringent standards.

David M. Buss

 **YES**

Psychological Sex Differences: Origins Through Sexual Selection

Sexual Selection Defines the Primary Domains in Which the Sexes Have Faced Different Adaptive Challenges

Although many who are not biologists equate evolution with natural selection or survival selection, Darwin (1871) sculpted what he believed to be a second theory of evolution—the theory of sexual selection. Sexual selection is the causal process of the evolution of characteristics on the basis of reproductive advantage, as opposed to survival advantage. Sexual selection occurs in two forms. First, members of one sex can successfully outcompete members of their own sex in a process of intrasexual competition. Whatever characteristics lead to success in these same-sex competitions—be they greater size, strength, cunning, or social skills—can evolve or increase in frequency by virtue of the reproductive advantage accrued by the winners through increased access to more numerous or more desirable mates.

Second, members of one sex can evolve preferences for desirable qualities in potential mates through the process of intersexual selection. If members of one sex exhibit some consensus about which qualities are desirable in the other sex, then members of the other sex who possess the desirable qualities will gain a preferential mating advantage. Hence, the desirable qualities—be they morphological features such as antlers or plumage or psychological features such as a lower threshold for risk taking to acquire resources—can evolve by virtue of the reproductive advantage attained by those who are preferentially chosen for possessing the desirable qualities. Among humans, both causal processes—preferential mate choice and same-sex competition for access to mates —are prevalent among both sexes, and probably have been throughout human evolutionary history (Buss, 1994).

From David M. Buss, "Psychological Sex Differences: Origins Through Sexual Selection," *American Psychologist*, vol. 50, no. 3 (March 1995), pp. 164-168. Copyright © 1995 by The American Psychological Association, Inc. Adapted with permission of the publisher and the author.

Hypotheses About Psychological Sex Differences Follow From Sexual Asymmetries in Mate Selection and Intrasexual Competition

Although a detailed analysis of psychological sex differences is well beyond the scope of this [selection] (see Buss, 1994), a few of the most obvious differences in adaptive problems include the following.

Paternity uncertainty   Because fertilization occurs internally within women, men are always less than 100% certain (again, no conscious awareness implied) that their putative children are genetically their own. Some cultures have phrases to describe this, such as "mama's baby, papa's maybe." Women are always 100% certain that the children they bear are their own.

Identifying reproductively valuable women   Because women's ovulation is concealed and there is no evidence that men can detect when women ovulate, ancestral men had the difficult adaptive challenge of identifying which women were more fertile. Although ancestral women would also have faced the problem of identifying fertile men, the problem is considerably less severe (a) because most men remain fertile throughout their life span, whereas fertility is steeply age graded among women and (b) because women invest more heavily in offspring, making them the more "valuable" sex, competed for more intensely by men seeking sexual access. Thus, there is rarely a shortage of men willing to contribute the sperm necessary for fertilization, whereas from a man's perspective, there is a pervasive shortage of fertile women.

Gaining sexual access to women   Because of the large asymmetry between men and women in their minimum obligatory parental investment—nine months gestation for women versus an act of sex for men—the direct reproductive benefits of gaining sexual access to a variety of mates would have been much higher for men than for women throughout human evolutionary history (Symons, 1979; Trivers, 1972). Therefore, in social contexts in which some short-term mating or polygynous mating were possible, men who succeeded in gaining sexual access to a variety of women, other things being equal, would have experienced greater reproductive success than men who failed to gain such access (see also Greiling, 1993, for adaptive benefits to women of short-term mating).

Identifying men who are able to invest   Because of the tremendous burdens of a nine-month pregnancy and subsequent lactation, women who selected men who were able to invest resources in them and their offspring would have been at a tremendous advantage in survival and reproductive currencies compared with women who were indifferent to the investment capabilities of the man with whom they chose to mate.

Identifying men who are willing to invest   Having resources is not enough. Copulating with a man who had resources but who displayed a hasty postcopulatory departure would have been detrimental to the woman, particularly if she became pregnant and faced raising a child without the aid and protection of an investing father. A man with excellent resource-accruing capacities might channel resources to another woman or pursue short-term sexual opportunities with a variety of women. A woman who had the ability to detect a man's willingness to invest in her and her children would have an adaptive advantage compared with women who were oblivious to a man's willingness or unwillingness to invest.

These are just a few of the adaptive problems that women and men have confronted differently or to differing degrees. Other examples of sex-linked adaptive problems include those of coalitional warfare, coalitional defense, hunting, gathering, combating sex-linked forms of reputational damage, embodying sex-linked prestige criteria, and attracting mates by fulfilling the differing desires of the other sex—domains that all have consequences for mating but are sufficiently wide-ranging to span a great deal of social psychology (Buss, 1994). It is in these domains that evolutionary psychologists anticipate the most pronounced sex differences—differences in solutions to sex-linked adaptive problems in the form of evolved psychological mechanisms.

Psychological Sex Differences Are Well Documented Empirically in the Domains Predicted by Theories Anchored in Sexual Selection

When Maccoby and Jacklin (1974) published their classic book on the psychology of sex differences, knowledge was spotty and methods for summarizing the literature were largely subjective and interpretive. Since that time, there has been a veritable explosion of empirical findings, along with quantitative meta-analytic procedures for evaluating them (e.g., Eagly, 1995; Feingold, 1990; Hall, 1978; Hyde, in press; Oliver & Hyde, 1993; Rosenthal, 1991). Although new domains of sex differences continue to surface, such as the recently documented female advantage in spatial location memory (Silverman & Eals, 1992), the outlines of where researchers find large, medium, small, and no sex differences are starting to emerge more clearly.

A few selected findings illustrate the heuristic power of evolutionary psychology. Cohen (1977) used the widely adopted d statistic as the index of magnitude of effect to propose a rule of thumb for evaluating effect sizes: $0.20 =$ "small," $0.50 =$ "medium," and $0.80 =$ "large." As Hyde (in press) has pointed out in a chapter titled "Where Are the Gender Differences? Where Are the Gender Similarities?," sex differences in the intellectual and cognitive ability domains tend to be small. Women's verbal skills tend to be slightly higher than men's ($d = -0.11$). Sex differences in math also tend to be small ($d = 0.15$). Most tests of general cognitive ability, in short, reveal small sex differences.

The primary exception to the general trend of small sex differences in the cognitive abilities domain occurs with spatial rotation. This ability is essential for successful hunting, in which the trajectory and velocity of a spear must anticipate correctly the trajectory of an animal as each moves with different speeds through space and time. For spatial rotation ability, $d = 0.73$. Other sorts of skills involved in hunting also show large magnitudes of sex differences, such as throwing velocity ($d = 2.18$), throwing distance ($d = 1.98$), and throwing accuracy ($d = 0.96$; Ashmore, 1990). Skilled hunters, as good providers, are known to be sexually attractive to women in current and traditional tribal societies (Hill & Hurtado, 1989; Symons, 1979).

Large sex differences appear reliably for precisely the aspects of sexuality and mating predicted by evolutionary theories of sexual strategies (Buss & Schmitt, 1993). Oliver and Hyde (1993), for example, documented a large sex difference in attitudes toward casual sex ($d = 0.81$). Similar sex differences have been found with other measures of men's desire for casual sex partners, a psychological solution to the problem of seeking sexual access to a variety of partners (Buss & Schmitt, 1993; Symons, 1979). For example, men state that they would ideally like to have more than 18 sex partners in their lifetimes, whereas women state that they would desire only 4 or 5 ($d = 0.87$; Buss & Schmitt, 1993). In another study that has been replicated twice, 75% of the men but 0% of the women approached by an attractive stranger of the opposite sex consented to a request for sex (Clark & Hatfield, 1989).

Women tend to be more exacting than men, as predicted, in their standards for a short-term mate ($d - 0.79$). Women tend to place greater value on good financial prospects in a mate—a finding confirmed in a study of 10,047 individuals residing in 37 cultures located on six continents and five islands from around the world (Buss, 1989a). More so than men, women especially disdain qualities in a potential mate that signal inability to accrue resources, such as lack of ambition ($d = 1.38$) and lack of education ($d = 1.06$). Women desire physical protection abilities more than men, both in short-term mating ($d - 0.94$) and in long-term mating ($d = 0.66$).

Men and women also differ in the weighting given to cues that trigger sexual jealousy. Buss, Larsen, Westen, and Semmelroth (1992) presented men and women with the following dilemma: "What would upset or distress you more: (a) imagining your partner forming a deep emotional attachment to someone else or (b) imagining your partner enjoying passionate sexual intercourse with that other person" (p. 252). Men expressed greater distress about sexual than emotional infidelity, whereas women showed the opposite pattern. The difference between the sexes in which scenario was more distressing was 43% ($d = 0.98$). These sex differences have been replicated by different investigators (Wiederman & Allgeier, 1993) with physiological recording devices (Buss et al., 1992) and have been replicated in other cultures (Buunk, Angleitner, Oubaid, & Buss, 1994).

These sex differences are precisely those predicted by evolutionary psychological theories based on sexual selection. They represent only a sampling from a larger body of supporting evidence. The sexes also differ substantially in a wide variety of other ways that are predicted by sexual selection theory, such as in thresholds for physical risk taking (Wilson & Daly, 1985), in frequency of perpetrating homicides (Daly & Wilson, 1988), in thresholds for inferring sexual intent in others (Abby, 1982), in perceptions of the magnitude of upset people experience as the victims of sexual aggression (Buss, 1989b), and in the frequency of committing violent crimes of all sorts (Daly & Wilson, 1988). As noted by Donald Brown (1991), "it will be irresponsible to continue shunting these [findings] aside, fraud to deny that they exist" (p. 156). Evolutionary psychology sheds light on why these differences exist.

Conclusions

Strong sex differences occur reliably in domains closely linked with sex and mating, precisely as predicted by psychological theories based on sexual selection (Buss, 1994). Within these domains, the psychological sex differences are patterned in a manner that maps precisely onto the adaptive problems men and women have faced over human evolutionary history. Indeed, in most cases, the evolutionary hypotheses about sex differences were generated a decade or more before the empirical tests of them were conducted and the sex differences discovered. These models thus have heuristic and predictive power.

The evolutionary psychology perspective also offers several insights into the broader discourse on sex differences. First, neither women nor men can be considered "superior" or "inferior" to the other, any more than a bird's wings can be considered superior or inferior to a fish's fins or a kangaroo's legs. Each sex possesses mechanisms designed to deal with its own adaptive challenges— some similar and some different—and so notions of superiority or inferiority are logically incoherent from the vantage point of evolutionary psychology. The meta-theory of evolutionary psychology is descriptive, not prescriptive—it carries no values in its teeth.

Second, contrary to common misconceptions about evolutionary psychology, finding that sex differences originated through a causal process of sexual selection does not imply that the differences are unchangeable or intractable. On the contrary, understanding their origins provides a powerful heuristic to the contexts in which the sex differences are most likely to be manifested (e.g., in the context of mate competition) and hence provides a guide to effective loci for intervention if change is judged to be desirable.

Third, although some worry that inquiries into the existence and evolutionary origins of sex differences will lead to justification for the status quo, it is hard to believe that attempts to change the status quo can be very effective if they are undertaken in ignorance of sex differences that actually exist. Knowledge is power, and attempts to intervene in the absence of knowledge may resemble a surgeon operating blindfolded—there may be more bloodshed than healing (Tooby & Cosmides, 1992).

The perspective of evolutionary psychology jettisons the outmoded dualistic thinking inherent in much current discourse by getting rid of the false dichotomy between biological and social. It offers a truly interactionist position that specifies the particular features of social context that are especially critical for processing by our evolved psychological mechanisms. No other theory of sex differences has been capable of predicting and explaining the large number of precise, detailed, patterned sex differences discovered by research guided by evolutionary psychology (e.g., Bailey, Gaulin, Agyei, & Gladue, 1994; Buss & Schmitt, 1993; Daly & Wilson, 1988; Ellis & Symons, 1990; Gangestad

& Simpson, 1990; Greer & Buss, 1994; Kenrick & Keefe, 1992; Symons, 1979). Evolutionary psychology possesses the heuristic power to guide investigators to the particular domains in which the most pronounced sex differences, as well as similarities, will be found. People grappling with the existence and implications of psychological sex differences cannot afford to ignore their most likely evolutionary origins through sexual selection.

References

Abby, A. (1982). Sex differences in attributions for friendly behavior: Do males misperceive females' friendliness? *Journal of Personality and Social Psychology, 32,* 830–838.

Ashmore, R. D. (1990). Sex, gender, and the individual. In L. A. Pervin (Ed.), *Handbook of personality: Theory and research* (pp. 486–526). New York: Guilford Press.

Bailey, J. M., Gaulin, S., Agyei, Y., & Gladue, B. A. (1994). Effects of gender and sexual orientation on evolutionarily relevant aspects of human mating psychology. *Journal of Personality and Social Psychology, 66,* 1074–1080.

Brown, D. (1991). *Human universals.* Philadelphia: Temple University Press.

Buss, D. M. (1989a). Sex differences in human mate preferences: Evolutionary hypotheses tested in 37 cultures. *Behavioral and Brain Sciences, 12,* 1–49.

Buss, D. M. (1989b). Conflict between the sexes: Strategic interference and the evocation of anger and upset. *Journal of Personality and Social Psychology, 56,* 735–747.

Buss, D. M. (1994). *The evolution of desire: Strategies of human mating.* New York; Basic Books.

Buss, D. M., Larsen, R., Westen, D., & Semmelroth, J. (1992). Sex differences in jealousy: Evolution, physiology, and psychology. *Psychological Science, 3,* 251–255.

Buss, D. M., & Schmitt, D. P. (1993). Sexual strategies theory: An evolutionary perspective on human mating. *Psychological Review, 100,* 204–232.

Buunk, B., Angleitner, A., Oubaid, V., & Buss, D. M. (1994). *Sexual and cultural differences in jealousy: Tests from the Netherlands, Germany, and the United States.* Manuscript submitted for publication.

Clark, R. D., & Hatfield, E. (1989). Gender differences in receptivity to sexual offers. *Journal of Psychology and Human Sexuality, 2,* 39–55.

Cohen, J. (1977). *Statistical power analysis for the behavioral sciences.* San Diego, CA: Academic Press.

Daly, M., & Wilson, M. (1988). *Homicide.* New York: Aldine de Gruyter.

Darwin, C. (1871). *The descent of man and selection in relation to sex.* London: Murray.

Eagly, A. H. (1995). The science and politics of comparing women and men. *American Psychologist, 50,* 145–158.

Ellis, B. J., & Symons, D. (1990). Sex differences in sexual fantasy: An evolutionary psychological approach. *Journal of Sex Research, 27,* 527–556.

Feingold, A. (1990). Gender differences in effects of physical attractiveness on romantic attraction: A comparison across five research paradigms. *Journal of Personality and Social Psychology, 59,* 981–993.

Gangestad, S. W., & Simpson, J. A. (1990). Toward an evolutionary history of female sociosexual variation. *Journal of Personality, 58,* 69–96.

Greer, A., & Buss, D. M. (1994). Tactics for promoting sexual encounters. *Journal of Sex Research, 5,* 185–201.

Greiling, H. (1993, June). *Women's short-term sexual strategies.* Paper presented at the Conference on Evolution and the Social Sciences, London School of Economics, London, England.

Hall, J. A. (1978). Gender effects in decoding nonverbal cues. *Psychological Bulletin, 85,* 845–852.

Hill, K., & Hurtado, M. (1989). Hunter-gatherers of the new world. *American Scientist, 77,* 437–443.

Hyde, J. S. (in press). Where are the gender differences? Where are the gender similarities? In D. M. Buss & N. Malamuth (Eds.), *Sex, power, conflict: Feminist and evolutionary perspectives.* New York: Oxford University Press.

Kenrick, D. T., & Keefe, R. C. (1992). Age preferences in mates reflect sex differences in reproductive strategies. *Behavioral and Brain Sciences, 15,* 75–133.

Maccoby, E. E., & Jacklin, C. N. (1974). *The psychology of sex differences.* Stanford, CA: Stanford University Press.

Oliver, M. B., & Hyde, J. S. (1993). Gender differences in sexuality: A meta-analysis. *Psychological Bulletin, 114,* 29–51.

Rosenthal, R. (1991). *Meta-analytic procedures for social research* (rev. ed.). Newbury Park, CA: Sage.

Silverman, I., & Eals, M. (1992). Sex differences in spatial abilities: Evolutionary theory and data. In J. Barkow, L. Cosmides, & J. Tooby (Eds.), *The adapted mind: Evolutionary psychology and the generation of culture* (pp. 539–549). New York: Oxford University Press.

Symons, D. (1979). *The evolution of human sexuality.* New York: Oxford University Press.

Tooby, J., & Cosmides, L. (1992). Psychological foundations of culture. In J. Barkow, L. Cosmides, & J. Tooby (Eds.), *The adapted mind: Evolutionary psychology and the generation of culture* (pp. 119–136). New York: Oxford University Press.

Trivers, R. (1972). Parental investment and sexual selection. In B. Campbell (Ed.), *Sexual selection and the descent of man* (pp. 136–179). New York: Aldine de Gruyter.

Wiederman, M. W., & Allgeier, E. R. (1993). Gender differences in sexual jealousy: Adaptationist or social learning explanation? *Ethology and Sociobiology, 14,* 115–140.

Wilson, M., & Daly, M. (1985). Competitiveness, risk taking, and violence: The young male syndrome. *Ethology and Sociobiology, 6,* 59–73.

NO ↩

Anne Fausto-Sterling

Beyond Difference:
A Biologist's Perspective

Do biologists know things of use to social scientists who study gender? Answering this question requires a bit of context. During the past few years we have been subjected to a series of blows, both within the academy and without. The left hook hits us from the media. Lead stories in *Time* (August 15, 1994), *Newsweek* (March 27, 1995; June 3, 1996), and *The New Republic* (Wright, 1994a) (to name but a few) tell us that infidelity and physical desire are both in our genes, that feminists have hopelessly misled their flock by attacking the first wave of sociobiological claims about gender and social change, and that differences in brain anatomy might "explain why women are more intuitive" (*Newsweek*, 1995, p. 54)....

The popular media's publicity blitz describes the encroachment of biological understandings on arenas of social behavior previously seen to be the bailiwick of the social sciences. Some reporters and scientists present these new biological understandings as certain beyond question. To be sure, according to this view, some gaps in our knowledge remain, but the current wave of findings has solidified the biological framework on which we hang our understandings of sex differences. Shouldn't we be happy to have these vexing questions settled once and for all?...

What tools can I, as a biologist, offer to social scientists wishing to understand the thought currents of the past few years? What can biology tell us about human sex differences? My quarrels with many of the arguments about innate human differences and their evolution stem from understandings of the nature of biological explanation, which differ significantly from those of writers such as [journalist Robert] Wright, [J. Richard] Udry, and the various *Time* and *Newsweek* authors. The biological work to which I am drawn contains solid theory and detailed empirical information; using such work as a starting point enables us to build complex, interesting accounts of behavior....

From Anne Fausto-Sterling, "Beyond Difference: A Biologist's Perspective," *Journal of Social Issues*, vol. 53, no. 2 (1997), pp. 233, 235-245, 248. Copyright © 1997 by The Society for the Psychological Study of Social Issues. Reprinted by permission of Blackwell Publishers Ltd.

79

Why Frogs Jump

I'll start with a seemingly simple question: "Why does a frog jump?" The answer can be given at several different levels. Within the moment of watching the frog jump, we can suggest a holistic answer—the frog jumps as part of an ecosystem. It senses a predator nearby and gets out of the way. A more mechanistic, reductionist approach would focus on the frog's leg muscles: it jumps because its muscles twitch. Even more specifically, we can reduce the level of explanation to a discussion of how and why muscles twitch, and we can say it's jumping because two proteins, actin and myosin, have molecular properties that allow them to contract, something they do in response to a nerve impulse. Each of these levels of explanation is valid for particular purposes, but one cannot necessarily substitute for the other. . . .

Focusing on either the contemporary ecosystem or adult muscle function leaves out two important types of biological analysis and explanation—development (embryological, juvenile, and adult) and evolution. Both mechanistic and holistic analyses of current behaviors describe *what is*. In contrast, examining individual development or species evolution allows us to talk about how things get to be the way they are. . . .

Evolutionists . . . describe events that take place over many generations. An evolutionist would speak in terms of genetic variation, natural selection, adaptation, and geographic isolation (to name the most commonly studied mechanisms of evolution). . . .

Developmental answers respond to the "why" question for individual frogs within a particular generation, while evolutionists look at changes in gene frequency at the population level. Suppose I ask why two groups of frogs jump differently. Why, for example, do bullfrogs jump further than leopard frogs? One can stick with a strictly reductionist explanation. On average, bullfrogs jump further because they are a lot bigger. And one could reduce that answer to details about the number of muscle fibers and the comparative biophysics of fibers of different lengths and thicknesses. But one could add in a second question: why are bullfrogs larger than leopard frogs? One answer might be development—they are bigger because bullfrogs spend two years as tadpoles and thus have a much longer growing period than leopard frogs, which metamorphose in a single growing season. Both explanations are valid, but offer different kinds of information. One could push matters further, asking why the bullfrog life cycle differs from that of the leopard frog. An answer here would require data about the evolution of the two species. When and under what circumstances did they diverge from a common ancestor? What kind of life cycle did the progenitor species have, i.e., did leopard frogs lose a year of development or did bullfrogs gain one? And why? Was it due to natural selection, geographical isolation or genetic drift? Or, does each species even now exhibit developmental plasticity—the ability to change its life cycle in appropriate environmental circumstances? Answers to these questions can be acquired empirically. Indeed, solving problems such as these is what many evolutionary biologists do for a living. It will not do simply to assume the answer.

Many social scientists study gender inequity. Some hope to figure out how to equalize difference. Others believe that whatever differences they've observed cannot (and perhaps should not) change. Each of these groups has an underlying and not always articulated theory about the biological basis of difference; when pressed, they will invoke it to their advantage. But when dueling social scientists use biological tools to do battle, they do not always think clearly about the level and type of biological explanation with which they argue.

Thus the first thing social scientists need to think through when they use biology to ask the difference question is for which level of explanation do they seek an answer. Such a question is neither innocent nor far-removed from questions of policy. If one finds a sex difference, does it help to know its immediate physiological cause, or does one really seek a developmental or even an evolutionary explanation? I assume that in a trivial sense anything we do has an immediate physiological cause, i.e., if I run from danger, it is not only because I can recognize the cultural signs of a dangerous situation. It is also because I am physically able to see, hear, and run, in the same way that a frog can jump because of the actin and myosin in its muscles. But that knowledge is not particularly interesting if what we want to understand is why I consider a particular situation to be dangerous in the first place. The answer to such a question depends very much on why one wants to study difference in the first place. Does one want to learn about it in order to explain the way things are, or to design policies to change the status quo? I suggest that currently available types of evolutionary explanations work best in the former case, whereas developmental understandings are most useful in the latter. As the following discussion makes plain, understandings at the level of molecular physiology are usually the least useful for a researcher interested in designing effective social policy.

From Mice to Bats and Beyond

Geneticists look at evolution in a number of different ways. The following discussion comes from the work of C.H. Waddington (1975). Animal populations consist of individuals with unique genotypes—the sum of all the genes in a cell. During any particular generation, populations participate in different kinds of systems. Waddington named one of these "the exploitative system." Animals, within the limits of their genetic makeup (e.g., mice can't fly from one tree top to the next; to colonize tree tops they must climb or jump to nearby branches), choose among and modify possible environments, thus creating an environmental niche. At the same time, animals in any particular generation develop under particular stresses and strains. Waddington called this development within a single generation "the epigenetic system." During development, a chance environmental stress might reveal a developmental potential not ordinarily visible. Suppose, for example, our hypothetical tree mice hadn't found much food during a particular year. Some females might go through pregnancy in a condition of near starvation. As a result of that, some fetuses would die, others would develop normally, and still others might survive but exhibit some sort of limb defects, say a failure of the skin connecting the limb digits to degenerate during development as it normally does. Perhaps these abnormalities show up only when a particular genotype develops in combination with low protein availability. The result: webbed feet. (Such a scenario is not particularly far-fetched. Rats subjected to prenatal heat stress, for example, developed longer limbs.) (Siegel, Doyle & Kelley, 1977)

Webbed feet might make mice slow climbers, rendering them more vulnerable to predation by a passing hawk.... But that disadvantage might be balanced out by an emerging ability—the webbed feet enable the mouse to glide when jumping from tree to tree, thereby avoiding birds in the habit of scanning tree trunks for passing mice, *and* increasing their food options by enabling them to reach more distant tree tops. The mouse-hawk interactions and the ability to improve survival by niche extension form part of what Waddington called "the natural selective system." If the environmental stress of low food availability remained for several generations, mice with an epigenetic system (i.e., an interaction between environment and genes to produce a new phenotype) in which development during protein deprivation produced webbed feet, might survive with higher frequency than that of same genotype developing under high food conditions. (Note how the same genotype can produce different phenotypes under different developmental conditions.) Thus the low protein–webbed feet epigenetic system would become more frequent in future generations. If the selection went on for long enough, these mice might even develop a new niche, forgoing climbing altogether. Waddington demonstrated that in some cases, new phenotypes induced by epigenetic stresses stabilize even if the original stress disappears (Waddington, 1975). Thus a new variety of webbed-footed gliding mouse might emerge and, with further selection for more efficient gliding, might even evolve into what is called in German a *fledermaus,* a flying mouse, or bat. I do not suggest that this is how bats actually evolved; I have merely created a plausible scenario in order to illustrate the varied biological systems involved in evolution.

Using Waddington's framework, let's turn to some of the modern-day theorizing about the evolution of the human psyche. Robert Wright (1994b) champions a new group of academics that call themselves evolutionary psychologists. In 1992, Barkow, Cosmides and Tooby published *The Adapted Mind,* arguably the scholarly founding volume for this emerging field. Their central premise is that "there is a universal human nature, but that this universality exists primarily at the level of evolved psychological mechanisms, not of expressed cultural behaviors" (p. 5). They also postulate that psychological mechanisms evolved as adaptations via natural selection and "that the evolved structure of the human mind is adapted to the way of life of Pleistocene hunter-gatherers...." (p. 5). These academics argue that we can only understand contemporary human psychology by understanding how the mind evolved.

Some evolutionary psychologists have a lot to say about sex and gender. Recently, David Buss (1995), a prominent evolutionary psychologist, discussed the natural selective system faced by primitive humans:

> Women face the problem of securing a reliable or replenishable supply of resources to carry them through pregnancy, and lactation.... especially when food resources were scarce, that is, during droughts or harsh winters. All people are descendants of a long and unbroken line of women who successively solved this adaptive challenge; for example, by preferring mates who show the ability to accrue resources and to share them. (p. 164)

Buss tells a story of much the same quality as the one I just invented about the evolution of bats. It has a certain plausibility. Proto-human females must, indeed, have had the challenge of finding enough nutrition to sustain pregnancy and lactation. But as does my bat tale, Buss's lacks essential information. Without knowing when the traits of interest became a permanent part of the human lineage, we can know little about the actual environmental variations, little about the degree to which nutritional needs, via an epigenetic system, might have sharpened foraging abilities dormant within some of the genotypes in particular populations, and/or whether systems of natural selection worked to make food utilization more physiologically efficient. If Buss's selective scenario played out, perhaps it fueled the development of foraging skills, including the ability to hold three-dimensional maps in one's mind's eye—returning even after many years, to a spot which had previously contained a good food source. Certainly Buss can hypothesize that pregnancy and lactation led females to select males who were good providers, just as I can hypothesize that it led females to evolve well-developed spatial and memory skills. We might both be wrong, or right, but without more data and a far more specific hypothesis, we have no way of knowing.

There are a lot of data about prehistoric human culture and protohominids, and it is appropriate to use them to devise hypotheses about human evolution. It is not unreasonable to ask the hypothesis-builders of evolutionary psychology to at least postulate at what point in human or hominid history they imagine contemporary reproductive behaviors to have first appeared. "Throughout the Pleistocene" is pretty vague. What is the evidence that it wasn't earlier or later? What, if any, animal systems provide unnamed models? What were the food and predator stresses at that moment? Data on these points can be gleaned from the archeological and geological record. How did humans respond? Biogeographic data can be brought to bear on this point. Was there a division of labor during this early period of evolution? Or did gender-based divisions of labor evolve later (Leibowitz, 1978)?

Over how long a period of time did human mating systems evolve? Or are they still evolving? For example, the earliest humans living in the heart of Africa certainly did not, as Buss suggests, experience harsh winters. How do the events of interest to evolutionary psychology relate in time to the expansion and geographical radiation of human populations? What evidence is there for a long, unbroken line of women? When and where were there genetic bottlenecks during the course of human evolution? How many of them were there?

Table 1

Latour and Strum's Nine Questions

1. What are the initial units of evolution (genes? individuals? the family? the species?)

2. Which qualities do the authors think the units possess? (selfishness? self-regulation? harmony? aggressiveness?)

3. Units with particular qualities enter into relationships with one another. Explicitly, what form do these relationships take? (exploitative, trade-offs, parasitical, competitive, cooperative?)

4. What time delays are involved in exchanges which take place in the established relationships between fundamental units? (pre-hominid? hominid? Homo? Homo sapiens? prehistorical? last week?)

5. What method of measurement can be used to assess answers to questions 1-4? (L&S write, for example, "It is one thing to state that a baboon behaves as if to improve this reproductive success, but quite another to decide how he can implement his directive when he does not know who his offspring are" (p. 174).

6. In what framework of events, is the evolutionary story embedded? L&S note that most evolutionary stories are logical, but usually not specifically historical.

7. What agents or causes are said to play a role within the framework of events? (e.g., a shift from forest to savannah as a trigger for the evolution of socialness).

8. What is the stated explicit methodology?

9. What explicit political lessons do the authors of a theory draw?

The use of molecular evidence to trace human evolution has created a great deal of ferment during recent years (Ayala, 1995; Culotta, 1995; Dorit, Akashi & Gilbert, 1995; Gibbons, 1994, 1995, 1996; Hammer, 1995; Piazza, 1993; Tishkoff et al., 1996). It would be nice if evolutionary psychologists were specifically to incorporate this new information into their theory building. Which evolutionary lines or kinds of adaptive behavior were lost or selected for? How much of our current gene pool do we have because of genetic drift or geographic isolation, how much because of adaptation and natural selection? Some prior work at least attempts to situate theory-making within a time line and a set of postulates about which organisms (chimps? bonobos? Australopithecus? Homo habilis?) evolved modern human mating patterns (Leibowitz, 1978; Tanner, 1981; Fedigan, 1986). Let's engage in current discussions using the best available knowledge base and the most highly detailed hypotheses available.

Without addressing some of these questions, evaluating hypotheses becomes very difficult. For example, given how precarious early human existence must have been, isn't it possible that females realized that no individual male would live long enough or stay healthy enough to provide over a period of years for his offspring? Isn't it just as likely then that the females who passed on more genes to the next generation were the ones who hedged their bets and slept with more than one male? Buss and other evolutionary psychologists engage in what are, in essence, thought-experiments, but unless much more carefully specified hypotheses are presented, there's no way to know how the postulated starting-points relate to the actual starting-points.

The development of scientifically sound theories about the evolution of human behavioral patterns and their relationship to contemporary behavior could emerge from collaborations between social scientists, evolutionists, and behavioral biologists. Specifically, those experts in the social studies of science who have been so bitterly attacked in the current science wars have a great deal to offer. One model collaboration, developed in the halcyon days before science studies were taken seriously enough to be attacked, is a paper written by Bruno Latour (Mr. Science Studies!! See Latour, 1987) and Sharon Strum (Strum, 1987), a primatologist who studies baboon behavior. Latour and Strum (1986) devised a set of questions aimed at making specific hypotheses about human evolution. Using their questionnaire, they evaluated the quality of the theories constructed by both social scientists and biologists. (All failed the test pretty miserably.) I urge anyone devising theories about evolution and human behavior to use Latour and Strum's nine questions [Table 1] to measure the scientific quality of their hypotheses. As Latour and Strum conclude, "the difficulties of tracing human social origins goes beyond the mere speculative nature of the endeavor. Scientists have not yet come to terms with what makes an account scientific or convincing . . . when scientists are unaware of the mythic character and function of origin accounts . . . the coherence of the scientific account suffers" (p. 186).

When, instead of hypothesizing about past evolutionary events, biologists study evolution in contemporary populations, they collect very particular kinds of data. They monitor food supply, shelter, rainfall, predator levels—sometimes for as long as a decade. At the same time, they follow individual animals as they mate, raise offspring, and die. They observe the animals, use DNA fingerprinting to see who fathered the offspring, and measure changes in animal shape, size, and behavior over several generations (Clutton-Brock, Guinness & Albon, 1982; Davies, 1992). Evolutionary psychologists also obtain data about contemporary humans and try to reason backwards from what they find. But because their data come from present-day humans, they need to attend especially carefully to human epigenetic systems—to what degree specific behaviors appear in specific environments. Buss writes, "Women's current mate preferences provide a window for viewing our mating past" (1994, p. 23). Buss conducted surveys in both the United States and in 37 cultures worldwide, obtaining a total sample size of more than 10,000. Both men and women rated the importance of 18 different mate characteristics. In all cases women placed a higher value on men with good financial prospects than vice versa. Buss argues that the present state of affairs resulted from sexual selection. "Evolution," he writes "has favored women who prefer men who possess attributes that confer benefits and who dislike men who possess attributes that impose costs" (p. 21). Buss further argues that the evolution of female preference for resource-rich males is ancient and not likely to change. Evidence for the latter claim comes from his observation that the feminist revolution of the 1970's and 1980's did not change this particular preference.

One can look at Buss's data and arguments from several points of view. Social scientists are more than competent to make judgments about data quality, sampling techniques, cross-cultural diversity, propriety of chosen statistical evaluations and such; indeed, some have made pointed criticisms of his research (numerous authors in *Behavioral and Brain Sciences,* 1989). But evolutionary biologists also have standards for evaluating Buss-like hypotheses. Four, in particular, have been suggested as essential to the acceptance of conjectures about the evolution of human reproductive behaviors (Wallen, 1989). First, of course, is there a good fit between the hypothesis and data? Second, is the evolutionary explanation as good as or better than some proposed alternative? Third, when using questionnaires to obtain data in support of hypotheses about reproduction, do observed or independently documented behaviors correlate with answers on the questionnaire? Fourth, do postulated characters actually relate to reproductive fitness (e.g., does marrying a wealthier man really increase a woman's chance of producing more and fitter children)? In the case of Buss's hypothesis that, during human evolution, natural selection favored women who prefer wealthier men, only the first of the four criteria has been reasonably met.

Evolutionary arguments that meet the highest standards of evolutionary science must always hold clear the difference between obtaining data to demonstrate the workings of contemporary selective events, and using contemporary data to devise hypotheses about the past. In his popular writing, Buss often blurs this distinction. For example, he begins his discussion of human female preference for males with financial resources by reference to a field study of a bird called the gray shrike. He cites an elegant experiment in which a field biologist demonstrated that female shrikes preferred males with larger caches of food. The study shows sexual selection at work in a contemporary bird population. Buss then moves from his account of shrike behavior, to imagine a scenario that might have taken place during early human evolution. For female preference for richer mates to have evolved, he stipulates that prehistoric men would have had to have been able to accrue and control resources, that different men would have had different resource levels and that there would have been an advantage to monogamy for the female.... (He never specifies just when during human evolution this might have been going on, so we cannot use the archeological record to evaluate his assumptions.) These conditions, he feels, are easily met among humans, and he reaches back to the contemporary world to grab as an example a Donald Trump or some Rockefeller or other. He then returns to "women over evolutionary history" and then back again to contemporary studies of female preference.

What we have, in the end, is a mish-mash of argument in which often very beautifully done contemporary studies of mating behaviors in animals are thrown in with far less elegant surveys of contemporary human behavior. The latter are then combined with unsubstantiated but plausible postulates (like my mouse to bat story) about some unspecified earlier period of human evolution in which contemporary behavior might have had its origin. I do not argue that it is wrong to think about the evolution of human behavior. Rather, one must do it using the high standards of the best studies of behavioral evolution in animals (Fausto-Sterling, 1997; Fausto-Sterling, Gowaty & Zuk, 1997). And if one is going to build hypotheses about prehistoric evolution, then too, one must use the standards of the field and the rich, albeit imperfect, information already obtained from the fossil record.

On Genes and Development

Many biologists, sociologists and psychologists bracket the question of evolution in order to study contemporary development. Even if Buss, Wright, and others are 100% on target about the selective forces that led to our current sex/gender systems, broad sweep evolutionary arguments tell us little about specific mechanisms. In the evolutionary psychologist's scenario, individual females who learned to recognize high-resource males survived and reproduced more frequently than those who didn't. But what, precisely, were the recognition mechanisms that evolved? Again, one can imagine a variety of possibilities. There might be something about the physique or physiognomy of high-resource males that females could spot (just as . . . frog retina cells were selected to tell the difference between birds of prey and potential food). Or, perhaps something a lot more indirect and potentially transformative of the human or hominid way of life happened. Perhaps women who talked a lot with other women could gather information through social and cultural networks; in this scenario, what would have evolved was the ability to gossip and trade information about nearby males. (Barkow, 1992, also discusses the evolution of gossip.) The result might be the evolution of elaborate cultural mechanisms, not some built-in hard-wired unchangeable brain response.

　　Most psychologists and sociologists are interested in contemporary mechanisms—how an individual develops throughout his or her life span (Waddington's epigenetic system). What can biologists tell us about this process, the process of producing a phenotype? Let's first look, through the lens of the developmental geneticist, at the relationship between genes and environment. . . . [G]eneticists study . . . "the norm of reaction." They look at development as it occurs in different environments.

　　. . . Studying norms of reaction reminds us that most of the time there is no such thing as a fixed genetic trait. Genetic traits can only be defined in a particular environment. . . .

　　Knowing about norms of reaction highlights the most common fallacy encountered in discussions about the genetic basis of behavior—the presumption that individuals have constant environments, and that, in the absence of empirical measures, one can predict for any or all environments, the phenotype produced by a particular gene. If physical phenotypes are plastic, isn't it likely that behavioral phenotypes are plastic in spades? . . . [I]t makes more sense to think of the plasticity, rather than the specific behavior, as being under genetic control. In fact, geneticists studying animals and plants have amassed experimental data showing that plasticity *is* a trait under genetic control, and can evolve via natural selection. Among ecologists and quantitative geneticists, the evolution and genetics of plasticity is a very hot topic right now (for example: Newman, 1988; Gomulkiewicz & Kirkpatrick, 1992; Scheiner, 1993; Schlichting & Pigliucci, 1994; West-Eberhard, 1989). Yet neither the concepts of the norm of reaction or phenotypic plasticity have appeared as a serious part of evolutionary theories about human sex differences.

How an individual looks or behaves, then, results from the full panoply of gene expression evoked in a particular environment. Having the gene is not enough. If it stays silent throughout the life cycle, its effect is never seen, and we certainly do not express all of the gene sequences found in our DNA. But even within a carefully defined environment and with (hypothetically) full knowledge of all interacting genes, a third factor contributes to the outcome— random chemical fluctuation. Random processes occur in every developmental generation, but they are not part of a genetically controlled developmental program. Thus they are not directly selected for. Biologists sometimes refer to these one-time events as "developmental noise." . . .

Conclusion

The discussions of sex differences that one reads in various settings, from scholarly texts to the media, frequently slip from one category of biological explanation to another. This slippage makes it difficult to assess the strengths and limitations of particular knowledge claims. One finds oneself simultaneously coping with reductionist explanations for behavior (frogs jump because their muscles twitch) and evolutionary explanations, which address rather different biological questions and demand different types of proof. To have intelligent discussions and arguments about the role of biological difference in the genesis of gender difference, we must attend to what level of explanation is being offered, and to hold those with whom we debate these questions to a higher standard of explanatory clarity than has hitherto been offered.

Evolutionary explanations of difference often entail elegant theories based on very partial knowledge of contemporary cultures and on analogies from animals, but without any foundation in the specific history of human evolution. There are no studies of human evolution comparable to those on red deer (Clutton-Brock, Guinness & Albon, 1982) or chimpanzees (Goodall, 1986). And the two species of chimps, for example, have strikingly different mating systems. Who shall we choose as our model female? Females of the better-known chimp species have an associated pattern of hormones and copulation, but the bonobo female has sex constantly with both males and females, she apparently uses sex not just for reproduction, but as a medium of social mediation (Parish, 1994; de Waal, 1995). Evolutionary explanations of human sex differences usually ignore an entire literature on norms of reaction and phenotypic plasticity. Using this strong and interesting literature in basic genetics and ecology could lead to a very different kind of story-telling. It is primarily the feminist Darwinists such as Jane Lancaster, Barbara Smuts, and Patricia Gowaty who have incorporated contextual diversity and polymorphism into their evolutionary accounts of human behavior (Fausto-Sterling, Gowaty & Zuk, 1997).

So, do biologists know things of use to social scientists? The answer is certainly "yes." But which aspects of biological knowledge are most useful for social scientists? The answer depends on what the knowledge project is in the first place. Suppose one is interested in educational reform. If one's unstated starting assumption is that there are likely to be irreducible cognitive differences between boys and girls, one is more likely to incorporate biological knowledge which suggests fixed brain differences between males and females and which goes on to offer evolutionary explanations for the origins of such difference. Belief in hormonally-induced, hard-wired brain differences of very ancient evolutionary origin is easiest to reconcile with difference-based reform —encouraging boys and girls to develop their special but rather different skills. If, on the other hand, one assumes that on average anyone can learn just about anything (and ought to do so if they want to), then the views of geneticists who focus on norms of reaction, adaptive plasticity and context-dependent gene action will appeal. These latter understandings of biology are more compatible with equity-based reform—the belief that given the right circumstances almost all students can excel.

We each gravitate to the accounts of biology that most suit our social belief systems. Rather than becoming mired in often inaccurate or partial renditions of biological knowledge, social scientists can offer something to the world that biologists cannot—thick, complex, multivariate descriptions of human behavior. It would be a shame if social scientists gave up their skills and knowledge base in favor of strictly biological accounts of complex human behaviors. Were biological approaches to stand alone as our sole method of understanding, however interesting they may sometimes be, they would provide impoverished versions, indeed, of the knowledge systems offered us by anthropologists, sociologists and psychologists.

References

Ayala, F. (1995). The myth of Eve: Molecular biology and human origins. *Science, 270,* 1930–1936.

Barkow, J. H. (1992). Beneath new culture is old psychology: Gossip and social stratification. In J. H. Barkow, L. Cosmides, & J. Tooby, (Eds.), *The adapted mind: Evolutionary psychology and the generation of culture* (pp. 627–637). New York: Oxford University Press.

Barkow, J. H., Cosmides, L., & Tooby, J., Eds. (1992). *The adapted mind: Evolutionary psychology and the generation of culture.* New York: Oxford University Press.

Behavioral and Brain Sciences, 12 (1989) pp. 1–49. (Target article by David Buss and responses)

Buss, D. M. (1995). Psychological sex differences: Origins through sexual selection. *American Psychologist, 50,* 164–168.

Buss, D. M. (1994). *The evolution of desire.* New York: Basic.

Clutton-Brock. T. H., Guinness, F. E., & Albon, S. E. (1982). *Red deer: The behavior and ecology of two sexes.* Chicago: University of Chicago Press.

Cowley, G. (1996, June 3). The biology of beauty. *Newsweek,* 60–66.

Culotta, E. (1995). Asian hominids grow older. *Science, 270,* 1116–1117.

Davies, N. B. (1992). *Dunnock behavior and social evolution.* New York: Oxford University Press.

de Waal, F. B. M. (1995, March). Bonobo sex and society. *Scientific American,* 82–88.

Dorit, R. L., Akashi, H., & Gilbert, W. (1995). Absence of polymorphism at the ZFY locus on the human Y chromosome. *Science, 268,* 1183–1185.

Fausto-Sterling, A. (1997) Feminism and behavioral evolution: A taxonomy. In P. A. Gowaty, (Ed.), *Evolution and Feminism* (pp. 42–60). New York: Chapman Hall.

Fausto-Sterling, A., Gowaty, P., & Zuk, M. (1997). Evolutionary psychology and Darwinian feminism. *Feminist Studies.* (Forthcoming)

Fedigan, L. (1986). The changing role of women in models of human evolution. *Annual Review of Anthropology, 15,* 25–66.

Gibbons, A. (1996). The peopling of the Americas. *Science, 274,* 31–33.

Gibbons, A. (1995). The mystery of humanity's missing mutations. *Science, 267,* 35–36.

Gibbons, A. (1994). Rewriting—and redating—prehistory. *Science, 263,* 1087–1088.

Gomulkiewicz, R., & Kirkpatrick, M. (1992). Quantitative genetics and the evolution of reaction norms. *Evolution, 46,* 390–411.

Goodall, J. (1986). *The chimpanzees of Gombe: Patterns of behavior.* Cambridge: Harvard University Press.

Hammer, M. F. (1995). A recent common ancestry for human Y chromosomes. *Nature, 378,* 376–378.

Latour, B. (1987). *Science in Action.* Cambridge: Harvard University Press.

Latour, B., & Strum, S. C. (1986). Human social origins: Oh please, tell us another story. *Journal of Social Biological Structure, 9,* 169–187.

Leibowitz, L. (1978). *Females, males, families: A biosocial approach.* North Scituate, MA: Duxbury Press.

Newman, R. A. (1988). Adaptive plasticity in development of *Scaphiopus couchii* tadpoles in desert ponds. *Evolution, 42,* 774–783.

Newsweek. (1995, March 27). The new science of the brain. *Newsweek,* 48–54.

Newsweek. (1996, June 3). The biology of beauty: What science has discovered about sex appeal. *Newsweek,* 61–69.

Parish, A. R. (1994). Sex and food control in the "uncommon chimpanzee": How bonobo females overcome a phylogentic legacy of male dominance. *Ethology and Sociobiology, 15,* 157–179.

Piazza, A. (1993). Who are the Europeans? *Science, 260,* 1767–1769.

Scheiner, S. M. (1993). Genetics and the evolution of phenotypic plasticity. *Annual Review of Ecology and Systematics, 24,* 35–68.

Schlichting, C. D., & Pigliucci, M. (1994). Gene regulation, quantitative genetics and the evolution of reaction norms. *Trends in Ecology and Evolution, 9,* 154–168.

Siegel, M. I., Doyle, W. J., & Kelley, C. (1977). Heat stress, fluctuating asymmetry and prenatal selection in the laboratory rat. *American Journal of Physical Anthropology, 46,* 121–126.

Strum, S. (1987) *Almost Human.* New York: Random House.

Tanner, N. M. (1981). *On Becoming Human.* Cambridge: Cambridge University Press. (1994, August 15). Infidelity: It may be in our genes. *Time,* 44–52.

Tishkoff, S. A., et al. (1996). Global patterns of linkage disequilibrium at the CD4 locus and modern human origins. *Science, 271,* 1380–1385.

Waddington, C. H. (1975). *The evolution of an evolutionist.* Ithaca, NY: Cornell University Press.

Wallen, K. (1989). Mate selection, economics and selection. *Behavioral and Brain Sciences, 12,* 37–38.

West-Eberhard, M. J. (1989). Phenotypic plasticity and the origins of diversity. *Annual Review of Ecology and Systematics, 20,* 249–278.

Wright, R. (1994a, November 28). The Female Mind. *The New Republic,* 34–36.

Wright, R. (1994b). *The moral animal: Why we are the way we are: The new science of evolutionary psychology.* New York: Pantheon.

POSTSCRIPT

Does Evolutionary Theory Explain Psychological Sex Differences in Humans?

Perhaps one of the most troubling implications of evolutionary psychological theory for feminist and other critics is the seeming improbability of social change. Is it inevitable, for example, that males will aggress against females? A subgroup of feminists ("Darwinian feminists") adapt evolutionary theory to guide their scientific inquiry while being conscious of sexist assumptions and concerned about the problem of social change. Their goal goes beyond just describing the role of evolutionary mechanisms in creating sex differentials to identifying strategies for social change.

Darwinian feminists focus on variability and developmental flexibility of psychological and behavioral repertoires. They believe that we are capable of a wide range of behaviors and possess the ability to adapt behavior to context. Moreover, organisms do not just experience one environment but many different environments with different pressures. Thus, the choice of behavior depends on specific environmental conditions.

Questions remain about how evolutionary psychological theoretical propositions about human sex and gender ought to be tested. What constitutes supportive evidence of evolutionary explanations of human sex differences? Evolutionary psychologists have taken two general approaches in research. They have built hypotheses about sex-differentiated behaviors and psychological mechanisms based on assumptions about the environmental pressures and functional adaptations of hunter-gatherers and tested them by examining contemporary analogs of sex differences. They started by identifying contemporary sex-differentiated behavior patterns and then developing evolutionary accounts to explain them. Can contemporary data be used to test these hypotheses about ancestral conditions and behaviors?

Suggested Readings

J. H. Barkow, L. Cosmides, and J. Tooby, eds., *The Adapted Mind: Evolutionary Psychology and the Generation of Culture* (Oxford University Press, 1992).

D. M. Buss and N. M. Malamuth, eds., *Sex, Power, Conflict: Evolutionary and Feminist Perspectives* (Oxford University Press, 1996).

A. Fausto-Sterling, P. A. Gowaty, and M. Zuk, "Evolutionary Psychology and Darwinian Feminism," *Feminist Studies* (Summer 1997).

ISSUE 5

Are Sex Differences in the Brain Primarily Responsible for Males' and Females' Differing Cognitive Abilities?

YES: Doreen Kimura, from *Sex and Cognition* (MIT Press, 2000)

NO: MaryAnn Baenninger and Nora Newcombe, from "Environmental Input to the Development of Sex-Related Differences in Spatial and Mathematical Ability," *Learning and Individual Differences* (1995)

ISSUE SUMMARY

YES: Clinical neurologist Doreen Kimura states that early effects of sex hormones on brain organization establish differences between males' and females' cognitive abilities.

NO: Psychologists MaryAnn Baenninger and Nora Newcombe assert that social and environmental factors contribute greatly to sex-related differences in spatial and mathematical ability.

$\mathbf{C}$ognition represents a complex system of skills that enable the processing of different types of information. Cognitive processes underlie our intellectual activities and many other daily tasks. For three decades, researchers have actively explored whether or not males and females differ in their cognitive abilities. The most common taxonomy of cognitive processes used in cognitive sex differences research is based on the type of information used in a cognitive task: verbal (words), quantitative (numbers), and visual-spatial (figural representations).

The study of cognitive sex differences became especially active after the publication of Eleanor Emmons Maccoby and Carol Nagy Jacklin's now famous book entitled *The Psychology of Sex Differences* (Stanford University Press, 1974). Their aim in constructing this tome was to catalog and synthesize the main findings from studies of sex comparisons in numerous domains, with the underlying aim of dispelling sexist stereotypes and redressing inequalities between the sexes. While concluding with a generally skeptical perspective on the existence of sex differences, the authors maintained that one area in which the sexes did appear to differ was intellectual ability and functioning. Specifically, the sexes appeared to differ in verbal, quantitative, and spatial abilities.

This compilation and synthesis of sex comparison findings spawned extensive research on sex differences in numerous areas of functioning but especially in the domain of cognitive abilities. Study after study aimed to determine whether or not the sexes differed on specific verbal, quantitative, and spatial cognitive tasks. Moreover, many researchers followed the tradition of Maccoby and Jacklin by trying to amass large collections of individual studies and reach an overall conclusion about whether or not (and how much) the sexes differ in this domain. Rather than use the informal synthesis approach used by Maccoby and Jacklin, researchers began to use the quantitative technique of meta-analysis, which has been used to explore whether or not any sex differences change in magnitude over the life cycle or over time, whether or not there is cross-cultural consistency in any sex differences, and whether or not cognitive sex differences are found across various ethnic groups.

There has been contradiction among findings. Some researchers document what they describe as important sex differences; others report negligible sex differences that have become smaller over time. When sex differences are described, males show better visual spatial ability, especially the ability to mentally rotate three-dimensional figures. Males are also found to have greater mathematical ability. Females show better verbal fluency.

This is a politically charged area of research because the stakes are high for the more and less cognitively able. Cognitive abilities relate to valued and "marketable" occupational and societal skills, often putting males at an advantage for higher social status and advancement. This "cognitive ability hierarchy" is not determined by findings of sex differences but reflect differential societal valuation of different cognitive abilities. It so happens that the cognitive abilities on which some evidence shows that males excel (spatial and mathematical skills) are more highly valued (and drive the economy) than females' superior verbal abilities. Critical questions are, What causes cognitive sex differences? Must cognitive ability differences between the sexes, and thus societal inequalities, continue?

A criticism of explanatory research (including both biological and sociocultural studies) is the lack of direct testing of causal links. For example, sex differences in brain structure may exist, as might sex differences in spatial test performance. But do sex differences in brain structure *cause* sex-differentiated performance on spatial tests? Evidence is lacking for such causal claims. Observers caution that we must discriminate between causal theory and scientific evidence when evaluating causal claims.

In the following selections, Doreen Kimura reviews evidence in support of the biological argument that cognitive sex differences are rooted in the brain. In contrast, MaryAnn Baenninger and Nora Newcombe document the powerful role of social and environmental factors in sex differentials in cognitive abilities.

Doreen Kimura

Sex and Cognition

[Elsewhere] we summarized the main differences in cognitive or problem-solving skills between men and women, and boys and girls, and reviewed the evidence for biological influences on these differences. Currently the most compelling evidence for a biological role is the fact that cognitive patterns are affected by past and current exposure to sex hormones. We also discussed the extent to which certain brain differences may account for the differing cognitive makeup of the sexes, and considered some of the common sociological explanations for sex differences in cognition.

To begin, we recap the story of hormonal contributions to male-favoring abilities. The evidence from persons with early hormonal anomalies such as congenital adrenal hyperplasia (CAH), idiopathic hypogonadotrophic hypogonadism (IHH) and androgen insensitivity indicates that early exposure to androgens contributes significantly to scores on several paper-and-pencil spatial tasks. Similarly, studies of normal young men and women have established that different levels of testosterone are consistently associated with different spatial scores. Fluctuations in sex hormones across seasons or at different phases of the menstrual cycle are also associated with predictable changes in cognitive patterns, including changes in spatial performance.

In addition there is some evidence that math reasoning is related to testosterone levels in men, though perhaps not in women. Finally, although we have as yet no information that hormones influence accuracy of targeting, we have ruled out sports history, male physique, and male "gender" identity as critical factors in producing the sex difference consistently found in this ability.

On female-favoring tasks, we know that fluctuations in estrogen levels are associated with changes in verbal fluency, perceptual speed, and manual dexterity. So far, we have almost no studies relating the reliably found female advantage in verbal memory to levels of sex hormones, though recent reports that taking estrogen therapeutically may enhance memory in older women are suggestive.

Besides sex hormones, we proposed other ways of linking cognitive pattern to prenatal events. Since dermatoglyphic (fingerprint) patterns are fixed early in the second trimester before birth, we can reasonably assume from correlations between aspects of cognitive function and fingerprint characteristics, that there is a prenatal contribution to such functions. In fact, the direction of finger-ridge asymmetry—that is, whether there are more ridges on the left or right hand—is reliably related to whether a person is more likely to show a so-called masculine cognitive pattern or a feminine one, even within a sex. Math reasoning is one ability strongly related to rightward ridge asymmetry, suggesting a prenatal contribution to this math skill. Other abilities which are related to finger-ridge asymmetry include the sexually differentiated motor skills—targeting (rightward asymmetry) and fine motor function (leftward asymmetry). It is a fair assumption that brain systems developing at the same time as the finger ridges are responsible for these effects. At present we don't know whether these brain events are hormonally linked.

Of course, differences in behavior between individuals or groups must in some way be mediated by the nervous system. Much is known in rodents about the effect of hormones on brain structure and function. We know, for example, a fair amount about how the hypothalamus mediates sexual behavior, about the hormonal mechanism in the amygdala's mediation of rough-and-tumble play, and about the role of the hippocampal complex in certain spatial maze-solving functions. We can manipulate hormones in nonhumans and look at the effects on brain and behavior as we cannot do in people. Such experiments provide us with very useful models of how similar functions may operate in people, though ultimately these ideas must somehow be tested on humans.

Several contrasts in human brain structure and function between the sexes were described, with special reference to commissural systems, anterior-posterior function, and left-right lateralization of function. Although we would expect such brain differences to be related to differences in human cognitive patterns, we have up to now had little in the way of solid evidence linking sex variations in brain organization to cognitive abilities. The absence of such evidence is most likely due to the difficulty of collecting it. Some of the best information we have about the functions of particular brain regions comes from persons with neurological damage. Most studies of this kind, however, have not compared men and women—perhaps in part because larger numbers of patients would be needed to make such a comparison.

The widely held assumption that there are major differences in the degree of brain lateralization of function between men and women is debatable. Even where sex differences in brain lateralization clearly exist, no convincing case has yet been made that they influence cognitive pattern. Nonetheless, it is likely that in the near future new brain-imaging techniques will help uncover relationships between individual brain organization and cognitive abilities.

Taking all these facts together, we can say with certainty that there are substantial stable sex differences in cognitive functions like spatial rotation ability, mathematical reasoning, and verbal memory; and in motor skills requiring accurate targeting and finger dexterity. We can also state with certainty that most of these sexually differentiated functions are strongly influenced by early and/or current hormonal environments. Other factors may contribute to these abilities prenatal through nonhormonal mechanisms.

Evidence for socialization influences on such differences between the sexes is meagre, and most often focuses on relating past life experience (preferred sports, school courses taken, presumed parental influence) to current abilities. All such associations are of course open to alternative interpretations. Some people have also claimed that cognitive sex differences have been declining, implying that as men's and women's environments become more alike, they will differ less. We pointed out other reasons for reduced sex differences, when they occur, including the changing of test items to favor one group (typically females). Often the arguments for socializing influences consist in simply insisting that such explanations be given priority.

What evidence we have does not suggest that the male superiority on imaginal rotation and mathematical reasoning has declined over the last few decades. The very early appearance in life of sex differences in imaginal rotation ability and in certain motor skills is probably more easily reconcilable with pre- and perinatal biological influences than with gendered socialization. However, it must also be said that "natural experiments" relevant to socializing influences are less likely to occur than those relevant to the role of sex hormones. The effect of sex-of-rearing in persons with anomalous genital structure, for example, has simply not been sufficiently studied.

**MaryAnn Baenninger
and Nora Newcombe**

Environmental Input to the Development of Sex-Related Differences in Spatial and Mathematical Ability

In 1974, Maccoby and Jacklin published *The Psychology of Sex Differences,* a massive literature review which reached the conclusion that males perform reliably better than females on tests of mathematical and spatial ability. The potential biological and social causes of those differences have been debated ever since, often vociferously and with a focus on an "either/or" approach in which one of these explanations must be primary. Biological differences are generally more prominently featured in the popular media (e.g., *Time's* cover of January 20, 1992, emblazoned with the teaser "Why are men and women so different? It isn't just upbringing. New studies show they are born that way.") On the other hand, however, the possible social causes of sex-related differences have recently been highlighted in the popular press's reporting of the American Association of University Women's (1991) report, *Shortchanging Girls: Shortchanging America.* The AAUW argued that girls receive less favorable treatment in classrooms, compared to boys, and that, somewhere during early adolescence, girls suffer a dramatic loss of self-esteem, especially in mathematics and science.

The purpose of this review is to examine the social and environmental contribution to sex-related differences in spatial and mathematical ability. We show that there is strong evidence that environmental input is essential for the development of high levels of mathematical and spatial ability, in both sexes, and strong evidence that this environmental input is more common in the lives of boys than of girls. However, although a causal link between these facts, in which sex-stereotyped input leads to sex-related ability differences, seems natural to many observers, including the AAUW, the evidential basis for this argument needs to be stronger. Sex-differentiated input may maintain or widen an already-existing biological predisposition, rather than create a difference from nothing. Key empirical studies on this issue remain to be done.

Fine delineation of how biology and environment interact in the development of sex differences in spatial and mathematical ability is, however, not as important to educators as one might think. We argue that, whatever the story

From MaryAnn Baenninger and Nora Newcombe, "Environmental Input to the Development of Sex-Related Differences in Spatial and Mathematical Ability," *Learning and Individual Differences,* vol. 7, no. 4 (1995). Copyright © 1995 by JAI Press, Inc. Reprinted by permission of Elsevier Science.

on the interaction of biological and social factors in the development of cognitive sex differences turns out to be, the key message for people concerned with effective schooling is that, currently, neither girls nor boys develop their spatial or mathematical ability to the full extent possible. Thus, whatever the cause of sex-related differences, the central social issue is to nurture such abilities more intensively in both girls and boys.

Experience Has Clear Effects on Mathematics and Spatial Ability

Performance in mathematics and spatial tasks depends on environmental input. For mathematics, such a conclusion may appear almost self-evident, in that counting and arithmetic notation systems, not to mention calculus and algebra, are invented symbolic tools culturally transmitted in the schools. Nevertheless, a strong commitment by many Americans to a view of mathematical ability as innate sometimes obscures recognition of this fact (Stevenson & Stigler 1992; Geary in press). Spatial competence is less obviously taught in the schools than is mathematics, and the temptation to view it as innate in a very strong sense may be even greater than for mathematics. For instance, people will frequently comment that they have difficulty finding their way or following directions, in a fashion that attributes these facts to native ability and discounts the possibility that they simply haven't worked to develop skills in these areas.

There is clear evidence, however, that, contrary to these popular assumptions, environmental input is crucial for both the mathematical and spatial domains. First, gains in spatial and mathematical ability are tied directly to school experiences, for both boys and girls. Second, training of spatial ability in various types of experimental interventions results in substantial change in spatial ability scores for both sexes....

Boys and Girls Have Different Experiences

In evaluating sex-differentiated experiences, one needs to take into account both formal experience, including classroom learning and other lessons, and informal experiences, including activities and recreation that facilitate spatial and mathematical ability. One needs to look at these formal and informal settings both in terms of the content of what children do, and also in terms of the nature of the social interactions that occur around these experiences.

Formal Experience...

Course Taking Decisions   Boys take more math courses than girls beginning at the time they are able to make choices about which courses they take (e.g., Armstrong 1981; Benbow & Stanley 1982; Fennema & Carpenter 1981; Fennema & Sherman 1977; Pallas & Alexander 1983). This decision seems to depend on perceptions of the usefulness of math for one's future life, as well as to self-assessments of one's abilities and liking for the subject. These perceptions and self-assessments are likely influenced by parents and teachers, as discussed below.

Parents   Parents make attributions about the causes of their children's success, they exert pressure for achievement on their children, they express varying levels of satisfaction with their children's performance, and they model their own sex-role orientations for their children (Holloway 1986). There is a relation between parental estimates of children's ability and the children's own expectations for their performance and their own self-concepts concerning their math ability (Parsons, Adler, & Kaczala 1982).

Given these facts, it is significant that parents of boys believe that math comes more naturally to their sons, and think that their boys had to exert less effort to do well, compared to parents of girls (Parsons, Adler, & Kaczala 1982). Parents of boys also make more unstable, external attributions about their sons' performance in math; relative to parents of girls, for instance, they are more likely to believe that a specific test grade is high or low because of the teacher, rather than because of the child's ability (Holloway 1986). In contrast, mothers of girls believe that their children's performance in math is more a function of their children's effort and achievement orientation in school than do mothers of boys (Holloway & Hess 1982).

It might be argued that these differences reflect facts about children, not social stereotypes. However, girls themselves, at least at young ages, are more motivated to achieve in math than are boys, even when their level of ability is equal to that of boys; their liking of math is higher than that of boys (Holloway 1986). Yet, the mothers of these same children hold higher aspirations, and exert more pressure for later achievement on their male children than they do their female children (Holloway 1986).

Even when girls like math and excel at it, as in high-ability samples, there are indications that they have sex stereotyped expectations about it. High-ability children tend to view math as a male domain, and their fathers are more likely to engage in math-related activity than are their mothers (Raymond & Benbow 1989; Raymond & Benbow 1986).

Teachers   There are many investigations concerning teachers' differential use of evaluative feedback in the classroom (e.g. Becker 1981; Brophy 1985; Brophy & Good 1970; Dweck, Davidson, Nelson, & Enna 1978; Heller & Parsons 1981).... We focus illustratively on the outcome of one investigation that used a large sample of teachers (ten), a large sample of class periods (100), and quantitative and qualitative measures (Becker 1981).

Becker (1981)... code[d] student-teacher interaction [and conducted] qualitative analyses of transcripts of classroom dialogue. She studied ninth and tenth grade geometry classes because geometry represents a choice point for students: it is required, but further study in math after geometry is usually not required. Geometry has large spatial and conceptual components as well, so the implications of this study are particularly relevant here.

Becker (1981) found that boys responded to more open questions (where the teacher waits for a student to volunteer a response), more process questions (requiring "higher-order" thought), and made more "call-outs" (responses to questions before they were called on) than girls. Males also received more sustained interaction than girls, and more teacher-initiated contacts. In terms of encouragement for later participation and success in mathematics, boys had many more positive interchanges with teachers, whereas girls received 90% of the negative interactions.

Particularly poignant were Becker's (1981) reports of lost opportunities to encourage girls in later mathematical pursuits. . . .

Becker (1981) reports that teachers made frequent remarks about females' lesser ability and experience with things mathematical, spatial, and mechanical, and that female teachers even engaged in self-deprecating remarks about their own abilities in geometry and other spatially and mechanically oriented tasks, thereby sending the message that girls and women are not expected to have such competencies and experiences. Again, all of these differential expectations are unrelated to the actual ability and performance of girls and boys, because at this age level, girls are performing equal to or better than boys, in math . . . (Kimball 1989). . . .

Self-Expectations and Feelings of Competence   Girls and women, relative to boys and men, express reduced feelings of competence and self-efficacy about their abilities in mathematics (Lent, Lopez, & Bieschke 1993). The masculine label on mathematics appears to be responsible for females' reduced feelings of competency, because when presented with a gender-neutral task, females express equally high feelings of competency as males (Hackett & Campbell 1987).

There are also sex differences in attributions for success and failure in mathematics. When success and failure feedback are manipulated, girls are more likely than boys to attribute their successes to unstable factors like effort, whereas boys are likely to attribute their successes to ability. The reverse effect occurs for failures: girls attribute them to ability, boys to unstable factors like effort or task characteristics (Hackett & Campbell 1987; Wolleat, Pedro, Becker, & Fennema 1980). This effect occurs also when girls' and boys' performance levels are controlled (Wolleat et al. 1980). Thus, real success in math does not reduce girls' tendency to disregard natural ability as a cause for their high performance.

Motivational factors appear to interact with students' attributions. Students with "mastery orientations" are more likely to do well in situations where novel concepts or new instructional units are challenging. Since math is a discipline that continually presents new challenges, boys may fare better because they adopt a mastery orientation, rather than a helpless orientation (Licht & Dweck 1984).

It has been argued, however, that the subjective value of a task is more important than attributions for success, or other motivational factors in determining effort (Eccles, Adler, & Meece 1984). When social forces act to reduce the desirability or value of a specific activity for a certain group, that group will choose not to pursue the activity. Even when girls express confidence in their abilities in math, they may choose to avoid it in favor of another discipline (e.g.,

English) that has a higher subjective value for them (Eccles et al. 1984; Meece, Parsons, Kaczala, Goff, & Futterman 1982).

These attributional and motivational factors translate into reduced expectations for success in mathematics in girls. It makes sense that girls would choose disciplines seen as not requiring mathematics if they believe their successes in math are the result of effort, not ability, that their future math grades are going to be lower than they actually are (Mura 1987), and that they have little control over their eventual performance.

Informal Experience

Mathematical Activity   Boys take more math classes than girls, but outside the classroom they appear to engage in more math and science-related activity as well (Kimball 1989). Hilton and Berglund (1974) found that, when questioned about outside-the-classroom activity, girls consistently reported reading fewer books on science, spending less time reading science magazines, talking less about science and math to friends and parents, and finding math more boring and less interesting than boys find it. Sadly, these differences were minimal in grade seven and quite pronounced in grade 11....

Casserly (1980), on interviewing girls in Advanced Placement math and science courses found that they lamented the fact that their parents were unlikely to buy them math and science-related toys, even after considerable pleading, and that they were often forced to appropriate things like Legos, erector sets, and chemistry sets that were originally bought for their brothers....

Causal Linkages?

To this point, we have shown that environmental input is crucial to mathematical and spatial development, and that boys and girls differ in their mathematical and spatial input. Do sex differences in input cause sex differences in ability, or vice versa? Or, as is most likely, are there complicated interactions between biological and social facts? In this section, we evaluate arguments that the linkage goes, at least to some extent, from experiences to ability, leaving to the next section the task of considering interactions.

Impact of Course-Taking Decisions on Sex Differences in Mathematics   As we have seen, boys take more math courses than girls, beginning at the time they are able to make choices about which courses they take (e.g., Armstrong 1981; Benbow & Stanley 1982; Fennema & Carpenter 1981; Fennema & Sherman 1977; Pallas & Alexander 1983). Pallas and Alexander (1983), analyzing data from the Educational Testing Service's Study of Academic Prediction and Growth (Hilton 1979), found that sex differences of 35 points on the SAT-M favoring boys were reduced to 14 points when the amount of coursework taken was controlled. Furthermore, they found that when girls and boys in this sample started out in ninth grade there were no sex differences, but girls were at a significant disadvantage by twelfth grade. They also found that girls took fewer math courses than boys and that the more advanced the coursework for girls, the less the difference between boys' and girls' twelfth grade scores.

When coursework is "naturally" controlled for by studying male and female samples with equivalent coursework there appears to be essentially no difference between the sexes. For instance, Smith and Walker (1988) found that on the New York State Regents Mathematics Examination, girls slightly outperformed boys in both ninth and eleventh grades, whereas the reverse was true for tenth grade scores. Kimball (1989) concluded that differential course taking accounts for some of the sex-differences in mathematics ability, but that other factors, possibly including differential course taking in the sciences, and other mathematics-related experience outside the classroom, may also account for some of the difference.

Spatial Ability Training   It has often been argued that experiential hypotheses about sex differences predict that spatial test training should raise females' scores more than males' scores, since males came into the training with the benefit of more prior experience than did females. Contrary to this hypothesis, Baenninger and Newcombe (1989) found that while training of all types raised spatial test performance above pre-training levels, females and males improved equally....

Correlations of Informal Spatial Experience and Ability   Baenninger and Newcombe (1989) conducted a meta-analysis on all of the studies they could find that examined the relationships between scores on spatial experience scales and various measures of spatial ability....

Baenninger and Newcombe (1989) concluded that there was a statistically significant, but small, relation between degree of participation in spatial activities and spatial ability....

Participation in video games and computer programming has also been shown to increase spatial ability scores.... Dorval and Pépin (1986) showed that eight video game playing sessions improved the performance of college-aged novice video game players on the space relations subtests of the DAT [Differential Aptitude Tests], and Subrahmanyam and Greenfield (1994) found that fifth-graders' spatial skills improved following playing the game *Marble Madness*. This improvement did not differ for the sexes, however, in either study, echoing Baenninger and Newcombe's (1989) finding that spatial ability training did not produce significantly different degrees of improvement for females and males. Law, Pellegrino, and Hunt (1993) also found a relation between reported levels of video game playing and judgments of a target's velocity, but not the distance it had traveled. In this task, males outperformed females, but differential experience with video game playing accounted for more of the variance in velocity judgments than did sex.

Historical Change   In an article with the eye-catching title "Cognitive Gender Differences are Disappearing," Feingold (1988) examined the data from nationwide representative samples of students taking the Differential Aptitude Tests (DAT) between the years 1947 and 1980, and the Preliminary Scholastic

Aptitude Test and the Scholastic Aptitude Test (PSAT/SAT) between 1960 and 1983.... [I]n all cases, but the notable exception of SAT Math scores, the gap between the sexes has been closing consistently since the first administration of the tests (Feingold 1988). Thus, for the most part, on nationally administered standardized tests, "cognitive gender differences are disappearing" (Feingold 1988)....

What about the notable exception, in Feingold's (1988) sample of data, that sex differences in SAT-M scores have slightly increased...? This change can be accounted for by the selectivity of the SAT sample, relative to the PSAT sample. As noted above, sex-related differences favoring males are more dramatic at the high end of the distribution (Benbow 1988). Students taking the SAT represent a sample that is closer to the high end of the distribution than the more nationally representative sample of students taking the PSAT. In addition, SAT-M scores may, in fact, reflect sex-related differences in experience, rather than biology, as some have claimed (Benbow 1988), because they could be a reflection of differential course taking in the later high school years.

Biological-Social Interactions

Numerous biological hypotheses have been put forth to explain sex-related differences in spatial and mathematics abilities. These include sex differences in cerebral laterality (Benbow 1988; Geschwind & Behan 1982; McGee 1979; McGlone 1980; Ozer 1987), and its impact on processing strategies (e.g., Newcombe, Dubas, & Baenninger 1989), and the organizing and activating effects of hormones (Collaer & Hines 1995; Hines & Shipley 1984; Newcombe & Baenninger 1989; Resnick, Berenbaum, Gottesman, & Bouchard 1986). A "timing of puberty" hypothesis that incorporates hormonal and cerebral laterality explanations has also been advanced (Waber 1977), but has not received consistent support (Newcombe & Dubas 1987). All of the proposed biological causes have been studied extensively for their own sake, but they are relevant here primarily because it is reasonable to assume that biological factors interact, in not so clear cut ways, with social factors to produce a final outcome. It is likely that any biological foundations for spatial and mathematical abilities are enhanced (or obscured) by social and experiential forces.

The "bent twig" conceptualization of sex-related differences in mathematics and spatial ability embodies this interactive approach (Casey & Brabeck 1990; Sherman 1978). In this approach, biological factors "bend the twig" towards the development of certain kinds of abilities, and experience encourages growth in the "bent" direction.... This biosocial hypothesis is important, not only because it is interesting in itself but also because it confirms the potential value of an interactionist approach to sex differences.

Integrating the Evidence

Two strong conclusions can be drawn from this review. First, mathematics and spatial ability are clearly influenced by experience. For spatial ability, training (even simple practice) results in definite improvements in performance on spatial tests. Exposure to a school curriculum also increases spatial ability scores (but not performance in other areas like memory) and skill at addition (but not understanding of conservation of number).

Second, it is clear that boys and girls are differentially exposed to spatial and mathematics-related training and activity. Boys engage in more spatial and mathematics-related activity than girls, and they take more math courses, beginning at the time when they are able to choose. Perhaps the most profound contrast between boys' and girls' experiences, however, is the differential expectations that their parents and teachers hold for them, and their differential feelings of self-efficacy, and attributions of their own performance in these domains. For girls who are in elementary school or junior high, the attributions and expectations they, their parents, and their teachers hold may translate into "good girls" who are conscientious, neat, obedient, and who answer correctly. Fulfilling these expectations in later years may include the development of a self-concept that includes reduced aspirations for and involvement in math and spatially-oriented courses, activity, and careers.

Showing that sex-differentiated experience leads to sex-differentiated levels of skill in a quantitative fashion is trickier than demonstrating the truth of the first two conclusions. The relation between early participation in spatial activity and later performance on spatial tests is not strong, but it is significant. For mathematical ability, number of courses taken is related to performance on standardized mathematics tests. These facts suggest a causal link between experience and skill, but evaluating self-selection explanations of the associations is not easy.

While it may seem hardly surprising that a student who took advanced algebra, trigonometry, and calculus would perform better, on average, on the SAT-M than a student who took only elementary algebra and geometry, the finding that male students outperform female students on the SAT-M is often presented, at least implicitly, as if biology accounted for the difference. In fact, filtered-down versions of media reports of such differences negatively influence mothers' beliefs about their daughters' math ability and future achievement potential (Eccles & Jacobs 1986).

More research is needed to link hypothesized biological bases for the development of spatial skill to the ability to take advantage of (and the propensity to seek out) environmental experiences engaging and fostering components of spatial skill. We need to identify specific experiences that engage spatial skill, rather than merely speculating on, for instance, the role of aiming sports or puzzles. The finding of school-related effects on spatial development suggests that some particularly crucial kinds of spatial experience may be more common at school than at home. Having identified the sorts of environmental input that foster the growth of spatial ability, we need to determine if the input has equivalent effects on biologically-defined groups, or, as suggested by Casey and Brabeck, differential effects.

Information of the sort we sketched above, when available, may help educators to design finely-tuned mathematical and spatial curricula to foster the growth of spatial and mathematical skill in all of the children they seek to educate. On the basis of current data, however, we believe caution is in order in advocating different curricula for different groups (e.g., mathematics for females). Environmental enrichment seems to, by and large, help everyone. When mathematical and spatial experiences and expectations are gender-blind, there is reason to hope that the educational potential of all children will be better realized.

References

American Association of University Women (1991). *Shortchanging girls, shortchanging America: A call to action.* Washington, DC: American Association of University Women.

Armstrong, J. M. (1981). "Achievement and participation of women in mathematics: Results of two national surveys." *Journal for Research in Mathematics Education, 12,* 356–372.

Baenninger, M. & N. Newcombe. (1989). "The role of experience in spatial test performance: A meta-analysis." *Sex Roles, 20,* 327–343.

Becker, J. R. (1981). "Differential treatment of males and females in mathematics classes." *Journal for Research in Mathematics Education, 12,* 40–53.

Benbow, C. P. (1988). "Sex differences in mathematical reasoning ability among the intellectually talented: Their characterization, consequences, and possible explanations." *Behavioral and Brain Sciences, 11,* 169–232.

Benbow, C. P. & J. C. Stanley. (1982). "Consequences in high school and college of sex differences in mathematical reasoning ability: Longitudinal perspective." *American Education Research Journal, 19,* 598–622.

Brophy, J. E. (1985). "Interactions of male and female students with male and female teachers." Pp. 115–142 in *Gender influences in classroom interaction,* edited by L. C. Wilkinson & C. B. Marrett. Orlando, FL: Academic Press.

Brophy, J. E. & T. L. Good. (1970). "Teachers' communication of differential expectations of children's classroom performance: Some behavioral data." *Journal of Educational Psychology, 61,* 365–374.

Casey, M. B. & M. M. Brabeck. (1990). "Women who excel on a spatial task: Proposed genetic and environmental factors." *Brain and Cognition, 12,* 73–84.

Casserly, P. L. (1980). "Factors affecting female participation in advanced placement programs in mathematics, chemistry, and physics." Pp. 138–163 in *Women and the mathematical mystique,* edited by L. H. Fox, L. Brody, & D. Tobin. Baltimore, MD: Johns Hopkins University Press.

Collaer, M. L. & M. Hines. (1995). "Human behavioral sex differences: Relationships to gonadal hormone levels during early development." *Psychological Bulletin, 118,* 55–107.

Dorval, M. & M. Pépin. (1986). "Effect of playing a video game on a measure of spatial visualization." *Perceptual Motor Skills, 62,* 159–162.

Dweck, C. S., W. Davidson, S. Nelson, & B. Enna. (1978). "Sex differences in learned helplessness: II. The contingencies of evaluative feedback in the classroom and III. An experimental analysis." *Developmental Psychology, 14,* 268–276.

Eccles (Parsons), J., T. A. Adler, & J. L. Meece. (1984). "Sex differences in achievement: A test of alternate theories." *Journal of Personality and Social Psychology, 46,* 1, 26–33.

Eccles, J. S. & J. E. Jacobs. (1986). "Social forces shape math attitudes and performance." *Signs, 11,* 367–380.

Feingold, A. (1988). "Cognitive gender differences are disappearing." *American Psychologist, 43,* 95–103.

Fennema, E. & T. P. Carpenter. (1981). "Sex-related differences in mathematics: Results from the national assessment." *Mathematics Teacher, 74,* 554–559.

Fennema, E. & J. Sherman. (1977). "Sex related differences in mathematics achievement, spatial visualization and affective factors." *American Educational Research Journal, 14,* 1, 51–71.

Geary, D. C. (in press). "Sexual selection and sex differences in mathematical abilities." *Behavioral and Brain Sciences.*

Geschwind, N. & P. Behan. (1982). "Left-handedness: Association with immune disease, migraine, and developmental learning disorder." *Proceedings of the National Academy of Sciences, 79,* 5097–5100.

Hackett, G. & N. K. Campbell. (1987). "Task self-efficacy and task-interest as a function of performance on a gender-neutral task." *Journal of Vocational Behavior, 30,* 203–215.

Heller, K. A. & J. E. Parsons. (1981). "Sex differences in teachers' evaluative feedback and students' expectancies for success in mathematics." *Child Development, 52,* 1015–1019.

Hilton, T. L. (1979). "ETS study of academic prediction and growth." *New Directions for Testing and Measurement, 2,* 27–44.

Hilton, T. L. & G. W. Berglund. (1974). "Sex differences in mathematics achievement: A longitudinal study." *Journal of Educational Research, 67,* 231–237.

Hines, M. & C. Shipley. (1984). "Prenatal exposure to diethylstilbestrol (DES) and the development of sexually dimorphic cognitive abilities and cerebral lateralization." *Developmental Psychology, 20,* 81–94.

Holloway, S. D. (1986). "The relationship of mothers' beliefs to children's mathematics achievement: Some effects of sex differences." *Merrill-Palmer Quarterly, 32,* 231–250.

Holloway, S. D. & R. D. Hess. (1982). "Causal explanations for school performance: Contrasts between mothers and children." *Journal of Applied Developmental Psychology, 3,* 319–327.

Kimball, M. M. (1989). "A new perspective on women's math achievement." *Psychological Bulletin, 105,* 2, 198–214.

Law, D. J., J. W. Pellegrino, & E. B. Hunt. (1993). "Comparing the tortoise and the hare: Gender differences and experience in dynamic spatial reasoning tasks." *Psychological Science, 4,* 1, 35–40.

Lent, R. W., F. G. Lopez, & K. J. Bieschke. (1993). "Predicting the mathematics related choice and success behaviors: Test of an expanded social cognitive model." *Journal of Vocational Behavior, 42,* 223–236.

Licht, B. G. & C. S. Dweck. (1984). "Determinants of academic achievement: The interaction of children's achievement orientations with skill area." *Developmental Psychology, 20,* 4, 628–636.

Maccoby, E. E. & C. N. Jacklin. (1974). *The psychology of sex differences.* Stanford, CA: Stanford University Press.

McGee, M. G. (1979). "Human spatial abilities: Psychometric studies and environmental, genetic, hormonal, and neurological influences." *Psychological Bulletin, 86,* 5, 889–918.

McGlone, J. (1980). "Sex differences in human brain asymmetry: A critical survey." *Behavioral and Brain Sciences, 3,* 215–263.

Meece, J. L., J. E. Parsons, C. M. Kaczala, S. B. Goff, & R. Futterman. (1982). "Sex differences in math achievement: Toward a model of academic choice." *Psychological Bulletin, 91,* 2, 324–348.

Mura, R. (1987). "Sex-related differences in expectations of success in undergraduate mathematics." *Journal for Research in Mathematics Education, 18,* 1, 15–24.

Newcombe, N. & M. Baenninger. (1989). "Biological change and cognitive ability in adolescence." Pp. 168–191 in *Biology of adolescent behavior and development,* edited by G. R. Adams, R. Montemayor, & T. P. Gullota. London: Sage.

Newcombe, N. & N. Dubas. (1987). "Individual differences in cognitive ability: Are they related to timing of puberty?" Pp. 249–302. in *Biological-psychosocial interactions in early adolescence,* edited by R. M. Lerner & T. T. Foch. Hillsdale, NJ: Erlbaum.

Newcombe, N., J. S. Dubas, & M. Baenninger. (1989). "Associations of timing of puberty with spatial ability: do they persist into adulthood?" *Child Development, 60,* 246–254.

Ozer, D. (1987). "Personality, intelligence, and spatial visualization: Correlates of mental rotations performance." *Journal of Personality and Social Psychology, 53,* 1, 129–243.

Pallas, A. M. & K. L. Alexander. (1983). "Sex differences in quantitative SAT performance: New evidence on the differential coursework hypothesis." *American Educational Research Journal, 20,* 165–182.

Parsons, J. E., T. F. Adler, & C. M. Kaczala. (1982). "Socialization of achievement attitudes and beliefs: Parental influences." *Child Development, 53,* 322–339.

Raymond, C. L. & C. P. Denbow. (1986). "Gender differences in mathematics: A function of parental support and student sex-typing?" *Developmental Psychology, 22,* 6, 808–819.

———. (1989). "Educational encouragement by parents: Its relationship to precocity and gender." *Gifted Child Quarterly, 33,* 4, 144–151.

Resnick, S. M., S. A. Berenbaum, I. I. Gottesman, & T. J. Bouchard. (1986). "Early hormonal influences on cognitive functioning in congenital adrenal hyperplasia." *Developmental Psychology, 22,* 2, 191–198.

Sherman, J. A. (1978). *Sex-related cognitive differences.* Springfield, IL: Charles C. Thomas.

Smith S. E. & W. J. Walker. (1988). "Sex differences on New York state regents examinations. Support for the differential course-taking hypothesis." *Journal for Research in Mathematics Education, 19,* 81–85.

Stevenson, H. W. & J. W. Stigler. (1992). *The learning gap: Why our schools are failing and what we can learn from Japanese and Chinese education.* New York: Summit Books

Subrahmanyam, K. & P. M. Greenfield. (1994). "Effect of video game practice on spatial skills in girls and boys." *Journal of Applied Developmental Psychology, 15,* 13–32.

Waber, D. P. (1977). "Sex differences in mental abilities, hemispheric specialization and rate of physical growth at adolescence." *Developmental Psychology, 13,* 29–38.

Wolleat, P. L., J. D. Pedro, A. D. Becker, & E. Fennema. (1980). "Sex differences in high school students causal attributions of performance in mathematics." *Journal for Research in Mathematics Education, 11,* 357–366.

POSTSCRIPT

Are Sex Differences in the Brain Primarily Responsible for Males' and Females' Differing Cognitive Abilities?

What does it mean if we find that cognitive sex differences are more heavily accounted for by biology or by environmental reasons? If individuals are differently predisposed for cognitive skill, should we and can we do something about it? If so, what? For example, evidence suggests that testosterone is implicated in spatial abilities. Should we give females more testosterone to boost their spatial abilities? Does this sound preposterous considering that thousands of athletes (predominantly males) inject themselves with steroids daily to boost their muscle mass?

Feminist scholars are fearful of biological causal evidence because it renders the environment irrelevant and implies that cognitive sex differences are unchangeable. Rather, they believe that sociocultural evidence provides more hope for social change. How much truth can be found in either claim? Psychosocially caused behavior has often been very difficult to reduce or eliminate (e.g., sex and racial bias). Furthermore, biological mechanisms (e.g., hormones and brain structure) change in response to environmental input. Recent evidence shows, for example, that just as brain structures and functions have been found to impact the way people select and respond to the environment, environmental input and experience alter brain structure and function throughout the life course. If so, then a radical move like injecting females with testosterone is not necessary. Simply engaging individuals in certain activities (even the performance of cognitive tasks) can boost testosterone levels naturally. Thus, many scholars have argued for an interactionist approach to studying cognition, examining the interaction of biology and environment.

Rather than think of sociocultural and biological arguments as necessarily in opposition and mutually exclusive, we must consider how they interact to explain cognitive sex differences. For example, individuals differ in their genetic potential or predisposition for good spatial skills. But genetically predisposed children might select environments that provide more spatial opportunity, augmenting brain structure and further fostering the development of spatial ability. The environment also intercedes in either developing or thwarting this potential. The biological makeup of individuals in the home may also influence the family environment (e.g., parents' and siblings' biological predisposition as impacted by past experiences and environmental inputs). Likewise, individuals might recognize and directly respond to the child's predisposition for spatial ability and provide spatial experiences. Macro-level cultural influences may also act on biological predisposition (e.g., cultural prohibition of certain experiences).

Scholars also urge that we need to go beyond descriptive and explanatory research to a consideration of what the differences *mean* for individuals and society, especially given differential societal valuation of the cognitive differences. Indeed, cognitive sex differences research has revealed the powerful effects of identification and reinforcement of sex role–appropriate behaviors, expectations, motivational variables, and explicit and implicit messages in cognitive sex differences. If individuals have poor mathematical or spatial skill, what does it mean to be excluded from opportunities because of these cognitive deficits (whether actual or presumed based on stereotypes)? Having cognitive deficits impacts identity and self-esteem: how we feel about our abilities, our role in society, and our potential for success. It also creates dependencies. (Think about how much more expensive life is for individuals who are not mechanically inclined.) Spending so much time in a devaluing environment provides constant reminders of the jeopardy incurred by cognitive sex differences to future income, status, and happiness. The restrictions to societal and occupational opportunities based on cognitive functioning have repercussions for individuals and also for society at large. How is society impacted by the fact that the majority of engineers, mathematicians, chemists, mechanics, and airplane pilots are male? Of course, critics point out that the sex differences in occupational representation are grossly disproportionate to the magnitude of cognitive sex differences. Thus, even if there is biological evidence for cognitive sex differences, there seem to be other social factors at work in creating this gulf.

Professor of psychology Diane F. Halpern maintains that sex is a poor predictor of cognitive performance (given large within-sex variability and large overlap between males and females); cognition benefits from education; and expectations, identification, and reinforcements of sex role–appropriate behaviors have powerful effects on sex differences in cognitive performance and self-perceptions. She also warns that we must not let findings of sex differences or causes limit anyone's intellectual potential.

Suggested Readings

J. E. Foss, "Is There a Natural Sexual Inequality of Intellect? A Reply to Kimura," *Hypatia* (Summer 1996).

D. F. Halpern, ed., "Psychological and Psychobiological Perspectives on Sex Differences in Cognition: I. Theory and Research" (Special Issue), *Learning and Individual Differences* (1995).

D. F. Halpern, ed., "Psychological and Psychobiological Perspectives on Sex Differences in Cognition: I. Controversies and Commentaries" (Special Issue), *Learning and Individual Differences* (1996).

ISSUE 6

Do Women and Men Communicate Differently?

YES: Philip Yancey, from "Do Men and Women Speak the Same Language?" *Marriage Partnership* (Fall 1993)

NO: Mary Crawford, from *Talking Difference: On Gender and Language* (Sage, 1995)

ISSUE SUMMARY

YES: Author Philip Yancey maintains that men and women have different conversational styles.

NO: Psychologist Mary Crawford critically evaluates the assertion that men and women have different conversational styles, arguing that it is invalid and inflammatory.

Feminists view the study of communication and gender as very important since language is a powerful agent in the creation and maintenance of the gender system. In 1978, a major review of the scientific literature on gender and language by Cheris Kramer, Barrie Thorne, and Nancy Henley entitled, "Perspectives on Language and Communication," *Signs: Journal of Women in Culture and Society* (vol. 3, 1978) was published. This review summarized the three central research questions:

1. Do men and women use language in different ways?
2. In what ways does language—in structure, content, and daily usage—reflect and help constitute sexual inequality?
3. How can sexist language be changed?

Over twenty years later, these three questions continue to dominate the field, but they have been reframed in part because of the assumption underlying earlier work that the social categories of men and women are internally homogeneous groups. Rather, more contemporary work has sparked an interest in *specificity* and *complexity*. Rather than studying "generic" groups of males and females, we must study particular men and women in particular settings and examine the interactions of gender and other identity categories and power relations.

Some of the most popular work on gender and language is that of author Deborah Tannen. She describes extensive differences between men's and women's communication styles, presenting illustrations from heterosexual romantic relationships and the workplace in *You Just Don't Understand: Women and Men in Conversation* (Ballantine Books, 1991). In "She Just Doesn't Understand," *The New Republic* (December 12, 1994), Alan Wolfe reviews the complexity involved in the different communication styles described by Tannen, including "how loudly or softly we speak, when and how we pause, whether we use irony or humor, whether we make a request in the form of a question or a declaration, how we take turns, whether we interrupt, the forms of address we use, how we frame what we say: all are capable of being misunderstood."

Tannen parallels male-female difference to cultural difference and regards males and females as different but equal. She explores how this cultural difference manifests itself in male-female (mis)communication. Her aim in her popular publications is to reassure men and women that they are not alone in experiencing miscommunication and communication problems because of sex-differentiated communication styles. Moreover, she says that she does not value one style over the other. If anything, she praises women's communication styles. Tannen urges that males and females need to respect each other's differences so that they understand why they misunderstand each other.

Critics have observed that in Tannen's scholarly work, she argues that, given the complexity of human behavior, universalizing and generalizing is inappropriate and not helpful. Rather, localizing specific cases yields better insight. Yet in her popular work she creates generic individuals, generalizing from case studies. Tannen argues that men and women grow up with different cultural backgrounds as evidenced by the sex-segregated nature of children's play in which girls cooperate and boys compete. Tannen concludes that men and women communicate using different languages or "genderlects" because they think differently.

In contrast, Mary Crawford asserts that questions of difference are misguided and counterproductive not only because they are invariably marked by a political agenda but also because sex comparisons locate gender in the individual rather than in social relations and processes. Thus, she observes, responses to claims of sex difference in communication styles frequently involve blaming women for deficiencies or minimizing conflicts between men and women by reframing them as miscommunication for which we must develop tolerance. Sociocultural inequalities are not addressed.

What do we *know* about differences between males' and females' communication styles? Do men's and women's communication styles differ? In the following selections, Philip Yancey draws on the personal experience of himself and his wife and a group of couples to test Tannen's claims. Regarding the question of sex differentiation in communication styles, Yancey indicates unequivocally yes; Mary Crawford implores us to look again and to ask different questions.

Philip Yancey  **YES**

Do Men and Women Speak
the Same Language?

For five years my wife, Janet, and I met in a small group with three other couples. Sometimes we studied the Bible, sometimes we read books together, sometimes we spontaneously discussed topics like money and sex. Almost always we ended up talking about our marriages. Finally we decided the time had come to investigate an explosive topic we had always avoided: the differences between men and women. We used the book *You Just Don't Understand* [William Morrow & Company, 1990], by Deborah Tannen, as the springboard for our discussions. That study of the different communication styles of men and women had risen to the top of The New York Times bestseller list. Books on gender differences tend to portray one party as the "right" party. Women are sensitive, compassionate, peace-loving, responsible, nurturing; men are boorish slobs whose idea of "bonding" is to slouch in front of a TV with their buddies watching other men chase little round balls. Or, men are rational, organizational geniuses who run the world because they are "hardwired" with leadership skills that women can never hope to master. But in her book, Tannen strives to avoid such bias, focusing instead on what it takes for men and women to understand each other.

She sees males as more competitive, aggressive, hierarchical and emotionally withdrawn. Females, she concludes, are quieter, more relational and mutually supportive. Naturally, any generalities about gender differences do not apply to all men or all women. Yet we found one point of commonality that helped us all: Male/female relationships represent a classic case of cross-cultural communication. The key to effective relationships is to understand the vast "cultural" gap between male and female.

Anyone who has traveled overseas knows that barriers exist between cultures, language being the most obvious. The barriers between men and women can be just as real, and just as frustrating. Typically, says Tannen, men and women don't recognize these differences; they tend to repeat the same patterns of miscommunication, only more forcefully. As a result, marriages often resemble the stereotypical tourist encounter: One party speaks loudly and slowly in a language the other does not comprehend.

From Philip Yancey, "Do Men and Women Speak the Same Language?" *Marriage Partnership*, vol. 10, no. 4 (Fall 1993). Copyright © 1993 by Philip Yancey. Reprinted by permission of the author.

The Male/Female Culture Gap

"Shared meaning" is a good, concise definition of culture. By virtue of growing up in the United States, I share the meaning of things like Bart Simpson, baseball and the Fourth of July with 250 million other people, and no one else in the world. Our couples group found that some problems come about because one spouse enters marriage with a different set of "shared meanings" than the other. Consider routine dinner conversation. For some of us, interrupting another's conversation seems an act of impoliteness or hostility; for others, it expresses friendly engagement. Angie, one of the women in our group, said, "When Greg first came to my Italian family's get-togethers he would hardly speak. We usually had a fight on the way home. We later figured out he felt shut down whenever someone interrupted him in the middle of a story or a comment. Well, in my family interrupting is a sign of involvement. It means we're listening to you, egging you on.

"Greg comes from a German family where everyone politely takes turns responding to the previous comment. I go crazy—their conversation seems so boring and stilted. It helped us both to realize there is no 'right' or 'wrong' style of conversation—we were simply acting out of different cultural styles."

Everyone grows up with "rules" or assumptions about how life is supposed to operate. Marriage forces into close contact two people with different sets of shared meanings and then requires them to negotiate a common ground. Bill and Holly told of a disagreement that nearly ruined their Christmas vacation. Bill said, "We visited Holly's family, which is huge and intimidating. That Christmas, one of the sisters bought a VCR and television to present to the parents, without consulting the rest of the family. 'You guys can chip in anything you want,' she told her siblings and in-laws. 'I'll sign the card and present the gift as being from all of us.'

"To me this looked like a set-up job," Bill continued. "I felt pressure to come up with our fair share, which was a lot more than we would have spent on our own. I felt manipulated and angry, and Holly couldn't understand my feelings. She said her sister was absolutely sincere. 'Our family doesn't keep score,' she said. 'Ellen spontaneously felt like buying a present, and she'll be content whether everyone chips in one-eighth or if no one contributes anything. It's not 'tit-for-tat' like your family.'

"Holly was probably right. My family does keep score. You send a letter, you expect one in return. You give a gift, you expect one of equal value. I'm finally coming to grasp that Holly's family doesn't operate like mine."

Another couple, Gayle and Don, identified on-timeness as their major cross-cultural disagreement. Gayle grew up in a family that didn't notice if they were 10 or 15 minutes late, but Don wears a digital watch and follows it punctually. Several times a week they clash over this common cross-cultural difference. In Germany the trains run on time; in Mexico they get there—eventually.

Cross-cultural differences may seem trivial but, as many couples learn, on small rocks great ships wreck. It helps to know in advance where the rocks are.

Cross-Gender Communication

Communication can either span—or widen—the gender gap. Research shows that boys and girls grow up learning different styles of communicating. Boys tend to play in large groups that are hierarchically structured, with a leader who tells the others what to do and how to do it. Boys reinforce status by giving orders and enforcing them; their games have winners and losers and are run by elaborate rules. In contrast, girls play in small groups or in pairs, with "best friends." They strive for intimacy, not status.

These gender patterns continue into adulthood. A man relates to the world as an individual within a hierarchy; he measures himself against others and judges success or failure by his movement up or down the ladder. A woman approaches the world as a network of many social connections. For women, writes Deborah Tannen, "conversations are negotiations for closeness in which people try to seek and give confirmation and support, and to reach consensus."

Tannen's studies of the corporate world show it to be a male-dominated culture where men tend to make pronouncements, to surround themselves with symbols of status, to position themselves against one another, and to improve their standing by opposition. Women, though, tend to seek approval from others and thereby gain their sense of worth. Women are more inclined to be givers of praise than givers of information.

Our couples group agreed that Tannen's observations about the corporate world ring true. "I feel trapped," said Gayle, a management consultant. "At work I find myself changing in order to meet male expectations. I can't be tentative or solicit other people's reactions. I have to appear strong and confident whether I genuinely feel that way or not. I feel I'm losing my femininity."

Because women rely so strongly on feedback from others, they may hesitate to express themselves in a forthright, direct manner. As one psychologist says, "A man might ask a woman, 'Will you please go the store?' where a woman might say, 'I really need a few things from the store, but I'm so tired.'" A man might judge such behavior sneaky or underhanded, but such indirectness is actually the norm in many cultures.

For example, a direct approach such as, "I want to buy that cabbage for 50 cents" will get you nowhere in a Middle Eastern or African market. Both parties expect an elaborate social dance of bluff and innuendo. "If indirectness is understood by both parties, then there is nothing covert about it," Tannen concludes. The challenge in marriage is for both parties to recognize a communication style and learn to work within it.

Battle of the Sexes

We discovered that each couple in our group had what we called a Blamer and a Blamee; two of the Blamers were husbands, two were wives. The Blamer was usually a perfectionist, very detail- and task-oriented, who expected unrealistically high standards of the spouse. "No matter what I do," said one Blamee, "I can never measure up to my husband's standard of cooking or housekeeping or reading or sex, or anything. It's like I'm constantly being graded on my performance. And it doesn't motivate me to improve. I figure I'm not going to satisfy him anyway, so why try?"

All of us would like to make a few changes in the person we live with, but attempts to coax those changes often lead to conflict. And in conflict, gender differences rise quickly to the surface. Men, who grow up in a hierarchical environment, are accustomed to conflict. Women, concerned more with relationship and connection, prefer the role of peacemaker.

In my own marriage, for example, Janet and I view conflict through different eyes. As a writer, I thrive on criticism. I exchange manuscripts with other writers, and I've learned the best editors are the least diplomatic ones. I have two friends who pepper my manuscripts with words like "Ugh!" and "Awk!", and I would hesitate to publish any book without first running it through their gauntlet. In addition, I've gotten used to receiving heated letters from readers. Complimentary letters sound alike; angry letters fascinate me.

Janet, though, tends to feel criticism as a personal attack. I have learned much by watching her manage other people. Sensitive to criticism herself, she has become masterful at communicating criticism to others. When I managed employees in an office setting I would tend to blunder in with a straightforward approach: "There are five things you're doing right and five things you're doing wrong." After numerous failures, I began to see that the goal in criticism is to help the other person see the problem and desire to change. I have learned the necessity of communicating cross-culturally in my conflicts. When dealing with gluttons for punishment like me, I can be as direct as I want. For more sensitive persons, I need to exercise the skills I've gleaned from diplomats like my wife.

As our small group discussed various styles, we arrived at the following "guidelines" for conflict:

First, identify your fighting style. We tend to learn fighting styles from the family we grow up in. In Angie's Italian family, the fighting style was obvious: yell, argue and, if necessary, punch your brother in the nose. She approached marriage much the same way, only without the punches. Meanwhile, her husband would clam up and walk away from an argument. Angie thought Greg was deliberately ignoring her, and their conflicts never got resolved until they sought counseling. There, they realized that Greg was walking away because he knew he had no chance against Angie's well-honed fighting skills. Once both of them realized the dynamics behind their dead-end conflicts, they were able to make appropriate adjustments and change the "rules of engagement."

Second, agree on rules of engagement. Every couple needs to negotiate what constitutes "fighting fair." The couples in our group agreed to avoid these things: fighting in public, straying from the topic at hand, bringing up old history, threatening divorce and using sex as a way to paper over conflict. It's also helpful to consider additional rules, such as "Don't pretend to go along with a decision and then bring it up later as a matter of blame;" and "Don't resort to 'guerrilla warfare'—getting revenge by taking cheap shots after an argument is over."

Third, identify the real issue behind the conflict. A hidden message often underlies conflict. For example, women are sometimes accused of "nagging." On the surface, their message is the specific complaint at hand: not spending enough time with the kids, not helping with housework, coming home late from work. Actually, Deborah Tannen writes, there is another message at work:

"That women have been labeled 'nags' may result from the interplay of men's and women's styles, whereby many women are inclined to do what is asked of them and many men are inclined to resist even the slightest hint that anyone, especially a woman, is telling them what to do. A woman will be inclined to repeat a request that doesn't get a response because she is convinced that her husband would do what she asks if he only understood that she really wants him to do it. But a man who wants to avoid feeling that he is following orders may instinctively wait before doing what she asked in order to imagine that he is doing it of his own free will. Nagging is the result, because each time she repeats the request, he again puts off fulfilling it."

Spouses need to ask themselves questions like, "Is taking out the garbage really the issue, or is it a husband's crusty resistance to anything that infringes on his independence?"

Man Talk, and Woman Talk

In conversation, men and women appear to be doing the same thing—they open their mouths and produce noise. However, they actually use conversation for quite different purposes. Women use conversation primarily to form and solidify connections with other people. Men, on the other hand, tend to use words to navigate their way within the hierarchy. They do so by communicating their knowledge and skill, imparting information to others.

Women excel at what Tannen calls "private speaking" or "rapport-talk." Men feel most comfortable in "public speaking" or "report talk." Even though women may have more confidence in verbal ability (aptitude tests prove their superior skill), they are less likely to use that ability in a public context. Men feel comfortable giving reports to groups or interrupting a speaker with an objection—these are skills learned in the male hierarchy. Many women might perceive the same behavior as putting themselves on display. For example, at a party the men tell stories, share their expertise and tell jokes while the women usually converse in smaller groups about more personal subjects. They are busy connecting while the men are positioning themselves.

Our couples' group discussion became heated when we brought up another female trait that commonly goes by the name "bitching" (Tannen substituted the much more respectable term "ritual lament"). "Yeah, let's talk about this!" Greg said. "I remember one ski trip when I met some of my buddies in Colorado. We spent three days together before our wives joined us. We guys were having a great time, but when the women showed up everything changed. Nothing was right: The weather was too cold and the snow too crusty, the condo was drafty, the grocery store understocked, the hot tub dirty. Every night we heard them complain about sore muscles and raw places where the ski boots rubbed.

"The guys would listen to the griping, then just look at each other and say, 'The women are here!' It was incredible. We were living and skiing in exactly the same conditions. But before the women arrived, we had peace. Afterward, we heard nothing but gripes."

Tannen's explanation is that women tend to bond in pain. Through griping, they reaffirm connections with each other. For men, the immediate response to a complaint is to fix the problem. Otherwise, why complain? Women don't necessarily want the problem solved—who can "fix" the weather, for example? They merely want to feel understood and sympathized with.

Coming Together

Over several months our couples group gained an appreciation for the profound differences between male and female, but also a respect for how difficult it can be to pin down those differences.

 **NO**

Two Sexes, Two Cultures

Cross-Cultural Talk

Consider the difficulties of talk between, say, a person of Italian background and one from Japan. Even if the two share a common language, they may have trouble communicating because they are likely to have different ways of expressing politeness, conversational involvement, and so forth. The 'two-cultures' approach proposes that talk between women and men is fraught with potential misunderstanding for much the same reasons that communication across ethnic groups is.

... Talk shows and best-sellers proclaim the frustrations of cross-sex talk (*You just don't Understand*) and describe a gender gap so great that the two sexes might as well be from different planets (*Men are from Mars, Women are from Venus*)....

Talking Across the Gender Divide

... When we think of distinct female and male subcultures we tend to think of societies in which women and men spend virtually their entire lives spatially and interactionally segregated.... In Western societies, however, girls and boys are brought up together. They share the use of common space in their homes; eat, work, and play with their siblings of both sexes; generally attend coeducational schools in which they are aggregated in many classes and activities; and usually participate in religious meetings and activities together. Both sexes are supervised, cared for, and taught largely by women in infancy and early childhood, with male teachers and other authority figures becoming more visible as children grow older. Moreover, they see these social patterns mirrored and even exaggerated in the mass media. How can the talk of Western women and men be seen as talk across cultures?

The two-cultures model was first applied to the speech of North American women and men by Daniel Maltz and Ruth Borker, who proposed that difficulties in cross-sex and cross-ethnic communication are 'two examples of the same larger phenomenon: cultural difference and miscommunication' (1982: 196). Maltz and Borker acknowledge the argument that American women and men

From Mary Crawford, *Talking Difference: On Gender and Language* (Sage, 1995), pp. 86–94, 97, 101–108. Copyright © 1995 by Sage Publications, Inc. Reprinted by permission of Sage Publishing Ltd. Some references omitted.

interact with each other far too much to be characterized as living in different subcultures. However, they maintain that the social rules for friendly conversation are learned between the ages of approximately 5 and 15, precisely the time when children's play groups are maximally segregated by sex. Not only do children voluntarily choose to play in same-sex groups, they consciously exaggerate differences as they differentiate themselves from the other sex. Because of the very different social contexts in which they learn the meanings and goals of conversational interaction, boys and girls learn to use language in different ways.

Citing research on children's play, Maltz and Borker (1982) argue that girls learn to do three things with words:

1. to create and maintain relationships of closeness and equality;
2. to criticize others in acceptable (indirect) ways;
3. to interpret accurately and sensitively the speech of other girls.

In contrast, boys learn to do three very different things with words:

1. to assert one's position of dominance;
2. to attract and maintain an audience;
3. to assert oneself when another person has the floor.

The Two-Cultures Approach as Bandwagon

... The new twist in the two-cultures model of communication is to conceive relationship difficulties not as women's deficiencies but as an inevitable result of deeply ingrained male–female differences. The self-help books that encode a two-cultures model make the paradoxical claim that difference between the sexes is deeply socialized and/or fundamental to masculine and feminine natures, and at the same time subject to change and manipulation if the reader only follows prescribed ways of talking. ...

A best-selling exemplar of the genre is *Men are from Mars, Women are from Venus* (Gray, 1992). As its title proclaims, this book dichotomizes and stereotypes women and men to extremes....

Every aspect of personality, motivation, and language is polarized. Women's speech is indirect, men's is direct. Women respond to stress by becoming overwhelmed and emotionally involved, men by becoming focused and withdrawn. Women and men even lunch in restaurants for different reasons: for men, it is an efficient way to approach the task of eating; for women, it is an opportunity to build a relationship.

Women and men are so irredeemably and fundamentally different that they need translators to help them communicate.... They also need rules and routines to bridge the gender gap. (Oddly, some of these rules and routines are opposite to those endorsed in assertiveness training books. Instead of 'I would like you to take out the trash,' a wife is exhorted to ask, 'Would you take out the trash?' Like assertiveness prescriptions, however, they are promulgated with detailed specificity and total conviction. If she unthinkingly asks '*Could* you take out the trash?' the wife has doomed her relationship to a period of resistance and resentment.) ...

Although the book makes prescriptions for both sexes, it leaves little doubt about its intended readership: women in middle-class heterosexual marriages. In this book, Martians come home after a long day at the office to waiting Venusians. Martians are obsessed with paid work and money, Venusians with home and feelings. Venusians seem to do almost all the domestic work, from taking children to the dentist to cooking, cleaning, and calling elderly relatives. Martians may be asked to help, but only if Venusians use carefully circumscribed request forms and recognize that Martians have every right to refuse. Helpful tips are provided for 'Programming a Man to Say Yes' and 'The Art of Empowering a Man.' If all else fails, one can read the section on 'How to Give up Trying to Change a Man.'

... Despite the endless lists of how to change each other, the ultimate promise is that women can earn love through acceptance of the status quo. Individual change is not really necessary, much less the restructuring of masculinity and femininity. 'Through understanding the hidden differences of the opposite [sic] sex we can ... give and receive ... love. Love is magical, and it can last, if we remember our differences' (Gray, 1992: 14).

Academic psychologists and linguists have tended to ignore self-help materials. The path along the journey to enlightenment and communication heaven in these books is not likely to be cluttered with any actual references to research. ...

The situation would be different if a prominent and well-respected academic were to claim expertise in male–female communication and write about it for the general public. And that is just what has happened with Deborah Tannen's *You just don't Understand: Women and Men in Conversation* (1990). ... *You just don't Understand* has been on the *New York Times* bestseller list for over three years and claims over one million copies in print. ... It seems that the state of gender relations among the middle-class book-buying public demanded an explanation of communication difficulties and frustrations, an explanation that books like *Men are from Mars, Women are from Venus* and *You just don't Understand* promised to provide.

Although Tannen is a much-published and respected linguist, this particular work has been quite controversial among her peers. Scholarly review and commentary have been mixed. ...

Tannen claims that childhood play has shaped world views so that, when adult women and men are in relationships 'women speak and hear a language of connection and intimacy, while men speak and hear a language of status and independence' (1990: 42). The contrasting conversational goals of intimacy and independence lead to contrasting conversational styles. Women tell each other of their troubles, freely ask for information and help, and show appreciation of others' helping efforts. Men prefer to solve problems rather than talk about them, are reluctant to ask for help or advice, and are more comfortable in the roles of expert, lecturer, and teacher than learner or listener. Men are more talkative in public, women in private. These different styles are labelled 'report talk' (men's) and 'rapport talk' (women's).

Given the stylistic dichotomy between the sexes, miscommunication is almost inevitable; however, no one is to blame. Rather, another banner proclaims, 'The Key is Understanding:' 'Although each style is valid on its own terms, misunderstandings arise because the styles are different. Taking a cross-cultural approach to male–female conversations makes it possible to explain why dissatisfactions are justified without accusing anyone of being wrong or crazy' (1990: 47).

You just don't Understand makes its case for the two-cultures model skillfully and well using techniques that have become standard in popular writing about behavior: characterizations of 'most' women and men, entertaining anecdotes, and the presentation of research findings as fact. However, it is better written than most....

The Two-Cultures Approach: An Evaluation

Beyond Deficiencies and Blame

Proponents of the two-cultures model maintain that it is an advance over approaches that blame particular groups for miscommunication....

Unlike earlier approaches, the two-cultures model does not characterize women's talk as deficient in comparison to a male norm.... To John Gray, neither Mars nor Venus is a superior home. To Deborah Tannen, 'report talk,' and 'rapport talk' are equally limiting for their users in cross-sex communication. The speech style attributed to men is no longer 'standard' speech or 'the language,' but merely one way of negotiating the social landscape.

... Although *Men are from Mars, Women are from Venus* prescribes rigid rules for talk, the much more sophisticated *You just don't Understand* presents a view of language that stresses its flexibility....

Doing Gender, Doing Power

The two-cultures approach fails to theorize how power relations at the structural level are recreated and maintained at the interactional level....

This failure to recognize structural power and connect it with interactional power has provoked the strongest criticisms of the two-cultures approach. In a review of *You just don't Understand,* Senta Troemel-Ploetz (1991) pointed out that if the majority of relationships between women and men in our society were not fundamentally asymmetrical to the advantage of men,

> we would not need a women's liberation movement, women's commissions, houses for battered women, legislation for equal opportunity, antidiscrimination laws, family therapy, couple therapy, divorce.... If you leave out power, you do not understand any talk, be it the discussion after your speech, the conversation at your own dinner-table, in a doctor's office, in the back yards of West Philadelphia, in an Italian village, on a street in Turkey, in a court room or in a day-care center, in a women's group or at a UN conference....

No one involved in debating the two-cultures approach denies that men have more social and political power than women. Maltz and Borker (1982: 199) acknowledge that power differentials 'may make some contribution' to communication patterns. However, they do not theorize the workings of power in interaction or advocate structural changes to reduce inequity.

The Bandwagon Revisited

... Deborah Tannen's critics have charged that, despite the absence of overt woman-blaming and the positive evaluation of 'feminine' modes of talk, the interpretations she offers often disguise or gloss over inequity, and privilege men's interpretations. They have accused her of being an apologist for men, excusing their insensitivity, rudeness, and dominance as mere stylistic quirks, and encouraging women to make the adjustments when needs conflict....

Differences and Dichotomies

In both *You just don't Understand* and *Men are from Mars, Women are from Venus,* women and men are presented as having non-overlapping and inherently conflictual conversational goals and styles....

Both books position cross-sex communication as fundamental. They do not set out to deal with communication across other categories that separate people: class, 'race,' ethnicity, age, sexual orientation, and so on.... With their erasure, the complexities of social position and situation are backgrounded; women become a global category and sex can take center stage....

When sex is the only conceptual category, differences attributable to situations and power relationships are made invisible....

The language of both books further constructs gender as difference. Gray repeatedly characterizes men and women as 'opposite sexes,' describes gender-differentiated behavior as 'instinctive,' and indulges in classic gender polarities: Martians are hard, Venusians soft; Martians are angular, Venusians round; Martians are cool, Venusians warm. 'In a magical and perfect way their differences seemed to complement each other' (1992: 44). Tannen's much more responsible and scholarly work is guilty of none of these excesses; it constructs gender as difference more subtly. The overlap between women and men is obscured by chapter titles ('Different Words, Different Worlds') and banner headings ('Male–Female Conversation is Cross-Cultural Communication') that suggest categorically different speech styles. The demands of mass-market writing preclude the use of numbers, tables, statistical analyses, graphs of distributions of results, or discussions of how persons and situations interact. Without these aids to conceptualizing *degrees* of differences and fluctuation, difference cannot readily be described except in terms of most/many women/men. This contributes to the fundamental attribution error. Instead of a flexible, situation-specific behavior, speech style becomes a static personality trait.

... Although Tannen notes that some women fear *with justification* that 'different' will be heard in reference to an implicit male norm, and that the conceptual step between 'different' and 'worse' is a short and perhaps inevitable one (1990: 14–15), she never develops these insights. Like the acknowledgment of status and power disparities, acknowledgement that difference may be read as women's deficiency appears, then disappears, without becoming a vehicle for further analysis.

... Tannen defends her choice not to write about dominance, control, and the politics of gender.

Asymmetries of Power

... In a chapter titled 'Damned if You Do,' Tannen reviews some of the research showing that the same behavior may be interpreted differently depending on whether it is done by a woman or a man, and that such interpretation is usually to women's disadvantage. The styles more typical of men, she acknowledges, are taken as the norm. Moreover, when women and men interact in mixed-sex groups, men's norms prevail. Women adjust to them, and it is this that gives the *appearance* of male dominance. Women who attempt to emulate the male norms may be disliked and disparaged as unfeminine and aggressive. Although Tannen makes the poignant observation that 'The road to authority is tough for women, and once they get there it's a bed of thorns,' this observation *ends* her chapter on the double bind rather than providing a starting point for further analysis.

> These are important areas of research, and many books have been written about them; they are not new, and they are not the field in which I work. I wrote a book about the role of what I call 'conversational style' in everyday conversation, especially in the context of close relationships, because that has been the subject of my research throughout my academic career. (Tannen, 1992: 249)

... Thirty years of social science research has shown that men have more power in heterosexual marriage and dating relationships due to their ability to access external resources and their higher social status generally.... Though Tannen briefly and belatedly... acknowledges research showing that earning more money is probably the greatest source of marital power, she does not appear to recognize that the actual result of this phenomenon, which she presents as a gender-neutral fact, is greater *male* power....

A Rhetoric of Reassurance

The rhetoric of difference makes everyone—and no one—responsible for interpersonal problems. Men are not to blame for communication difficulties; neither is a social system in which gender governs access to resources. Instead, difference is reified: 'The culprit, then is not an individual man or even men's styles alone, but the difference between women and men's styles' (Tannen, 1990: 95).

One of the most striking effects achieved in these books is to reassure women that their lot in heterosexual relationships is normal. Again and again, it is stressed that no one is to blame, that miscommunication is inevitable, that unsatisfactory results may stem from the best of intentions....

Tannen explains that when men do most of the talking in a group, it is not because they intend to prevent women from speaking or believe that women have nothing important to say. Rather, they see the women as *equals,* and expect them to compete in the same style they themselves use. Thus, an inequity that feminists have conceptualized in terms of power differentials is acknowledged, but explained as an accidental imbalance created by style and having little to do with a gendered social order.

... In the separate worlds of 'report talk' and 'rapport talk', the goal may be sex-specific but the desire is the same: to be understood and responded to in kind. In *You just don't Understand,* each anecdote is followed by an analysis of the intentions of *both* speakers, a practice that Tannen (1992) feels reflects her fairness to both sexes. But this symmetry is false, because the one kind of intention that is never imputed to any speaker is the intent to dominate. Yet people are aware of such intentions in their talk, and, when asked, can readily describe the verbal tactics they use to 'get their own way' in heterosexual interactions....

Many of the most compelling anecdotes describe situations in which a woman is hurt, frustrated or angered by a man's apparently selfish or dominating behavior, only to find that her feelings were unwarranted because the man's intentions were good. This is psychologically naive. There is no reason to believe that *post hoc* stated intentions are a complete and sufficient description of conversational motives. Accounts of one's intentions are a socially constructed product in which face-saving and self-justification surely play a part. And even if intentions are innocent, language is a form of social action. Speech acts do things, and these things cannot be undone by declaring good intentions.

The emphasis on interpreting a partner's intentions is problematic in other ways as well. As Nancy Henley and Cheris Kramarae (1991: 42) point out, '[F]emales are required to develop special sensitivity to interpret males' silence, lack of emotional expressiveness, or brutality, and to help men express themselves, while men often seem to be trained deliberately to misinterpret much of women's meaning.' Young girls are told that hitting, teasing, and insults are to be read as signs of boys' 'liking.' Adolescent girls are taught to take responsibility for boys' inexpressiveness by drawing them out in conversation, steering talk to topics that will make them feel comfortable, and being a good listener. Girls and women learn from the discourse of popular fiction to reinterpret men's verbal and physical abuse. Indeed, a central theme in the romance novel is that cold, insensitive and rejecting behavior by men is to be read as evidence of their love (Unger and Crawford, 1992). Interpreting their partners' behavior in these ways may function to keep women in unrewarding relationships by making them more bearable.

Analyzing conversation in terms of intentions has a very important implication: it deflects attention from *effects,* including the ways that everyday action and talk serve to recreate and maintain current gender arrangements. Instead, readers are left to analyze what goes on in people's heads—what they say they intend to accomplish, not what they do accomplish, when they are engaged in 'doing gender.' Entering a larger discourse in which women are blamed for the consequences of societal sexism and for their own powerlessness, popularizations of the two-cultures model may be used to deflect responsibility from men.

References

Gray, J. (1992) *Men are from Mars, women are from Venus.* New York: HarperCollins.

Henley, N. M. and Kramarae, C. (1991) Gender, power, and miscommunication. In N. Coupland, H. Giles, and J. M. Wiemann (eds.), *Miscommunication and problematic talk* (pp. 18–43). Newbury Park, CA: Sage.

Maltz, D. N. and Borker, R. A. (1982) A cultural approach to male–female miscommunication. In J. Gumperz (ed.), *Language and social identity.* Cambridge: Cambridge University Press.

Tannen, D. (1990) *You just don't understand: women and men in conversation.* New York: Ballantine.

Tannen, D. (1992) Response to Senta Troemel-Ploetz's 'Selling the apolitical' (1991). *Discourse and Society,* 3, 249–254.

Troemel-Ploetz, S. (1991) Review essay: selling the apolitical. *Discourse and Society,* 2, 489–502.

Unger, R. and Crawford, M. (1992) *Women and gender: a feminist psychology.* New York and Philadelphia: McGraw-Hill and Temple University Press. [2nd edn in press]

POSTSCRIPT

Do Women and Men Communicate Differently?

It is important to situate discourse about sex differences in communication (indeed in any domain) in a sociopolitical context. Beliefs that the sexes differ, whether supported by empirical evidence or not, are deeply entrenched in our society. Indeed, while academic critics signal the lack of a scientific basis to Tannen's sweeping claims, her popular works have shot to the top of the best-seller list. We, the consumers, have to be very careful about scrutinizing how knowledge has been constructed and used. There is no such thing as a "simple" yes or no answer to a question of sex difference.

Scholarly and popular writing on sex differences is impacted greatly by what can be called the "hall of mirrors" effect. As described by Deborah Cameron in "Gender and Language: Gender, Language, and Discourse: A Review Essay," *Signs: Journal of Women in Culture and Society* (1998), "in the course of being cited, discussed, and popularized over time, originally modest claims have been progressively represented as more and more absolute, while hypotheses have been given the status of facts." Thus, for example, the originally modest claim made by researchers Don Zimmerman and Candace West in "Sex Roles, Interruptions and Silences in Conversation," in Barrie Thorne and Nancy Henley, eds., *In Language and Sex: Differences and Dominance* (Newbury House, 1975), that men interrupt women more than the reverse may have been exaggerated by constant repetition and then critiqued for being overstated (much like the "telephone" game played by children).

Suggested Readings

D. Cameron, "Gender and Language: Gender, Language, and Discourse: A Review Essay," *Signs: Journal of Women in Culture and Society* (1998).

K. Hall and M. Bucholtz, eds., *Gender Articulated: Language and the Socially Constructed Self* (Routledge, 1995).

H. Kotthoff and R. Wodak, eds., *Communicating Gender in Context* (John Benjamins, 1997).

D. Tannen, *Gender and Discourse* (Oxford University Press, 1994).

S. Wilkinson and C. Kitzinger, eds., *Feminism and Discourse: Psychological Perspectives* (Sage Publications, 1995).

ISSUE 7

Should We Continue to Study Sex Differences?

YES: Alice H. Eagly, from "The Science and Politics of Comparing Women and Men," *American Psychologist* (March 1995)

NO: Bernice Lott, from "The Personal and Social Correlates of a Gender Difference Ideology," *Journal of Social Issues* (1997)

ISSUE SUMMARY

YES: Professor of psychology Alice H. Eagly examines the potential usefulness of research on sex differences for fostering social change.

NO: Professor of psychology Bernice Lott argues that the continued emphasis on describing sex differences is problematic.

Some feminist scholars warn of the overrepresentation of findings of sex differences in published scholarship. Many scholars argue that the comparison of males and females is as much a political as a scientific enterprise. Findings of similarities between groups is thought to be a "null" finding and thus not publishable in its own right. The popular press is eager to disseminate evidence of sex differences; indeed, findings of sex similarity are viewed as not newsworthy. Often, the description of a sex difference is accompanied by a presumption that the difference is innate and thus immutable.

What are the origins of this difference model? The early impetus for studying sex differences in the 1970s was to expose and amend inequalities between the sexes. The difference model served its purpose of drawing attention to women's experiences at a time in social scientific inquiry when most research was conducted on all-male samples, sometimes even generalizing the results to "people." In 1974, the difference model was brought to psychology's center stage by Eleanor Emmons Maccoby and Carol Nagy Jacklin's book *The Psychology of Sex Differences* (Stanford University Press). Their ambitious goal was to draw together, catalog, and synthesize all psychological research reporting sex comparisons. In their evaluation of overall trends in this large body of research, they concluded that there were both similarities and differences between the sexes, varying in magnitude and sometimes in contrast to cultural stereotypes.

Maccoby and Jacklin's work triggered other in-depth analyses of the existence or lack thereof of sex differences in numerous areas. In general, conclusions reflected skepticism about the presence of sex differences. In the 1980s this area of research took another step forward by moving from an impressionistic normative reviewing process to a more formal, quantitative technique for synthesizing research: meta-analysis. Meta-analysis provides a common metric with which studies can be directly compared and the magnitude of sex differences can be represented. Moreover, meta-analysis looks at the consistency of findings across studies and tries to identify variables (such as measurement strategies, the historical moment when the study was conducted, and sample characteristics) that explain inconsistencies and even contradictions across studies.

Researcher and psychologist Jacquelyn James in "What Are the Social Issues Involved in Focusing on *Difference* in the Study of Gender?" *Journal of Social Issues* (Summer 1997), outlines five critical issues to consider when reviewing the status of the difference model:

1. *Very Small Differences Can Be Statistically Significant.* Because of the social weight of scientific evidence, even misrepresented and statistically weak differences get exaggerated by public accounts and therefore misused.

2. *False Universalism.* Interpretations of group differences often presume within-group similarity. In fact, other individual differences (e.g., social power) may explain differences better than sex.

3. *The "Tyranny of Averages."* Sex differences are usually based on group averages, interpreted as if they represent absolutes. Within-group variability or the overlap between distributions of males and females is not examined.

4. *The Revelations of Within-Group Differences.* Careful examination of within-group variation can be very effective in challenging gender stereotypes and examining the conditions under which differences do and do not occur. Furthermore, methodological practices may skew the meaning of sex differences (e.g., measurement bias).

5. *Some Differences Are Diminishing Over Time.* Weakening differences over time suggest that sociohistorical change is relevant to the "why" of difference.

In light of such critical review, we return to the original impetus of sex difference research in the 1970s—to expose and eliminate inequalities between the sexes. Can sex difference research help to better understand sex and gender and contribute to beneficial social change? Or, are the negative social consequences of such a research paradigm too great?

In the following selections, Alice H. Eagly argues that while we must be aware of the potentially problematic social consequences of sex difference research, the benefits of such research for social change outweigh the costs. In contrast, Bernice Lott urges that the costly consequences of sex difference research call for moving beyond a difference model.

129

Alice H. Eagly

The Science and Politics of Comparing
Women and Men

The Political Context of Research
That Compares the Sexes

... Placing this research area in context produces a political story, the story of
why research psychologists have taken so much interest in comparing the sexes
and why some now suggest that this interest is misplaced.

Understood in its cultural context, this research area should be viewed as
intertwined with the history of feminism as a social and intellectual movement
in American society. Just as feminist empiricists active in the early decades
of the century were important contributors to the intellectual side of the first
women's movement of the 20th century (see Rosenberg, 1982; Scarborough &
Furumoto, 1987), it was as part of a broader feminist movement that contemporary researchers have challenged assumptions about women's inferiority. The
timing of Maccoby and Jacklin's (1974) book was hardly accidental but reflected
the emergence of the modern feminist movement in the United States. As the society and the media questioned traditional assumptions about women's roles,
feminist researchers in psychology questioned their discipline's assumptions
about women's abilities and behavior.

Maccoby and Jacklin's (1974) skeptical message about the existence of sex
differences should be understood in the context of the larger critique that feminism provided of psychologists' rather limited efforts to understand gender.
One central target of feminist criticism was research and writing on sex differences. Feminists argued that psychologists' claims about sex differences falsely
portrayed women as inferior to men. Some of the rhetoric was heated: Bernard
(1974), for example, called studies of sex differences "battle weapons against
women" (p. 13). Shields (1975a), in a widely read article, exposed the sexist biases in early writing about maternal instinct and sex differences in the size and
structure of the human brain. Feminist writing of the 1970s generally portrayed
research purportedly demonstrating sex differences as largely prescientific and
obviously faulty or, if the research was more modern, as riddled with artifacts,

From Alice H. Eagly, "The Science and Politics of Comparing Women and Men," *American Psychologist*, vol. 50, no. 3 (March 1995), pp. 149-150, 155-158. Copyright © 1995 by The American
Psychological Association, Inc. Adapted with permission of the publisher and the author.

methodological deficiencies, and unexplained inconsistencies in findings (e.g., Sherif, 1979).

Many psychologists, for the most part women, then started studying sex differences and similarities from a feminist perspective. Implicit or explicit in much of this work was the expectation that methodologically sound comparisons of women and men would raise women's status by dispelling people's stereotypes about women. In fact, much gender research reflected two missions: revealing people's damaging stereotypes and attitudes concerning women and displaying the absence of stereotypic sex differences in behavior, traits, and abilities (see Eagly, 1987). Much feminist research on sex differences was (and still is) intended to shatter stereotypes about women's characteristics and change people's attitudes by proving that women and men are essentially equivalent in their personalities, behavioral tendencies, and intellectual abilities (e.g., Caplan et al., 1985; Fischer, 1993). Caught up in the passions of a burgeoning social movement, many feminist psychologists, including the author of this [selection] (Eagly, 1978), had a relatively uncomplicated vision of what empirical research on sex differences would yield. Properly analyzed to remove artifacts, this research would yield null findings or, at least, differences that could be described as trivially small.

Null findings were congenial to many feminist psychologists not only because they would challenge gender stereotypes but also because sameness was thought to increase women's chances for equal opportunity in the society. To the extent that the "gender-neutral" strategy of making no distinctions between women and men leads to gender equality (see Bem, 1993), scientific research showing that women are not different from men should help ensure women equal access to a variety of roles from which they were excluded. In contrast, evidence of differences might be seen as disqualifying women in relation to certain roles and opportunities and as justifying unequal treatment under the law. For other psychologists, scientific demonstrations that women and men differ seemed to conflict with the ideals of egalitarianism (e.g., Baumeister, 1988). Indeed, the equalitarianism issue can be raised in relation to virtually all research examining differences between social groups.

Despite most feminist empiricists' advocacy of the view that sex differences are small or null, psychology has offered a countertheme in the writings of other feminists who have accepted the existence of certain sex-related differences, primarily those that display women's nurturance and concern for other people. Much of this writing has reflected mainly qualitative methods of producing and examining evidence and thus reflects a different tradition than the formal empiricism that underlies the writing of feminist empiricists. For example, Gilligan (1982) argued that the moral reasoning of women and men differs, with women tending to adopt a care perspective and men a justice perspective. Chodorow (1978) maintained that women's relational skills and desire to form close relationships follow from their experiences as mothers and their successful re-creation of these aspects of personality in their daughters. Other feminist writers have similarly argued that behavior is sex differentiated and praised those aspects of behavior that they ascribed to women (e.g., Helgesen, 1990; Ruddick, 1989). Indeed, the disjunction between those feminist psychologists who have argued in favor of difference and the feminist empiricists, who generally have argued in favor of similarity, led Hare-Mustin and Mare-cek (1988) to describe the psychology of gender in terms of contrasting biases, which they named *alpha bias,* a preference to exaggerate differences, and *beta bias,* a preference to minimize them.

Questions Underlying the Contemporary Stresses Between Science and Politics

The flood of scientific research on sex differences that followed the modern reemergence of the feminist movement has failed to present psychologists with an absence of differences between the sexes but instead has provided considerably more varied and challenging outcomes. The new wave of research on sex-related differences has encountered a negative reaction from many feminist psychologists (see Hare-Mustin & Marecek, 1988; Kahn & Yoder, 1989; Matlin, 1993a; Mednick 1991), and this lack of enthusiasm should not be surprising. During the 1970s research psychologists had already enjoyed some success in shaping a scientific consensus about the triviality of sex differences.

... [T]he specific points most commonly made by critics when countering the onslaught of contemporary research documenting sex-differentiated behavior [are reflected in the conclusion to this selection]....

Conclusion

The common description of empirical research as showing that sex-related differences are small, unusually unstable across studies, very often artifactual, and inconsistent with gender stereotypes arose in part from a feminist commitment to gender similarity as a route to political equality. It also arose from piecemeal and inadequate interpretations of the relevant empirical research. These interpretations failed to place research on sex-related differences in the context of other psychological research and often implied that findings that were very ordinary (in terms of magnitude, consistency, etc.) were rather exceptional. Given the new understanding of empirical findings that is evolving, research psychologists should think more deeply about the purposes for which their research may be used. Is psychological research that compares the sexes beneficial or harmful? Does this research foster or hinder the social change that would increase gender equality? These are many-sided questions that are addressed only in preliminary fashion in this [selection] to stimulate debate.

The fear is often expressed in feminist writing that differences become deficiencies for women because women are an oppressed group (e.g., Unger & Crawford, 1992). Anxiety about sex differences is especially strong to the extent that scientists favor biological explanations, because this approach might produce a portrayal of women as innately inferior to men. Yet, contemporary research that has systematically examined whether the traits and behaviors ascribed to women are regarded as inferior to those ascribed to men has not found evidence for this generalized unfavorable perception of women (Eagly & Mladinic, 1994; Eagly, Mladinic, & Otto, 1991). This research has shown that the stereotype of women is more positive overall than the stereotype of men, at least in contemporary samples of U.S. and Canadian college students. To the extent that behavioral differences truly do mirror people's stereotypes, scientific research may thus reveal a pattern of differences that shows both sexes to have strengths and deficiencies but that portrays women somewhat more favorably than men, on the whole. Nonetheless, the favorability of the female stereotype may be a mixed blessing because the particular kinds of positive characteristics most often ascribed to women, primarily "niceness–nurturance" qualities, probably contribute to the exclusion of women from certain kinds of high-status roles (e.g., those that are thought to require toughness and aggressiveness). At any rate, the sex differences that scientists have documented do not tell a simple tale of female inferiority.

The possible uses for findings that have demonstrated sex-differentiated behavior will be enhanced to the extent that psychologists understand the causes of the differences. For example, a case has been made for the biological mediation of sex differences in spatial skills (e.g., Gaulin, 1993; H. Thomas & Kail, 1991). If this position is correct, women should prefer a different cue system for negotiating spatial tasks, as Kimura (1992) has argued. If so, gender-informed programs to train women in tasks that have an important spatial component could take account of these female preferences. Alternatively, to the extent that sex differences in spatial ability arise from experience (Baeninger & Newcombe, 1989), psychologists might help devise ways to give girls and women more equal access to experiences that train high spatial ability. Still, despite these possibilities of positive outcomes, knowledge of sex differences in spatial ability could decrease women's access to jobs and professions for which excellent spatial ability is a prerequisite.

Another example of the potential usefulness of research on sex differences can be found in social psychological investigations of small group behavior. This research documents in exquisite detail how men take charge in task-oriented groups (e.g., Eagly & Karau, 1991; Wood & Rhodes, 1992). Women who learn about the specific behaviors that mediate male dominance and the causal factors that underlie these behaviors may be prepared to find the points in the sequence of processes where they can intervene to produce a more equal sharing of power. Some women may even seek out specific training programs designed to increase their dominance (e.g., assertiveness training). Nonetheless, knowledge of men's more dominant behavior could contribute to exclusion of women from some kinds of leadership roles. Which type of outcome would predominate would depend on many factors, including the strength of the women's desire to change their status, their political power, and their interest in using psychological research to help them effect change.

In concert with Scarr's (1988) optimistic analysis, social scientific knowledge of sex differences could enhance women's ability to understand the antecedents of inequality and to improve their status in society. Nonetheless, the aura of danger surrounds research on sex differences. Some critics urge psychologists to stop this dangerous work or at least censor it in various ways (e.g., Baumeister, 1988; McHugh et al., 1986). Each researcher must of course weigh the potential costs and potential benefits. If enough research psychologists conclude that the costs outweigh the benefits, research comparing the sexes will recede once again because it is too politically relevant. However, the scientific work now possesses a momentum of its own, as more investigators become caught up in the sheer excitement of discovery and theory testing.

Contemporary psychology has produced a large amount of research revealing that behavior is sex differentiated to varying extents. The knowledge produced in this area of science can be beneficial both in helping women and men to understand their natures and their society and in suggesting ways to enhance gender equality. Yet there surely are dangers that the new research will be used in far less beneficial ways by the misogynist forces of the society. Therefore, the stresses between gender politics and the science of gender are not going to disappear. Never before in the history of psychology has such a formidable body of scientific information encountered such a powerful political agenda. The results of this encounter should be instructive to all psychologists who believe that psychology should serve human welfare as it advances scientific understanding.

References

Baenninger, M., & Newcombe, N. (1989). The role of experience in spatial test performance: A meta-analysis. *Sex Roles, 20,* 327–344.

Baumeister, R. F. (1988). Should we stop studying sex differences altogether? *American Psychologist, 43,* 1092–1095.

Bem, S. L. (1993). *The lenses of gender: Transforming the debate on sexual inequality.* New Haven, CT: Yale University Press.

Bernard, J. (1974). *Sex differences: An overview* (Module 26). New York: MSS Modular Publications.

Caplan, P. J., MacPherson, G. M., & Tobin, P. (1985). Do sex-related differences in spatial abilities exist? A multilevel critique with new data. *American Psychologist, 40,* 786–799.

Chodorow, N. (1978). *The reproduction of mothering: Psychoanalysis and the sociology of gender.* Berkeley: University of California Press.

Eagly, A. H. (1978). Sex differences in influenceability. *Psychological Bulletin, 85,* 86–116.

Eagly, A. H. (1987). *Sex differences in social behavior: A social-role interpretation.* Hillsdale, NJ: Erlbaum.

Eagly, A. H., & Karau, S. J. (1991). Gender and the emergence of leaders: A meta-analysis. *Journal of Personality and Social Psychology, 60,* 685–710.

Eagly, A. H., & Mladinic, A. (1994). Are people prejudiced against women? Some answers from research on attitudes, gender stereotypes, and judgments of competence. In W. Stroebe & M. Hewstone (Eds.), *European review of social psychology* (Vol. 5, pp. 1–35). New York: Wiley.

Eagly, A. H., Mladinic, A., & Otto, S. (1991). Are women evaluated more favorably than men? An analysis of attitudes, beliefs, and emotions. *Psychology of Women Quarterly, 15,* 203–216.

Fischer, A. H. (1993). Sex differences in emotionality: Fact or stereotype? *Feminism & Psychology, 3,* 303–318.

Gaulin, S. J. C. (1993). How and why sex differences evolve, with spatial ability as a paradigm example. In M. Haug, R. E. Whalen, C. Aron, & K. L. Olsen (Eds.), *The development of sex differences and similarities in behaviour* (pp. 111–130). London, England: Kluwer Academic.

Gilligan, C. (1982). *In a different voice: Psychological theory and women's development.* Cambridge, MA: Harvard University Press.

Hare-Mustin, R. T., & Marecek, J. (1988). The meaning of difference: Gender theory, postmodernism, and psychology. *American Psychologist, 43,* 455–464.

Helgesen, S. (1990). *The female advantage: Women's ways of leadership.* New York: Doubleday/Currency.

Kahn, A. S., & Yoder, J. D. (1989). The psychology of women and conservatism: Rediscovering social change. *Psychology of Women Quarterly, 13,* 417–432.

Kimura, D. (1992). Sex differences in the brain. *Scientific American, 267*(3), 118–125.

Maccoby, E. E., & Jacklin, C. N. (1974). *The psychology of sex differences.* Stanford, CA: Stanford University Press.

Matlin, M. W. (1993a, May). *Looking into the crystal ball: The psychology of women and gender in the 21st century.* Invited address at the conference on Psychology in the 21st Century, York University, Ontario, Canada.

McHugh, M. C., Koeske, R. D., & Frieze, I. H. (1986). Issues to consider in conducting nonsexist psychological research: A guide for researchers. *American Psychologist, 41,* 879–890.

Mednick, M. T. (1991). Currents and futures in American feminist psychology: State of the art revisited. *Psychology of Women Quarterly, 15,* 611–621.

Rosenberg, R. (1982). *Beyond separate spheres: The intellectual roots of modern feminism.* New Haven, CT: Yale University Press.

Ruddick, S. (1989). *Maternal thinking: Toward a politics of peace.* New York: Ballantine Books.

Scarborough, E., & Furumoto, L. (1987). *Untold lives: The first generation of American women psychologists.* New York: Columbia University Press.

Scarr, S. (1988). Race and gender as psychological variables: Social and ethical issues. *American Psychologist, 43,* 56–59.

Sherif, C. W. (1979). Bias in psychology. In J. A. Sherman & E. T. Beck (Eds.), *The prism of sex: Essays in the sociology of knowledge* (pp. 93–133). Madison: University of Wisconsin Press.

Shields, S. A. (1975a). Functionalism, Darwinism, and the psychology of women. *American Psychologist, 30,* 739–754.

Thomas, H., & Kail, R. (1991). Sex differences in speed of mental rotation and the X-linked genetic hypothesis. *Intelligence, 15,* 17–32.

Unger, R., & Crawford, M. (1992). *Women and gender: A feminist psychology.* New York: McGraw-Hill.

Wood, W., & Rhodes, N. (1992). Sex differences in interaction style in task groups. In C. L. Ridgeway (Ed.), *Gender, interaction, and inequality* (pp. 97–121). New York: Springer-Verlag.

Bernice Lott

 **NO**

The Personal and Social Correlates of a Gender Difference Ideology

The ideology of gender difference is ubiquitous in mainstream and minority United States cultures and has enormous significance for personal and social life. Our widely shared and strong beliefs about differences between women and men in interests, competencies, and roles are not benign or neutral, and their consequences are profound and continuous throughout the course of one's life. My objective here is to explore the powerful and problematic, overt and subtle, widespread influence of this ideology on a sample of institutions, behaviors, social interactions, and relationships.

As noted by Morawski (1994), while the idea of difference is understood as a comparison of persons on some dimension, it also "is *evaluative* and *prescriptive*" (p. 156) and embedded in a history in which one gender is valued over the other. Thus, the significance of gender difference ideology for social life results not only from the idea of difference, per se, but from the inextricable union of difference and inequality, in both the origin of a gender difference ideology and in its operation in contemporary life. As argued so well by MacKinnon (1987), if difference were really the issue, then it would not be the case, as it is that "women and men are equally different but not equally powerful ... [Gender differences would not] be the social issue it is or have the social meaning it has—were it not for male dominance" (p. 51).

I choose to use the term gender rather than sex to emphasize clearly that what is being discussed are the attributions and meanings a society gives to the concepts of woman and man, girl and boy. Sex denotes female and male and divides animals across all species into two groups on the basis of structural criteria related to reproductive functions and capacities. Gender, on the other hand, is a distinction that is specific and unique to human beings, and "does not flow automatically from genitalia and reproductive organs, the main physiological differences of females and males" (Lorber, 1994, p. 17). Gender is identified, first, by differential power and, second, is associated with prescribed roles and with implicit and explicit meanings that cultures provide the necessary conditions for learning and maintaining. Such a distinction between sex and gender is based not at all on a separation between biology and culture. I do

From Bernice Lott, "The Personal and Social Correlates of a Gender Difference Ideology," *Journal of Social Issues*, vol. 53, no. 2 (1997), pp. 279-285, 291-297. Copyright © 1997 by The Society for the Psychological Study of Social Issues. Reprinted by permission of Blackwell Publishers Ltd.

not accept "the idea of an external world divisible into the biological and the social and cultural, the natural and artificial" (Morawski, 1994, p. 153), since, as we know (but sometimes forget), culture is made possible only because of the enormous biological capacity of human beings for learning.

Some have suggested (e.g., Murray, 1996) that gender may be examined at three different levels: (1) as a system of social relationships in which gender interacts with, and influences, institutional structures; (2) as what people "do" in social interactions in accord with norms about what is appropriate for them; and (3) as an attribute used by individuals for self identification within their culture. Feminist theorists propose further that, across these levels, gender, as a social construction, is less "a property of individuals" than it is a consequence or an effect "emerging from social relations" (Morawski, 1994, p. 161) that are grounded in inequality. In the words of MacKinnon (1987), "Gender is an inequality of power, a social status based on who is permitted to do what to whom" (p. 8).

The beliefs we share about gender are learned early, are subscribed to widely, and are so difficult to change because they are reinforced by social consensus, by structural arrangements that support and demand them, and by the operation of self-fulfilling prophecies. These are the attributes of stereotypes. As noted by Hilton and von Hippel (1996), the generally accepted position is that "stereotypes are beliefs about the characteristics, attributes, and behaviors of members of certain groups" (p. 240) that simplify the demands on perceivers and emerge in response to such factors as different social roles, differences in power, or as a way of justifying the status quo. A related approach is the view that stereotypes are beliefs about "everyday base rates, or ... the relative prevalence of traits, behaviors, or other attributes among a particular category of people, as compared to people in general" (Nelson, Acker, & Manis, 1996). Beliefs about gender qualify as stereotypes, and function as such for individuals. In this [selection], however, I prefer to use the more general term, belief, and to refer to the collection of related beliefs about women and men as an ideology.

This [selection] will present examples of our gender ideology's apparent influence on, and reflection in, social behavior but I do not assume that beliefs necessarily precede behavior and directly influence what one does nor that our actions necessarily reflect what we think. The evidence for a lack of simple concordance between beliefs and behavior is extensive, convincing, and not surprising. As I have noted elsewhere (Lott, 1995), it is to be expected that attitudes, beliefs, and behaviors (relative to the same stimulus or class of stimuli) will be relatively independent, but will be correlated to the extent that they have been learned under the same set of conditions. An individual may learn affective, cognitive, and behavioral reactions to a stimulus under different conditions, or, as is even more likely, these separate reactions may be maintained, or influenced by, separate sets of contextual cues and contingencies. For example, a man may believe that a woman is more capable than he is of changing a diaper, or he may not believe this but still hand his baby to its mother, aunt, or grandmother for a diaper change because this behavior on his part is expected, and will be positively reinforced.

What I am suggesting is a complex relationship between our gender ideology and behavior in which the latter is influenced sometimes directly by what we believe about women and men and, more often, indirectly by what we anticipate will be the likely consequences of our actions in the light of a prevailing set of gender beliefs and further, in which beliefs are influenced by the actions we observe ourselves and others engaged in. As noted by Lorber (1994) "Gendered norms and expectations are enforced through informal [and formal] sanctions ... [and] Everyday gendered interactions build gender into the family, the work process, and other organizations and institutions, which in turn reinforce gender expectations for individuals" (p. 32). What adds even further to the complexity of this analysis is the role of differential power, i.e., gender inequality as both an antecedent of beliefs about gender and a consequence of gender-related behavior by persons "doing" gender and by persons responding to the cue of gender.

Eagly (1994) tells us that feminists have been surprised to find evidence that women and men sometimes behave differently. On the contrary, we certainly expect our gender ideology to have consequences and to underlie gendered behavior in certain places, times, and under particular kinds of circumstances. Of course we expect, along with Eagly (1987), that social roles will shape gender-related behavior and that behavior will be "constrained by its social context and, in particular, by men's more dominant social position" (Eagly, 1994, p. 518). Or, as noted by Hoyenga and Hoyenga (1993), "Even if stereotypes do not directly create sex differences, the stereotypic assumptions of others may sometimes impel us to act out their stereotypic beliefs" (p. 10). The truly surprising phenomenon, however, as I have noted elsewhere (Lott, 1997), is that, despite the systematic and relentless pairing of gender with particular attributes and competencies by our mainstream culture, despite all the conditions in our society that push girls and boys, and then women and men, into different spheres, the differences so painstakingly searched for by gender difference researchers are small indeed and always overshadowed by the much larger overlap between genders and by within-gender variability.

While our gender difference ideology is only sometimes apparent in how women and men actually behave in various situations and interactions, there are nevertheless serious negative consequences of the cultural pressures to maintain this ideology, i.e., consequences that inhibit or constrain constructive action.... My concern here is not with the behavior of women and men, which is sometimes found to differ in gender-related situations, but rather with the *differential responses to women and men that reflect an ideology of difference,* and on the gender inequalities that precede and result from this ideology....

Hyde's (1994) assessment, that "the study of gender differences in psychology has been nothing but a growth industry ... It's here to stay" (p. 508), is chilling since such study is intimately related to our culture's determined effort that gender differences be maintained despite evidence against their inevitability and in support of gender as a social construction. Bem (1996) has traced the ebb and flow of our society's, and our discipline's, "obsession with the questions of biological difference" (p. 11), which continues as an obsession simply with difference, whether presumed to be innate or learned. Elsewhere I have argued (Lott, 1997) that cataloging sameness and difference serves a primarily political, not scientific, purpose as it rationalizes and perpetuates differences in power, and contributes to the continuation of separate spheres for women and men. In this [selection] I attend to some of the significant destructive outcomes of differential responses to women and men and of our gender difference beliefs. This focus can also be seen as part of a more general effort in psychology to understand "the consequences of stereotyping for the stereotyped individual," a subject about which, according to Hilton and von Hippel (1996), "we still know little" (p. 263).

Personal Experience

Our gender beliefs mandate different expectations of the personal attributes, interests, and behaviors of women and men, and, not surprisingly, they also mandate differential perceptions of our daughters and sons beginning at birth. A recent replication by Karraker, Vogel and Lake (1995) of the now classic study by Rubin, Provenzano, and Luria on "the eye of the beholder" phenomenon found that, despite the lack of objective differences, a sample of parents of newborns who were individually interviewed two days and one week after the birth of their first born child tended to see girls and boys differently. The parents of newborn girls rated them as finer featured, less strong, more delicate, and more feminine than the parents of newborn boys, and these perceptions persisted for at least one week after the babies were home from the hospital. We know, of course, that this is just the beginning and that most parents go on "to create a gendered world for their newborn by naming, birth announcements, and dress" (Lorber, 1994, p. 25).

What is especially compelling about these data on parental perceptions is that they illustrate how gender stereotypes affect *individual experience* for which feminist psychologists have great respect, and value as an important source of empirical data. We have no reason to question the authenticity of the parents' reports. The newborn girl and boy babies are perceived differently, and the parents of the infant wrapped in a pink blanket experience her as more delicate than the parents of the infant wrapped in a blue blanket experience him. Yet, gender beliefs are clearly the mediators of such "experience." It is reasonable to assume that this is not unique to our perceptions of newborns but that personal experience generally is mediated by beliefs about gender. . . .

That gender beliefs permeate and intersect with "experience" would seem to be an obvious proposition that most psychologists would accept; at the same time, however, it must give us pause to recognize that experience is "already an interpretation," that it cannot be taken "as a given," or located simply in the individual (Scott, 1992, as cited by Markens, 1996). An example from the experimental literature provides a striking illustration of this theoretical proposition. A study of aggressive behavior with a college sample by Lightdale and Prentice (1994), in which participants played a video game permitting them to drop bombs on an enemy, found that under conditions of deindividuation (anonymity) there was no difference between women and men in the average number of bombs they dropped. Nevertheless, the women and men differed in what they said they did; their self-assessments indicated that the men believed they had behaved significantly more aggressively than the women believed about themselves despite the fact that this was not the case. Thus, "experience" is not free of gender ideology but is enmeshed in it. How, indeed, could it be otherwise, and how can we fail to recognize the enormous significance of the consequences? As noted by Lightdale and Prentice (1994), "the failure of women's self-reports to reflect their own high levels of aggression in the deindividuated condition is striking given our behavioral evidence that they were at least as aggressive as males" (p. 42). . . .

Family Life

Our gender ideology includes the expectation that women and men will have different domestic responsibilities in both quantity and quality. A well designed study by Perkins and DeMeis (1996) gathered data relevant to the question of whether the often observed difference between women and men in the amount of housekeeping work done is a reflection of differential socialization (assumed to result in different "feminine" and "masculine" traits) or a reflection of "doing gender." Survey data obtained from over 1100 graduates of a liberal arts college found an almost identical pattern for single women and men in the number of hours they spent on domestic household activities, more differences between married or cohabiting women and men, and the most difference between women and men who were parents (with outside employment hours controlled). While women increased their household chore activities as family relationships increased, men decreased their domestic activity. The authors concluded that their findings "challenge the view that gender differences in household work simply reflect a culturally learned pattern whereby women are taught that doing housework . . . is part of their gender identity" (p. 86). Rather, both genders appear to be behaving in accord with a gender ideology that prescribes a greater share of housework for women who are in relationships with men and even more housework for women who are parents. These findings thus illustrate the argument of Lorber (1994) that "responsibility for the work in the domestic sphere is an outcome of women's gender status, not its cause" (p. 285). . . .

Our gender ideology mandates that women do the domestic family work of household chores and child care while men who are fathers are defined by the provider role and by their paid employment. Wives, across ethnic groups in the United States, are responsible for more housework and child care hours per week than are husbands, regardless of employment status and regardless of financial contribution to the household. The consequences of this division of labor have been explored by Silverstein (1996) who notes that men's failure to assume equal responsibility in the private world is "one of the most significant impediments to equality for women in the public world" (p. 5). Mothers are the ones who typically begin to limit their paid work commitments, producing incremental differences with fathers in job experience, skills, and earning capacity. That there is nothing inherently natural about women's increasing domestic involvement and men's decreasing involvement when they become parents is apparent from research findings that, according to Silverstein, have not reliably demonstrated gender differences in competent parenting but point instead to necessary on-the-job training for parents of both genders. Noteworthy is a study of gay father couples by Silverstein and her colleagues that documents an intimate and supportive environment provided by these men to their children....

Challenges to a Gender Difference Ideology

A gender difference ideology, which has such destructive consequences, can be challenged through the painstaking work of social scientists who continue to present empirical evidence of behavioral similarity between women and men with similar backgrounds, in similar positions and similar situations. I have dealt with this issue in several previous papers (e.g., Lott, 1985, 1990; Lott & Maluso, 1993) beginning with a critical examination of the stereotypes implicit in the idea and assessment of androgyny (Lott, 1981) and most recently in a discussion of the political agenda inherent in the continuing obsession with cataloging gender differences (Lott, 1997). The literature presenting such evidence is vast and far too numerous to be discussed in this [selection], but a few examples from disparate areas can be cited here.

Among the most stubbornly defended assumptions is that men are better at spatial tasks than women. It is therefore instructive to find that among an ethnically heterogeneous sample of college students, in a study by Sharps, Price, and Williams (1994), there were no gender differences observed on the Mental Image Rotation task under conditions in which the spatial cognitive nature of the task was deemphasized in the instructions and when the figures to be rotated were familiar ones. In another variation, instructions that emphasized the relationship between the task and skills needed in traditionally feminine jobs were also found to be associated with no gender difference in performance. These findings, the authors concluded, "demonstrate the importance of implicit sociocultural factors for the spatial cognitive performance of women and men" (p. 421).

That women and men differ significantly in mathematics ability is also a much emphasized part of our gender ideology, especially the assumption that women can never reach the same high level of performance in this area as men. Steele (1996) has referred to this as a stereotype of limitation rather than of lack, and argues that this is particularly threatening to women for whom this domain is important and who, because of the stereotype, are never sure that their performance will continue to improve. In a series of studies, Steele had women and men college students with equally high academic records in math take tests. Under one set of conditions, the women were told that they were taking a difficult math test on which women and men were known to do equally well. Their scores on this test were dramatically higher than those of comparable women who took the same test without such prior information.

Another series of laboratory studies shed light on a dichotomous attribute that is basic to our culture's assumptions about gender, that women manifest communality while men behave with agency. Conway, Pizzamiglio, and Mount

(1996) found that these attributes are constitutive of status, with low status persons perceived as more communal, like women, and high status persons perceived as more agentic, like men. And in the laboratory of "real life," an in-depth interview and survey study by Barnett (Barnett & Rivers, 1996) of 300 primarily White dual-earner couples in the Boston area found that women and men tended to feel pretty much the same about relationships with children and spouses, that they reported similar concerns, and similar sources of satisfaction and stress from their marriages, children, and jobs. Such data seriously challenge the easy and so-popular cliche that women are from Venus while men are from Mars.

My position is similar to that presented by others who propose that we actively resist the continued efforts to keep cultures (whether mainstream or minority) organized around the ideology of dichotomous gender. Gender can be deconstructed and, as Lorber (1994) suggests, "The most obvious way would be to deliberately and self-consciously not use gender to organize social life" (p. 297). A provocative fictional example of this can be found in the novel "Woman on the Edge of Time" by Marge Piercy (1976) which depicts a society in which whether one is male or female has no bearing on the jobs one does, the interests one has, or one's role in child rearing. Outside of fiction, however, resistance to gendering can only be done with great difficulty since, as noted by Lorber (1994), "The process of gendering and its outcome are legitimated by religion, law, science, and the society's entire set of values" (p. 15). That this process continues despite our everyday experiences and observations of the wide array of attributes, skills, and actions common to both women and men speaks to the powerful motivation of our society to maintain the illusion of difference. Bem (1995) argues that we need to reduce the male-female distinction so that it rests primarily on reproductive differences. I would add that anything short of such a revolutionary objective continues to reinforce the belief that anatomy is indeed destiny and serves to bolster the institutional maintenance of inequality.

I take issue with those who suggest that movement from one gender to another through surgical or transvestite transformations is a way of bending gender or demonstrating its fluidity. Bem (1995) has proposed that gender categories can best be eliminated by their proliferation, e.g., recognition of the full "kaleidoscope" of butches, femmes, lipstick lesbians, drag queens, leather dykes, etc, etc. These very categories, however, depend on an unquestioned acceptance of a gender difference ideology, and, indeed, take such an ideology to caricatured extremes. Gender boundaries are writ large and not eroded, repudiated, or dispensed with by those who ostensibly and dramatically pass between them. As Lorber (1994) argues, "Without gender differentiation, transvestism and transsexuality would be meaningless ... There would be no need to reconstruct genitalia to match identity if interests and life-styles were not gendered" (p. 27). To construct gender, and its multiple associations with behavior, on the basis of genitalia is, again, to subscribe to the belief that anatomy is destiny.

So, what should we do about gender? With this question, I return to where this [selection] began, with a definition of gender in terms of social relations of inequality dependent upon the acceptance of difference. MacKinnon (1987) has said it most eloquently: Differences are inequality's post hoc excuse, its

> conclusory artifact, its outcome presented as its origin, the damage that is pointed to as the justification for doing the damage after the damage has been done, the distinctions that perception is socially organized to notice because inequality gives them the consequences for social power. (p. 8)

An ideology of gender difference serves inequality and power differentials through its proscriptions and prescriptions, by limiting our vision and restricting our possibilities. But, in addition, a gender difference ideology is a source of personal confusion, stress, interpersonal difficulties, and social unease since our gender beliefs are often not reliable predictors of how individuals actually behave.

Gender is the imposition of cultural meaning onto reproductive distinctiveness. As a social process, variations in the construction of gender are possible, as illustrated by the data of cultural anthropology, and are susceptible to change. Does questioning the meaning and social function of gender imply that women (or men) should no longer recognize the common gender-specific experiences, problems, values, or directions that define us within the cultural, historical space we inhabit? Of course not, and, in fact, it is only by doing so that we gain the knowledge necessary to ask the important questions. As Frye (1996) has pointed out, women "continue to meet and gather to form and maintain social and political organizations of women, for women, as women, and in such settings to refashion continuously what it is to be a women, a woman-among-women" (p. 1007). One of the outcomes of the continued effort to understand gender is recognition of the fact that contrast is not a necessary constituent of self-recognition or self-definition. As Frye puts it, "a self is not constituted by negating an Other" (p. 1007). And genders need not be understood through dichotomous opposition.

Similarly, minority groups of Color need not be understood in terms of how each differs from a European American norm but rather in terms of the historical, social, political, and economic forces that have influenced them, as suggested by Thomas and Miles (1995). Landrine (1995) argues persuasively that the outcome of a continued focus on "difference" is the production of a "psychological hierarchy in which the Other occupies a lower status than the dominant group" and which "thus perpetuates the very social arrangements purported to be challenged by the focus on differences" (p. 6).

It is because our construction of gender is inextricably tied to inequality that our study of gender must focus on the process and conditions that underlie the construction. The typical focus, a descriptive delineation of the socialized outcomes, i.e., ways in which women and men are "different," does not really help us celebrate diversity. Attention to women's previously unrecognized contributions to music, art, history, science, technology, etc. is an essential route to such celebration. Recognition of women's unsung past and present accomplishments, however, requires, first, that we understand the politics of *why* women's work has been ignored and, second, that we pay serious attention to the complexity of the category "woman" (and "man") and fully appreciate the significance of within-gender differences. An informed appreciation of gender-related diversity requires that we understand the continuing relationships between inequality and gender categories, that we always examine gender in its cultural (learned) context, and that we recognize the full range of gender diversity.

We must insist that diversity, a term now much in vogue, refers to an appreciation of human possibilities, and not to a parade of socially constructed differences. The ways in which we vary needs to be understood as illustrating the potential of human organisms of both sexes for learning so that we can appreciate our commonalities as equal members of the human family.

References

Barnett, R. C., & Rivers, C. (1996). *She works/he works: How two-income families are happier, healthier and better off.* San Francisco: Harper Collins.

Bem, S. L. (1995). Dismantling gender polarization and compulsory heterosexuality: Should we turn the volume down or up? *The Journal of Sex Research, 32,* 329–334.

Bem, S. L. (1996). Transforming the debate on sexual inequality: From biological difference to institutionalized androcentrism. In J. C. Chrisler, C. Golden, & P. D. Rozee (Eds.), *Lectures on the Psychology of Women* (pp. 9–21). New York: McGraw Hill.

Conway, M., Pizzamiglio, M. T., & Mount, L. (1996). Status, communality, and agency: Implications for stereotypes of gender and other groups. *Journal of Personality and Social Psychology, 71,* 25–38.

Eagly, A. H. (1987). *Sex differences in social behavior: A social-role interpretation.* Hillsdale, NJ: Lawrence Erlbaum.

Eagly, A. H. (1994). On comparing women and men. *Feminism and Psychology, 4,* 513–522.

Frye, M. (1996). The necessity of differences: Constructing a positive category of women. *Signs, 21,* 991–1010.

Hilton, J. L., & von Hippel, W. (1996). Stereotypes. *Annual Review of Psychology, 47,* 237–271.

Hoyenga, K. B., & Hoyenga, K. T. (1993). *Gender-related differences.* Needham Heights, MA: Allyn & Bacon.

Hyde, J. S. (1994). Should psychologists study gender differences? Yes, with some guidelines. *Feminism and Psychology, 4,* 507–512.

Karraker, K. H., Vogel, D. A., & Lake, M. A. (1995). Parents' gender-stereotyped perceptions of newborns: The eye of the beholder revisited. *Sex Roles, 33,* 687–701.

Landrine, H. (1995). Introduction: Cultural diversity, contextualism, and feminist psychology. In H. Landrine (Ed.), *Bringing cultural diversity to feminist psychology* (pp. 1–20). Washington, DC: American Psychological Association.

Lightdale, J., & Prentice, D. A. (1994). Rethinking sex differences in aggression: Aggressive behavior in the absence of social roles. *Personality and Social Psychology Bulletin, 20,* 34–44.

Lorber, J. (1994). *Paradoxes of gender.* New Haven: Yale University Press.

Lott, B. (1981). A feminist critique of androgyny: Toward the elimination of gender attributions for learned behavior. In C. Mayo & N. N. Henley (Eds.), *Gender and nonverbal behavior* (pp. 171–180). New York: Springer.

Lott, B. (1985). The potential enrichment of social/personality psychology through feminist research, and vice versa. *American Psychologist, 40,* 155–164.

Lott, B. (1990). Dual natures or learned behavior: The challenge to feminist psychology. In R. T. Hare-Mustin & J. Marecek (Eds.), *Making a difference: Psychology and the construction of gender* (pp. 65–101). New Haven: Yale University Press.

Lott, B. (1995). Distancing from women: Interpersonal sexist discrimination. In B. Lott & D. Maluso (Eds.), *The social psychology of interpersonal discrimination* (pp. 12–49). New York: Guilford.

Lott, B. (1997). Cataloging gender differences: Science or politics? In M. R. Walsh (Ed.), *Women, men, and gender: Ongoing debates* (pp. 19–23). New Haven: Yale University Press.

Lott, B., & Maluso, D. (1993). The social learning of gender. In A. E. Beall & R. J. Sternberg (Eds.), *The psychology of gender* (pp. 99–123). New York: Guilford.

MacKinnon, C. A. (1987). *Feminism unmodified: Discourses on life and law.* Cambridge, MA: Harvard University Press.

Markens, S. (1996). The problematic of "experience:" A political and cultural critique of PMS. *Gender & Society, 10,* 42–58.

Morawski, J. G. (1994). *Practicing feminisms, reconstructing psychology.* Ann Arbor: University of Michigan Press.

Murray, S. B. (1996). "We all love Charles": Men in child care and the social construction of gender. *Gender & Society, 10,* 368–385.

Nelson, T. E., Acker, M., & Manis, M. (1996). Irrepressible stereotypes. *Journal of Experimental Social Psychology, 32,* 13–38.

Perkins, H. W., & DeMeis, D. K. (1996). Gender and family effects on the "second-shift" domestic activity of college-educated young adults. *Gender & Society, 10,* 78–93.

Piercy, M. (1976). *Woman on the edge of time.* New York: Fawcett.

Sharps, M. J., Price, J. L., & Williams, J. K. (1994). Spatial cognition and gender: Instructional and stimulus influences on mental image rotation performance. *Psychology of Women Quarterly, 18,* 413–425.

Silverstein, L. B. (1996). Fatherhood is a feminist issue. *Psychology of Women Quarterly, 20,* 3–37.

Steele, C. (1996, August). *A Burden of Suspicion: The Role of Stereotypes in Shaping Intellectual Identity.* Master lecture, 104th annual conference of the American Psychological Association, Toronto, Canada.

Thomas, V. G., & Miles, S. E. (1995). Psychology of Black women: Past, present, and future. In H. Landrine (Ed.), *Bringing cultural diversity to feminist psychology* (pp. 303–330). Washington, DC: American Psychological Association.

POSTSCRIPT

Should We Continue to Study Sex Differences?

Should we move beyond the difference model for studying sex and gender? Debate has focused on social costs and benefits incurred as a consequence of sex difference findings, the statistical and social meaning of sex difference findings, the overemphasis on difference and underrepresentation of findings of similarity, and the questionable efficacy of sex difference findings in elucidating the phenomena of sex and gender.

Whether or not scholars believe that the continuation of sex difference research would be beneficial or at least benign, there is widespread agreement that this research alone is insufficient to explore the complexities of sex and gender as social categories and processes. Difference research has been primarily descriptive in nature, even though assumptions abound about the "natural" causes of sex differences. But knowing what differences exist between males and females does not help us to understand why, how, when, and for whom they exist. Furthermore, descriptive research alone does not help us understand the social meaning or significance of such differences. Some assert that sex comparisons obscure an understanding of gender as social relations and do little to help us understand the processes that expand or delimit the significance of the difference. Others argue that focusing on categorical differences helps us to avoid the hard work we have to do to improve our society. At the very least, scholars urge that we move beyond the individual as the focus of difference research to examine the way gender is produced in interpersonal and institutional contexts.

In moving beyond the difference model, what other approaches can be used to better understand sex and gender? One suggestion calls for an approach to studying gender that transcends the difference model. The focus is on the *process* of gender. Research should explore and document "gender coding," or how society is gendered (e.g., unequal expectations, opportunities, power), and how individuals (particularly those who are disenfranchised) cope with or negotiate such inequality (ranging from acceptance to resistance). It is important to view individuals as having some agency to affect their environment but also as being constrained or shaped by social situations and structures.

Another suggested innovation reflects an effort to move beyond essentialist overgeneralizations about "generic" men and women as distinct groups. What does a categorical variable like sex actually mean? Many argue that such variables are too simplistic and therefore meaningless for representing the complexity among individuals, identities, and experiences that make up the group.

Some state that assertions about sex differences are usually based on comparisons of white middle-class men and women and therefore have limited generalizability. Thus, some scholars advocate exploring within-sex diversity and attending to a host of contextual and structural variables that are inseparable from sex.

This kind of approach has led some to ask, Can we move to a point where difference no longer makes so much of a difference? How do we get there? One view differentiates between approaches that "turn the volume up" versus "turn the volume down" on categories of difference. Should we eliminate sex and gender dichotomies from the definition of normal and natural (turn the volume down) or proliferate categories of sex and gender into as many categories as needed to capture human complexity? Or is the focus on categories obscuring more specific and critical concepts such as privilege, conflict of interest, oppression, subordination, and even cooperation?

Suggested Readings

C. F. Epstein, *Deceptive Distinctions: Sex, Gender, and the Social Order* (Yale University Press, 1988).

R. T. Hare-Mustin and J. Marecek, eds., *Making a Difference: Psychology and the Construction of Gender* (Yale University Press, 1990).

J. B. James, ed., "The Significance of Gender: Theory and Research About Difference" (Special Issue), *Journal of Social Issues* (Summer 1997).

C. Kitzinger, ed., "Should Psychologists Study Sex Differences?" *Feminism & Psychology* (1994).

D. L. Rhode, *Theoretical Perspectives on Sexual Difference* (Yale University Press, 1990).

J. Worell and C. Etaugh, eds., "Gender Transformations" (Special Issue), *Psychology of Women Quarterly* (1994).

The World Wide Web Virtual Library: Sexual Harassment Issues

This portion of the Men's Issues Page of the World Wide Web Virtual Library includes men's commentaries on and analyses of sexual harassment. Included is a section on frequencies of sexual harassment by sex of harasser and harassed, and a discussion of male-on-male harassment.

http://www.vix.com/pub/men/harass/harass.html

Overview of Women's Health and Development: Female Genital Mutilation

Sponsored by the World Health Organization (WHO), this Web page includes information on the classification and definition of Female Genital Surgery (FGS), World Health Organization activities against Female Genital Mutilation, and a sizable bibliographic database of articles on Female Genital Mutilation.

http://www.who.int/frh-whd/FGM/infopack/English/
fgm_infopack.htm

Go Ask Alice!

Go Ask Alice! is a health question-and-answer site and is sponsored by Columbia University's Health Education Program. The mission of this site is to provide in-depth, factual, and nonjudgmental information to assist individuals' decisionmaking about their physical, sexual, emotional, and spiritual health. Questions about sexuality, sexual health, and relationships are frequent. This site includes hundreds of relevant links.

http://www.goaskalice.columbia.edu

PART 3

Culture Says: "Gender Matters"

*M*any contemporary scholars view gender as a cultural construction. Cultures provide individuals with knowledge and "lenses" that structure institutions, social interactions, beliefs, and behaviors. Through cultural lenses or meaning systems, individuals perceive the "facts" of gender. Conceptualizations of sex and gender and the importance of sex and gender as social categories vary from culture to culture. However, within a particular culture, since individuals are usually limited to their own cultural lens, definitions of sex and gender seem fixed or even natural. In fact, cultural scholars argue, culture so completely defines us that we are usually oblivious to its presence in our own society. We think of culture as something that other societies have.

In this section, we examine cultural constructions of gender. Specifically, how are cultural institutions and mores structured by cultural definitions of the importance of sex and gender and by cultural gender proscriptions? What does culture dictate about the significance and characteristics of the social categories "male" and "female"? Does one's standpoint or location within the culture prescribe one's gender experiences?

- Should Title VII Apply to Sexual Harassment Between Individuals of the Same Sex?

- Is Female Circumcision Universally Wrong?

- Can Women's Sexuality Be Free From Traditional Gender Constraints?

ISSUE 8

Should Title VII Apply to Sexual Harassment Between Individuals of the Same Sex?

YES: Catharine A. MacKinnon, from *Joseph Oncale v. Sundowner Offshore Services, Incorporated*, U.S. Court of Appeals for the Fifth Circuit (August 12, 1997)

NO: Equal Employment Advisory Council, from *Joseph Oncale v. Sundowner Offshore Services, Incorporated*, U.S. Court of Appeals for the Fifth Circuit (October 14, 1997)

ISSUE SUMMARY

YES: Attorney Catharine A. MacKinnon argues that same-sex sexual harassment violates civil rights to sex equality under the law, highlighting that male-on-male sexual abuse is a neglected and serious social problem that is inextricably connected to male-on-female sexual abuse.

NO: Attorneys for the Equal Employment Advisory Council contend that same-sex harassment does not constitute unlawful sex discrimination under Title VII because it does not occur "because of sex." They caution that courts must carefully distinguish between sex and sexual orientation.

In the interest of ensuring equality of employment opportunities, Title VII of the Civil Rights Act of 1964 prohibits discrimination in the terms or conditions of employment based on race, religion, national origin, or sex. Two categories of sexual harassment are covered in Title VII: (1) quid pro quo propositions and (2) hostile work environment. Unwelcome sexual advances, requests for sexual favors, and other sexual verbal or physical contact are considered as harassment on the basis of sex by Title VII when (1) submission to the conduct is made a quid pro quo term of employment (implicitly or explicitly) and/or submission to or rejection of the conduct results in employment decisions affecting the individual, and/or (2) the purpose or effect of the conduct is to unreasonably interfere with work performance or create a hostile, offensive, or intimidating working environment.

It is interesting to note that just prior to the final vote on the Civil Rights Act by the House of Representatives, Representative Howard Smith (D-Virginia) introduced an amendment to include the term "sex" in the hopes of defeating the passage of the entire Civil Rights Act. This political maneuver backfired, as the Civil Rights Act was passed. Brief House debate revealed Congress's intention of including sex discrimination in Title VII to prevent discrimination against women and to protect the employment rights of all women. The provision in Title VII for sex discrimination was needed to redress inequities faced by women in the workforce from overt discrimination or indirectly resultant of male-dominated culture.

Defining the scope of Title VII as it applies to sex has been problematic. What is the meaning of "sex"? Do courts think of sex (defined as the biological statuses of male and female) and gender (societal meaning associated with being male or female) as synonymous? What does it mean to be discriminated against "because of sex"?

Within the last decade, heated debate has been sparked about whether or not same-sex harassment is actionable under Title VII. This debate has accentuated the definitional questions already raised by Title VII. It also adds questions about heterosexist bias in the definition of sex and the association between sexual orientation (of both the harasser and the harassed) and sex.

The U.S. Supreme Court case *Oncale v. Sundowner Offshore Services Incorporated* brought many of the controversies to the fore. Joseph Oncale began employment by Sundowner in 1991 as a new roustabout on an eight-man rig crew working offshore for seven days at a time. John Lyons, a crane operator, supervised Oncale and two other roustabouts (the lowest ranking positions on the crew). Danny Pippen, a driller, and Brandon Johnson, a floor hand, had no supervisory authority over Oncale.

Oncale's allegations included verbal abuse by Lyons and three incidents of sexual harassment in the presence of the entire crew. Oncale eventually quit, asking that his pink slip reflect that he resigned voluntarily due to sexual harassment and verbal abuse. During deposition, Oncale reported that he left Sundowner because he was afraid of being raped.

Oncale filed a sexual harassment complaint against his former employer, stating that sexual harassment directed against him by coworkers constituted discrimination because of sex. The district court held that Oncale had no Title VII cause of action for harassment because he and his coworkers are all male. The Fifth Circuit Federal Court affirmed this decision. The case was then appealed to the U.S. Supreme Court.

The following selections are taken from two opposing *amici curiae* briefs regarding the *Oncale v. Sundowner* case. Catherine A. MacKinnon, on behalf of many men's and sexual victimization activism groups, argues that same-sex harassment should be actionable under Title VII. Attorneys for the Equal Employment Advisory Council state that action on same-sex harassment is not provided for by Title VII. While weighing and evaluating the opposing assertions, examine carefully the assumptions each brief makes about definitions of and associations between sex and sexual orientation.

Catharine A. MacKinnon

 **YES**

Statement of Catharine A. MacKinnon

Summary of Argument

Men raping men is a serious and neglected social problem with deep roots in gender inequality. Courts generally permit men who have been sexually assaulted and otherwise sexually harassed by other men at work to sue under Title VII of the Civil Rights Act of 1964, as women can. The Fifth Circuit decision under review is a pernicious legal anomaly, categorically precluding equality relief on summary disposition simply because the victim and victimizer are of the same sex. Its double standard of gender justice denies men rights because they are men—with negative implications for gay and lesbian rights as well, as exemplified by the related Fourth Circuit approach, under which heterosexual perpetrators may commit acts for which homosexual perpetrators are held legally responsible. These decisions make accountability for sex discrimination turn on who one is, not on what is done.

The better approach advanced by amici, building on the vast body of judicial precedent, is not abstract but concrete. Whether an assault is "because of sex," triggering Title VII, is a factual determination. Other legal requisites being met, if acts are sexual and hurt one sex, they are sex-based, regardless of the gender and sexual orientation of the parties.

The Fifth Circuit decision at bar is bottomed on misconceptions about the gendered nature of the sexual abuse of men, particularly its connections to the inequality of women to men and of gays and lesbians to heterosexuals. Male rape—whether the victim is male or female—is an act of male dominance, marking such acts as obviously gender-based and making access to sex equality rights for Joseph Oncale indisputable.

The Equal Protection Clause of the Fourteenth Amendment as well as clear statutory principles, requires recognizing same-sex sexual assault as unquestionably actionable as sex discrimination under Title VII as a matter of law. The decision of the Fifth Circuit in this case must accordingly be reversed.

From *Joseph Oncale v. Sundowner Offshore Services, Incorporated*, 83 F.3d 118 (1998). Notes and some case citations omitted.

Argument

Introduction

The Fifth Circuit stands alone in precluding Title VII access for same-sex sexual harassment. Every other circuit that has considered the question... has found some allegations of harassment of men by men to state legally sufficient claims under Title VII's sex discrimination prohibition.

The foundation of Oncale and fountainhead of its legal error is *Goluszek v. Smith*, 697 F. Supp. 1452 (N.D. Ill. 1988). *Goluszek* held that while women sexually harassed by men have a Title VII remedy, because women are unequal to men at work, men sexually harassed by men have none, because an all-male male-dominated environment cannot discriminate against a man as a man. Sexually victimized men are thus denied access to civil rights remedies when other men sexually violate or demean them at work in circumstances in which identically situated women have clear claims....

The many courts that have recognized the actionability of same-sex harassment claims before and since *Goluszek* have relied on the plain language of the statute, the clear weight of authority in sexual harassment cases, and deference to E.E.O.C. [Equal Employment Opportunity Commission] guidelines. They have used simple logic, equality principle, life experience and common sense....

I. Sexual Abuse of Men by Men Is a Serious Social Problem of Gender Inequality

Amici [curiae]—as survivors of and experts on male-on-male sexual abuse—submit that *Goluszek*, hence the Fifth Circuit reliance on it, incorrectly analyzed the sexual abuse of men by men. Men are discriminated against based on their sex when sexually aggressed against by other men. They are targeted as men—usually as certain kinds of men—to be victimized through their masculinity, violated in their minds and bodies as individual members of their gender, as gender is socially defined.

A. Male Dominance in Society Includes Sexual Dominance of Some Men Over Other Men as Well as Over Women

Anthony Goluszek's male coworkers verbally tormented him in sexually explicit ways, demeaned his adequacy as a man, accused him of being gay or bisexual based on his reticence to have or discuss an interest in [having intercourse with] women, and poked his buttocks with a stick. *Goluszek*, 697 F. Supp. at 1454. Nonetheless the *Goluszek* court ruled that he was not discriminated against based on his sex because the purpose of Title VII is to redress an "imbalance of power and an abuse of that imbalance by the powerful which results in discrimination against a discrete and vulnerable group[,]" namely women. Id. at 1456. Because Goluszek was "a male in a male-dominated environment," id., he could not, the court found, have suffered an environment "that treated males as inferior[.]" Id. Conceding that *Goluszek* "may have been harassed 'because' he is a male," id., the court nonetheless dismissed his claims because the acts complained of could not have created "an anti-male environment" for him at work. Id.

Goluszek's workplace was unmistakably a male-dominated environment.... Sex segregation combined with gender hierarchy in the workforce ensures that many, perhaps most workplaces are dominated by men, in numbers or power or both.... Sex integration addresses the sex-discriminatory composition of all-male environments... but the sex-discriminatory norms long endemic to such settings—under which men may sexually victimize others —must also be addressed to make sex equality real.

Amici strongly agree with the *Goluszek* court that Title VII—certainly as amended and interpreted over time—is aimed at rectifying sex-based power imbalances and stopping male abuses of power in the workplace. But men abuse male power over other men as well as over women. To conclude, from the fact that women are differentially sexually abused at work, that men who are sexually abused are not abused as men, and should have no Title VII relief, reflects not only faulty analysis but false assumptions, misreadings and incomplete information.

The *Goluszek* opinion displays several common myths about male-on-male sexual abuse with which amici are familiar in their work: that men, acting as members of their gender, cannot and do not dominate other men as well as women; that when a man sexually abuses another man, the actions are not sexual and not gender-based; and that male domination of some men over other men is not part of the social system whereby men dominate women.

In the world of *Goluszek*, men in all-male environments do not oppress other men in sex-specific ways. As one district court, in following *Goluszek*, put it: "This theory focuses on whether there is an atmosphere of oppression by a "dominant gender," and thus assumes that the harasser and victim must be of opposing genders." *Martin v. Norfolk* S. Ry., 926 F. Supp. 1044, 1049 (N.D. Ala. 1996). Masculinity is assumed to be uniform, gender making all men sufficiently equal to one another that no man can be in a significant position of powerlessness relative to another man. But as study after study has shown, all-male environments are frequently characterized by extreme hierarchy well-documented to breed sexual abuse of men by men, whether from "a sense of macho competition, violence as a rite of passage, an expression of dominant status, or an initiation of hazing." *Michael Scarce, Male on Male Rape: The Hidden Toll of Stigma and Shame*, at 35 (1997)....

Men are most often raped by other men when there are no women around: in prisons, in confined and isolated work sites, in men's schools and colleges, in the military, in athletics, in fraternities.... Men sexually abuse those they have power over in society: first, women and children; then other men, typically on the basis of their status as men of a particular age...; physical stature...; ethnicity...; race...; disability...; or sexual orientation, perceived, or actual,... that makes them attractive for, or vulnerable to, male sexual aggression.

The *Goluszek* court held that a man cannot be made inferior as a man in an all-male setting. But both Goluszek and Oncale were treated as inferior men in very standard ways—Oncale more violently. Oncale's attackers were asserting male dominance through imposing sex on a man with less power. Men who are sexually assaulted are thereby stripped of their social status as men. They are feminized: made to serve the function and play the role customarily assigned to women as men's social inferiors. In terms that apply to male-on-male rape generally, Susan Brownmiller analyzes prison rape of men as "an acting out of power roles within an all-male, authoritarian environment in which the weaker, younger inmate... is forced to play the role that in the outside world is assigned to women." Susan Brownmiller, *Against our Will: Men, Women, and Rape,* at 258 (1975). This lowers the victim's status, making him inferior as a man by social standards. For a man to be sexually attacked, by placing him in a woman's role, demeans his masculinity; he loses it, so to speak. This cannot be done to a woman. What he loses, he loses through gender, as a man.

Often it is men perceived not to conform to stereotyped gender roles who are the targets of male sexual aggression. *Goluszek* was taunted for appearing unwilling to oppress women sexually. Because he did not conform to his male co-workers' view of what his gender behavior ought to be, because he was not seen to be practicing sexual objectification and subordination of women, he was seen as less a man according to their sex-stereotyped standards.... "Having his gender questioned" marked Goluszek's abuse as sex-based. Title VII's goal of "striking at the entire spectrum of disparate treatment of men and women resulting from sex stereotypes..." clearly intercepts such acts....

B. Denial of Sex and Gender in Male-on-Male Sexual Abuse Maintains Male Dominance

The gravamen of Goluszek is that male same-sex aggression is not gendered in the sense Title VII requires. Implicit is an insistence that men cannot be sexually dominated in their social status or roles as men. The denial that interactions among men can have a sexual component, and that sexual abuse of men is gendered, are twin features of the social ideology of male dominance with which amici are familiar as experts. In this ideology, men are seen as sexually invulnerable. This image protects men from much male sexual violence and naturalizes the sexual abuse of women, making it seem that women, biologically, are sexual victims. Denying that men can be sexually abused as men thus supports the gender hierarchy of men over women in society. The illusion is preserved that men are sexually inviolable, hence naturally superior, as the sexual abuse of men by men is kept invisible.

Accordingly, some courts jump to de-sexualize and de-gender male-on-male sexual aggression. In denying access to equality relief, they call the behavior at issue "horseplay;" ... "mere locker room antics," ... being "razzed," ... and "a personal grudge match." ... They pass it off as "puerile and repulsive," "diffuse" and "ambiguous," "offensive and tasteless." ...

The point is to call the behavior anything but sexual and attribute it to anything but gender. Amazingly, even gender is used to deny gender, for example, "boys will be boys"—a gendered description if ever there was one—being considered not gender-based. That the behavior described may be everything these courts say it is does not mean that it is not sexual and gendered, hence sex-based.

Denial that sexual abuse of men by men is sexual in nature is a common feature of male dominance. When a man's testicles are aggressively grabbed, it takes a lot to deny that the attack has something to do with the fact he is a man, but the district court managed it in *Quick v. Donaldson Co., Inc.* 895 F. Supp. 1288 (S.D. Ia. 1995), rev'd, 90 F.3d 1372 (8th Cir. 1996). Attacks focused on male sexual organs are sexual attacks, hence sexual. With the Seventh Circuit, "frankly, we find it hard to think of a situation in which someone intentionally grabs another's testicles for reasons entirely unrelated to that person's gender." *Doe* at *15. Similarly, when men rub another man's penis until it becomes erect, blindfold him and force him to his knees and put their fingers into his mouth in simulated fellatio, expose their genitals to him, put a broom handle between his buttocks, ask him for sex, offer to pay him money for sex, unzip their fly and invite him into a restroom stall, flick their tongue and say "I love you" while sex is discussed, see *McWilliams,* 72 F.3d at 1198–99 (Michael, J., dissenting) (facts), powerful denial is required to deem the conduct anything but sexual. But, in *McWilliams,* because the perpetrators "were" heterosexual, the Fourth Circuit imagined this aggression to be

> "because of" the victim's known or believed prudery, or shyness, or other form of vulnerability to sexually-focused speech or conduct. Perhaps "because of" the perpetrators' own sexual perversion, or obsession, or insecurity. Certainly, "because of" their vulgarity and insensitivity and meanness of spirit. But not specifically "because of" the victim's sex.

Id. at 1196. None of the conjectured motivations excludes gender as the driving force in all of them. Moreover, motivation need not be exclusively gender-based to be actionably gender-based. . . .

Moral disapprobation is no substitute for equality analysis and legal accountability. The acts against Mr. McWilliams were neither gender-neutral nor indiscriminate; they asserted male dominance. He was targeted as a man, a certain kind of man the court described as having "arrested . . . cognitive and emotional development." 72 F.3d at 1193. "Men's rape of women is a hateful act designed to reinforce male supremacy. So is men's rape of men." Rus Ervin Funk, *Men Who Are Raped,* in Scarce, at 222. He was abused as women are so often abused—except that women, when their sexuality hence their gender is assailed by men at work, have a Title VII remedy.

II. Sexual Harassment of Men by Men Is Sex-Based Abuse Under Sex Equality Guarantees as a Matter of Law

A. Sex Discrimination Law, Hence Sexual Harassment Law, Protects Both Sexes

Sexual harassment is legally recognized as a form of sex-based discrimination. There is no question that both Title VII and the Equal Protection Clause of the Fourteenth Amendment, under which sexual harassment is also actionable, . . . protect both sexes equally, even if, due to gender inequality in society, these provisions, as applied, do not always affect the sexes in precisely the same way.

The plain language of Title VII protects all individuals from sex discrimination: "It shall be an unlawful employment practice for an employer... to discriminate against any individual with respect to his... terms, conditions, or privileges of employment, because of such individual's... sex...." 42 U.S.C. § 2000e–2(a)(1) 78 Stat. 255 (1994). In deciding that this prohibition on discrimination "because of such individual's sex" applied to men, this Court stated: "Male as well as female employees are protected against discrimination." *Newport News Shipbuilding & Dry Dock Co. v. E.E.O.C.*, 462 U.S. 669, 682 (1983)....

No one has legal carte blanche to discriminate against members of their own racial or gender group.... Nor does any basic principle of equality law or the Supreme Court's recognition of the claim for a sexually hostile working environment restrict the relief available to survivors based on the gender of discriminator or victim.... As noted by the Eleventh Circuit in ruling that same-sex harassment is actionable under Title VII, "There is simply no suggestion in these statutory terms that the cause of action is limited to opposite gender contexts." *Fredette*, 112 F.3d at 1505. Accord *Caldwell*, 958 F. Supp. at 968....

Equality rights, while based on group membership, are personal rights.... While the Constitution, like Title VII, is rightly concerned for members of groups who have traditionally been subjected to systematic discrimination, it has never confined individual access to equality relief to members of such groups. Individual men may need equality rights particularly when, as here, their situation is exceptional among men and/or they are in situations in which women, as members of the subordinated gender group, are more typically found....

B. Same-Sex Harassment Is Facially Sex-Based When It Is Sexual and One Sex Is Victimized

To be actionable as sex discrimination, an impugned behavior must be "because of sex." When a man sexually harasses another man, how do we know it was "because of sex?"

Drawing on over twenty years of judicial development of the legal claim for sexual harassment, the answer is the same for men as for women, for gay men and lesbian women as for heterosexual women and men. It is a question of fact. For purposes of motions testing the legal sufficiency of sexual harassment claims, sexual allegations are facially gender-based. When, in addition, one sex is disadvantaged, sex-based discrimination is unambiguously claimed as a matter of law.

1. Whether alleged acts are "based on sex" is a question of fact   The first two appellate cases to establish the legal claim for sexual harassment, *Barnes*, [*v. Costle*, 561 F.2d 983, 990n.55] supra (quid pro quo), and *Bundy v. Jackson*, 641 F.2d 934 (D.C. Cir. 1981) (hostile environment), took the view that whether or not behavior was sex-based under Title VII was a question of fact. To overcome motions to dismiss arguing that sexual harassment of a woman by a man was not sex-based as a matter of law because the same thing could have been done to a man, the D.C. Circuit thought that what mattered was not what could have been done but what was done.

... In *Bundy*, the D.C. Circuit glossed this formulation, considering same-sex as well as opposite-sex harassment: "in each instance the question is one of but-for causation: would the complaining employee have suffered the harassment had he or she been of a different gender?" *Bundy*, 641 F.2d at 942 n.7. In other words, the conceptual possibility of bisexual or homosexual harassment was not allowed to preclude a trial on the facts of heterosexual harassment, in this case, of a woman by a man.

Later courts followed the "but for sex" test in case after case of male-on-female harassment.... The widely followed opinion in *Henson* formulated it: "In the typical case in which a male supervisor makes sexual overtures to a female worker, it is obvious that the supervisor did not treat male employees in a similar fashion. It will therefore be a simple matter for the plaintiff to prove that but for her sex, she would not have been subjected to sexual harassment." *Henson*, 682 F.2d at 904 (citing *Bundy*, 641 F.2d at 942 n.7). Why "obvious"? Do courts assume that if behavior is heterosexual, it is gendered? They may. But there was no allegation to the contrary. Nothing else appearing, courts infer that the behavior is gender-based as heterosexuality is gender-based....

Some judges believe that opposite-sex harassment cases make knowing that the behavior is sex-based relatively easy, while same-sex cases make it comparatively hard.... Amici disagree. The facts are no more likely to be clear or murky in same-sex than in opposite-sex cases. The view that opposite-sex settings are easily gendered while same-sex settings are not reflects a presumption of heterosexuality. Correctly understood, the same tests developed to determine whether harassment is gender-based in cases between women and men —is it sexual? is one sex harmed?—apply equally in cases between women and between men.

2. Aggression that is sexual has been treated by courts as facially sex-based

Sexuality is gendered in societies of sex inequality.... As a result, for better or worse, in most instances "it is the essence of sexual conduct between two individuals that the one initiating or inviting the conduct normally does so because of the other's sex." *Tietgen*, 921 F. Supp. at 1500–01. Courts adjudicating sexual harassment claims reflect this state of affairs when they unproblematically consider that sexual allegations are gender-based allegations. "Sexual harassment is ordinarily based on sex. What else could it be based on?" *Nichols*, 42 F.3d at 511.

Without requiring genital proof, courts routinely deem opposite-sex harassment "unquestionably based on gender..." simply because the facts alleged are sexual facts.... Sexuality is so obviously gendered that courts have sometimes felt the need to stress that sexuality isn't all there is to Title VII's gender-harassment prohibition.... Courts have properly rejected out of hand the argument that sexual initiatives by a man to a woman were not gender-based because "his actions were merely the result of his desire for King as an individual and, therefore, were not sex-based harassment." *King v. Bd. of Regents of the Univ. of Wis. Sys.*, 898 F.2d 533, 538 (7th Cir. 1990). Persons are sexually gendered as individuals.

The view "if it's sexual, it's gendered" has also guided same-sex cases....

The underlying question of whether impugned treatment is or is not sexual is itself a question of fact—subtle at times, often anything but. Sexually speaking, two men saying "we're going to [have sex with] you" and one pulling out his penis, Dep. at 58:23–24, 57, is hardly subtle. Behavior can be hostile, produce anguish or distress (and intend to) or aim to demean and still be sexual. Producing fear in another, or abusing power, . . . can be sexually arousing or potentiating to the perpetrator. . . .

But the genders of the perpetrator and the victim do not dispose of whether a given behavior is sexual or not. One cannot presume that behavior that is sexual in opposite-sex contexts is not sexual in same-sex contexts, as Judge Neimeyer does in *Hopkins,* 77 F.3d at 752–53. Just as acts do not automatically become sexual simply because they are engaged in by members of different sexes, acts do not become nonsexual simply because they are engaged in by members of the same sex. No differential presumptions are appropriate.

3. Harassment is sex-discriminatory when sexual and one sex is victimized

. . . Justice Ginsburg clarified that, in proving discrimination based on sex as required in *Meritor,* 477 U.S. at 66, "the critical issue, Title VII's text indicates, is whether members of one sex are exposed to disadvantageous terms or conditions of employment to which members of the other sex are not exposed." *Harris,* 510 U.S. at 25 (Ginsburg, J., concurring) (citation omitted). The E.E.O.C.'s directive on same sex harassment uses precisely these terms: "The victim does not have to be of the opposite sex of the harasser. Since sexual harassment is a form of sexual discrimination, the crucial inquiry is whether the harasser treats a member or members of one sex differently from members of the other sex." 2 EEOC Compliance Manual § 615.2(b)(3) (1974 & Supp. 1996). Same-sex harassment courts have applied this "singles out one sex" rule with no difficulty. . . .

C. Neither the Rights of Victims Nor the Liabilities of Perpetrators of Sexual Harassment Should Turn on Their Sexual Orientation

The sexual orientation of the parties inevitably arises in, and is implicated in ruling on, same-sex harassment. The sexual orientation of the parties is, however, properly irrelevant to the legal sufficiency of sexual harassment claims. An accused perpetrator's being gay or lesbian does not make that person's behavior sex-based, but sexual orientation may be pertinent in determining whether particular behavior is based on sex, . . . in the totality of the circumstances.

1. Access to sex equality relief for acts of sexual abuse depends on the acts, not on the sexual preference of the actors

Wright v. Methodist Youth Services, 511 F. Supp. 307 (N.D. Ill. 1981), the first reported case of same-sex sexual harassment, held that a man fired because he rejected the sexual advances of his male supervisor stated a claim for sex discrimination under Title VII. Wright described the behavior as "homosexual advances," id. at 308, 309, although so far as is known, most men who sexually abuse other men are heterosexual. Scarce at 17. . . . The *Wright* ruling thus established that same-sex sexual advances were sex-based within the meaning of Title VII in a context that linked that result to the sexual preference of the perpetrator.

The emerging rule is to regard sexual orientation as not determinative of the legal sufficiency of same-sex claims as a matter of law but to admit it as relevant on the facts. Perpetrator sexual orientation does not make unwanted sexual initiatives sex-based any more than victim sexual orientation makes unwanted advances welcome, although both can be relevant (if sometimes only minimally) to both factual determinations.... It is not categorically irrelevant because "when a homosexual supervisor is making offensive sexual advances to a subordinate of the same sex, and not doing so to employees of the opposite sex, it absolutely is a situation where, but for the subordinate's sex, he would not be subjected to that treatment." *E.E.O.C. v. Walden Book Co., Inc.,* 885 F. Supp. 1100, 1103–1104 (M.D. Tenn. 1995).... Although care must be taken that this approach does not create an opening for homophobic attacks, the role itself merely applies the same standard to everyone.

Sexual orientation on its face disposes of nothing. Gay men do not initiate unwanted sex to all men any more than lesbian women welcome sexual attention from all women. Needless to say, from knowing a person is gay, one cannot deduce that they sexually harassed another person. But the fact that a perpetrator of same-sex harassment is not gay—or not known to be gay or provably gay—also does not render same-sex sexual behavior not sex-based. Thus the Fourth Circuit's view that same-sex sexual harassment by heterosexual men cannot be sex-based, *McWilliams,* 90 F.3d at 1194–1195, but harassment by homosexual men can be, *Wrightson,* 99 F.3d at 143, is wrong on many grounds. Those boys who were just boys in the machine shop in *McWilliams* became sexual and gendered when they ran the restaurant in *Wrightson*? Beyond misreading social reality, the Fourth Circuit approach is impractical (courts are now to adjudicate a person's "real" sexual orientation?), incoherent (a victim's recovery for sexual abuse depends on what the perpetrator does with voluntary others?), and invidious (heterosexuals may sexually abuse people whom homosexuals may not?). On the Fourth Circuit's view, if a plaintiff could prove that one of the "faggots" in *Quick* actually "is" gay, would his testicle-grabbing become sex-based, while the identical act of the straight coworker next to him is not?

By definition, sexual harassment is unwanted, so victim orientation is as irrelevant on same-sex facial challenges on sex-basis as it is on opposite-sex ones. The sexual orientation of the victim cannot convert aggression that is sex-based into aggression that is not, or vice-versa.

Will Title VII access now turn on the sexual feelings and imagined or real sexual identities of perpetrators? Will it have one sexual harassment rule for gay sexual harassers and another for straight ones? One for those whose sexual feelings have coalesced, another for those whose sexual feelings are diverse, diffuse, denied, deniable, unknown, or simply unproveable? Oncale sued for forced sex. Why should the gender of those with whom [supervisor John] Lyons and [coworker Danny] Pippen are sexual, when others want to be sexual with them, determine Oncale's rights against them for violating (what is conventionally considered) his manhood?

2. Harassment because of homosexuality is harassment because of sex   In practical terms, harassment because of homosexuality cannot be separated from harassment because of sex. The gender of sexual object choice (although not all there is to sexual orientation) partly defines gender in society. The gender of a person with whom one has sex, or is thought to have sex, is a powerful constituent of whether one is considered a woman or a man in society.…

The pitfalls of trying to separate the two are illustrated by Dillon. Mr. Dillon was taunted, ostracized, and physically beaten by coworkers because they believed he was gay. They called him "fag" and other terms of homophobic abuse, he said, because he was a man. The Sixth Circuit, admitting his harassment was "clearly sexual in nature," Dillon, 1992 WL 5436 at *6, rejected his Title VII claim, saying it was because of homosexuality not sex. So far as is discernible in the opinion, Mr. Dillon is heterosexual. In the view of amici, he was harassed as a male. Women are not called "fag." When women are seen as effeminate, they are rewarded, or sexually harassed in ways clearly marked as sex-specific. Dillon should not have had to prove facts that did not exist, such as that "his coworkers would have treated a similarly situated woman… differently," or to argue that "a lesbian would have been accepted." Id. at *9. Hypothetical counterfactuals cannot be proven. That the behavior was sexual, and that no women were, in fact, subjected to it (supported in Dillon's case by evidence of clearly homophobic attacks) should be enough.

Only men are subject to denigration by gay-bashing taunts like "faggot." Only women are subject to denigration by the use of terms like "dyke" as epithet and insult. Such abuse is inherently socially gendered. Using sex with members of one's own sex as derision, insult, and hostility denigrates the target's gender-adequacy. Such terms, when part of sexual harassment, create a hostile environment for men as men and for women as women, whether directed at straights or gays. Because they attack individuals as members of their gender group, they are based on sex.…

Although this appeal does not require resolution of the question, amici submit that sexual harassment because of sexual orientation is sex-based discrimination. When individuals are sexually harassed because of the sex of their sexual partners, real or imagined, they are harassed because of sex. First, formally speaking, those harassed because they are gay men or lesbian women are harassed because of the gender of their sexual partners and identification. If their own gender, or that of their loved ones, were different, they would not be so treated. They are precisely similarly situated to heterosexuals in having sexual relationships based on gender yet are treated differently because of their own gender, the gender of their sexual partners, or both.… Second, more substantively, gay men and lesbian women, through challenging the naturalness and inevitability of gendered-unequal roles in sex, challenge the sexual dimension of gender inequality under which sexual violence by men against women, and some men, is widespread.… Third, usually both gay men and lesbian women are not sexually harassed by the same harasser. Equal oppression… may occur in this context scarcely more often than bisexual harassment appears to. In any case, sex equality rights are individual rights. It is no answer to victimization based on the supposed gender-inappropriateness of one's sexuality that others of another sex who make the corresponding "error" are also discriminated against. Equal discrimination in this sense is sex discrimination two times over, not no discrimination at all.

III. The Equal Protection Clause Forbids Exempting Same-Sex Harassment Claims From Title VII Coverage

The Fifth Circuit's approach in *Oncale* creates a blatant double standard in sexual harassment cases based on gender, and potentially on sexual orientation as well, that denies survivors equal protection of the laws. Men are denied legal protection women have. Under the Fourth Circuit's extension, straight perpetrators can freely commit sexual aggression for which gay perpetrators are held accountable. And because sexual harassment due to sexual orientation, wrongly, is regarded as not covered by Title VII, ... some courts have concluded that "Title VII does not protect homosexuals from harassment ... since such treatment arises from their affectional preference rather than their sex." *Polly v. Houston Lighting & Power Co.*, 825 F. Supp. 135, 139 n.2 (S.D. Tex. 1993).

A dual system of rights on an arbitrary ground violates every equal protection standard known.... Surely, if officially ignoring men's complaints of sexual harassment while taking women's seriously violates the sex equality component of the Equal Protection Clause, ... judicially interpreting Title VII to ignore men's complaints of sexual abuse by men, while allowing women's complaints of sexual abuse by men, does as well. And this Court taught in *Romer* that homosexuals, as such, may not be excluded from the ordinary civil processes for asserting their rights that are available to everyone else.

Without question, "the guarantee of equal protection cannot mean one thing when applied to one individual and something else when applied to [another] person[.] *Bakke*, 438 U.S. at 289–290 (Powell, J., with whom White, J., joined). But the parallel between this case and the "reverse discrimination" cases ... is more formal than substantive. Those who claim "reverse discrimination" say they are treated the way the historically powerless are treated. However, affirmative action designed to redress and end arbitrary social exclusion and white/male supremacy ... does not violate the legal equality rights of individual members of socially dominant groups who thereby lose their customary group-based privileges.... At the same time, it would be perverse to allow members of dominant groups to use equality laws to reassert their dominance while denying access to equality relief to individual members of dominant groups who fail to meet their group's standard for dominance and/ or are treated like members of historically powerless groups are so often treated.

Oncale presents a real, not imagined, a direct, not reverse, act of discrimination based on sex. It cannot be the case that whites, wrongly claiming racism, can destroy equality programs for people of color while sexually assaulted men, rightly claiming sexism, cannot sue their victimizers. And far from undermining the rights of those who most often need the claim, allowing Oncale to sue under Title VII not only takes nothing from them but, by reducing the stigma of sexual assault and increasing accountability for it, benefits all sexual abuse survivors.

Much sexual harassment jurisprudence reasons that, had a sexually harassed woman been a man, she would not have been so treated, therefore she is harassed "because of sex." The present case poses the question, What if she had been a man and the same thing happened? The answer is at once sex-specific and sex-neutral: both sexes are covered for injuries through their gender. Women do not have sex equality rights only because men couldn't be treated in the same way, this case suggests, but because men could be and are not. And when they are? Had he been a woman, Mr. Oncale might not have been treated the way he was. But if he were, his sex equality rights would be recognized.

Conclusion

For the foregoing reasons, the decision of the Court of Appeals for the Fifth Circuit should be reversed and the cause remanded for trial on the merits.

 **NO**

Brief Filed by the Equal Employment Advisory Council

Summary of Argument

Title VII's ban on sex discrimination applies only to conduct that occurs "because of" the discriminatee's sex. Consequently, to establish a case of sexual harassment of the hostile environment variety, a Title VII plaintiff must be able to show not only that he or she was subjected to unwelcome conduct of a sexual nature that was sufficiently severe and pervasive to meet the standards this Court set forth in *Meritor* [*Savings Bank, FSB v. Vinson*] and *Harris* [*v. Forklift Systems, Inc.*], but also that the conduct occurred because of his or her sex. The mere fact that harassing conduct involved sexually explicit language, gestures, or physical contact, without more, does not suffice to establish this essential element of a plaintiff's case.

Where a hostile working environment allegedly results from sexual conduct that involves a male perpetrator and a female victim (or vice versa), courts typically presume that the conduct is because of the victim's sex. But where perpetrator and victim are heterosexuals of the same gender, as in this case, no such inference properly can be drawn. A contrary rule effectively would convert Title VII from a focused mandate to end discrimination into an unmanageably broad code of working behavior.

In discussing and applying Title VII's ban against discrimination because of an individual's sex, moreover, courts must be careful to distinguish between sex and sexual orientation. Repeated efforts in Congress to amend Title VII to add protection against discrimination based on sexual orientation have been unsuccessful. Since Title VII does not cover discrimination based on sexual orientation, it follows that it does not cover harassment based on sexual orientation.

Congress left it up to employers to establish and maintain standards of behavior appropriate to their own workplaces, subject only to the requirement that they not subject employees to discrimination because of statutorily-protected characteristics such as sex and race. Conduct of the sort that Oncale alleges in this case would violate most employers' workplace standards and

---

From *Joseph Oncale v. Sundowner Offshore Services, Incorporated*, 83 F.3d 118 (1998). Some notes and case citations omitted.

subject the perpetrators to severe discipline or even discharge. Such conduct, if proved, also would be remediable under tort law in most, if not all, jurisdictions. But, absent evidence that Oncale was subjected to this conduct because of his sex, it does not fall within the specific focus of Title VII's antidiscrimination mandate.

Argument

I. This Court Should Confirm, in Keeping With the Plain Language of Title VII, That Only Harassment That Occurs "Because of" the Victim's Sex, and That Meets the Court's Standards of Severity and Pervasiveness, Can Constitute Unlawful Sexual Harassment

A. Title VII's Ban on Sex Discrimination Applies Only to Employment-Related Conduct That Is "Because of" Sex

Title VII of the Civil Rights Act of 1964, 42 U.S.C. § § 2000e et seq., makes it an "unlawful employment practice for an employer . . . to discriminate against any individual with respect to his compensation, terms, conditions or privileges of employment, because of such individual's race, color, religion, sex, or national origin." 42 U.S.C. § 2000e-2(a)(1) . . . Accordingly, under this Court's decisions allocating the burdens of proof in a Title VII case, the plaintiff at all times retains the burden of persuading the trier of fact that the challenged employment decision was made because of a characteristic protected by the statute. . . .

Under this Court's "simple test of Title VII discrimination," *Newport News Shipbuilding & Dry Dock Co. v. EEOC,* 462 U.S. 669, 683 (1983), sex discrimination occurs when a person is treated "in a manner which but for that person's sex would be different." Id. (quoting *Los Angeles Dep't of Water & Power v. Manhart,* 435 U.S. 702, 711 (1978)). See also *Price Waterhouse v. Hopkins,* 490 U.S. 228, 240 (1989) (In using the phrase "because of," "Congress meant to obligate [a sex discrimination plaintiff] to prove that the employer relied upon sex-based considerations in coming to its decision.").

Notably, Title VII prohibits discrimination against an individual because of that individual's sex. "The statute's focus on the individual is unambiguous." *Manhart,* 435 U.S. at 708. . . . Thus, the focus is on the sex of the alleged victim of the discrimination, not on that of the alleged discriminator.

B. Harassment May Constitute Unlawful Sex Discrimination Insofar as It Occurs "Because of" the Victim's Sex

In *Meritor Savings Bank, FSB v. Vinson,* 477 U.S. 57, 66 (1986), this Court ruled that "a plaintiff may establish a violation of Title VII by proving that discrimination based on sex has created a hostile or abusive work environment." Drawing on precedents involving harassment based on race, the Court reasoned that "nothing in Title VII suggests that a hostile environment based on discriminatory sexual harassment should not be likewise prohibited." Id. The Court quoted at length from an Eleventh Circuit opinion stating that:

> Sexual harassment which creates a hostile or offensive environment for members of one sex is every bit the arbitrary barrier to sexual equality at the workplace that racial harassment is to racial equality. Surely, a requirement that a man or woman run a gauntlet of sexual abuse in return for the privilege of being allowed to work and make a living can be as demeaning and disconcerting as the harshest of racial epithets.

Meritor, 477 U.S. at 67 (quoting *Henson v. Dundee,* 682 F.2d 897, 902 (1982)). As the Court later explained, Title VII's prohibition of discrimination in employment "because of [an] individual's ... sex ... 'is not limited to "economic" or "tangible" discrimination. The phrase "terms, conditions or privileges of employment" evinces a congressional intent "to strike at the entire spectrum of disparate treatment of men and women" in employment,' which includes requiring people to work in a discriminatorily hostile or abusive environment." *Harris v. Forklift Systems,* 510 U.S. 17, 21 (1993) (quoting *Meritor,* 477 U.S. at 64).

Precisely what discriminatory conduct will constitute unlawful sexual harassment under Title VII, however, is less than clear. The Court in *Harris* noted the difficulty of establishing a "mathematically precise test." *Harris,* 510 U.S. at 22–23. Instead, the Court directed, "whether an environment is 'hostile' or 'abusive' can be determined only by looking at all the circumstances. These may include the frequency of the discriminatory conduct; its severity; whether it is physically threatening or humiliating, or a mere offensive utterance; and whether it unreasonably interferes with an employee's work performance." Id.

C. Discrimination "Because of" Sex Is a Threshold Requirement for a Finding of Sexual Harassment in Violation of Title VII

Throughout the development of "sexual harassment" jurisprudence, one threshold point remains constant. Only a "discriminatory" hostile or abusive work environment violates Title VII....

Thus, when articulating in *Harris* that which makes "hostile" and "abusive" workplace conduct unlawful, this Court was careful to use the modifier "discriminatory" each time it addressed the issue. e.g., "requiring people to work in a discriminatorily hostile or abusive environment," *Harris,* 510 U.S. at 21; "When the workplace is permeated with 'discriminatory intimidation, ridicule, and insult...,'" id. (quoting *Meritor,* 477 U.S. at 65); "A discriminatorily abusive work environment, even one that does not seriously affect employees' psychological well-being...," id. at 22.

Determining whether or not the conduct was discriminatory is analytically distinct from determining whether or not it was severe and pervasive enough to create a hostile or abusive environment. It is the discriminatory nature of the conduct, and not simply the degree of hostility or abuse, that makes certain types of harassment actionable under Title VII. "The very fact that the discriminatory conduct was so severe or pervasive that it created a work environment abusive to employees because of their race, gender, religion, or national origin offends Title VII's broad rule of workplace equality." *Harris,* 510 U.S. at 22. . . .

Accordingly, proof that the challenged conduct occurred because of the purported victim's sex is an indispensable element of every sexual harassment case.

D. Not Every Workplace Act or Utterance That Has a Sexual Connotation or Component Amounts to Discrimination "Because of" Sex

Sex is part of life. Popular culture places a heavy emphasis on sexuality and sexual behavior, as is regularly evidenced in books, magazines, movies, on television, and on the Internet. Most foul language, in every language and culture for thousands of years, has had connotations of sexual activity, private body parts, or gender. In many places, routine use of vulgar language, crude jokes and gestures, and even physical horseplay are part of the fabric of daily life. Regrettably, but not surprisingly, then, such behavior occasionally creeps into the workplace as well.

Most employers today strive to maintain work environments in which employees treat one another with respect and refrain from use of crude language or harassing behavior of any sort. To an employer interested in maintaining order, efficiency, and harmony in its workplace, the important point is that such behaviors are inappropriate, whether or not they are unlawful.

But not every workplace act or utterance that has a sexual component or connotation involves gender-based discrimination. For example, several courts of appeals have concluded that use of the pejorative term "bitch" is not in and of itself evidence of sex discrimination. . . .

Where a "hostile" working environment is alleged as a result of sexual conduct that involves a male perpetrator and female victim, courts tend to presume that the conduct is "because of" the victim's sex. E.g., *Burns v. McGregor Electronic Industries, Inc.,* 955 F.2d 559, 564 (8th Cir. 1992) ("Sexual behavior directed at a woman raises the inference that the harassment is based on her sex."). But where perpetrator and victim are of the same gender, the connection is far from clear. (n1) As Justice Ginsburg noted in her concurring opinion in *Harris,* "The critical issue, Title VII's text indicates, is whether members of one sex are exposed to disadvantageous terms or conditions of employment to which members of the other sex are not exposed." *Harris,* 510 U.S. at 25 (Ginsburg, J., concurring).

As this Court considers the issue of harassment among persons of the same gender, it is important to keep in mind the core concept underlying *Meritor*—that discriminatory sexual harassment violates Title VII where it is an "arbitrary barrier to sexual equality." *Meritor,* 477 U.S. at 67 (quoting *Henson v. Dundee,* 682 F.2d 897, 902 (11th Cir. 1982)).

1. Among heterosexuals of the same gender, sexually explicit actions, comments, and gestures—no matter how crude or offensive—do not, without more, establish discrimination "because of" sex Typically, sexual conduct in the nature of jokes, comments, or horseplay among heterosexuals of the same gender—even when it involves language, conduct, or physical contact that the recipient finds highly offensive—does not amount to sexual harassment violative of Title VII. As the Fourth Circuit has observed:

> As a purely semantic matter, we do not believe that in common understanding the kind of shameful heterosexual-male-on-heterosexual-male conduct alleged here (nor comparable female-on-female conduct) is considered to be "because of the [target's] sex." Perhaps "because of" the victim's known or believed prudery, or shyness, or other form of vulnerability to sexually-focused speech or conduct. Perhaps "because of" the perpetrators' own sexual perversion, or obsession, or insecurity. Certainly, "because of" their vulgarity and insensitivity and meanness of spirit. But not specifically "because of" the victim's sex.

McWilliams v. Fairfax County Board of Supervisors, 72 F.3d 1191, 1195–96 (4th Cir.), cert. denied, 117 S. Ct. 72 (1996). Likewise, as the Seventh Circuit has pointed out:

> Although explicit sexual content or vulgarity may often take a factfinder a long way toward concluding that harassing comments were in fact based on gender . . . this need not necessarily be the case. Most unfortunately, expressions [explicitly involving sexual activity] are commonplace in certain circles, and more often than not, when these expressions are used (particularly when uttered by men speaking to other men) their use has no connection whatsoever with the sexual acts to which they make reference—even when they are accompanied, as they sometimes were here, with a crotch-grabbing gesture. Ordinarily, they are simply expressions of animosity or juvenile provocation. . . .

Johnson v. Hondo, Inc., 1997 U.S. App. LEXIS 22827 at* 10–11 (7th Cir. Aug. 28, 1997). (n2)

As the Fourth Circuit has noted, "To interpret Title VII to reach that conduct when only heterosexual males are involved as harasser and victim would be to extend this vital statute's protections beyond intentional discrimination 'because of' the offended worker's 'sex' to unmanageably broad protection of the sensibilities of workers simply 'in matters of sex.' " *McWilliams,* 72 F.3d 1191, 1196.

Any other result would defy common sense and, indeed, would convert Title VII into a generic code of workplace conduct unrelated to protection against sex discrimination. Harassment of an employee because he is new to the workplace, acts or dresses differently than other workers, or is perceived as unfriendly (or odd, or weak, or otherwise vulnerable) does not become harassment "because of" the individual's sex simply because it involves some use of language having sexual connotations or some physical contact with intimate body parts. Such teasing, bullying, or even molestation of other workers of the same gender may be reprehensible, but it is not "sex discrimination" as this Court has interpreted the term. Decency and respect toward one's fellow workers are important values that extend far beyond the focus of Title VII's mandate to eliminate specific forms of discrimination.

2. The lower courts properly have distinguished between sex and sexual orientation and recognized that Title VII does not address harassment based on an individual's sexual orientation In addressing the issue presented in this case, the Court should take care to distinguish, as have most lower federal courts, between sex and sexual orientation. Simply stated, Title VII's prohibition on discrimination based on sex does not extend to discrimination based on an individual's sexual orientation. . . .

Because discrimination on the basis of sexual orientation does not constitute discrimination "because of . . . sex" within the meaning of Title VII, it follows that harassment of an employee on the basis of that person's sexual orientation likewise is not covered.

E. The Court Below Properly Upheld the Dismissal of the Complaint in This Case, Because Oncale Presented No Facts From Which a Jury Reasonably Could Conclude That the Alleged Harassment Occurred "Because of" His Sex
In this case, Oncale alleged that his male supervisor and co-workers subjected him to treatment in the workplace that most people—including most employers—undoubtedly would regard as highly offensive, hostile, and even abusive. But he failed to establish any basis for concluding that they subjected him to this treatment because of his sex. Accordingly, the courts below properly concluded that he could not make out a case of sex discrimination violative of Title VII.

Oncale alleged no facts from which a jury reasonably could infer that his supervisor and co-workers treated him as they did because he was a male. It may have been that they disliked him. It may have been that they were mean-spirited. Perhaps they found it perversely amusing to torment him. Perhaps they were socially arrested individuals who lacked the capacity to cope in acceptable ways with the boredom and isolation of life on an offshore oil rig.

Whatever the explanation, right-minded employers certainly would deplore the type of behavior of which Oncale accuses his supervisor and co-workers. Indeed, most employers' standards of workplace conduct would make such behavior grounds for severe discipline or discharge, regardless of whether it was lawful or unlawful. Moreover, the conduct Oncale alleged might well have been tortious. The only issue before this Court, however, is whether Oncale alleged or adduced facts from which a jury reasonably could conclude that the alleged conduct constituted discrimination against him "because of" his sex. Since he was unable to point to any such facts, his complaint of unlawful sexual harassment under Title VII properly was dismissed.

Conclusion

For the foregoing reasons, amicus curiae Equal Employment Advisory Council respectfully submits that the judgment of the court below should be affirmed.

Notes

1. As Judge Manion observed in his opinion dissenting in part in *Doe* by *Doe v. City of Belleville,* 119 F.3d 563, 601 (7th Cir. 1997): " 'When someone sexually harasses

an individual of the opposite gender,' a 'presumption arises that the harassment is "because of" the victim's gender' " (quoting Judge Niemeyer's concurrence in *Hopkins v. Baltimore Gas & Elec. Co.*, 77 F.3d 745, 752 (4th Cir.), cert. denied, 117 S. Ct. 70 (1996), but "When a man harasses a man, or a woman harasses a woman, it is not reasonable to infer that the harassment was 'because of such individual's ... sex.' "

2. Amicus respectfully disagrees with the rationale of *Doe* by *Doe v. City of Belleville*, 119 F.3d 563, 576 (7th Cir. 1997), insofar as it suggests that "male on male" hostile environment harassment necessarily is "because of" the victim's sex whenever it "revolve[s] around his [or her] gender and specifically allude[s] to sexual conduct." The court's premise that any workplace harassment that an employee experiences "as a man [or as a woman]," amounts to harassment "because of" the victim's gender, id. at 578, is a classic non sequitur. Contrary to the court's assertion, "why the harassment was perpetrated (sexual interest? misogyny? personal vendetta? misguided humor? boredom?)" is not "beside the point." Id. It is the point. The court's declaration that "the harasser's motives are irrelevant" in this situation, id. at 579, effectively reads out of Title VII the requirement that a person claiming sexual harassment must show that the conduct was "because of" his or her sex.

POSTSCRIPT

Should Title VII Apply to Sexual Harassment Between Individuals of the Same Sex?

Title VII's provision for sexual harassment covers unwanted sexual behavior because of the harassed's *sex*. Is there a distinction between "sex" and "sexual" when determining whether or not a sexual harassment case is actionable under Title VII? One court has reasoned that the distinction makes little difference when dealing with opposite-sex harassment. In cases of opposite-sex harassment, "sex" and "sexual" are treated synonymously. If a man makes sexual advances to a woman, it is presumed that he is doing so specifically because she is a woman. But, some argue, in same-sex harassment, the distinction between "sex" and "sexual" becomes very important. While in opposite-sex harassment cases, details of the sexual content of conduct is enough proof of sexual harassment; in same-sex harassment cases, the courts require additional proof that the harasser acted "because of" the recipient's sex and not for other reasons, such as sexual orientation.

The logic of this argument has been charged as heterosexist in that it seems to assume that only homosexuals have a sexual orientation. Should we more carefully question whether or not it is a given in opposite-sex harassment cases that male-to-female (or female-to-male) harassment is always because of sex? Isn't it possible that in many opposite-sex harassment cases the harassment is as much because of sexual orientation as sex? Such logic also conflates sex and sexual orientation. Can sex and sexual orientation be distinguished in cases of sexual harassment? What if sex and sexual orientation motivate the harassment? Should sexual orientation become relevant to all sexual harassment cases to determine if the harassment was "because of sex," or should it be universally irrelevant?

Suggested Readings

C. R. Calleros, "The Meaning of 'Sex': Homosexual and Bisexual Harassment Under Title VII," *Vermont Law Review* (1995).

E. P. Johnson and M. M. Puchades, "Same Gender Sexual Harassment: But Is It Discrimination Based on Sex?" *Florida Bar Journal* (1995).

E. L. Perry, J. M. Schmidtke, and C. T. Kulik, "Propensity to Sexually Harass: An Exploration of Gender Differences," *Sex Roles* (1998).

ISSUE 9

Is Female Circumcision Universally Wrong?

YES: Loretta M. Kopelman, from "Female Circumcision/Genital Mutilation and Ethical Relativism," *Second Opinion* (October 1994)

NO: Stanlie M. James, from "Shades of Othering: Reflections on Female Circumcision/Genital Mutilation," *Signs: Journal of Women in Culture and Society* (Summer 1998)

ISSUE SUMMARY

YES: Professor of medical humanities Loretta M. Kopelman argues that all forms of female genital mutilation (FGM) should be eliminated. She concludes that given the serious health and cultural consequences, such a moral absolute is justified.

NO: Stanlie M. James, an Afro-American studies and women's studies scholar, asserts that a universal condemnation of female circumcision/genital mutilation is a form of "arrogant perception." She urges that rather than treating individuals in cultures embodying such traditions as oppressed "others," we need to carefully study the nuanced complexities of cultures.

The terms *female circumcision* and *female genital mutilation* (FGM) encompass three main categories of procedures that take place in a variety of countries and in a variety of circumstances: (1) "Sunna" (Arabic meaning "tradition") circumcision involves the removal of the prepuce and/or the top of the clitoris; (2) clitoridectomy (or excision) involves the removal of the entire clitoris (prepuce and glans) and removal of the labia minora; and (3) infibulation (or pharaonic circumcision) entails the removal of the clitoris and the labia (majora and minora), scraping the sides of the vulva, and joining the scraped vulva across the vagina by thorns or sewing with catgut or thread. A small opening is kept to allow urine and menstrual blood to pass through. On her wedding night, the infibulated woman is cut open (usually by the husband) to allow intercourse and sewn closed again (reinfibulated) at a later point to secure fidelity to the husband.

Female genital surgery (FGS) is practiced in more than 40 countries, including many African and some Asian societies. Estimates from the World Health Organization indicate that the practice of FGS increased in the 1990s. Increasingly, immigrant communities in Western countries (Europe, Australia, United States, and Canada) practice FGS. The type of FGS and the age at which the practice is done varies across countries and regions, ranging from birth to early adulthood. The targeted age varies by the cultural meaning of the ritual. For example, if FGS is thought of as a rite of passage into adult womanhood, FGS is done at the age of 14 or 15. If FGS is done to control female sexuality, the procedure is performed at age 7 or 8. FGS has a disproportionate impact on girls of color. Mothers, grandmothers, and other female kin typically control FGS. Women who are not medically trained usually perform the procedures.

There has been heated debate about FGS as being in violation of universal human rights. Are there certain fundamental, inviolable human rights that transcend all cultural boundaries? Cultural universalists argue *yes*. But cultural relativists respond *no*, arguing that Western liberal individualism has biased the delineation of human rights, and thus current delineations of human rights cannot be seen as universal but as Western impositions on non-Westerners. Cultural relativists also maintain that scholars' prioritization of human rights differs in Western and non-Western societies, whereby Westerners value civil and political rights over social and cultural rights; non-Westerners tend to do the opposite. Universalists retort that relativists' toleration of FGS and other harmful cultural practices perpetuates the violation of human rights and reinforces the subjugation of women to the interests of their larger sociocultural group.

On the question of justified reaction to FGS, the universalist position has largely prevailed. Many legal and nonlegal strides have been made in the international campaign against FGS, including the passage of the Female Genital Mutilation Act into U.S. law in 1996. But now the question has shifted from whether or not FGS is a human rights violation to how FGS can be eradicated, effecting lasting social change. Some argue that relativists' sensitivity to the cultural context may be more effective in bringing about change *from within,* since culture itself is the most formidable obstacle. Universalist critics argue that assertive condemnation is necessary to convey the moral imperative of the eradication of FGS; anything short of this stance may be counterproductive. In the following selections, Loretta M. Kopelman represents the universalist stance, and Stanlie M. James advocates a cultural relativist position on bringing about the eradication of FGS. As you read these selections, consider with which position you are most comfortable and why.

Loretta M. Kopelman

 **YES**

Female Circumcision/Genital Mutilation and Ethical Relativism

Reasons Given for Female Circumcision/Genital Mutilation

According to four independent series of studies conducted by investigators from countries where female circumcision is widely practiced (El Dareer 1982; Ntiri 1993; Koso-Thomas 1987; Abdalla 1982), the primary reasons given for performing this ritual surgery are that it (1) meets a religious requirement, (2) preserves group identity, (3) helps to maintain cleanliness and health, (4) preserves virginity and family honor and prevents immorality, and (5) furthers marriage goals including greater sexual pleasure for men.

El Dareer conducted her studies in the Sudan, Dr. Olayinka Koso-Thomas in and around Sierra Leone, and Raquiya Haji Dualeh Abdalla and Daphne Williams Ntiri in Somalia. They argue that the reasons for continuing this practice in their respective countries float on a sea of false beliefs, beliefs that thrive because of a lack of education and open discussion about reproduction and sexuality. Insofar as intercultural methods for evaluating factual and logical statements exist, people from other cultures should at least be able to understand these inconsistencies or mistaken factual beliefs and use them as a basis for making some judgments having intercultural moral authority.

First, according to these studies the main reason given for performing female circumcision/genital mutilation is that it is regarded as a religious requirement. Most of the people practicing this ritual are Muslims, but it is not a practice required by the Koran (El Dareer 1982; Ntiri 1993). El Dareer writes: "Circumcision of women is not explicitly enjoined in the Koran, but there are two implicit sayings of the Prophet Mohammed: 'Circumcision is an ordinance in men and an embellishment in women' and, reportedly Mohammed said to Om Attiya, a woman who circumcised girls in El Medina, 'Do not go deep. It is more illuminating to the face and more enjoyable to the husband.' Another version says, 'Reduce but do not destroy. This is enjoyable to the woman and preferable to the man.' But there is nothing in the Koran to suggest that the Prophet commanded that women be circumcised. He advised that it was

From Loretta M. Kopelman, "Female Circumcision/Genital Mutilation and Ethical Relativism," *Second Opinion*, vol. 20, no. 2 (October 1994). Copyright © 1994 by The Park Ridge Center for the Study of Health, Faith, and Ethics, 211 E. Ontario, Suite 800, Chicago, IL 60611. Reprinted by permission. Notes omitted.

174

important to both sexes that very little should be taken" (1982:72). Female circumcision/genital mutilation, moreover, is not practiced in the spiritual center of Islam, Saudi Arabia (Calder et al. 1993). Another reason for questioning this as a Muslim practice is that clitoridectomy and infibulation predate Islam, going back to the time of the pharaohs (Abdalla 1982; El Dareer 1992).

Second, many argue that the practice helps to preserve group identity. When Christian colonialists in Kenya introduced laws opposing the practice of female circumcision in the 1930s, African leader Kenyatta expressed a view still popular today: "This operation is still regarded as the very essence of an institution which has enormous educational, social, moral and religious implications, quite apart from the operation itself. For the present, it is impossible for a member of the [Kikuyu] tribe to imagine an initiation without clitoridectomy ... the abolition of IRUA [the ritual operation] will destroy the tribal symbol which identifies the age group and prevent the Kikuyu from perpetuating that spirit of collectivism and national solidarity which they have been able to maintain from time immemorial" (Scheper-Hughes 1991:27). In addition, the practice is of social and economic importance to older women who are paid for performing the rituals (El Dareer 1982; Koso-Thomas 1987; Abdalla 1982; Ginsberg 1991).

Drs. Koso-Thomas, El Dareer, and Abdalla agree that people in these countries support female circumcision as a good practice, but only because they do not understand that it is a leading cause of sickness or even death for girls, mothers, and infants, and a major cause of infertility, infection, and maternal-fetal and marital complications. They conclude that these facts are not confronted because these societies do not speak openly of such matters. Abdalla writes, "There is no longer any reason, given the present state of progress in science, to tolerate confusion and ignorance about reproduction and women's sexuality" (1982:2). Female circumcision/genital mutilation is intended to honor women as male circumcision honors men, and members of cultures where the surgery is practiced are shocked by the analogy of clitoridectomy to removal of the penis (El Dareer 1982).

Third, the belief that the practice advances health and hygiene is incompatible with stable data from surveys done in these cultures, where female circumcision/genital mutilation has been linked to mortality or morbidity such as shock, infertility, infections, incontinence, maternal-fetal complications, and protracted labor. The tiny hole generally left for blood and urine to pass is a constant source of infection (El Dareer 1982; Koso-Thomas 1987; Abdalla 1982; Calder et al. 1993; Ntiri 1993). Koso-Thomas writes, "As for cleanliness, the presence of these scars prevents urine and menstrual flow escaping by the normal channels. This may lead to acute retention of urine and menstrual flow, and to a condition known as hematocolpos, which is highly detrimental to the health of the girl or woman concerned and causes odors more offensive than any that can occur through the natural secretions" (Koso-Thomas 1987:10). Investigators completing a recent study wrote: "The risk of medical complications after female circumcision is very high as revealed by the present study [of 290 Somali women, conducted in the capital of Mogadishu]. Complications which cause the death of the young girls must be a common occurrence especially in the rural areas.... Dribbling urine incontinence, painful menstruations, hematocolpos and painful intercourse are facts that Somali women have to live with—facts that strongly motivate attempts to change the practice of female circumcision" (Dirie and Lindmark 1992:482).

Fourth, investigators found that circumcision is thought necessary in these cultures to preserve virginity and family honor and to prevent immorality. Type 3 circumcision [in which the clitoris, labia minora, and parts of the labia majora are removed, also called infibulation] is used to keep women from having sexual intercourse before marriage and conceiving illegitimate children. In addition, many believe that Types 2 [in which the clitoris and most or all of the labia minora are removed, also called intermediary] and 3 circumcision must be done because uncircumcised women have excessive and uncontrollable sexual drives. El Dareer, however, believes that this view is not consistently held—that women in the Sudan are respected and that Sudanese men would be shocked to apply this sometimes-held cultural view to members of their own families. This reason also seems incompatible with the general view, which investigators found was held by both men and women in these cultures, that sex cannot be pleasant for women (El Dareer 1982; Koso-Thomas 1987; Abdalla 1982). In addition, female circumcision/genital mutilation offers no foolproof way to promote chastity and can even lead to promiscuity because it does not diminish desire or libido even where it makes orgasms impossible (El Dareer 1982). Some women continually seek experiences with new sexual partners because they are left unsatisfied in their sexual encounters (Koso-Thomas 1987). Moreover, some pretend to be virgins by getting stitched up tightly again (El Dareer 1982).

Fifth, interviewers found that people practicing female circumcision/ genital mutilation believe that it furthers marriage goals, including greater sexual pleasure for men. To survive economically, women in these cultures must marry, and they will not be acceptable marriage partners unless they have undergone this ritual surgery (Abdalla 1982; Ntiri 1993). It is a curse, for example, to say that someone is the child of an uncircumcised woman (Koso-Thomas 1987). The widely held belief that infibulation enhances women's beauty and men's sexual pleasure makes it difficult for women who wish to marry to resist this practice (Koso-Thomas 1987; El Dareer 1992). Some men from these cultures, however, report that they enjoy sex more with uncircumcised women (Koso-Thomas 1987). Furthermore, female circumcision/genital mutilation is inconsistent with the established goals of some of these cultures because it is a leading cause of disability and contributes to the high mortality rate among mothers, fetuses, and children. Far from promoting the goals of marriage, it causes difficulty in consummating marriage, infertility, prolonged and obstructed labor, and morbidity and mortality.

Criticisms of Ethical Relativism

Examination of the debate concerning female circumcision suggests several conclusions about the extent to which people from outside a culture can understand or contribute to moral debates within it in a way that has moral force.

First, the fact that a culture's moral and religious views are often intertwined with beliefs that are open to rational and empirical evaluation can be a basis of cross-cultural examination and intercultural moral criticism (Bambrough 1979). Defenders of female circumcision/genital mutilation do not claim that this practice is a moral or religious requirement and end the discussion; they are willing to give and defend reasons for their views. For example, advocates of female circumcision/genital mutilation claim that it benefits women's health and well-being. Such claims are open to cross-cultural examination because information is available to determine whether the practice promotes health or causes morbidity or mortality. Beliefs that the practice enhances fertility and promotes health, that women cannot have orgasms, and that allowing the baby's head to touch the clitoris during delivery causes death to the baby are incompatible with stable medical data (Koso-Thomas 1987). Thus an opening is allowed for genuine cross-cultural discussion or criticism of the practice.

Some claims about female circumcision/genital mutilation, however, are not as easily open to cross-cultural understanding. For example, cultures practicing the Type 3 surgery, infibulation, believe that it makes women more beautiful. For those who are not from these cultures, this belief is difficult to understand, especially when surveys show that many women in these cultures, when interviewed, attribute to infibulation their keloid scars, urine retention, pelvic infections, puerperal sepsis, and obstetrical problems (Ntiri 1993; Abdalla 1982). Koso-Thomas writes: "None of the reasons put forward in favor of circumcision have any real scientific or logical basis. It is surprising that aesthetics and the maintenance of cleanliness are advanced as grounds for female circumcision. The scars could hardly be thought of as contributing to beauty. The hardened scar and stump usually seen where the clitoris should be, or in the case of the infibulated vulva, taut skin with an ugly long scar down the middle, present a horrifying picture" (Koso-Thomas 1987:10). Thus not everyone in these cultures believes that these rituals enhance beauty; some find such claims difficult to understand.

Second, the debate over female circumcision/genital mutilation illustrates another difficulty for defenders of this version of ethical relativism concerning the problem of differentiating cultures. People who brought the practice of female circumcision/genital mutilation with them when they moved to another nation still claim to be a distinct cultural group. Some who moved to Britain, for example, resent the interference in their culture represented by laws that condemn the practice as child abuse (Thompson 1989). If ethical relativists are to appeal to cultural approval in making the final determination of what is good or bad, right or wrong, they must tell us how to distinguish one culture from another.

How exactly do we count or separate cultures? A society is not a nation-state, because some social groups have distinctive identities within nations. If we do not define societies as nations, however, how do we distinguish among cultural groups, for example, well enough to say that an action is child abuse in one culture but not in another? Subcultures in nations typically overlap and have many variations. Even if we could count cultural groups well enough to say exactly how to distinguish one culture from another, how and when would this be relevant? How big or old or vital must a culture, subculture, group, or cult be in order to be recognized as a society whose moral distinctions are self-contained and self-justifying?

A related problem is that there can be passionate disagreement, ambivalence, or rapid changes within a culture or group over what is approved or disapproved. According to ethical relativism, where there is significant disagreement within a culture there is no way to determine what is right or wrong. But what disagreement is significant? As we saw, some people in these cultures, often those with higher education, strongly disapprove of female circumcision/ genital mutilation and work to stop it (El Dareer 1982; Koso-Thomas 1987; Ntiri 1993; Dirie and Lindmark 1992; Abdalla 1982). Are they in the same culture as their friends and relatives who approve of these rituals? It seems more accurate to say that people may belong to various groups that overlap and have many variations. This description, however, makes it difficult for ethical relativism to be regarded as a helpful theory for determining what is right or wrong. To say that something is right when it has cultural approval is useless if we cannot identify the relevant culture. Moreover, even where people agree about the rightness of certain practices, such as these rituals, they can sometimes be inconsistent. For example, in reviewing reasons given within cultures where female circumcision/genital mutilation is practiced, we saw that there was some inconsistency concerning whether women needed this surgery to control their sexual appetites, to make them more beautiful, or to prevent morbidity or mortality. Ethical relativists thus have extraordinary problems offering a useful account of what counts as a culture and establishes cultural approval or disapproval.

Third, despite some clear disagreement such as that over the rightness of female circumcision/genital mutilation, people from different parts of the world share common goals like the desirability of promoting people's health, happiness, opportunities, and cooperation, and the wisdom of stopping war, pollution, oppression, torture, and exploitation. These common goals make us a world community, and using shared methods of reasoning and evaluation, we can discuss how they are understood or how well they are implemented in different parts of our world community. We can use these shared goals to assess whether female circumcision/genital mutilation is more like respect or oppression, more like enhancement or diminishment of opportunities, or more like pleasure or torture. While there are, of course, genuine differences between citizens of the world, it is difficult to comprehend how they could be identified unless we could pick them out against a background of our similarities. Highlighting our differences, however useful for some purposes, should not eclipse the truth that we share many goals and values and are similar enough that we can assess each other's views as rational beings in a way that has moral force. Another way to express this is to say that we should recognize universal human rights or be respectful of each other as persons capable of reasoned discourse.

Fourth, this version of ethical relativism, if consistently held, leads to the abhorrent conclusion that we cannot make intercultural judgements with moral force about societies that start wars, practice torture, or exploit and oppress other groups; as long as these activities are approved in the society that does them, they are allegedly right. Yet the world community believed that it was making a cross-cultural judgment with moral force when it criticized the Communist Chinese government for crushing a pro-democracy student protest rally, the South Africans for upholding apartheid, the Soviets for using psychiatry to suppress dissent, and the Bosnian Serbs for carrying out the siege of Sarajevo. And the judgment was expressed without anyone's ascertaining whether the respective actions had widespread approval in those countries. In each case, representatives from the criticized society usually said something like, "You don't understand why this is morally justified in our culture even if it would not be in your society." If ethical relativism were convincing, these responses ought to be as well.

Relativists who want to defend sound social cross-cultural and moral judgments about the value of freedom and human rights in other cultures seem to have two choices. On the one hand, if they agree that some cross-cultural norms have moral authority, they should also agree that some intercultural judgments about female circumcision/genital mutilation may have moral authority. Some relativists take this route (see, for example, Sherwin 1992), thereby abandoning the version of ethical relativism being criticized herein. On the other hand, if they defend this version of ethical relativism yet make cross-cultural moral judgments about the importance of values like tolerance, group benefit, and the survival of cultures, they will have to admit to an inconsistency in their arguments. For example, anthropologist Scheper-Hughes (1991) advocates tolerance of other cultural value systems; she fails to see that she is saying that tolerance between cultures is right and that this is a cross-cultural moral judgment using a moral norm (tolerance). Similarly, relativists who say it is wrong to eliminate rituals that give meaning to other cultures are also inconsistent in making a judgment that presumes to have genuine cross-cultural moral authority. Even the sayings sometimes used by defenders of ethical relativism—such as "When in Rome do as the Romans" (Scheper-Hughes 1991)—mean it is morally permissible to adopt all the cultural norms in operation wherever one finds oneself. Thus it is not consistent for defenders of this version of ethical relativism to make intercultural moral judgments about tolerance, group benefit, intersocietal respect, or cultural diversity.

The burden of proof, then, is upon defenders of this version of ethical relativism to show why we cannot do something we think we sometimes do very well, namely, engage in intercultural moral discussion, cooperation, or criticism and give support to people whose welfare or rights are in jeopardy in other cultures. In addition, defenders of ethical relativism need to explain how we can justify the actions of international professional societies that take moral stands in adopting policy. For example, international groups may take moral stands that advocate fighting pandemics, stopping wars, halting oppression, promoting health education, or eliminating poverty, and they seem to have moral authority in some cases. Some might respond that our professional groups are themselves cultures of a sort. But this response raises the already discussed problem of how to individuate a culture or society....

Comment

We have sufficient reason, therefore, to conclude that these rituals of female circumcision/genital mutilation are wrong. For me to say they are wrong does not mean that they are disapproved by most people in my culture but wrong for reasons similar to those given by activists within these cultures who are working to stop these practices. They are wrong because the usual forms of the surgery deny women orgasms and because they cause medical complications and even death. It is one thing to say that these practices are wrong and that activists should be supported in their efforts to stop them; it is another matter to determine how to do this effectively. All agree that education may be the most important means to stop these practices. Some activists in these cultures want an immediate ban (Abdalla 1982). Other activists in these cultures encourage Type 1 circumcision (pricking or removing the clitoral hood) in order to "wean" people away from Types 2 and 3 by substitution. Type 1 has the least association with morbidity or mortality and, if there are no complications, does not preclude sexual orgasms in later life. The chance of success through this tactic is more promising and realistic, they hold, than what an outright ban would achieve; and people could continue many of their traditions and rituals of welcome without causing so much harm (El Dareer 1982). Other activists in these countries, such as Raquiya Abdalla, object to equating Type 1 circumcision in the female with male circumcision: "To me and to many others, the aim and results of any form of circumcision of women are quite different from those applying to the circumcision of men" (1982:8). Because of the hazards of even Type 1 circumcision, especially for infants, I agree with the World Health Organization and the American Medical Association that it would be best to stop all forms of ritual genital surgery on women. Bans have proven ineffective: this still-popular practice has been illegal in most countries for many years (Rushwan 1990; Ntiri 1993; El Dareer 1982). Other proposals by activists focus on education, fines, and carefully crafted legislation (El Dareer 1982; Abdalla 1982; Ozumba 1992; Dirie and Lindmark 1992; WHO 1992).

The critique of the reasons given to support female circumcision/genital mutilation in cultures where it is practiced shows us how to enter discussions, disputes, or assessments in ways that can have moral authority. We share common needs, goals, and methods of reasoning and evaluation. Together they enable us to evaluate many claims across cultures and sometimes to regard ourselves as part of a world community with interests in promoting people's health, happiness, empathy, and opportunities as well as desires to stop war, torture, pandemics, pollution, oppression, and injustice. Thus, ethical relativism—the view that to say something is right means it has cultural approval and to say it is wrong means it has cultural disapproval—is implausible as a useful theory, definition, or account of the meaning of moral judgments. The burden of proof therefore falls upon upholders of this version of ethical relativism to show why criticisms of other cultures always lack moral authority. Although many values are culturally determined and we should not impose moral judgments across cultures hastily, we sometimes know enough to condemn practices approved in other cultures. For example, we can understand enough of the debate about female circumcision/genital mutilation to draw some conclusions: it is wrong, oppressive, and not a voluntary practice in the sense that the people doing it comprehend information relevant to their decision. Moreover, it is a ritual, however well-meant, that violates justifiable and universal human rights or values supported in the human community, and we should promote international moral support for advocates working to stop the practice wherever it is carried out.

References

Abdalla, Raquiya H. D. 1982. Sisters in Affliction: Circumcision and Infibulation of Women in Africa. London: Zed Press.

Bambrough, Renford. 1979. Moral Skepticism and Moral Knowledge. London: Routledge and Kegan Paul.

Calder, Barbara L., Yvonne M. Brown, and Donna I. Rac. 1993. "Female Circumcision/Genital Mutilation: Culturally Sensitive Care." Health Care for Women International 14, no. 3 (May–June): 227–38.

Dirie, M. A., and G. Lindmark. 1992. "The Risk of Medical Complication after Female Circumcision." East African Medical Journal 69, no. 9 (September): 479–82.

El Dareer, Asma. 1982. Woman, Why Do You Weep? Circumcision and Its Consequences. London: Zed Press.

Ginsberg, Faye. 1991. "What Do Women Want?: Feminist Anthropology Confronts Clitoridectomy." Medical Anthropology Quarterly 5, no. 1 (March): 17–19.

Koso-Thomas, Olayinka. 1987. The Circumcision of Women. London: Zed Press.

Ntiri, Daphne Williams. 1993. "Circumcision and Health among Rural Women of Southern Somalia as Part of a Family Life Survey." Health Care for Women International 14, no. 3 (May–June): 215–16.

Ozumba, B. C. 1992. "Acquired Gynetresia in Eastern Nigeria." International Journal of Gynaecology and Obstetrics 37, no. 2. 105–9.

Rushwan, Hamid. 1990. "Female Circumcision." World Health, April–May, 24–25.

Scheper-Hughes, Nancy. 1991. "Virgin Territory: The Male Discovery of the Clitoris." Medical Anthropology Quarterly 5, no. 1 (March): 25–28.

Sherwin, Susan. 1992. No Longer Patient: Feminist Ethics and Health Care. Philadelphia: Temple University Press.

Thompson, June. 1989. "Torture by Tradition." Nursing Times 85, no. 15: 17–18.

World Health Organization. 1992. International Journal of Gynaecology and Obstetrics 37, no. 2: 149.

Stanlie M. James

 **NO**

Shades of Othering: Reflections on Female Circumcision/Genital Mutilation

Alice Walker has brought her considerable talent and resources to bear on the critical problem of female circumcision/genital mutilation by retrieving the character Tashi from the margins of *The Color Purple* (1982) and centralizing her story in the novel *Possessing the Secret of Joy* (1992). Through Tashi's fictional story, along with the documentary film and accompanying text *Warrior Marks* (Walker and Parmar 1993a, 1993b), Walker has managed to focus attention on this issue in ways that have eluded human rights activists who have toiled unheralded for years to effect change. In fact, Walker's successful efforts to generate national attention and discussion in the United States were cause for somber rejoicing and hope, although a variety of representatives from the mainstream media felt compelled to express horror and dismay that such "savage" practices continued to exist in those "exotic" places. Although I am delighted that my "shero" Alice Walker has become so publicly supportive of ongoing struggles to eradicate these harmful traditional practices, I am uneasy with the manner in which she has chosen to champion such a worthy cause.

Early in the film and companion text *Warrior Marks*, Walker recounts the unfortunate story of how her brother shot and blinded her in one eye; she rightly characterizes it as a "patriarchal wound." She suggests that her injury is analogous to the female circumcision/genital mutilation millions of women have experienced over thousands of years and that this "visual mutilation" has helped her to "see" more clearly the subject of genital mutilation (Walker and Parmar 1993a, 18; 1993b). I find the analogy drawn between her personal misfortune and pervasive traditions of circumcision/mutilation to be particularly problematic. While little boys with BB guns are emblematic of violent patriarchal societies, the logic of the analogy suggests that boys shooting and blinding their sisters is a traditional ceremonial practice sanctioned by this society in much the same fashion as female circumcision is in other societies. Although Walker is certainly imbued with a sympathetic perspective, centering her own story within this international struggle for women's human rights seems to have the unintentional consequence of "othering" or marginalizing the very people she wishes her audience to support.

Walker compiled an impressive array of interviews for *Warrior Marks*, including women who have been circumcised/mutilated, the mother of a girl who will undergo the procedure, and activists who are struggling to eradicate these practices. Curiously, these interviews are interspersed with a dancer's most erotic depiction of the horrors of circumcision. One stunning interview was with a weeping young woman, Aminata Diop, who had refused to undergo circumcision/mutilation and was seeking sanctuary in Europe. She had been disowned by her parents, and her father had divorced her mother and thrown her into the street for failing to control her daughter's behavior, thereby bringing shame upon him. Aminata's fiancé had broken their engagement. In another interview, Walker spoke with a woman who had traumatic memories of her own experience but felt compelled, albeit regretfully, to continue the tradition with her own daughter. Outraged and censorious, Walker interviewed circumcisers in a manner that failed to articulate or even recognize that such traditional practices have provided some women with opportunities to attain respect and income in societies where there are often precious few avenues available to women to attain such critically limited resources.

...[Walker] challenges a deeply entrenched and difficult practice that is detrimental to the health and well-being of women and girls, but she does so in a way that invites the characterization of African women as victims without agency. Indeed, Walker seems "possessed" of the pernicious notion that she can and must rescue those unfortunate women from themselves, from their ignorance, and from their patriarchal traditions.

Patricia Stamp has argued that third world women have often been treated as "passive targets of oppressive practices and discriminatory structures," a conceptualization that "colludes with sexist ideologies that construct women as naturally inferior, passive and consigned to a private apolitical world" (1991, 845). Privileged Western women (and I must include myself at least at the margin of this particular category) must be mindful of the sin that Marilyn Frye has termed "arrogant perception" (1983) and that Isabelle R. Gunning describes as the view that one is the center of the universe, thus distancing herself from the "other" (1992).

In "The Discourse of the Veil at the Turn of Two Centuries" (1993), Leila Ahmed argues that nascent Western feminist stirrings were deflected from Western conditions to focus on the veil as the ultimate symbol of Islamic oppression of women. This redirected emphasis communicates too readily that oppression occurs only "elsewhere" and that "native" women can be rescued by encouraging them to abandon their own religion, customs, and culture and to adopt those of the West. Ultimately this form of arrogant perception is supportive of colonialism and its institutions (Ahmed 1993).

Arrogant perception is apparent in the West's horrified, condemnatory responses to practices such as the Indian tradition of sati, Chinese foot binding, and Arab customs of veiling and purdah. It is apparent in Western facile insensitivity to the unfamiliar. Arrogant perception nourishes ethnocentrism even as it obscures visions of the multifaceted complexity of those characterized as oppressed "others," as well as their inter- and intrarelationships within and between societies.

This [selection] emerges from my concern about whether others outside the culture can appropriately engage in nonimperialist critique of such unfamiliar traditions. Can outrage be legitimately expressed in a manner that does not other or alienate the very people within cultures who are engaged in efforts to promote change? I am convinced that the debates swirling around female circumcision/female genital mutilation can and must move beyond troubling stances of arrogant perception. I argue that such debates must be restructured in ways that are neither condemnatory nor demeaning but that foster perceptions illuminated by careful study of the nuanced complexities of cultures. To that end, this [selection] explores the literature for approaches that will inform efforts to achieve perceptual integrity and that can in turn be used to mount effective challenges that would ultimately result in the eradication of FGM [female genital mutilation].

...Walker presents her audience with a variety of women's voices that are divorced from the specificity of cultural context. The superficiality of her insights into African social, political, and economic institutions obscures the rich heritage of its many cultures and societies, and that in turn suggests an (unintentional) insensitivity to the complexities of the lives of African women. This crucial deficiency leads to the regrettable conclusion that *Warrior Marks* is contaminated by a subtle form of cultural imperialism. This conclusion is especially disappointing because Walker's womanist writings are typically characterized by sophisticated analyses of the concept of multiple oppressions. For example, her haunting and complex short story "Advancing Luna—and Ida B. Wells" exhibits subtly nuanced insights into the impact of race, class, and gender on rape as it is played out within the context of African American communities and the broader American society (1981).

Evading the dubious position of arrogant perceiver requires the capacity to conceptualize culture as complex, competing, dynamic, and historicized. Rigorous interrogation of the particulars of culture enables the development of sophisticated contextualized analyses while allowing for critique with careful specificity. The writings of Gunning (1992), Robyn Cerny Smith (1992), and Jean-Claude Muller (1993) provide intriguing examples of efforts to avoid the limitations of arrogant perception while enhancing understanding of this critical issue.

In her article "Arrogant Perception, World Traveling and Multicultural Feminism: The Case of Female Genital Surgeries" (1992), Gunning probes female circumcision/genital mutilation. In an exercise of sensitivity and conciliation, Gunning chooses to refer to such practices as "genital surgeries" and characterizes them as "culturally challenging," which she defines as any practice that someone outside a particular culture would view as negative largely because she or he is culturally unfamiliar with the custom (191). Gunning proposes to confront these culturally challenging practices by retrieving the obscure history of genital surgeries in Western societies and exploring similarities and interconnections across boundaries of nationality.

Citing Ben Barker-Benfield's article "Sexual Surgeries in Late Nineteenth Century America" (1975), Gunning alerts readers to the existence of clitoridectomies and other related surgeries in Western societies. Immediately following the Civil War, white American men were increasingly concerned about the rise of "hysteria" or "madness" among women and felt that this could be traced to their sexuality. These "disorderly women" were identified as women's rightists, bloomer wearers, midwives, and anyone who had a suspected aversion to men or who sought to rival men in manly sports and occupations. Within this context, gynecology, a new medical specialty, was developed to "cure" women's problems. Because women's "mental disorders" were equated with their sexual organs, one "cure" adopted in the late 1860s was clitoridectomy.

Although it would be easy to assume that this was "simply" an issue of gender oppression in the United States, Gunning's careful interrogation of the practice reveals the complexities of multiple oppression. Evidence suggests that during the 1840s clitoridectomies and other related forms of surgery were tested by a Dr. Sims on enslaved women borrowed from their masters or purchased for purposes of experimentation. Later, during the 1850s, destitute white immigrant women in New York's Woman's Hospital were also subjected to experimentation. Once he had "perfected" his methods, Dr. Sims employed these surgeries in his private practice to cure white middle- and upper-class women whose male guardians (i.e., fathers and husbands) could afford the fees (Barker-Benfield 1975, 288–89; Gunning 1992, 205–9; see also Slack 1988).

Gunning's strategy of moving beyond stances of arrogant perception emerges from her efforts to uncover interconnecting similarities across boundaries of nationality and culture. She argues that becoming familiar with these hitherto obscured aspects of Western history facilitates Westerners' ability to understand that although most of these specific practices have largely been discontinued, the attitudes and assumptions about gender roles that were used to justify the surgery remain largely in place within contemporary Western society.

In "Female Circumcision: Bringing Women's Perspectives into the International Debate," Robyn Cerny Smith (1992) examines prevalent anthropological arguments that defend such traditional practices as crucial to the continued survival of tribal groups as distinctive cultural entities. Noting that female circumcision has often been characterized by authorities as ritual, Smith explores the work of anthropologists such as Victor Turner (1967, 1969) and Clifford Geertz (1979) on rites of passage and ritual in order to explicate analytical frameworks that have often been employed to determine whether the practice was indeed central to a group's identity. Smith notes that on the basis of such analyses, ethnographies of the Kikuyu often support the notion that the practice of female circumcision that accompanies "the irua ceremony is crucial to the maintenance of the Kikuyu as a separate, distinct entity ... [and that] the ... tribe's distinct values and structure would probably disappear without the circumcision ceremony or age-sets" (1992, 2470). The nomadic Darod of Somalia, in contrast, base their practice of infibulation on their understanding of Islam and its emphasis on controlling female sexuality. Unlike the Kikuyu, female circumcision among the Darod is neither a rite of passage nor imbedded in ritual. Therefore, Smith argues, tribal unity cannot be dependent on female circumcision, but the practice "may contribute to the maintenance of a gender hierarchy, in which women are subordinate to men. It is not clear, however, that tribal identity would disintegrate in the absence of hierarchy in the long term" (2472).

Although Smith's review of this body of ethnographic literature is important, the significance of her work emerges from her willingness to explore feminism, postmodernism, and international human rights as alternative approaches to restructuring the debates surrounding female genital mutilation. She observes that feminist perspectives have managed to facilitate the understanding that in addition to maintaining tribal identity, female circumcision is employed to sustain male dominance and control female sexuality. At the same time, Smith reminds her readers that feminist theories "were [also] developed by Western white women and are therefore 'insufficiently attentive to ... cultural diversity, and they falsely universalize features of the theorist's own era, society, culture, class, sexual orientation, and ethnic, or racial group'" (2488). Smith restates Nancy Hartsock's important admonition to postmodernists who would criticize feminist theories while failing to replace them with theories "that will help oppressed and marginalized groups name their experiences and guide their actions in their fight against oppression" (2488).

Another alternative approach to restructuring the debates around FGM is international human rights law. Its purpose is to establish international standards of human rights and to obligate states to protect them.... The issue of human rights of women has recently achieved visibility within the international system....

Smith engages the struggle to move beyond arrogant perception by encouraging reliance on the voices of marginalized women and pursuit of redress within the international human rights system. Only when the experiences of these women become central to that discussion, she argues, will the debate be restructured in a manner that adequately expresses their oppression: "Perhaps if these women and girls have the power to name their true oppressions and experiences in the international community, they may be able to work together to reevaluate the traditions that silence them. Then they may choose which traditions truly are necessary for tribal unity from their point of view and reject those traditions that continue to oppress them" (1992, 2503).

The efforts of Gunning and Smith to restructure debates surrounding practices of female circumcision/genital mutilation resonate with cultural specificity and historicized voices of women within an international context....

Muller [examined] the circumcision practices of the Cameroonian Dii....

Dii practices of male circumcision and what Muller calls *female pseudoexcision* are designed to sustain patriarchy by producing (socially) gendered men and women. For men this goal is achieved through the removal of the foreskin. There is no corresponding practice of clitoridectomy because unlike other ethnic groups who believe that the clitoris is a male appendage that must be removed, the Dii believe that the very essence of femininity resides in the clitoris. According to Muller, the clitoris is perceived as an essential organ because it regulates sexual relations between men and women. Through the ceremony of pseudoexcision, a young girl is taught that she will feel no pain if she behaves appropriately but will suffer if she misbehaves. Muller's sources also stressed their belief that the clitoris reveals whether a woman behaves with dignity and in a feminine manner.

Muller notes that for divergent reasons a man must have his foreskin removed while a woman retains her clitoris as representations of the quintessence of masculinity and femininity. Both men and women must endure the unifying principles of pain and suffering that, according to Muller, serve to increase the masculinity in men while curbing the savage sexuality of women.

Some Western feminists have often understood female genital mutilation as a consequence of patriarchal dominance perpetrated by men on women. Muller's study indicates that mutilation is not confined to the female body, nor does it serve only to enforce patriarchal dominance. Thus, deceptively simple assumptions must be revisited and revised within the specificities of cultural context.

Cleanliness, aesthetics, hygiene, birth control, and fear that the "untrimmed" clitoris would grow down past a woman's knees are among the expressed reasons for practicing female circumcision. Transgressing geographical and cultural boundaries, the most frequently mentioned rationale for such traditional practices is the need to control women, especially their sexuality. Clearly, female circumcision must be recognized as a patriarchal practice embedded within the complexity of gender hierarchy. Muller's (perhaps unintentional) contribution to perceptions of the deeply entrenched and pervasive nature of patriarchy and gender hierarchy arises from his careful depiction of male circumcision among the Dii and the accompanying rite of passage (and the additional circumcision of the prospective leader). While other ethnographies (including Kenyatta 1965) have described male circumcision, Muller's work exposes a critical connection between male circumcision and female subordination through his exploration of the Dii conviction that an uncircumcised male would be unable to make his wife obey. Even the emphasis on equality between the sexes found in the jesting relationship could be viewed as a metaphorical safety valve designed to neutralize or institutionalize incipient challenges to male dominance. With the institution of these two distinctive characteristics, the Dii can afford to respect women's human right to bodily integrity because the maintenance of patriarchy, in their society, is not dependent on the mutilation of women. Rather, male privilege within this particular version of gender hierarchy is upheld by a tradition of penis mutilation.

Perceptions of patriarchy are richly informed by the specificity of Gunning's (1992) and Smith's (1992) treatments of FGM and are enhanced by Muller's (1993) examination of male circumcision practices. Alice Walker contributes a palpable sense of outrage to these discussions. While she enjoys a wide latitude for the expression of that outrage in the fictitious *Possessing the Secret of Joy* (1992), outrage almost obscures her laudable intentions of eradicating such practices in *Warrior Marks* (Walker and Parmar 1993a, 1993b). That is, her outrage provokes her to come dangerously close to demonizing women circumcisers, while characterizing African women as both bad mothers and child abusers. Such cultural insensitivity invites the animosity of many African women who have struggled so valiantly to bring about change and is viewed by some as cultural imperialism. Outrage may be necessary, but it is certainly not a sufficient condition for fostering perceptual integrity. In fact, one must take care to see that outrage does not support the arrogant perception deemed detrimental to the struggle for change.

The diversity of texts suggests that the task of achieving the necessary perceptual integrity so crucial not only to the elimination of FGM but to the struggles to eradicate patriarchy emerges from the creative synthesis of multiple approaches and strategies, including cognizance of similarities in historical traditions and boundary-transgressive interconnections. Perceptual integrity will also develop from attempts to listen carefully to the rarely heard voices of marginalized women, to interrogate cultural specificities with sensitivity, and to work to incorporate specific prohibitions against FGM in international human rights legislation. It may also be facilitated through the adoption of perspectives and strategies developing among black feminists.

Black feminisms have emerged from the margins of society and the academy as expressions of disaffection with common unilateral analytical frameworks of race-, gender-, and class-based discrimination. The failure of these analytical frameworks to capture the subtle complexities of experiences of oppression has served effectively to "other" black women. As a response, American black feminists have sought to place African American women at the center of analyses through the critical examination of their everyday lives.

Careful readings of African American women's histories reveal them to be political actors who have traditionally striven to forge what Chandra Mohanty (1991) refers to as "communities of resistance" in order to engage in profound struggles to eradicate oppressions and transform society. As active subjects who have transgressed arbitrary boundaries of objectification and victimology, African American women, when they have deemed it appropriate, have developed strategic alliances with other groups, including African American men, white women (sporadically), and other women of color who have had similar experiences of oppression. These alliances have been sensitive to political maneuverings designed to privilege certain groups or issues. Despite the fragility of such alliances, they represent critical efforts to transgress the boundaries of race, class, and gender and are instructive to the processes of developing sophisticated analyses of issues of multiple oppression. Lessons gleaned from this labor will not only enhance efforts to transcend the boundaries of nationality, ethnicity, and religion but will also facilitate our attempts to articulate the complexities of patriarchy.

Just as many African American theorists and activists continue to engage in analyzing the relations of gender, race, and class in order to resist and eradicate multiple oppressions, African women are likewise engaged in developing their own communities of resistance that have profound implications at both the material and ideological levels for the institutions of patriarchy. For example, Africa News Service (1997) reported that a growing number of rural Kenyan families are participating in an alternative rite *Ntanira na Mugumbo*, or "Circumcision Through Words." Rather than subjecting their daughters to the traditional rites of passage that include FGM, young candidates are spending a week in seclusion learning traditional teachings about their coming roles as women, parents, and adults in the community. They are also taught about personal health, hygiene, reproductive issues, communication skill, self-esteem, and how to deal with peer pressure. The week concludes with a community celebration of song, dancing, and feasting to affirm the girls and their new place in the community. Circumcision Through Words developed out of collaborations between rural families, Maendeleo ya Wanawake Organization, the Kenyan national women's group, and the international nongovernmental organization Program for Appropriate Technology in Health and received funding from several international donors including the Ford Foundation.

Unfortunately, as I have indicated, many of these struggles have been rendered invisible by unsympathetic, unconcerned, or ill-informed outsiders. As these stories are retrieved from the margins sometimes referred to as the third world, previously concealed domestic challenges to FGM and gender hierarchy at the level of individual households and within specific countries may be revealed. Knowledge of African women's agency, their varied and multiple challenges, will in turn inform conceptualizations of those broader, ongoing internal arguments over critical issues of cultural identity.

In the momentous struggle to move beyond arrogant perception and toward perceptual integrity, theorists and activists are challenged to understand the nuances of their own cultures even as they are becoming cognizant of the complexities and subtleties of other cultures. They must engage in multiple and multicultural dialogues in order to embrace ever more expansive roles as sensitive, knowledgeable, nonimperialist women who recognize that African and othered women around the world are making priorities among the hard choices as they design their own struggles. It is only after toiling to create the necessary profound insights into the interconnections of similarities and differences that feminists can begin the ultimate task of constructing the transformational, transnational consensus so critical to the dismantling of all aspects of multiple patriarchal oppressions including (but not limited to) female genital mutilation.

References

Africa News Service. 1997. "Alternative Rite to Female Circumcision Spreading in Kenya." November 19.

Ahmed, Leila. 1993. "The Discourse of the Veil at the Turn of Two Centuries." Paper presented at the University of Wisconsin—Madison, November 21.

Barker-Benfield, Ben. 1975. "Sexual Surgery in Late Nineteenth Century America." *International Journal of Health Services* 5(2):279–98.

Frye, Marilyn. 1983. "In and Out of Harm's Way." In her *The Politics of Reality: Essays in Feminist Theory,* 52–83. New York: Crossing.

Geertz, Clifford. 1979. "Religion as a Cultural System." In *Reader in Comparative Religion: Anthropological Approach,* ed. William A. Lessa and Evon Z. Vogt, 78–89. 4th ed. New York: Harper & Row.

Gunning, Isabelle R. 1992. "Arrogant Perception, World Traveling and Multicultural Feminism: The Case of Female Genital Surgeries." *Columbia Human Rights Law Review* 23(2):189–248.

Kenyatta, Jomo. 1965. *Facing Mount Kenya.* New York: Vintage.

Mohanty, Chandra Talpade. 1991. "Introduction: Cartographies of Struggle, Third World Women and the Politics of Feminism." In *Third World Women and the Politics of Feminism,* ed. Chandra Talpade Mohanty, Ann Russo, and Lourdes Torres, 1–47. Bloomington: Indiana University Press.

Muller, Jean-Claude. 1993. "Les deux fois circoncis et les presque excisees. Le cas des Dii de l'Adamaoua (Nord Cameroun)." *Cahiers d'Etudes africaines* 33(4):531–44.

Slack, Alison T. 1988. "Female Circumcision: A Critical Appraisal." *Human Rights Quarterly* 10:438–87.

Smith, Robyn Cerny. 1992. "Female Circumcision: Bringing Women's Perspectives into the International Debate." *Southern California Law Review* 65(5): 2449–2504.

Stamp, Patricia. 1991. "Burying Otiena: The Politics of Gender and Ethnicity in Kenya." *Signs* 16(4):808–45.

Turner, Victor. 1967. *The Forest of Symbols.* Ithaca, N.Y.: Cornell University Press.

———. 1969. *The Ritual Process: Structure and Anti Structure.* London: Routledge & Kegan Paul.

Walker, Alice. 1981. "Advancing Luna—and Ida B. Wells." In her *You Can't Keep a Good Woman Down,* 84–104. New York: Harcourt Brace Jovanovich.

———. 1982. *The Color Purple.* New York: Washington Square.

———. 1992. *Possessing the Secret of Joy.* New York: Harcourt Brace Jovanovich.

Walker, Alice, and Pratiba Parmar. 1993a. *Warrior Marks: Female Genital Mutilation and the Sexual Blinding of Women.* New York: Harcourt Brace.

———. 1993b. *Warrior Marks: Female Genital Mutilation and the Sexual Blinding of Women.* Color, 54 min. London: Hauer Rawlence Productions. Film.

POSTSCRIPT

Is Female Circumcision Universally Wrong?

W hen should a cultural practice that is a departure from established American culture be accepted or disallowed in the United States? Imagine you are a pediatrician and one of your new patients is a small female child whose family just immigrated to the United States from Northern Sudan, where FGS is very prevalent. Her mother asks you to perform FGS on the child. What would be your response? How far do U.S. principles of familial privacy and personal autonomy extend in such a situation? Should the parent's decision about her/his child be respected or rejected? How does this situation differ from the performance of surgical "correction" to intersexual infants and children? To what degree should the child's health and well-being and legal inability to consent be weighed in the decision?

Now imagine you are a gynecologist and an adult Sudanese woman of legal consenting age comes to you and asks to be reinfibulated. If the procedure to which she is consenting is prohibited under law, are we unconstitutionally limiting her personal autonomy? After all, Americans place high value on bodily autonomy and privacy.

Why has FGS been practiced for so long? What sociohistorical changes have made possible the recent campaigns against FGS? What are the major obstacles to the worldwide eradication of FGS?

Suggested Readings

C. L. Annas, "Irreversible Error: The Power and Prejudice of Female Genital Mutilation," *Contemporary Health Law and Policy* (1996).

S. D. Lane and R. A. Rubinstein, "Judging the Other: Responding to Traditional Female Genital Surgeries," *Hastings Center Report* (May/June 1996).

E. Sussman, "Contending With Culture: An Analysis of the Female Genital Mutilation Act of 1996," *Cornell International Law Journal* (1998).

A. Walker, *Possessing the Secret of Joy* (Harcourt Brace Jovanovich, 1992).

C. J. Walley, "Searching for 'Voices': Feminism, Anthropology, and the Global Debate Over Female Genital Operations," *Cultural Anthropology* (1997).

ISSUE 10

Can Women's Sexuality Be Free From Traditional Gender Constraints?

YES: Rebecca Walker, from "Lusting for Freedom," in Barbara Findlen, ed., *Listen Up: Voices From the Next Feminist Generation* (Seal Press, 1995)

NO: Athena Devlin, from "The Shame of Silence," in Amy Kesselman, Lily D. McNair, and Nancy Schniedewind, eds., *Women: Images and Realities: A Multicultural Anthology*, 2d ed. (Mayfield, 1999)

ISSUE SUMMARY

YES: Third-wave feminist and author Rebecca Walker describes her sexuality as free, pleasurable, and affirming.

NO: Author Athena Devlin recounts the devastating influences of a traditional sexual script on her sexuality.

Sexuality has been identified by feminists as a culturally important domain for gender relations and politics. In Victorian times, self-control, discipline, delayed gratification, self-sacrifice, and repression characterized sexuality. Religious authorities defined the moral boundaries of right and wrong sexual activities. Contemporary conservative religious perspectives continue to restrict sexuality to procreation in the family context. Women's individual pleasure, exploration, and sexual identity are seen as antithetical or even threatening to procreative sexuality within the family. The patriarchal influence of Victorian times castigated women into a role of sexual subordination and ignorance, shame, and passivity. The pleasures of the body were considered "dirty."

The locus of definition and control then shifted to a medical model, proscribing sexual activity outside of a procreative model as abnormal and evidence of illness. In the medical model, sexuality is seen as located within the person as a set of natural physiological drives. The dominant medical model of sexuality, the Human Sexual Response Cycle (HSRC) was advanced in 1966 by William Masters and Virginia Johnson. The HSRC describes the sequence of physiological changes that occur during sexual activity and presumes that the sexes have the same sexual response cycles. Critics argue that this model of sexuality is biased toward men's sexual interests. They argue that although men's and women's sexuality may be more similar than different physiologically, gender inequality is a social reality that impacts the HSRC. Furthermore, sexuality is not just an internal or genital sensation of desire, arousal, and orgasm. There are also important *social* sexual realities.

Some contemporary sexologists (scholars who engage in the scientific study of sexuality) challenge a biological or "natural" approach to sex by arguing that the sociocultural context is central in defining everything about sexual experience. The sociocultural context creates and shapes sexuality by defining "sexual scripts," which are enacted in physical performance. Sexual scripts, of which expectations are a key element, guide sexual behavior by helping participants define the situation and plot out appropriate behavior.

Males are socialized to be more sexually aware, active, assertive, and entitled. They learn to value varied sexual experience and sexual gratification, for which they are often rewarded with the esteem of peers. Females generally are socialized to limit sexual activity and to tie sex to romance in which there is greater concern for affection than for sex. They learn to value intimacy and emotional communion. Females are often treated as and consequently see themselves as sexual *objects,* not subjects with sexual agency of their own. Many scholars argue that sex role socialization creates fundamental gender differences and inequalities, impacting heterosexual scripts and experience.

Indeed, it seems that females are in a no-win situation regarding their sexuality. While heterosexual females are rewarded early on for abstinence, later they receive pressure from male partners to have sex. Such females are considered "prudes" if they do not have sex, "sluts" or "loose" if they do have sex. Females learn that sex is "dirty" but they feel like their worth as a female is determined by their ability to attract and please males. HIV prevention educator Carolyn Laub explains how such sexual gender ideology is related to the practice of safer sex strategies and sexual risk. According to Laub, a female who is prepared for sex (e.g., carrying condoms) signals that she is sexually aware and therefore "easy" or dirty. Likewise, a female who talks with a potential sex partner about safer-sex issues may imply that she has been sexually active and therefore "loose."

The following selections illustrate a stark contrast between patriarchally-delimited women's sexuality and the possibility of sexual freedom and power for women. Rebecca Walker provides a personal account that supports her conviction that females need not feel guilty concerning their sexuality. Instead, females can celebrate their sexuality regardless of traditional gender constraints. Athena Devlin, on the other hand, provides her own personal account that demonstrates the difficulty in overcoming traditional gender constraints. Both males and females contribute to the factors that cause sexual double standards to thrive.

Rebecca Walker

 **YES**

Lusting for Freedom

I had sex young and, after the initial awkwardness, loved it. For days and nights, I rolled around in a big bed with my first boyfriend, trying out every possible way to feel good body to body. I was able to carry that pleasure and confidence into my everyday life working at the hair salon, raising my hand in English class, hanging out with my best girlfriend, and flirting with boys. I never felt any great loss of innocence, only great rushes of the kind of power that comes with self-knowledge and shared intimacy.

But experiences like mine are all too rare. There are forces that subvert girls' access to freeing and empowering sex—forces like AIDS, limited access to health care, and parental notification laws that force thousands of young women to seek out illegal and sometimes fatal abortions. The way we experience, speak about and envision sex and sexuality can either kill us or help us to know and protect ourselves better. The responsibility is enormous. Unfortunately, moral codes and legal demarcations complicate rather than regulate desire. And judgments like "right" and "wrong" only build barriers between people and encourage shame within individuals. I personally have learned much more from examining my own life for signs of what was empowering for me and what was not, and from listening to and asking questions of my friends: What did you feel then, what did you learn from that?

When I look back at having sex during my teenage years, I find myself asking: What was it in my own life that created the impulse and the safety; the wanting that led me and the knowing that kept me from harm?

❦

If you are a girl, sex marks you, and I was marked young. I am ashamed to tell people how young I was, but I am too proud to lie. Eleven. I was eleven, and my mother was away working. One autumn night Kevin, a boy I had met in the neighborhood, called and said he had a sore throat. I told him I would make him some tea if he wanted to come over. He said he was on his way. I had told him that I was sixteen, so I ran around for a few minutes, panicking about what to wear. I settled on a satin leopard-print camisole from my mother's bureau and hid it beneath a big red terry-cloth robe.

I have a few vivid memories of that night: I remember being cold and my teeth chattering. I remember his black Nike high tops and red-and-gray football jersey, and the smell of him, male and musky, as he passed me coming through the front door. I remember sitting on our green sofa and telling him rather indignantly that I was not a virgin. I remember faking a fear that I might get pregnant (I didn't have my period yet). I remember his dry penis, both of us looking elsewhere as he pushed it inside of me. I remember that I wanted him to stay with me through the night, but that instead he had to rush home to make a curfew imposed upon him by his football coach.

Shocking, right? Not really. Sex begins much earlier than most people think, and it is far more extensive. It is more than the act of intercourse, much more than penis and vagina. Sex can look like love if you don't know what love looks like. It gives you someone to hold on to when you can't feel yourself. It is heat on your body when the coldness is inside of you. It is trying out trusting and being trusted. Sex can also be power because knowledge is power, and because yeah, as a girl, you can make it do different things: I can give it to you, and I can take it away. This sex is me, you can say. It is mine, take it. Take me. Please keep me.

By the time I was eighteen I was fluent in the language of sex and found myself in restaurants with men twice my age, drinking red wine and artfully playing Woman. By then I had learned about the limitations of male tenderness, men's expectations about black female desire, the taboo of loving other women, the violence of rape. And, like women all over the world, I had mastered the art of transforming myself into what I thought each man would fall in love with. Not at all in control of each affair, but very much in control of the mask I put on for each man, I tried on a dozen personas, played out a dozen roles, decided not to be a dozen people. When Bryan said I was too black, I straightened my hair. When Ray said I was too young, I added four years. For Miles I was a young virgin, nervous and giggly. For Jacob I was a self-assured student of modern art. For Robbie I was a club girl. I was Kevin's steady.

When I think of what determined my chameleonlike identity then, I think of the movie *Grease,* with the dolled-up Olivia Newton-John getting the guy and popularity too after she put on pumps and a push-up bra and became "sexy." I also think about my best girlfriend in the fourth grade who stopped speaking to me and "stole" my boyfriend over Christmas break. It was a tricky world of alliances in those younger years. You could never be sure of who was going to like you and why, so I tried my best to control what parts I could. That explains my attempts to be cool and sexy, my pretending to know everything, my smoking cigarettes, and of course, my doing it with boys. I did what I thought had to be done.

But there were also other elements, other factors. Like curiosity, desire and my body. These are the urges that account for the wet, tonguey ten-minute kiss outside the laundry room that I remembered with a quivering belly for weeks afterwards. Ditto for my desire to bury my face in my boyfriend's armpits in order to learn his smell well enough to recognize it anywhere. This very same desire to know also made me reach down and feel a penis for the first time, checking almost methodically for shape, sensitivity and any strange aberrations on the skin. My quest was not simply a search for popularity, but a definite assertion of my own nascent erotic power. This strange force, not always pleasurable but always mine, nudged me toward physical exploration and self-definition, risk taking and intimacy building, twisting each element into an inextricable whole.

Because my mother was often away, leaving me with a safe and private space to bring my boyfriends, and because my common sense and experience of nonabusive love led me to decent men, my relationships consisted of relatively safe explorations of sex that were, at the time, fulfilling physically and emotionally. I also began to play with different kinds of strength. While I learned about my partners' bodies, I learned that I had the power to make them need me. While I learned how much of myself to reveal, I learned how to draw them out. While I learned that they were not "right" for me, I learned that I was more than what they saw.

Did I know then that I was learning to negotiate the world around me and answering important questions about the women I would become? Probably not, but looking back, it seems obvious: I peeled back endless layers of contorted faces, checking out fully the possibilities of the roles I took on. I left them again and again when I felt I could not bring all of myself to the script. I couldn't just be the football player's cheerleader girlfriend, or the club girl friend of a bartender. I wasn't happy faking orgasm (self-deceit for male ego) or worrying about getting pregnant (unprotected ignorance) or having urinary tract infections (victim of pleasure) or sneaking around (living in fear). Instinctively I knew I wanted more pleasure and more freedom, and I intuitively knew I deserved and could get both.

When I think back, it is that impulse I am most proud of. The impulse that told me that I deserve to live free of shame, that my body is not my enemy and that pleasure is my friend and my right. Without this core, not even fully jelled in my teenage mind but powerful nonetheless, how else would I have learned to follow and cultivate my own desire? How else would I have learned to listen to and develop the language of my own body? How else would I have learned to initiate, sustain and develop healthy intimacy, that most valuable of human essences? I am proud that I did not stay in relationships when I couldn't grow. I moved on when the rest of me would emerge physically or intellectually and say, Enough! There isn't enough room in this outfit for all of us.

It is important to consider what happens when this kind of self-exploration is blocked by cultural taboo, government control or religious mandate. What happens when we are not allowed to know our own bodies, when we cannot safely respond to and explore our own desire? As evinced by the worldwide rape epidemic, the incredible number of teenage pregnancies, and the ever-increasing number of sexually transmitted diseases, sex can be an instrument of torture, the usher of unwanted responsibility or the carrier of fatal illness.

It is obvious that the suppression of sexual agency and exploration, from within or from without, is often used as a method of social control and domination. Witness widespread genital mutilation and the homophobia that dictatorially mandates heterosexuality; imagine the stolen power of the millions affected by just these two global murderers of self-authorization and determination. Without being able to respond to and honor the desires of our bodies and our selves, we become cut off from our instincts for pleasure, dissatisfied living under rules and thoughts that are not our own. When we deny ourselves safe and shameless exploration and access to reliable information, we damage our ability to even know what sexual pleasure feels or looks like.

Sex in silence and filled with shame is sex where our agency is denied. This is sex where we, young women, are powerless and at the mercy of our own desires. For giving our bodies what they want and crave, for exploring ourselves and others, we are punished like Eve reaching for more knowledge. We are called sluts and whores. We are considered impure or psychotic. Information about birth control is kept from us. Laws denying our right to control our bodies are enacted. We learn much of what we know from television, which debases sex and humiliates women.

We must decide that this is no longer acceptable, for sex is one of the places where we do our learning solo. Pried away from our parents and other authority figures, we look for answers about ourselves and how the world relates to us. We search for proper boundaries and create our very own slippery moral codes. We can begin to take control of this process and show responsibility only if we are encouraged to own our right to have a safe and self-created sexuality. The question is not whether young women are going to have sex, for this is far beyond any parental or societal control. The question is rather, what do young women need to make sex a dynamic, affirming, safe and pleasurable part of our lives? How do we build the bridge between sex and sexuality, between the isolated act and the powerful element that, when honed, can be an important tool for self-actualization?

Fortunately, there is no magic recipe for a healthy sexuality; each person comes into her or his own sexual power through a different route and at her or his own pace. There are, however, some basic requirements for sexual aware-ness and safe sexual practice. To begin with, young women need a safe space in which to explore our own bodies. A woman needs to be able to feel the soft smoothness of her belly, the exquisite softness of her inner thigh, the full roundness of her breasts. We need to learn that bodily pleasure belongs to us; it is our birthright.

Sex could also stand to be liberated from... marriage and procreation. It can be more: more sensual, more spiritual, more about communication and healing. Women and men both must learn to explore sexuality by making love in ways that are different from what we see on television and in the movies. If sex is about communicating, let us think about what we want to say and how will we say it. We need more words, images, ideas.

Finally, young women are more than inexperienced minors, more than property of the state or of legal guardians. We are growing, thinking, inquisi-tive, self-possessed beings who need information about sex and access to birth control and abortion. We deserve to have our self-esteem nurtured and our personal agency encouraged. We need "protection" only from poverty and violence.

And even beyond all of the many things that will have to change in the outside world to help people in general and young women in particular grow more in touch with their sexual power, we also need to have the courage to look closely and lovingly at our sexual history and practice. Where is the meaning? What dynamics have we created or participated in? Why did we do that? How did we feel? How much of the way we think about ourselves is based in someone else's perception or label of our sexual experiences?

It has meant a lot to me to affirm and acknowledge my experiences and to integrate them into an empowering understanding of where I have been and where I am going. Hiding in shame or running fast to keep from looking is a waste of what is most precious about life: its infinite ability to expand and give us more knowledge, more insight and more complexity.

NO ↩

The Shame of Silence

As in every high school, there was in mine a set of especially powerful boys who were "popular." At my school in Texas, they were all football stars. When I was a freshman, and dying to make a good impression, I was invited by one of them to come over to his house to watch television. I don't think I will ever be able to forget (much to my embarrassment these days) how excited I was. By the time I left my house, my room looked like a clothes bomb had exploded in it. I was smiling from ear to ear, probably having visions of becoming a cheerleader. I forgot to ask myself *why* he had called me. I forgot to remember that I was *not* what you would call a popular girl. I rang his doorbell with a pounding heart and ridiculous aspirations. Bill let me in and led me into the living room. There, sitting on couches, were about eight boys. They were all watching a porno film on the VCR. They looked at me with open dislike and said "hi" pretty much in unison. I just stood there, frozen with disappointment while a blond woman acted out ecstasy on the television screen. No one spoke. After what seemed like a very long time, I turned away and walked into the kitchen just off the living room and sat at the table. I was embarrassed by my expectations. I felt like I had forgotten my "place." Now I remembered. I knew why I had been invited over. Bill let me stay in the kitchen by myself for about 20 minutes. When he finally walked in he just looked at me and said "You wanna go outside?" I said yes because it felt like the only way out. We went out to his back yard; to reclining deck chairs by a lit pool. We started making out. His hands were everywhere, his breath stank. I felt worthless and just let it happen. Then, when he leaned over to get to the hook of my bra, I looked up and there they all were, all eight of them standing on the second floor balcony watching us. I started yelling. Bill didn't say anything. He didn't tell them to go away, he didn't offer me an explanation. I suddenly got the feeling that it had all been planned this way. I was trying to stand and get my shirt back on when Bill took my hand and pulled me behind a fence at the back of the yard. When we got there, he turned and told me he wanted a hand job. I gave him one and left. I felt only one thing, and it wasn't anger; it was shame.

To be a "successful" girl in Highland Park was to be successful with boys. So, undeniably the girls that I grew up with viewed each other as less important than the boys they dated and more often than not, as would-be enemies.

From Athena Devlin, "The Shame of Silence," in Amy Kesselman, Lily D. McNair, and Nancy Schniedewind, eds., *Women: Images and Realities: A Multicultural Anthology,* 2d ed. (Mayfield, 1999). Copyright © 1999, 1995 by Mayfield Publishing Company. Reprinted by permission of Athena Devlin.

Nothing was ever as important as being accepted by men. And this, quite effectively, alienated us from one another. The key to success with boys in my high school was having the right kind of reputation, and reputation for a girl was for the most part focused narrowly on her looks and her sexual life. Importantly, it was the boys who decided what "type" a girl was sexually—which, in a social setting like this one, gave them a lot of power. What put them in this position was exactly that thing the girls lacked: each other. Maybe it was from all those hours of football practice where they had to depend on one another that did it, or maybe it was just because they felt important enough not to seek female approval as desperately as we sought theirs that made some sort of solidarity among them more possible. But in any event, it was to their distinct advantage. For girls, trying to please the powers that be was very confusing because we were supposed to be attractive and sexually exciting in order to be accepted, while simultaneously prudish and innocent. We were supposed to be sweet and deferential towards them when they went too far. I suppose I never got that delicate balance down. I got one side of the equation but not the other.

Not surprisingly, then, the shame I felt by having been treated as worthless by boys was something I desperately wanted to *hide*. I had failed, it seemed in the most important way. I never told any of my girl friends about that night and, because of my shame, which covered everything, I wasn't even really aware of my anger, and it certainly did not occur to me to *show* any anger towards these boys. I had never heard a girl publicly denounce a boy for his behavior towards her, though I had seen many a girl be thoroughly disgraced in those hallways of Highland Park High. So, when the story of my night with the football stars got passed along by the boys, the girls who heard about it never tried to comfort me. They whispered about me instead, often to the very boys that had been involved. They were gaining points by disassociating themselves from me, because I was the one at fault. Boys will be boys after all. It's the girls who say yes that were held accountable at my high school—by both sexes.

About six months later when my reputation as a "slut" had been firmly established, I began hanging out with a girl named Cindy who had a similar public identity. Some of the boys from the group that participated in that horrible night often asked us out when their regular girl friends were away or safely tucked behind curfews. I usually said no, although I occasionally agreed because going out with them still felt like a form of acceptance. At least they thought I was pretty enough to make out with. But Cindy went out with them a lot. One Friday night something happened. To this day I do not know what actually went on (no surprise). I just knew she was upset and the following Monday, Will, one of the boys she went out with, started hassling her in the hall. She began to cry in the middle of passing period with everyone staring. Suddenly, and for the first time, I felt incredibly angry and before fear held me back, I began to yell at Will. I don't remember what I said exactly, but it was something to the effect of who did he think he was, and that I thought he was an asshole. I don't think he had ever been so surprised. He stared at me in complete amazement. And so did Cindy. Unfortunately, it didn't take him too long to recover and he told me in a voice loud enough for everyone in the building to hear, that I was a whore and everyone knew it, that I would sleep with anyone (I was still a virgin at the time), and that I was completely disgusting. The contempt in his voice was incredible. I started to feel ashamed again. One did not have scenes like this at Highland Park. But the surprise was Cindy hated me for it. In her opinion I had done an unforgivable thing in sticking up for her. And, what I learned was that girls didn't want each other's protection because it made them less attractive to boys. They feared focusing on each other too much.

For me, however, this incident was a turning point because afterwards these boys left me alone completely. I was released from the painful confusion of boys wanting me and disliking me at the same time—ignoring me or talking about me behind my back and then calling me up late on Friday night. I had yelled at a football star in front of everyone. That made me completely unacceptable as opposed to only marginally so. People began to make sure they didn't cross my path. I was left alone. Moreover, I was feared. It was then that I began to realize just how much the boys depended on the girls not to do anything to defend themselves, that they depended heavily on our passivity. I saw that they lived in fear of us taking action. Any action. And I began to suspect that the isolation I noticed so many of the girls at my high school in Dallas feeling served a purpose useful enough to be a consequence of deliberateness. Still, I never made another scene.

But that was not really the greatest tragedy. Rather it was, and is, that girls grow up not knowing each other very well. And that while going through the same things, they are without both the benefit of each other's comfort and understanding, and more vulnerable to abuse. I am close to only one girl who went to high school with me, and that is probably only because we ended up at the same college. When I told her about writing this essay she told me, for the first time, some of her experiences at Highland Park. They were as tortured and humiliating as mine, but I had never heard her stories before and she had never heard mine. High school obviously wasn't a great experience for either of us, and while we sat there tracing the damage through to our present lives, I desperately wished it had been different. And it could have been if we could have shaken off the terrible trap of shame and talked about our lives and found ways to support each other. It seems clear to me now that not only were the boys protecting each other, but we girls were protecting the boys through the silence that existed between us.

POSTSCRIPT

Can Women's Sexuality Be Free From Traditional Gender Constraints?

Within feminism, women's sexual freedom was initially advanced as a central cause. Shortly thereafter, women's sexual victimization was added to the feminist agenda. Many say that although women's sexual victimization is a critical cause, attention to it supplanted the advancement of women's sexual freedom.

Over the last two decades, women's sexuality has changed—by some accounts dramatically—in some ways becoming more commensurate with men's sexuality. In general, women are gaining greater sexual experience. They engage in intercourse at a younger age, they have more sex partners, they engage in sexual intercourse more frequently, and they are increasingly likely to engage in casual sex. Yet, despite this trend toward sex equality in behaviors, traditional gender socialization and the sexual double standard continue to act as an interpretive filter for sexual experience. Women continue to experience guilt and shame in response to sexual experience and be seen by others as "dirty" or promiscuous.

Caution must be exercised in defining sexual equality for women. Many argue for commensurate sexual permissiveness for males and females. But does that necessarily mean women achieving a sexuality akin to men? Competitiveness, assertiveness, and coercion often characterize males' sexual experience. Males' self- and peer-esteem are linked to sexual experience and performance. Many future-oriented sexologists caution that in striving for sexual equality, we must not limit ourselves to a preset "male" definition of sexual freedom.

Psychologist and sex researcher Leonore Tiefer argues in *Sex Is Not a Natural Act and Other Essays* (Westview Press, 1995) that we need to encourage women's sexual experimentation and explore sexual possibilities. Furthermore, new ideas need to be developed about desire and pleasure. To facilitate this, there needs to be freely available information, ideas, images, and open sexual talk. Tiefer asserts that if women develop sexual knowledge and self-knowledge, they can take more responsibility for their own pleasure.

Sex education for youth has been targeted as a central arena for working toward greater sexual freedom for women. Traditional sex education programming has overlooked the possibility of female desire and sexual pleasure. Some argue that sex education programs can be used to help females not allow themselves to be treated as objects but think of themselves as sexual subjects. Women as sexual subjects would feel free to seek out sexual pleasure and know that they have a right to this pleasure. This argument supports the assertion that we also need to raise boys to avoid treating females as sexual objects. The challenge for sex education programming is to inform women about the possible risks of sexual relationships without supporting the double standard that limits, inhibits, and controls their sexuality.

Carolyn Laub states that future sex education programming must include education specifically about gender ideology, as it influences sexual perceptions, decisions, and experiences. She asserts that conformity to gender-based norms and ideals for sexual activity is the most important source of peer sexual pressure and risky sex among youth; youth "perform" gendered roles in sexual relations to secure gender affirmation. Gunter Schmidt, who studies sexuality, argues that as one's need for gender affirmation is frustrated elsewhere, sex will become an even more important arena for gender affirmation.

Other scholars also argue that catalyzing women's sexual freedom necessitates more far-reaching changes in gender role socialization. Tiefer comments, "A person would have to feel comfortable, safe, and entitled in order to focus wholly on his or her tactile experience. Can we assume that most women can be thoroughly relaxed in sexual situations given the inequality of so many relationships, given women's concern with their appearance, given women's worries about safety and contraception?"

Advocates of sex education reform also call for incorporating definitions of "good sex"—sex that is not coercive, exploitative, or harmful. They caution not to impose rigid definitions of "sexual normality"; rather, identify some dimensions of healthy sexuality as examples upon which individuals can explore and develop their own unique sexual identity and style. It has been observed that a central practice in the social construction of gender inequality is *compulsory heterosexuality* or societal pressure to be heterosexual. Many sexual revolutionaries argue that an important condition of sexual freedom is freedom from pressures to be a particular "type" of sexual being.

What cultural pressures exist to be a certain kind of sexual being? How can these cultural pressures be transcended? What would women's sexuality be like if it were not so socially restricted?

Suggested Readings

M. Fine, "Sexuality, Schooling, and Adolescent Females: The Missing Discourse of Desire," *Disruptive Voices: The Possibilities of Feminist Research* (University of Michigan Press, 1992).

J. Irvine, ed., *Sexual Cultures and the Construction of Adolescent Identities* (Temple University Press, 1994).

W. Simon and J. H. Gagnon, "Sexual Scripts: Performance and Change," *Archives of Sexual Behavior* (1986).

S. Thompson, *Going All the Way: Teenage Girls' Tales of Sex, Romance, and Pregnancy* (Hill & Wang, 1995).

D. Tolman, "Doing Desire: Adolescent Girls' Struggles for/With Sexuality," *Gender & Society* (1994).

On the Internet ...

Ethics and Genetics: A Global Conversation

This Bioethics.net interactive site is sponsored by The University of Pennsylvania Center for Bioethics and The MIT Press. It includes articles and readers' comments on a variety of bioethical issues. Read the commentary on John Robertson's article entitled "Preconception Gender Selection." Read others' comments and submit your own comment. Site visitors can also join live conversation about a variety of bioethical issues. This is an opportunity to pose your own question or issue.

```
http://bioethics.net
```

Young and Male in America: It's Hard Being a Boy

This informative article entitled "Young and Male in America: It's Hard Being a Boy" is by Brad Knickerbocker of *The Christian Science Monitor*. This article concerns contemporary boy's issues and addresses the role of gender in the Littleton, Colorado, school killings.

```
http://www.csmonitor.com/durable/1999/04/29/
fp1s3-csm.shtml
```

PART 4

Sex, Gender, and Youth

*G*ender is influenced before conception, in making decisions to carry
a fetus to term, and in the life expectancy of male and female children.
The potency of sex and gender as explanations for differences between
males and females escalates early in life. By early childhood, a host of
differences are observed between boys and girls as children internalize
a sense of themselves and others as gendered. Concern has been raised
about inequities and deficits resulting from the effects of sex and gender.
Is higher value placed on male versus female offspring? Does masculinity
put boys at an emotional disadvantage and lead them to social problems
and even deadly violence?

In this section, the effects of sex and gender on fetuses, children,
and adolescents are examined. Is fetal sex selection ethical? Are sex differences located in biology and/or culture? Can children's gender roles be
redefined? How does race interact with gender youths' experience?

- Is Fetal Sex Selection Harmful to Society?

- Is Gender the Most Critical Factor in the Recent Spate of School
  Shootings?

ISSUE 11

Is Fetal Sex Selection Harmful to Society?

YES: Gail Vines, from "The Hidden Cost of Sex Selection," *New Scientist* (May 1, 1993)

NO: Editors of *Lancet*, from "Jack or Jill?" *Lancet* (March 20, 1993)

ISSUE SUMMARY

YES: Author Gail Vines argues that sex selection of unborn fetuses and efforts to "create" fetuses of a particular sex may have unforeseen consequences for parenting, societal gender relations, and the use and abuse of technology.

NO: In this editorial the editors of *Lancet* review acceptable reasons for sex selection, refuting arguments about societal dangers of such practices.

Research has consistently documented the preference and desire for sons in twentieth-century America and in other cultures. In many cultures, such as India and China, maleness means social, political, and economic entitlement. Men are expected to support their parents in their old age. Moreover, men remain with their family throughout life; women, upon marriage, become part of the husband's family. Thus, women are traditionally seen as a continuing economic burden on the family—particularly in the custom of large dowry payments at weddings. In some cultures if a bride's family cannot pay the demanded dowry, the brides are often killed (usually by burning). Although dowries and dowry deaths are illegal, the laws are rarely enforced.

In such cultures, there is an expressed desire for male children and an urgency to select fetal sex. Recently, sex-determination technology is most commonly used to assay the sex of fetuses, even though in many cultures the use of such technology has been banned. When the fetus is determined to be female, abortion often follows because of cultural pressures to have sons. The decision about sex selection is ultimately the father's; many women are coerced into fetal sex determination and abortion. Such sex-determination practices have led to many more male than female infants being born. The gap grows even wider because of a high childhood death rate of girls, often from neglect or killing by strangulation, suffocation, or poisoning. Furthermore, women are blamed for the birth of a female child and are often punished for it (even though, biologically, it is the male's sperm, carrying either X or Y chromosomes, that determines sex).

Research shows that in contemporary America, 78 percent of adults prefer their firstborn to be a boy. Moreover, parents are more likely to continue having children if they have all girls versus if they have all boys. Faced with having only one child, many Americans prefer a boy. But there is also a high preference for a "sex-balanced" family—the "perfect" family having a firstborn son and a second-born daughter. The availability of sex-selection technology in the last quarter of the twentieth century was met with growing interest and widespread willingness to make use of the technology.

Available technologies for sex selection include preconception, preimplantation, and postconception techniques. Preconception selection techniques include folkloric approaches like intercourse timing, administering an acid or alkaline douche, and enriching maternal diets with potassium or calcium/ magnesium, all thought to create a uterine environment conducive to producing male or female fetuses. There are also sperm-separating technologies whereby X- and Y-bearing sperm are separated, and the desired sperm are artificially inseminated into the woman, increasing the chance of having a child of the chosen sex. Sound empirical evidence is limited for many of these techniques. Some research shows a recent sperm-separation technique to improve the chance to have a girl to 69 percent and to have a boy to 75 percent.

Preimplantation technologies identify the sex of embryos as early as three days after fertilization. For sex-selection purposes, the choice of an embryo for implantation is based on sex. Postconception approaches use prenatal diagnostic technologies to determine the sex of the fetus. The three most common technologies are amniocentesis (available after the 20th week of pregnancy), chorionic villi sampling (available earlier but riskier), and ultrasound (which can determine sex as early as 12 weeks but is not 100 percent accurate). Fetuses of the undesired sex are eliminated by selective abortion. A more extreme sex-selection approach, common in many cultures, is infanticide or willful neglect.

The American demand for and social acceptance of sex-selection technologies have increased in the last decade. Preconception selection techniques are becoming quite popular in the United States, and preimplantation technologies (though more expensive) are also more frequently used. It has become more and more socially accepted to use prenatal diagnostic technologies to determine fetal sex. But incidence rates for sex-selective abortions are difficult to obtain. There is mixed opinion about the frequency of sex-selective abortions, tinged by political controversy.

In the following selections, Gail Vines urges caution about sex-selection technologies, uncovering some unforeseen consequences for parenting and societal gender relations. In contrast, the editors of *Lancet* provide in their editorial acceptable reasons for sex selection, quelling fears of supposed dangers of sex selection to society.

Gail Vines  **YES**

The Hidden Cost of Sex Selection

U p to now, most speculation over the consequences [of choosing the sex of a child] has focused on what will happen if one sex proves more popular than the other. [Embryologist Anne] McLaren's prophecy of more aggression if boys are the preferred choice has been widely echoed. Michael Freeman, professor of English Law at University College London, says: "If we are trying to move away from a society where aggression and violence prevail, we would be moving in the wrong direction in creating a society with a preponderance of males." Others, however, see little cause for concern.

"Let's not panic about it until there is some evidence," says Bernadette Modell, a leading medical geneticist from University College Hospital in London who runs a clinic for couples at risk of passing on thalassaemia, a severe inherited form of anaemia. "My experience suggests that preferences for boys or girls would be perfectly balanced in our society," she says. "We have had very few requests for terminations on grounds of sex—which, by the way, we will not do."

Modell agrees that the concerns of parents at risk of having seriously ill children may not reflect those of the general public. Nonetheless, she doubts that the advent of sperm sorting will change things. "Getting pregnant by artificial insemination is quite a step. Most people don't want to interfere with nature if they don't have to." She suspects that people will use the technology only if they already have two children of the same sex, and that there will be no overall impact on the sex ratio.

In support of her views, Modell quotes the work of Andrew Czeizel of the National Institute of Hygiene in Budapest. He kept note of the women visiting his clinic who were pregnant for the third time, and already had two children of the same sex. He found that most women seeking an abortion for social reasons said they would be happy to keep a child of the opposite sex from their existing children, but would seek an abortion if it were the same.

But another survey of 1500 couples in Hungary in the late 1970s, also conducted by Czeizel, hinted at a sex bias. He asked the childless couples whether they would use an accurate and harmless method for choosing a child's sex, if it was available. Only 21 per cent said yes. But, of these, most favoured boys. Among couples wanting a single child, 65 per cent wanted it to be a male. The percentage fell to 57 per cent if more were planned. Overall, a significant 87 per cent wanted the first baby to be a boy. The consequence, Czeizel says, would be a shift in the ratio of boys to girls at birth from the present 106:100, to 142:100. And more boys would be first-borns.

Yet an American study presented at the American Association for the Advancement of Science in Detroit in 1983 concluded that many women pregnant with their first child had no preference, and that the number wanting boys was matched by those who preferred girls. And earlier this year, researchers from the University of Cambridge, Helen Statham, Josephine Green and colleagues, reported in *The Lancet* (27 February, p 564) that their survey of more than 2000 pregnant women suggests that most British women have no particular preference for boys or girls. In their postal questionnaire, the researchers asked if the women would "mind" the sex of their child. Most replied no, and most said they did not even want to know the baby's sex before birth. Those who expressed a preference were as likely to prefer a girl as a boy.

The Cambridge researchers stress that their survey of pregnant women "tells us nothing of what women would do if they could select the sex of their baby." Teresa Marteau, who is director of the Wellcome Psychology and Genetics Research Group at Guy's Hospital in London, agrees. She says asking someone if they would rather have a boy or a girl when they already have one or the other in their womb is different from saying, "I've got a new technology, would you like it?" Yet this is the crux of the matter. "These studies throw us off the scent," says Marteau. "We cannot assume from one sort of situation how people would respond to the other."

What's more, Marteau argues, "most of these studies have asked women what they would like, but we don't even know that it would be women who would make the decisions, were the technology available." One thing is certain, she says: "If we had this technology 70 years ago, we certainly wouldn't have the Queen as monarch."

Predicting the impact of a new technology is difficult. Marilyn Strathern, professor of social anthropology at the University of Manchester, argues that the availability of choice can shift the way people think about themselves and their relationships. "When there is choice things are altered fundamentally," Strathern said last week at a conference on sex selection at the British Medical Association, organised by a European Community project on fertility, infertility and the embryo. Strathern argues that even if the technique leaves the sex ratio unchanged, it may have unforeseen and insidious social consequences.

"At the moment, when you don't have to think about choosing the sex of a child, all kinds of hopes and fears about what the child would be like are possible. Parents, grandparents and siblings might all have different desires, but none have to be acted upon—you don't have to prioritise different viewpoints, and you can resolve to make the best of whatever comes," she says. But with sex selection there is the impression that you can easily prioritise these desires. "But you can't," she says. "It is not like deciding whether you prefer potatoes or spaghetti."

One difficulty is that partners may not agree about the desired sex of the child. Of course, it is likely that they will sort it out between them—but possibly to one person's advantage. "Without sex selection, there is a sporting chance that someone will end up with what they want; with sex selection, there is a sporting chance that the choices one partner would have made will be permanently disadvantaged with respect to those of the other."

Allowing people to choose the sex of their children may also have blatant social effects. Choice turns on comparisons, so sex selection will encourage comparisons between the sexes, a development that could easily worsen the position of girls and women in society. "Comparisons go on all the time—we call it discrimination," says Strathern. "To make sex an issue at the point of conception, to select on gender grounds, will reinforce discrimination... By even saying that one sex is preferable to another, we could be legitimising discrimination."

Sex selection could also alter parenting for the worse, argues Marteau. A document produced by the HFEA [Human Fertilisation and Embryology Authority] suggests that if parents can choose the sex of their children, they will love them more. "This is a very naive argument," she says. "Do we want to encourage conditional parenting, the kind of parent who says, 'I will love you only if you're a boy or a girl?'" The idea, she says "eats a tiny bit into our humanity."

Choosing the sex of their child might also give parents a spurious sense of control over reproduction, leaving them less able to cope when things go wrong.

There is a clear financial incentive for those who run sex selection services to push hard for public acceptance. The advent of a reliable technique will also bring with it the notion that "since we have the technology we ought to use it," says Marteau. To monitor this, there must be independent assessment. "During its first few years of use there must be very tight evaluation of the effects on families," she says.

Marteau warns against uncritical acceptance of sex selection. Its benefit to individuals will be tiny compared with its great potential social disadvantages, she suspects. "I don't think there is great misery in this country from not being able to choose the sex of your child, and it could possibly make things significantly worse."

NO ⬅

Editors of *Lancet*

Jack or Jill?

T he birth of a girl—or a boy—can be guaranteed only by selective destruction of conceptuses or fetuses of the undesired sex. This is done by selecting the appropriate conceptuses for implantation after invitro fertilization, or by abortion of fetuses conceived naturally, the sex having been determined by chorionic villus biopsy, amniocentesis, or ultrasound scanning. Such methods are generally regarded as acceptable when used to prevent the birth of a boy to a mother who is a carrier of a seriously handicapping X-linked condition such as haemophilia or Duchenne muscular dystrophy. Few people would sanction such action if the only reason for sex selection was cultural pressure or personal inclination.

... [S]uppose a completely effective method of sex selection at conception were to become available, should a couple be allowed to choose the sex of their baby? Would this be harmful for them, for their children, or for society as a whole? The happiness of individuals and the stability of the population depends on nearly equal numbers of boys and girls being born. The sex ratio at birth could be seriously disturbed if couples preferred boys to girls and if an appreciable proportion were to use sex selection. This is unlikely. Sex selection at conception would necessitate careful organisation of sexual activity, something that many couples find very difficult, as is shown by the observation that up to 50% of pregnancies are unplanned and to some extent unwanted. Most couples would continue to leave the sex of their children to chance and only a minority would use sex selection.

Careful surveys in 1970 and 1975 of a national sample of about 3500 ever-married women in the USA showed that, for first pregnancies, 45% preferred a boy and 34% had no preference and, for second pregnancies, of those with a girl, 68% preferred a boy and 18% had no preference and of those with a boy 72% preferred a girl and 9% had no preference. Most women did not want sex selection, but these results suggest that if this was available there would be a minuscule effect on the sex ratio of the population. 84% of the highly selected couples who sought treatment from Gametrics Ltd wanted a boy, perhaps because the method offered a greater chance of being successful (with no increased risk of twins) for male sex selection. Another possibility is that couples

From Editors of *Lancet*, "Jack or Jill?" *Lancet*, vol. 341, no. 8847 (March 20, 1993), pp. 727-728.

were more prepared to pay, and to experience considerable inconvenience, to have their family balanced by a boy than by a girl.

Sex selection might be considered harmful if it helped to perpetuate the view that boys have more value to the family than girls. This is a theoretical and simplistic ethical position. In practice the prohibition of sex selection at conception would have only a very small effect on the status of women. Within some cultures there is much unhappiness, especially for the woman, if a couple do not have a son. The woman who has only daughters often feels obliged to have repeated pregnancies in the hope that a son will be born. Consequently, families become too large for the available resources; the woman is placed at considerable risk as she becomes more parous and older; and some marriages break down if the wife does not give birth to a male child. The inconvenience and cost of sex selection would limit the use of this approach to situations when a child of a particular sex was considered necessary. If the use of sex selection were to increase the proportion of boys significantly, women would benefit from the wider choice of marriage partners and would acquire greater social value. The long-term outcome would be an increase in the birth of girls and restoration of balance.

Being able to choose whether to have a boy or a girl would add an acceptable new dimension to family planning. Couples could satisfy their wishes for the size and composition of their family and the children might benefit by being wanted, not only for themselves but also because of their gender. During pregnancy many prospective parents become convinced that they are going to have a child of one sex and are disconcerted when the opposite is revealed at delivery. Most adjust rapidly but a few remain disappointed and this is reflected in the relationship they form with their child.

Our increasing ability to modify human biology causes much anguish in some sections of society, as when chloroform was introduced for the relief of pain of childbirth, when effective contraception became available, and when abortion was made legal. In the UK the Human Fertilisation and Embryology Authority published a consultation document . . . and has asked for response. . . . Some people will always regard the selection of the sex of a baby at the time of conception as wrong and will seek prohibitive legislation; others will feel that there is a limited place for such methods and that regulations that restrict use are necessary. Many will prefer to leave the decision to use sex selection to individual couples because the benefits are likely to exceed any harmful effects. Law is not necessary to define who should be allowed to use sex selection but some regulation might be desirable to ensure that those requesting such a service received high quality professional care. A method offered to the public should have been subjected to a randomised controlled trial to prove effectiveness and safety, with the results published after peer review. Perhaps clinics will have to be licensed and monitored. The Office of Population Censuses and Surveys already publishes annual data from which the sex ratio of the population in the UK can be derived and this would allow action if significant imbalance developed. The possibility of effective sex selection provides a rare opportunity to plan in advance how a potentially valuable technique could be monitored and made available to the public.'

POSTSCRIPT

Is Fetal Sex Selection Harmful to Society?

Aprimary focus of critics' concern about sex-selection technologies (and cultural biases toward males) is their impact on population sex ratios. A skewed sex ratio, they fear, will cause dire consequences for a society, particularly for heterosexual mating (although it is ironic that the same class of reproductive technological advances not only facilitate sex selection but also make reproduction less reliant on conventional heterosexual mating). But what about social concerns about sex selection? How will the increasing frequency of the use of sex-selection technologies impact families? How will it affect gender assumptions and sex discrimination?

Is the acceptability of sex-selection conditional? If Americans were not as biased toward having just boys or just girls, and therefore the population sex ratio would not be threatened, would sex selection be acceptable to control the birth order of the sexes, to ensure a mixture of boys and girls, or to have an only child of a certain desired sex? Sex-selection technology might reduce overpopulation by helping families who already have a child of one sex "balance" their family with a second child of the other sex, rather than continue to have children "naturally" until they get the sex they want. Is using sex selection as a "small family planning tool" an acceptable use of sex-selection technologies? Many feel that using sex selection to balance a family is not sexist. But others argue that it is sexist because it promotes gender stereotyping, which undermines equality between the sexes.

Should abortions solely for the purpose of sex selection be allowed? This is a profound dilemma for many pro-choice feminists for whom a woman's right to choose an abortion for any reason is opposed to gross sex discrimination in the form of sex-selective abortions (usually of female fetuses). It is interesting to note that when parents choose to abort based on fetal sex in an effort to "balance" their family, sex selection is regarded as more acceptable than when only female fetuses are aborted because of a preference for males. What assumptions about sex and gender underlie this judgment?

Suggested Readings

A. L. Cherry, "A Feminist Understanding of Sex-Selective Abortion: Solely a Matter of Choice?" *Wisconsin Women's Law Journal* (1995).

J. Danis, "Sexism and 'The Superfluous Female': Arguments for Regulating Pre-Implantation Sex Selection," *Harvard Women's Law Journal* (1995).

A. M. Gillis, "Sex Selection and Demographics," *Bioscience* (June 1995).

ISSUE 12

Is Gender the Most Critical Factor in the Recent Spate of School Shootings?

YES: Michael Kimmel, from "Snips and Snails. . . and Violent Urges," *Newsday* (March 8, 2001)

NO: Alvin Poussaint, from Judge Baker Children's Center, http://www.jbcc.harvard.edu/articles/oct/school_shootings.htm (May 10, 2001)

ISSUE SUMMARY

YES: Sociologist Michael Kimmel observes that most of the perpetrators in recent school killings have been white boys. He argues that we must examine the social construction of white masculinity to better address such social problems.

NO: Clinical professor of psychiatry Alvin Poussaint describes youth violence as the result of festering anger and aggression fueled by family violence and violence portrayed in the media.

In March 1998 four girls and a teacher were shot and killed by two male teens in Jonesboro, Arkansas. Classmates explained the act as one of revenge because one of the deceased girls had recently broken up with one of the male perpetrators. A similar school killing occurred in October 1997 in Norwalk, California.

In May 1999 a 15-year-old boy in Conyers, Georgia, wounded six students with his stepfather's rifle. He was being treated for depression at the time of the shooting. The shooting followed an incident in which a popular athlete, to whom he believed his girlfriend was attracted, teased him.

In February 2000 a six-year-old boy in Mount Morris Township, Michigan, left his home (a crack house), went to school, and called out to another first grader, "I don't like you!" She replied, "So?" as the boy shot her with a loaded handgun, fatally wounding her. The boy had a history of violent behavior against other children. He lived with his mother, who was a drug addict; his father was in prison.

In March 2001 a 14-year-old girl in Williamsport, Pennsylvania, took her father's gun to the school cafeteria and shot a female classmate in the shoulder.

She had been threatened and teased at her old school in New Jersey, prompting her family to transfer her to a small Roman Catholic school in Pennsylvania. She continued to be teased and became depressed. "No one thought I would go through with this," she said as she fired the gun.

Has American society become a "violence culture," marked by the prevalence of family and school violence and the omnipresence of aggression and violence in the media? Are youths learning to react to the acute stressfulness of everyday life with aggression and violence? Research has documented the connection between stress and aggression, even lethal aggression. Compounding factors are alcohol and drug consumption, increased access to guns, and gender expectations and the status of women.

Surely there are many factors contributing to school violence. Examining the profiles of the teen perpetrators of school shootings over the last few years reveals some common patterns. The perpetrators were typically white, middle-class, suburban males. Most were described by peers as "outcasts" who had been taunted and bullied (especially among boys) and excluded (especially among girls). Recent school shootings have occurred in big schools where these problems are more difficult to detect.

Some attribute school violence to the deep social disconnect plaguing contemporary society. Increasing time without parental supervision and premature expectations for responsibility and independence are weakening children's sense of belonging to their families and communities and leaving them alone to cope with stress, frustration, and crisis.

Some lament that "boys will be boys," believing that boys' aggressive nature is bound to result in violence from time to time. Others believe boys' violence results from societal rules and expectations for boys' behavior. One result of these expectations is that any feminine characteristics or behaviors (e.g., emotional expression, gentleness) in males leads to rejection and ridicule. Social desirability restricts the boys' actions, often leading to displays of anger, aggression, and violence. Boys face a Catch-22; expressing their fears and frustrations is unacceptable for "real men," but such expression and attention is what they so desperately need.

Still others attribute school violence to the epidemic of family violence that models aggression and violence as ways to respond to problems. Interpersonal skills are rarely formally taught, leaving youths to learn through example.

In the following selections, different perspectives on the causes of the recent spate of school killings are presented. Michael Kimmel observes that most of the perpetrators in recent school killings have been white boys. He therefore argues that we must examine the social construction of white masculinity to better address such social problems. In contrast, Alvin Poussaint describes youth violence as the result of festering anger and aggression, which has been fueled by family violence and violence as shown in the media.

Michael Kimmel

 **YES**

Snips and Snails. . . and Violent Urges

For the next few days, the nation will once again stare at the photograph of a slight, confused-looking teenage boy, trying to understand the unfathomable—how Charles Andrew Williams, age 15, could open fire on his classmates, killing two and wounding 13 other people. We'll stare at his picture as the explanations for his murderous behavior pour in from experts and pundits alike.

We'll hear from psychologists, who'll draw elaborate profiles of misfits and loners, of adolescent depression and acting out. Cultural critics will blame a host of problems—violent video games, the Internet, guns.

All the while we will continue to miss the point—even though it is staring right back at us: Charles Andrew Williams is a middle-class, white boy.

That these latest murders and the ones in Littleton, Colo., Pearl, Miss., Paducah, Ky., Springfield, Ore., and Jonesboro, Ark., were all committed by young boys raises not a ripple. It's worth noting that what might seem to be a timely exception to the rule, yesterday's non-fatal shooting of one girl by another at a Catholic school in Williamsport, Pa., appears to have been a one-on-one incident.

We continue to speak about "teen violence," "youth violence" and "school violence" without ever noting the fact that the vast majority of the "teens" and "youth" we're talking about are boys. One expert, already consulted about the Santana High School tragedy, equally missed the point: Paul Mones, author of the book "When a Child Kills," suggested that the motivation for such deadly violence is that "kids want to vent their anger, their worries, their frustrations, their fantasies."

Exactly what "kids" is he talking about?

Gender is the single most obvious and intractable difference when it comes to violence in America. Men and boys are responsible for 95 percent of all violent crimes in this country. Every day, 12 boys and young men commit suicide—seven times the number of girls. Every day, 18 boys and young men die from homicide—10 times the number of girls.

From an early age, boys learn that violence is not only an acceptable form of conflict resolution, but one that is admired. Four times more teenage boys than teenage girls think fighting is appropriate when someone cuts into the front of the line. Half of all teenage boys get into a physical fight each year.

But what causes the unleashing of such homicidal rage? For the past few months, I have been investigating all school shootings that took place in the United States during the 1990s, as described in a report released by the FBI this past fall. All the shooters were boys. And most described their school days as a relentless gauntlet of bullying, gay-baiting epithets, physical assault and harassment until they snapped. Their days were spent, apparently, fending off constant criticism of their masculinity.

Reports indicate that Williams, too, was constantly picked on by his classmates. In that sense, President George W. Bush's compassionless characterization of Williams' attack as "a disgraceful act of cowardice" actually makes matters worse, decrying his ostensible lack of manhood yet again.

In the coming days, we will likely learn more about the daily indignities and assaults that Williams endured. In the meantime, we might remember the words of Evan Todd, a 255-pound linebacker on the football team at Columbine High School, a representative of the "jock culture" that Dylan Harris and Eric Klebold found such an interminable torment.

"Columbine is a clean, good place, except for those rejects," Todd told a Time magazine reporter in late 1999. "Sure we teased them. But what do you expect with kids who come to school with weird hairdos and horns on their hats? It's not just jocks; the whole school's disgusted with them. They're a bunch of homos . . . If you want to get rid of someone, usually you tease 'em. So the whole school would call them homos."

In most cases, boys learn any number of coping strategies to deal with the daily taunts of their classmates. Some turn inward, self-medicate with drugs or alcohol, become loners. A large number of teen suicides contain stories of such daily abuse. And, in a very few cases, the anguish of having one's masculinity challenged, ridiculed and denigrated builds until it explodes in a cathartic rage that seeks to destroy the entire world.

The belief that retaliatory violence is manly is not a trait carried on any chromosome, not soldered into the wiring of the brain's right or left hemisphere. It is not juiced by testosterone (it's still the case that half of boys don't fight, most don't carry weapons, and almost all don't kill). Boys learn it.

They learn it from a media that glorifies it, from sports heroes who commit felonies and get big contracts, from a culture saturated in images of heroic and redemptive violence. They learn it from each other. And they learn it from their fathers, nearly half of whom own a gun. Williams lived with his divorced father, whose gun he reportedly used in the school attack.

And this parallel education is made more lethal in states where gun-control laws are most lax, where gun lobbyists are most powerful. All available evidence suggests that the increases in the deadliness of school violence is attributable to guns.

Boys have resorted to violence for a long time, but sticks and fists and even the occasional switchblade do not create the bloodbaths of the past few years.

Nearly 90 percent of all homicides committed by boys ages 15 to 19 are firearm-related, and 80 percent of the victims are boys. If the rumble in "West Side Story" were to take place today, the death toll would not be just Riff and Bernardo, but all the Sharks and all the Jets—and probably several dozen bystanders.

Some will throw up their hands and sigh that boys will be boys. But in the face of these tragic killings, such resignation is unacceptable. Far more sweeping—and necessary—is a national meditation on how our ideals of manhood became so entangled with violence.

Make no mistake: Charles Andrew Williams is a real boy. In a sense, he is not deviant. Instead, he over-conforms to a definition of masculinity that prescribes violence as a solution. Recall that famous bumper sticker: "I don't get mad. I get even." Until we transform that definition of manhood, this terrible equation of masculinity and violence will add up to an increasing death toll at our nation's schools.

NO ⤶

Alvin Poussaint

Dr. Alvin Poussaint Talks About the School Shootings

Dr. Alvin Poussaint came to AOL Live to assist families and teens [in] discuss[ing] their emotions regarding the Colorado school shootings.

AOLiveMC4: Welcome to AOL Live, Dr. Alvin Poussaint. Do you have an opening comment?

Dr. Poussaint: I think with the pressure now with the cluster of school shootings around the country, that we have to be very concerned with warning signs and take very seriously children who are chronically angry, alienated, who make threats and have weapons, particularly guns. I think that such children, when they identify the children, should be sent to get help or counseling.

AOLiveMC4: Let's start with this audience question:

Question: Dr. Poussaint—would you address the issue of depression in instances such as this one? I have heard that suicide is depression turned inward and acts of violence is often depression turned outward.

Dr. Poussaint: I feel that children with depression, teenagers in particular, may sometimes be suicidal and sometimes homicidal because in both instances they are trying to cope with a great deal of internal anger and rage. But most depressed children do not act out violently. I think those who externalize, who put their anger on other people, are the ones most at risk for committing violence. But teens with depression should be referred for help. Murder, suicide basically go together. If a person values their own life, they may also value the lives of others.

Question: The question is how do we get our high schoolers to report what they see as possible dangerous kids?

Dr. Poussaint: I think that students should be encouraged by the principal, school teachers, to report other students who they know are carrying weapons or students who make threats of violence. That they don't feel like snitches and the school should make it as simple and safe as possible for students to report such information. The schools need to take that information seriously and intervene.

Warning Signs

Question: Doctor, what are the warning signs we as parents should be looking for?

Dr. Poussaint: I think if your child seems alienated from other people, if they are chronically angry most of the time, if they are getting into fights and making threats to other students, and if the child has access to weapons, especially guns, I would be very concerned as a parent. The parent should do something and understand their child needs help and has an emotional problem. The help may be of benefit.

Question: What, as a neighbor or friend, is my responsibility to those whose parents are not active in their child's life and they have little or no supervision?

Dr. Poussaint: That is a tough one because of the privacy of families. If the relationship is one where you know the child has no place to go and no supervision, you could create a safe haven for them and be concerned with the children. If the parents are truly neglecting or abusing their children, they should be reported to a social service agency, as that is a violation of the care of children. I think that many people are comfortable reporting abuse and neglect of younger children, but often do [not] understand the need to report the same things for older children or teens. It would be a good idea if more of those cases were reported.

Question: What kind of structured outlets are there for these children who suffer from this chronic anger?

Dr. Poussaint: The outlets are often several. They can become interested in sports to channel their aggression, they should talk to their families and friends about their anger, getting it out of their system by talking. And some children need to be directed to anger management programs in the school or community. Families need to examine why their particular child is so angry. Is there something that has gone wrong in the family?

Question: I've heard it said that today's teenagers can't fully plan for the future, they do not understand death is forever. What do you think of this?

Dr. Poussaint: I think that all of our children from an early age see a great deal of violence on TV and in the movies. Many of them adopt or see violence as something that is normal, sometimes they see it as glamorous, and they see it as entertainment and fun, and they see violence as a legitimate way of resolving conflict. From this media exposure, often children don't realize that death is real, as actors show up next week in another movie or TV show. Also, the effects of violence when seen in the media do not sufficiently show children the reality and tragic effects of committing violence. Some of the children may, in fact, see violence like they see or play a violent video game.

Dealing With Prejudice

Question: These children had racial prejudices that played a part in their rampage. How can we deprogram racially biased teenagers when they have been so negatively influenced?

Dr. Poussaint: I think the question of combating racism and prejudice is one that the whole society needs to be concerned about. Extreme bigotry toward any group, I see as disturbing; if a young person needs bigotry to feel self-esteem, they are emotionally troubled. So schools, families and the community should have programs to combat prejudice and promote friendship and tolerance. Often young people committing such violence have a history of bigotry, which means they are quite paranoid and easily scapegoat and demonize others, making it easier for them to kill.

Question: Dr. Poussaint, I am a clinical psychologist specializing in the family. I find much of the media coverage of this and other tragedies focuses on the individual child. Could you comment on what is known about the families of violent children? Thanks!

Dr. Poussaint: There are certain things we know, but not in all cases. Children who come from families where they have been physically abused and psychologically abused and neglected are more likely to commit violence. Children who witness a lot of violence in the home, like domestic violence, or in the community, are also more likely to be violent. Often children who feel totally rejected by their peers and others will feel a great deal of anger that may lead to violence. Sometimes families encourage their boys, in particular, to stand up and physically fight to defend their honor. I think families need to discourage violence everywhere and not do this in their own home, and parents should not condone or approve of their children enjoying a great deal of violence in the media as entertainment. Some parents may take children as young as 5 or 6 years old to R-rated movies with a great deal of graphic violence which may traumatize the children but may plant seeds of violent behavior in them.

Question: Why is it that they were allowed to dress like that on a daily basis and no one thought this could be the beginning of a problem?

Dr. Poussaint: That is unfortunate, it would have been helpful if someone had seen that as a clue to a potential problem, or a signal of their increasing alienation from the school and from their peers. Of course that is hindsight, but I think schools need to be more alert to the problems of their students who give indication and signals that they are troubled. When able, they should also involve the students' parents and families in terms of their concerns.

Safety vs. Rights

Question: Will this time be sufficient to make Americans wake up to the fact that civil rights can not be all-encompassing and must be weighed against morals and safety?

Dr. Poussaint: I think in response to that question, if you are talking about freedom of speech and the First Amendment, I think that is sacred and fundamental to American democracy. But I feel the need for there to be more moral education of children in families and also in the schools. Much of the antisocial behavior that children display is learned behavior, including violence, which they may learn from the media.

Question: How do I send my child to school with him not worrying if someone is going to kill him because he is smart, or black, or an athlete? I am at a lost for words.

Dr. Poussaint: I think your child should be reassured. Parents who are concerned should become more involved in the school. They should be at school looking at the guidelines for safe schools and making sure that the local school is knowledgable about them, and parents should become encouraged and involved in anger management and violence management programs in the school. They should also make sure they have strict rules against weapons in the school, and strict rules about assaultive behavior by students.

POSTSCRIPT

Is Gender the Most Critical Factor in the Recent Spate of School Shootings?

It is striking that two perpetrator characteristics (white and male) are common to most of the recent school shootings.

Kimmel observes that analyses of the school shootings have often either avoided or overlooked the fact that the shooters were white. Had the perpetrators been black, the school shootings quickly would have been deemed a "racial problem." But this part of the perpetrator profile does not match our stereotype of what danger looks like, creating a false sense of security that leads us to ignore warning signs. Classism has also contributed to this false sense of security, that violent crime happens only among the urban poor.

But we do expect aggression and violence to be perpetrated by males. Boys are at greater risk than girls for numerous problematic behaviors, including dropping out of school, committing suicide, being victimized by violence, and committing violent crimes. Whether we believe boys' behavior is innate or socially constructed, there is increasing recognition that gender impacts boys' development and experiences. In fact, it is generally agreed that the pressures of gender conformity are greater for boys than girls.

Michael Thompson and Dan Kindlon, authors of *Raising Cain: Protecting the Emotional Life of Boys* (Ballantine Books, 1999), observe great pressure on young males to prove that they are "real men." They describe young adolescent males as taking part in a "culture of cruelty" whereby male stereotypes are enforced. Their actions are replete with homophobia; anything compassionate or soft (i.e., feminine) in a male is labeled "gay."

Controversy continues about whether male behavior is based in biology or even evolution, the result of internalized gender role expectations, or the exaggeration of biological predispositions by a highly gendered society. But with the changing definitions of acceptable female behaviors, we have witnessed the malleability of gender for females. Why has gender been less malleable for males? How do we broaden opportunities for boys as we have for girls? How do notions of masculinity and femininity undermine raising "good humans"?

Suggested Readings

R. W. Connell, *Masculinities* (Allen & Unwin, 1995).

M. Fine and L. Weis, "(In)secure Times," *Gender & Society* (February 1997).

D. Perlstein, "Saying the Unsaid: Girl Killing and the Curriculum," *Journal of Curriculum and Supervision* (Fall 1998).

Minnesota Center Against Violence and Abuse (MINCAVA)

This Web site from the Minnesota Center Against Violence and Abuse (MINCAVA) contains extensive resources on violence and abuse, including such topics as batterer intervention, survivor resources, and connections between welfare and domestic violence.

http://www.mincava.umn.edu/vaw.asp

FatherWork

FatherWork is a Web page on "generative fathering" and was developed by family science professors David Dollahite and Alan Hawkins and their students at Brigham Young University. Start with the conceptual framework for generative fathering. Included in the site are insightful personal stories about fatherhood across the life span, and ideas and activities to encourage generative fathering. Many useful discussion questions are provided.

http://fatherwork.byu.edu

Work and Family: National Partnership for Women and Families

This public education and advocacy site by the National Partnership for Women and Families aims "to promote fairness in the workplace, quality heath care, and policies that help women and men meet the dual demands of work and family." This site includes a wealth of information about relevant public policy issues, including the Family Medical Leave Act. See the research report entitled "Family Matters: A National Survey of Women and Men" for some interesting national statistics.

http://www.nationalpartnership.org

NetWorking Moms

A primary feature of the NetWorking Moms site is an archive of threads from an active discussion list on issues relevant to working mothers. Also included are personal stories about managing work and family responsibilities.

http://networkingmoms.com

Welfare Made a Difference National Campaign

The Web site for the Welfare Made a Difference National Campaign includes personal stories of diverse individuals who are former welfare recipients.

http://www.wmadcampaign.org/mission.html

PART 5

All in the Family

*I*n contemporary America, the "ideal" family continues to be defined as one in which mother and father are married, father is the breadwinner, and mother maintains the home and cares for the children. This ideal is no longer matched by actual family structure, with more and more alternative family structures, including families with same-sex parents and single-parent families being developed to meet personal desires and needs and to cope with societal pressures and changes. Nonetheless, traditional family ideology remains dominant in America. Traditional family ideology institutionalizes conventional gender roles, so much so that many gender scholars view the family as a "gender factory."

In this section, we examine gender in the context of families. How is gender reflected in the revered traditional family model? How do gender expectations affect desired and actual family structure? What is the role of power differentials between men and women and gendered relational dynamics in domestic violence? How does gender shape the roles, rights, and responsibilities of mother and father? In what ways does gender influence families' efforts to balance work and family interests and responsibilities? What are the ramifications of this question for poor people, especially women? How has the swift development of reproductive technologies affected family formation and structure and the determination of parental rights? In what ways have families challenged traditional gender roles and developed new nongendered family models?

- Is Domestic Violence Best Treated as a Gender Crime?

- Should Men and Women Have Equal Parental Rights?

- Can Fathers "Mother"?

- Are Welfare Reforms Ineffective Because Welfare Mothers Are Irresponsible and Lazy?

ISSUE 13

Is Domestic Violence Best Treated as a Gender Crime?

YES: Lori Heise, Mary Ellsberg, and Megan Gottemoeller, from "Ending Violence Against Women," *Population Reports* (December 1999)

NO: A. E. Eyler and Marian Cohen, from American Academy of Family Physicians, http://www.aafp.org/afp/991201ap/2569.html (December 1, 1999)

ISSUE SUMMARY

YES: Lori Heise, codirector of the Center for Health and Gender Equity (CHANGE), Mary Ellsberg, senior associate at CHANGE, and Megan Gottemoeller, program associate at CHANGE, describe domestic violence as endemic to broader cultural issues, such as gender norms, expectations, and pressures, thereby arguing that it is only "treatable" through social change.

NO: A. E. Eyler, clinical associate professor of family medicine, and social worker Marian Cohen provide guidelines for treating domestic violence as an interpersonal problem in couple relationships.

In recent decades, scholars, practitioners, and activists have called for careful examination of and prevention and intervention efforts directed toward the epidemic of domestic violence. Most research, education, and services focus on physical aggression in heterosexual couples, whether dating, cohabiting, or married. Moreover, the typical pattern of violence is thought to involve a male perpetrator and a female victim. Battered women's shelters have served millions of women in the United States while batterers' groups focus on men.

Yet in the last decade, there has been great contention and debate among researchers about whether or not domestic violence is "gendered." Is domestic violence equally common from males to females as from females to males, or does domestic violence usually involve male perpetrators and female victims? What is the role of patriarchy and gendered power differentials and dynamics in the causes of domestic violence? Is gender (as socially constructed) the primary root of domestic violence, or is domestic violence the result of mishandling of interpersonal conflict?

Sparking this controversy were research findings challenging the prototypical pattern of domestic violence. For example, Richard Gelles and Murray Straus found in a national representative sample of adults that heterosexual men and women do not differ in their perpetration of partner-directed physical aggression. Revealing the incidence of women's abuse of men has been highly controversial, spawning many critiques and refutations of such findings. In fact, findings of spousal parity contradict other studies of domestic violence, including U.S. National Crime Survey data.

Psychologist John Archer conducted a major meta-analysis of domestic violence research to try to understand sources of contradiction among studies of domestic violence incidence rates, concluding that results vary by (1) sampling differences (female victims' reports, criminal surveys, and reports versus representative samples of married or dating couples not selected for their high level of violence), and (2) measurement differences (act-based measures versus assessments of physical aggression consequences). For example, Gelles and Straus's use of the Conflict Tactics Scale to assess partner aggression has been contested and charged with skewing domestic violence statistics. The Conflict Tactics Scale asks respondents to report on whether they emitted specific behaviors (hit, kick) to their partner within a certain time period (i.e., one year). Critics argue that the Conflict Tactics Scale simply counts acts of violence without distinguishing different meanings, motives, consequences, or contexts (including economic dependence) of such behaviors. Thus, for example, women are much more likely to suffer severe, even life-threatening, injury at the hands of male perpetrators than are abused husbands. Further, some argue that the majority of violence committed by women is rarely initiated by women but rather is in self-defense and often follows wife abuse.

Assertions of parity between men and women in the perpetration of domestic violence has triggered a passionate debate about whether domestic violence is a "gender crime," as defined in the U.S. Federal Violence Against Women Act, or something else. Gelles argues that rather than an example of "patriarchal coercive control" of women by men, domestic violence may be, regardless of gender, the consequence of poor conflict-management skills. In contrast, Scott Coltrane and Randall Collins assert in their book *Sociology of Marriage and the Family* (2000) that "in light of the general pattern of greater harm to wives, it is inappropriate to label examples of women hitting men as 'husband abuse' or to consider marital violence simply a case of 'mutual combat.' "

Statistics on the incidence rates of domestic violence and the profile of the "typical" perpetrator contribute to the development of theories about the occurrence of domestic violence. In turn, theories about why domestic violence occurs determine approaches to prevention and intervention. Is domestic violence best "treated" as a problem in specific couple relationships, as reflected in the guidelines provided by the American Academy of Family Physicians? Or, is domestic violence endemic to broader cultural issues such as gender norms, expectations, and pressures and thus, only "treatable" through social change?

Lori Heise, Mary Ellsberg, and Megan Gottemoeller

 **YES**

Ending Violence Against Women

Editor's Summary

Around the world at least one woman in every three has been beaten, coerced into sex, or otherwise abused in her lifetime. Most often the abuser is a member of her own family. Increasingly, gender-based violence is recognized as a major public health concern and a violation of human rights.

The effects of violence can be devastating to a woman's reproductive health as well as to other aspects of her physical and mental well-being. In addition to causing injury, violence increases women's long-term risk of a number of other health problems, including chronic pain, physical disability, drug and alcohol abuse, and depression. Women with a history of physical or sexual abuse are also at increased risk for unintended pregnancy, sexually transmitted infections, and adverse pregnancy outcomes. Yet victims of violence who seek care from health professionals often have needs that providers do not recognize, do not ask about, and do not know how to address.

What Is Gender-Based Violence?

Violence against women and girls includes physical, sexual, psychological, and economic abuse. It is often known as "gender-based" violence because it evolves in part from women's subordinate status in society. Many cultures have beliefs, norms, and social institutions that legitimize and therefore perpetuate violence against women. The same acts that would be punished if directed at an employer, a neighbor, or an acquaintance often go unchallenged when men direct them at women, especially within the family....

Intimate Partner Abuse

Worldwide, one of the most common forms of violence against women is abuse by their husbands or other intimate male partners. Partner violence occurs in all countries and transcends social, economic, religious, and cultural groups. Although women can also be violent and abuse exists in some same-sex relationships, the vast majority of partner abuse is perpetrated by men against their female partners.

While research into intimate partner abuse is in its early stages, there is growing agreement about its nature and the various factors that cause it. Often referred to as "wife-beating," "battering," or "domestic violence," intimate partner abuse is generally part of a pattern of abusive behavior and control rather than an isolated act of physical aggression. Partner abuse can take a variety of forms including physical assault such as hits, slaps, kicks, and beatings; psychological abuse, such as constant belittling, intimidation, and humiliation; and coercive sex. It frequently includes controlling behaviors such as isolating a woman from family and friends, monitoring her movements, and restricting her access to resources.

Magnitude of the Problem

In nearly 50 population-based surveys from around the world, 10% to over 50% of women report being hit or otherwise physically harmed by an intimate male partner at some point in their lives. . . . Research into partner violence is so new that comparable data on psychological and sexual abuse by intimate partners are few.

Physical violence in intimate relationships almost always is accompanied by psychological abuse and, in one-third to over one-half of cases, by sexual abuse. For example, among 613 abused women in Japan, 57% had suffered all three types of abuse—physical, psychological, and sexual. Only 8% had experienced physical abuse alone. In Monterrey, Mexico, 52% of physically abused women had also been sexually abused by their partners. In León, Nicaragua, among 188 women who were physically abused by their partners, only 5 were not also abused sexually, psychologically, or both.

Most women who suffer any physical aggression generally experience multiple acts over time. In the León study, for example, 60% of women abused in the previous year were abused more than once, and 20% experienced severe violence more than six times. Among women reporting any physical aggression, 70% reported severe abuse. The average number of physical assaults in the previous year among currently abused women surveyed in London was seven; in the US in 1997, three.

In surveys of partner violence, women usually are asked whether or not they have experienced any of a list of specific actions, such a being slapped, pushed, punched, beaten, or threatened with a weapon. Asking behavioral questions—for example, "Has your partner ever physically forced you to have sex against your will?"—yields more accurate responses than asking women whether they have been "abused" or "raped." Surveys generally define physical acts more severe than slapping, pushing, shoving, or throwing objects as "severe violence."

Measuring "acts" of violence does not describe the atmosphere of terror that often permeates abusive relationships. For example, in Canada's 1993 national violence survey one-third of women who had been physically assaulted by a partner said that they had feared for their lives at some point in the relationship. Women often say that the psychological abuse and degradation are even more difficult to bear than the physical abuse.

Dynamics of Abuse

Many cultures hold that men have the right to control their wives' behavior and that women who challenge that right—even by asking for household money or by expressing the needs of the children—may be punished. In countries as different as Bangladesh, Cambodia, India, Mexico, Nigeria, Pakistan, Papua New Guinea, Tanzania, and Zimbabwe, studies find that violence is frequently viewed as physical chastisement—the husband's right to "correct" an erring wife. As one husband said in a focus-group discussion in Tamil Nadu, India, "If it is a great mistake, then the husband is justified in beating his wife. Why not? A cow will not be obedient without beatings."

Justifications for violence frequently evolve from gender norms—that is, social norms about the proper roles and responsibilities of men and women. Typically, men are given relatively free reign as long as they provide financially for the family. Women are expected to tend the house and mind the children and to show their husbands obedience and respect. If a man perceives that his wife has somehow failed in her role, stepped beyond her bounds, or challenged his rights, then he may react violently.

Worldwide, studies identify a consistent list of events that are said to "trigger" violence. These include: not obeying her husband, talking back, not having food ready on time, failing to care adequately for the children or home, questioning him about money or girlfriends, going somewhere without his permission, refusing him sex, or expressing suspicions of infidelity. All of these constitute transgression of gender norms.

In many developing countries women share the notion that men have the right to discipline their wives by using force. In rural Egypt, for example, at least 80% of women say that beatings are justified under certain circumstances. One of the circumstances that women most often cite is refusing a man sex. Not surprisingly, refusing sex is also one of the reasons women cite most often as triggering beatings.

Societies often distinguish between just and unjust reasons for violence, as well as between acceptable and unacceptable amounts of aggression. The notion of "just cause" permeates findings on violence in many countries. Certain individuals, usually husbands and elders, may have the right to chastise a woman physically for certain transgressions, but only within limits. If a man oversteps these limits by becoming too violent or for beating a woman without "just cause," others have cause to intervene. As a woman in Mexico put it, "If I have done something wrong..., nobody should defend me. But if I haven't done something wrong, I have a right to be defended."

Even where culture itself grants men substantial control over female behavior, abusive men generally exceed the norm. For example, data from the Nicaragua Demographic and Health Survey (DHS) show that, among women who were abused physically, 32% had husbands who scored high on a scale of marital control compared with only 2% among women who were not abused physically. The scale included such behavior as the husband's continually accusing his wife of being unfaithful and limiting her access to family and friends.

A FRAMEWORK FOR UNDERSTANDING
PARTNER VIOLENCE

What causes violence against women? Increasingly, researchers are using an "ecological framework" to understand the interplay of personal, situational, and sociocultural factors that combine to cause abuse. In this model, violence against women results from the interaction of factors at different levels of the social environment.

The model can best be visualized as four concentric circles. The innermost circle represents the biological and personal history that each individual brings to his or her behavior in relationships. The second circle represents the immediate context in which abuse takes place—frequently the family or other intimate or acquaintance relationship. The third circle represents the institutions and social structures, both formal and informal, in which relationships are embedded—neighborhood, workplace, social networks, and peer groups. The fourth, outermost circle is the economic and social environment, including cultural norms.

A wide range of studies agrees on several factors at each of these levels that increase the likelihood that a man will abuse his partner:

- **At the individual level** these include being abused as a child or witnessing marital violence in the home, having an absent or rejecting father, and frequent use of alcohol.

- **At the level of the family and relationship** cross-cultural studies have cited male control of wealth and decision-making within the family and marital conflict as strong predictors of abuse.

- **At the community level** women's isolation and lack of social support, together with male peer groups that condone and legitimize men's violence, predict higher rates of violence.

- **At the societal level** studies around the world have found that violence against women is most common where gender roles are rigidly defined and enforced and where the concept of masculinity is linked to toughness, male honor, or dominance. Other cultural norms associated with abuse include tolerance of physical punishment of women and children, acceptance of violence as a means to settle interpersonal disputes, and the perception that men have "ownership" of women.

By combining individual-level risk factors with findings of cross-cultural studies, the ecological model contributes to understanding why some societies and some individuals are more violent than others and why women—especially wives—are so consistently the victims of abuse.

Women's Response to Abuse

Most abused women are not passive victims but use active strategies to maximize their safety and that of their children. Some women resist, others flee, and still others attempt to keep the peace by capitulating to their husbands' demands. What may seem to an observer to be lack of response to living with violence may in fact be strategic assessment of what it takes for the woman to survive in the marriage and to protect herself and her children.

A woman's response to abuse is often limited by the options available to her. Women consistently cite similar reasons that they remain in abusive relationships: fear of retribution, lack of other means of economic support, concern for the children, emotional dependence, lack of support from family and friends, and an abiding hope that "he will change." In developing countries women cite the unacceptability of being single or unmarried as an additional barrier that keeps them in destructive marriages.

At the same time, denial and fear of social stigma often prevent women from reaching out for help. In surveys, for example, from 22% to almost 70% of abused women say that they have never told anyone about their abuse before being asked in the interview. Those who reach out do so primarily to family members and friends. Few have ever contacted the police.

Despite the obstacles, many women eventually do leave violent partners— even if after many years, once the children are grown. In León, Nicaragua, for example, the likelihood that an abused woman will eventually leave her abuser is 70%. The median time that women spend in a violent relationship is five years. Younger women are more likely to leave sooner.

Studies suggest a consistent set of factors that propel women to leave an abusive relationship: The violence gets more severe and triggers a realization that "he" is not going to change, or the violence begins to take a toll on the children. Women also cite emotional and logistical support from family or friends as pivotal in their decisions to leave.

Leaving an abusive relationship is a process. The process often includes periods of denial, self-blame, and endurance before women come to recognize the abuse as a pattern and to identify with other women in the same situation. This is the beginning of disengagement and recovery. Most women leave and return several times before they finally leave once and for all.

Regrettably, leaving does not necessarily guarantee a woman's safety. Violence sometimes continues and may even escalate after a woman leaves her partner. In fact, a woman's risk of being murdered is greatest immediately after separation.

Explaining Intimate Partner Abuse

While intimate partner abuse is widespread, it is not universal. Anthropologists have documented small-scale societies—such as the Wape of Papua New Guinea —where domestic violence is virtually absent. This finding stands as testament to the fact that social relations can be organized in a way that minimizes partner abuse.

In many places the prevalence of such violence varies substantially among neighboring areas. These local differences are often greater than the differences among countries. For example, in Uttar Pradesh, India, the percentage of men who said they beat their wives varied from 18% in Naintal District to 45% in

Banda. The percentage that physically forced their wives to have sex varied from 14% to 36% among districts.

CULTURE: A DOUBLE-EDGED SWORD

In all societies there are cultural institutions, beliefs, and practices that undermine women's autonomy and contribute to gender-based violence. Certain marriage practices, for example, can disadvantage women and girls, especially where customs, such as dowry and bridewealth, have been corrupted by Western "consumer" culture.

In recent years, for example, dowry has become an expected part of the marriage transaction in some countries, with future husbands demanding ever-increasing dowry both before and after marriage. Dowry demands can escalate into harassment, threats, and abuse; in extreme cases the woman is killed or driven to suicide, freeing the husband to pursue another marriage and dowry.

Elsewhere, husbands are expected to pay "bridewealth" to compensate the bride's family for the loss of labor in her natal home. In parts of Africa and Asia this exchange has likewise become commercialized, with inflated bridewealth leaving many men with the impression that they have "purchased" a wife. In a recent survey in the Eastern Cape Province of South Africa, 82% of women said it is culturally accepted that, if a man pays *lobola* (bridewealth) for his wife, it means that he owns her. Some 72% of women themselves agreed with this statement.

Both marriage traditions undermine the ability of women to escape abusive relationships. For example, parents on the Indian subcontinent are reluctant to allow their daughters to return home for fear of having to pay a second dowry, whereas in bridewealth cultures, women's parents must repay the man if their daughter leaves the marriage. As an abused woman in India observed, "One often feels like running away from it all. But where does one go? The only place is your parents' house, but they will always try to send you back."

Cultural attitudes toward female chastity and male honor also serve to justify violence against women and to exacerbate its consequences. In parts of Latin American and the Near East, a man's honor is often linked to the sexual "purity" of the women in his family. If a woman is "defiled" sexually —either through rape or by engaging voluntarily in sex outside of marriage —she disgraces the family honor.

For example, in some Arab societies the only way to "cleanse" the family honor is to kill the "offending" woman or girl. A study of female homicide in Alexandria, Egypt, found that 47% of all women killed were murdered by a relative after they had been raped. At a recent conference in Jordan, experts from six Arab countries estimated that at least several hundred Arab women die each year as a result of honor killings.

Culture is neither static nor monolithic, however. Women's rights activists argue that communities must dismantle those aspects of culture that oppress women while preserving what is good. In the words of Ghanaian lawyer Rosemary Ofibea Ofei-Afboagye, "A culture that teaches male mastery and domination over women must be altered."

Women at the forefront of the women's human rights movement point out that appeals to culture are often an excuse to justify practices oppressive to women. Sudanese physician Nahid Toubia asks, "Why is it only when women want to bring about change for their own benefit that culture and custom become sacred and unchangeable?"

Although culture can aggravate women's vulnerability, it can also serve as a creative resource for intervention. Many traditional cultures have mechanisms—such as public shaming or community healing—that can be mobilized as resources to confront abuse. Activists from Canada's Yukon Territory, for example, have developed Circle Sentencing, an updated version of the traditional sanctioning and healing practices of the Canadian aboriginal peoples. Within the "circle," crime victims, offenders, justice and social service personnel, as well as community residents, listen to the victim's story and deliberate about how best to "restore justice" to the victim and the community. Sentencing often includes reparation, community service, jail time, treatment requirements, and community healing rituals.

Activists in India and Bangladesh likewise have adapted the *salishe*—a traditional system of local justice—to address domestic violence. For example, when a woman is beaten, the West Bengali NGO Shramajibee Mahila Samity sends a female organizer to the village to consult with the individuals and families involved. The organizer then facilitates a *salishe,* attempting to steer the discussion in a pro-woman direction. Collectively, the community arrives at a proposed solution, which is formalized in writing and monitored by a local committee.

NO ↩

A. E. Eyler and Marian Cohen

Case Studies in Partner Violence

The American Medical Association's Diagnostic and Treatment Guidelines on Domestic Violence state that, "Family violence usually results from the abuse of power or the domination and victimization of a physically less powerful person by a physically more powerful person."[1] Other factors that create or maintain a power differential, such as unequal financial resources, family connections or health status, can also foster situations in which the more powerful person exerts inappropriate control or intimidation over the less powerful person. Any misuse of power, especially that which involves physical violence or psychologic intimidation, constitutes abuse. A perpetrator is a person who performs or permits the actions that constitute abuse or neglect. The term "batterer" refers more specifically to a perpetrator who engages in physical violence. It should be noted that, although the most familiar constellation for partner violence is one in which the (current or ex-) husband or boyfriend is the perpetrator and the wife or girlfriend is the victim, partner abuse also occurs in homosexual relationships and in heterosexual relationships in which men are the victims. Unless specifically mentioned, the remarks in this article are true for situations in which men and women are the abusers....

Medical Management Guidelines

.... Clinical interventions specific to the problems of partner violence are discussed ... in the context of two case presentations....

Illustrative Cases

The following two cases, drawn from the clinical experiences of the authors, illustrate techniques for the diagnosis and management of patients experiencing interpersonal violence in partnered relationships. The discussion that follows each case is designed to assist family physicians with practical approaches to preventing violence and promoting victim safety.

Table 1

Interviewing Patients for Partner Abuse Risk

Does your partner physically hurt you or threaten you?

Have you ever been in a relationship where you were hurt or threatened?

Are you (or have you been) treated badly in other ways?

Has your partner ever destroyed things you cared about or stolen your things?

Has your partner ever threatened or abused your children?

Has your partner ever forced you to have sex when you didn't want to, or made you do something sexually that you didn't like?

We all get into arguments–what happens when you and your partner fight at home?

Do you ever feel afraid of your partner?

Has your partner ever prevented you from leaving the house, getting a job, seeking friends or continuing your education?

How does your partner act when he (or she) has been drinking or using other drugs?

Are there guns (or other weapons) in your home?

Has your partner (or anyone else) ever threatened to use them?

Source: Adapted with permission from Diagnostic and treatment guidelines on domestic violence. (American Medical Association, 1992)

Case 1

An 18-year-old woman presented to her family physician for an initial obstetric examination, accompanied by her 27-year-old boyfriend. Initial history revealed that she was a gravida [pregnancies] 1, para [births] 0, at 16 weeks of gestation and living in a mobile home with her partner. She was strongly considering giving up the baby for adoption because of "financial and other" reasons. Answers to screening violence history questions (*Table 1*)[1] indicated that she had been beaten by her father from preschool age until she was 13 years of age; her parents then divorced. The patient stated that her present partner had "slapped her around" on several occasions and that once she was "accidentally dragged by his truck" during an argument. He had slammed the driver's door, started the truck and put it in gear, reportedly without realizing that her dress was caught in the car door. On further questioning the patient stated that she was not happy in this relationship and in fact did not feel safe. However, she stated that she "had no place else to go" and expressed optimism about the future because her partner had begun to attend church and stated that he wanted to be a good father.

Discussion

Battering is frequent during pregnancy[2-4] and is more common if, as in this case, the pregnancy is unintended.[5] Battering can result in pregnancy complications, delayed entry into prenatal care[6,7] and unintended, rapid-repeat pregnancy in adolescent mothers.[9] Simple screening questions, administered in a private setting, often identify pregnant women who are being abused.[7] Furthermore, because battering may begin late in pregnancy, a discussion of personal safety should be included at multiple times during the course of obstetric care.

This patient is a survivor of an abusive childhood. She lives with a partner who controls her behavior and who is on occasion physically abusive to her. She is also financially dependent on him. Her vulnerability is further increased, physically and psychologically, by her unplanned pregnancy and her lack of family or other emotional support.

Because battering usually does not abate during pregnancy, the physician can best intervene by providing her with information regarding the potential danger of her situation and by assisting her in safety planning, including a facilitated referral to a shelter for battered women.[9] One useful technique is for the physician to contact the shelter while the patient is in the examination room or a private office. The physician can then hand the telephone to the patient and leave the room, allowing the patient to talk to a counselor in private. Thus, the patient's autonomy and privacy are respected, but an additional barrier to seeking help is removed.

The physician should inquire about the presence of firearms in the home or in the possession of the battering partner. This step is crucial in preventing serious injury and homicide.[10–12] Statistics from the Federal Bureau of Investigation indicate that over one half of female murder victims are killed by firearms in the hands of a current male partner or ex-husband.

It is also crucial that, throughout the course of the pregnancy, the physician avoid communicating to the patient that she is in any way responsible for, or deserving of, the abuse.[13] For example, asking her why she is still living with her partner may be interpreted as a judgment of her failure to end the relationship. Furthermore, as most men who batter will from time to time express goodwill or intent to change, it may be helpful to ask the patient if her partner has previously made promises of improved behavior and inquire if he has kept such promises. The physician may wish to review the elements of abuse outlined in *Table 2* with the patient and ask about her partner's behaviors. This table illustrates the many faces of abuse and may help her visualize and assess her risk in light of the overall circumstances, rather than focusing on her partner's latest promises. She may be unaware that the main issues in abusive relationships are power and control.

Many batterers who eventually stop using physical violence substitute psychologic abuse and intimidation.[14] Thus, it may further help the patient to understand that even in relationships in which the physical violence has ceased, a climate of fear may persist to a level where the formerly battered partner continues to comply with the requests of the dominant partner out of fear that the physical violence will resume....

Factors that specifically relate to partner abuse include the following: (1) a power differential in the relationship in which one partner is financially or emotionally dependent on the other; (2) a temporary or permanent disability (including pregnancy); (3) a force orientation—a belief on the part of the perpetrator that violence is an acceptable solution to conflicts and problems; and

Table 2

Power and Control Issues in Partner Violence

Physical Abuse

* Tripping	* Twisting arms
* Punching	* Kicking
* Grabbing	* Using a weapon against partner
* Beating	* Throwing partner down
* Pulling hair	* Choking
* Slapping	* Hitting
* Shoving	* Pushing
* Biting	

Power and Control

Threats

* Making and/or carrying out threats to do something to hurt partner emotionally	* Threatening to take away the children
* Threatening to commit suicide	* Threatening to report partner to a governmental agency, or betraying other important secrets

Emotional abuse

* Putting partner down	* Making partner feel bad about self
* Making partner think she or he is crazy	* Playing "mind games"

Using male privilege

* Treating partner like a servant	* Making all the "big" decisions
* Acting like the "master of the castle"	

Isolation

* Controlling what partner does	* Controlling who partner sees
* Controlling who partner talks to	* Controlling where partner goes

Sexual abuse

* Making partner do sexual things against her or his will	* Physically attacking the sexual parts of partner's body
* Treating partner like a sex object	

Using the children

* Making partner feel guilty about the children	* Using the children to give messages
* Using visitation as a way to harass partner	

Economic abuse

* Trying to keep partner from getting a job	* Making partner ask for money
* Taking partner's money	* Giving partner an "allowance"

Intimidation–putting partner in fear, by

* Looks, actions, gestures and a loud voice	* Smashing things
* Destroying partner's property	* Killing, hurting or threatening pets

Source: Information from a figure developed by The Domestic Abuse Intervention Project, Duluth, Minn.

(4) a personal or family history of abuse. It may be useful to ask the patient how her partner manages frustration or stress. Does he blame others (including her) or does he take responsibility for his mistakes? Does he use aggression (including threats or put-downs) to resolve conflicts in the relationship?

Case 2

A 45-year-old man presented to his physician with a complaint of worsening depression. The patient had been taking antidepressant medications for many years, was receiving ongoing psychotherapy from a clinical social worker and attending Alcoholics Anonymous meetings. The patient complained of insomnia, loss of appetite and thoughts of guilt and suicide since his spouse had "kicked him out." He was especially concerned because she has multiple sclerosis, relies on him for some physical assistance and, in his opinion, should not be left alone. Further discussion revealed that during an argument, he verbally threatened to harm her, then threw a large lamp at her (although he missed and did not actually hit her). She called the police, had him removed from the home and told him she would soon be filing for divorce.

Discussion

A positive outcome is possible for this couple because of the confluence of several helpful events and interventions. The patient had previously received treatment for alcoholism, had not resumed drinking and was under care for depression. Furthermore, his wife had worked as a teacher before her illness, was receiving retirement benefits and was not financially dependent on him. Perhaps most significantly, she called the police during the first violent episode rather than excuse her husband's actions and allow a pattern of threats and intimidation to become established. She also received a prompt response and support from the police and the courts.

The patient's depression worsened during the court proceedings, eventually requiring inpatient psychiatric treatment for suicide prevention. During the course of his therapy, he received psychologic support for his stressful personal situation, but his behavior toward his wife was not excused in any way by his treating physicians. Eventually, this couple began marital therapy together, after the goals of establishing a non-violent and equitable relationship were defined.

Family physicians can play a crucial role in referring batterers to appropriate services for behavior modification interventions and treatment of co-morbidities, such as depression and alcoholism. If the abusive patient's wife or partner is also a patient in the physician's practice, asking that person questions about her experiences of violence and providing information about safety planning and resources may be lifesaving.[9,15]

Studies have not identified any consistent psychiatric diagnoses among batterers, but abusive men share some common characteristics such as rigid sex-role stereotypes, low self-esteem, depression, a high need for power and control, a tendency to minimize and deny their problems or the extent of their violence, a tendency to blame others for their behavior, violence in the family of origin (particularly witnessing parental violence), and drug and alcohol abuse (which are not causative but are often associated).[16] Some but not all batterers meet the criteria in the *Diagnostic and Statistical Manual of Mental Disorders,* 4th ed. (DSM IV) for personality disorders or depression.[17]

Men who have alcoholism combined with a major depressive disorder or antisocial personality disorder are more likely to commit domestic violence than men with either of these conditions alone.[18] Most researchers believe that abusive behavior is the result of multiple factors, including individual characteristics, a family history of violence, the culturally rooted belief that violence is an acceptable means of solving problems and that violence toward women is acceptable or tolerated.[19,20] The patient in this case did not hold these beliefs and was eventually able to participate successfully in couples' therapy.

Batterers are often difficult to identify because they rarely present with symptoms that suggest problems with violence; however, they may seek care for injuries received from a violent episode where the victim's attempts at self-defense result in injuries to the batterer (e.g., hand fractures, bites, lacerations, eye injuries).

Family physicians can also screen for violent behavior by asking direct questions[21] or by inquiring about related beliefs and behaviors while conducting a routine patient history. One such approach is the funneling technique, which begins with less threatening questions and progresses to questions about more serious violence, depending on the patient's responses. Batterers often minimize or deny their abuse by using euphemisms for violence such as "not getting along," "loss of temper," "fighting" and "self-defense," when in fact they are referring to their own violent actions.[14] Therefore, questioning does not always result in identification of battering behavior. Nevertheless, this approach allows the physician to broach the subject, and further questioning about what the patient means by a specific term may sometimes provide the opportunity for the patient to disclose abusive actions and seek help.

Patients who batter should be advised that their behavior is illegal and should be given information about treatment programs. Family physicians should bear in mind that the usefulness of batterer treatment programs remains controversial.[22] Many perpetrators do not change their beliefs or behavior, and the immediate goal is protection of the battered patient and dependents (children and elderly relatives) from further harm. Early referral to community resources (e.g., safe houses and legal aid) and follow-up until the situation is resolved can be crucial. Encouraging the battered victim to call the police or involve sympathetic family members or friends may help alleviate the isolation that often accompanies domestic violence and also help prevent retaliation....

Prevention

Occasional conflict is a universal feature of intimate relationships. However, coercion, violence and unwanted sexual activity are not a normal part of marriage or other relationships and must not be tolerated. Many alternatives exist for handling conflict that do not involve violence, intimidation or domination of one person by the other. Prevention of abuse and neglect depends on the early recognition of risk and on timely, appropriate response.

Physicians frequently report that dealing with domestic violence is a frustrating experience. Persons who have been abused are often not "ideal" patients—they miss appointments, request tranquilizers, offer vague somatic complaints, do not follow through with treatment and often do not leave their batterers.

In contrast, perpetrators are often articulate, interesting community figures who present themselves more favorably.[15] In order to deal most effectively with the problem of partner abuse and to maintain a balanced perspective, family physicians must remain aware that appearances can be deceiving. Incorporating routine screening for violence risk into clinical practice may minimize the risk that a physician will fall prey to unconscious stereotypes about abused persons.

Domestic violence is a criminal offense. Patient education about these straightforward facts, during office visits or through written materials and timely referral, can be lifesaving.

References

1. Flitcraft AH, Hadley SM, Hendricks-Matthews MK, McLeer SV, Warshaw C, et al. Diagnostic and treatment guidelines on domestic violence. Chicago: American Medical Association, 1992.
2. Gazmararian JA, Lazorick S, Spitz AM, Ballard TJ, Saltzman LE, Marks JS. Prevalence of violence against pregnant women. JAMA 1996;275:1915–20.
3. McFarlane J, Parker B, Soeken K. Abuse during pregnancy: associations with maternal health and infant birth weight. Nurs Res 1996;45:37–42.
4. Physical violence during the 12 months preceding childbirth—Alaska, Maine, Oklahoma, and West Virginia, 1990–1991. MMWR Morb Mortal Wkly Rep 1994;43(8):132–7.
5. Gazmararian JA, Adams MM, Saltzman LE, Johnson CH, Bruce FC, Marks JS, et al. The relationship between pregnancy intendedness and physical violence in mothers of newborns. The PRAMS Working Group. Obstet Gynecol 1995;85:1031–8.
6. McFarlane J, Parker B, Soeken K, Bullock L. Assessing for abuse during pregnancy. Severity and frequency of injuries and associated entry into prenatal care. JAMA 1992;267:3176–8.
7. Dietz PM, Gazmararian JA, Goodwin MM, Bruce FC, Johnson CH, Rochat RW. Delayed entry into prenatal care. Obstet Gynecol 1997;90:221–4.
8. Jacoby M, Gorenflo D, Black E, Wunderlich C, Eyler AE. Rapid repeat pregnancy and experiences of interpersonal violence among low-income adolescents. Am J Prev Med 1999;16:318–21.
9. McFarlane J, Soeken K, Reel S, Parker B, Silva C. Resource use by abused women following an intervention program: associated severity of abuse and reports of abuse ending. Public Health Nurs 1997;14:244–50.
10. McFarlane J, Parker B, Soeken K. Abuse during pregnancy: frequency, severity, perpetrator, and risk factors of homicide. Public Health Nurs 1995;12:284–9.
11. McFarlane J, Soeken K, Campbell J, Parker B, Reel S, Silva C. Severity of abuse to pregnant women and associated gun access of the perpetrator. Public Health Nurs 1998;15:201–6.
12. Saltzman LE, Mercy JA, O'Carroll PW, Rosenberg ML, Rhodes PH. Weapon involvement and injury outcome in family and intimate assaults. JAMA 1992;267:3043–7.
13. Hamberger LK, Ambuel B, Marbella A, Donze J. Physician interaction with battered women. 1998; 7:575–82.

14. Adams D. Guidelines for doctors on identifying and helping their patients who batter. J Am Med Womens Assoc 1996;51:123-6.
15. Ferris LE, Norton PG, Dunn EV, Gort EH, Degani N. Guidelines for managing domestic abuse when male and female partners are patients of the same physician. The Delphi Panel and the Consulting Group. JAMA 1997;278:851-7.
16. Bennett LW, Substance abuse and the domestic assault of women. So Work, 1995;40:760-71.
17. American Psychiatric Association. Diagnostic and statistical manual of mental disorders. 4th ed. Washington, D.C.: American Psychiatric Association, 1994:317-92,629-74.
18. Keller LE. Invisible victims: battered women in psychiatric and medical emergency rooms. Bull Menninger Clinic 1996;60:1-21.
19. Chell D. Who are the batterers? Iowa Med 1995;85:28-30.
20. Hamberger LK. Identifying and intervening with men who batter. In: Hendricks-Matthews MK, Brewster A. Violence education: toward a solution. Kansas City, Mo.: Society of Teachers of Family Medicine, 1992:55-62.
21. Oriel KA, Fleming MF. Screening men for partner violence in a primary care setting. J Fam Pract 1998; 46:493-8.
22. Tolman R, Edleson J. Intervention for men who batter: a review of research. In: Stith SM, Straus MA, eds. Understanding partner violence: prevalence, causes, consequences, and solutions. Minneapolis, Minn.: National Council on Family Relations 1995:262-74.

POSTSCRIPT

Is Domestic Violence Best Treated as a Gender Crime?

While there is controversy about the incidence rates of female violence against males, there is little argument that some men are victims of partner violence (U.S. crime statistics consistently find that approximately 5 percent of men are victims of domestic violence, while research on representative samples using an act-based measure find that more men—similar to the rate of women —are victims of aggressive behaviors from their partner). What is potentially problematic about statistics on male *and* female perpetrators of domestic violence is how they are interpreted and used. Gender scholars urge that the statistics cannot be interpreted fairly without a detailed, contextual framework for understanding the causes of male and female violence. A dangerous assumption sometimes drawn from evidence that both men and women are potential perpetrators of violence is that the forms and levels of such violence are identical whether perpetrated by men or women. Used in several instances as a justification for the reallocation of domestic violence services and resources, such an assumption breaches the real needs of the domestic violence victims who suffer extreme physical and psychological harm, usually women.

In a decade review of domestic violence research, Michael Johnson and Kathleen Ferraro assert that future research on partner violence must distinguish among a complex array of experiences, including distinctions among types of violence, perpetrator motives, the social locations of both partners, and the cultural context in which violence occurs.

Various scholars argue that the richest vantage point from which to understand the complex phenomenon of domestic violence is a global analysis. For example, cultures differ in the existence of traditions inhibiting men from hitting women and in the strength of patriarchal values. Johnson and Ferraro urge us to broaden our examination of domestic violence to consider cultural differences, economic and social structures, effects of conflict and welfare, and the position of immigrant and refugee populations as critical delineators in the incidence rates and experiences of domestic violence.

Suggested Readings

J. Archer, "Sex Differences in Aggression Between Heterosexual Partners: A Meta-Analytic Review," *Psychological Bulletin,* 126 (2000): 651–680.

M. P. Johnson and K. J. Ferraro, "Research on Domestic Violence in the 1990s: Making Distinctions," *Journal of Marriage and the Family,* 62 (2000): 948–964.

ISSUE 14

Should Men and Women Have Equal Parental Rights?

YES: Marjorie Maguire Shultz, from "Reproductive Technology and Intent-Based Parenthood: An Opportunity for Gender Neutrality," *Wisconsin Law Review* (1990)

NO: Martha Albertson Fineman, from "The Neutered Mother," *University of Miami Law Review* (1992)

ISSUE SUMMARY

YES: Professor of law Marjorie Maquire Shultz argues that parental status should be determined on the basis of expressed intentions rather than biological factors. She reasons that since the ability to form and express intentions is gender neutral, this approach brings greater gender equity to parenting roles.

NO: Professor of law Martha Albertson Fineman asserts that the rhetoric of gender neutrality among liberal legal feminists undermines the unique and powerful role of Mother. As a result, women who are mothers are represented poorly in the context of law and policy.

Questions that once seemed simplistic but have recently become much more complex include: How is a baby made? Who is involved in making a baby? Who are the baby's parents? In determining the parents, does it matter whether or not the individuals *intended* to make the baby? Are the same criteria for establishing motherhood useful for establishing fatherhood?

Two types of legal cases are most challenging to traditional decisions about parental rights: Paternal rights of unwed fathers and parental rights of parties to surrogacy arrangements. Consider the parental rights' decisions made in the following four legal cases. Observe the similar or different criteria for determining maternal and paternal rights.

Lehr v. Robertson, 463 U.S. 248 (1983) (unwed father paternal rights case). Jonathan Lehr petitioned to prevent the adoption of his daughter by the husband of the child's mother. Lehr had not established a substantial relationship with his daughter; the mother had. Lehr's "mere biological relationship" was not enough to establish legal paternity. The court's ruling implied that Lehr had passed up his right as the biological father to develop a relationship with his child. Thus, his paternal rights could not be upheld.

Michael H. v. Gerald D., 491 U.S. 110 (1989) (unwed father parental rights case). Michael H. impregnated Carol who was married to Gerald D. at the time of conception. Gerald D. was listed as the father on the child's birth certificate. A blood test revealed with near certainty that Michael H. was the biological father. Michael H. and Carol lived together for nearly a year during the child's infancy. Carol then left with the child to return to Gerald D. There were several moves back and forth between the two men and another man, Scott. Michael H. financially supported and had a relationship with the child for three years. Within 18 months of the child's birth, Michael H. filed a petition for a declaration of paternity. The court assigned paternal rights to Gerald D., regardless of the biological father's established and intended relationship with the child. The "marital presumption" states that if a child is conceived during and born into an existing marriage, even if the child has a different biological father, the husband is the legal father. The state of California's interest in "preserving the integrity of the matrimonial family" outweighed other interests.

Baby M (surrogacy case decided in New Jersey in 1987). This case was a high-profile custody battle between Mary Beth Whitehead (surrogate) and William Stern (contracting father). Eggs from Whitehead were fertilized with sperm from Stern. Initially, a New Jersey trial court granted custody to William Stern and allowed his wife to adopt the baby; Whitehead's parental rights were terminated. However, the New Jersey Supreme Court reversed the trial court decision. The Court ruled that Whitehead's rights should not be terminated; she was the mother since she had conceived and gestated the child. The Court also declared that the surrogacy contract, in which money was paid to a surrogate mother, was illegal and degrading to women. Custody was awarded to William Stern. Liberal visitation rights were given to Whitehead. No legal maternal rights were granted to Elizabeth Stern.

Anna J. v. Mark C. et. al., 12 Cal. App. 4th 977 (gestational surrogacy case decided in California in 1990). This case was a gestational surrogacy arrangement in which eggs from the contracting mother were fertilized with the contracting father's sperm. The resultant zygote was implanted in the uterus of Anna J. (the gestational surrogate). During the pregnancy, the contracting and genetic parents, the Calverts, learned that Anna J. had withheld information from them about previous miscarriages and pregnancy-related problems. At this time, the Calverts sought a legal declaration as legal parents of the unborn baby. In response, Anna J. filed an action seeking a declaration as legal mother. The court consolidated the cases, making Anna J. the leading case. A California trial court ruled that the surrogate had no legal parental rights since she had no other biological link other than gestation.

Marjorie Maguire Schultz asserts that expressed intentions should take precedence over biological relationships in determining parental status. Martha Albertson Fineman counters that the effect of gender-neutral determinations of parental status would result in damaging consequences for women who are mothers. Laws and policies would cease to represent these women fairly.

Marjorie Maguire Shultz

Reproductive Technology and Intent-Based Parenthood: An Opportunity for Gender Neutrality

Modern reproductive techniques subdivide what was previously unitary. Various stages of the biological process can now be severed, allowing specific impaired aspects of the procreative process to be replaced by workable substitutes. As a result, more than two persons can now be biologically involved in a given instance of reproduction. Furthermore, because processes that previously were bundled can now be separated, procreation can be depersonalized: biological reproduction can be separated from the social and physical context of interpersonal intimacy. Whenever subdivision occurs, choices emerge. Developments in reproductive technology have created new biological and social options that in turn challenge old assumptions and pose new dilemmas for legal doctrine and policy.

One particularly significant theme emerges from this array of developments: the choices generated by modern reproductive technology have made personal intention a far more significant factor in procreation and parenthood.... Legal rules governing modern procreative arrangements and parental status should recognize the importance and the legitimacy of individual efforts to project intentions and decisions into the future. Where such intentions are deliberate, explicit and bargained for, where they are the catalyst for reliance and expectations, as is the case in technologically-assisted reproductive arrangements, they should be honored....

By embracing the emerging opportunities provided by advancing technology, the law would enhance individual freedom, fulfillment and responsibility. Important additional gains would also accrue. Rules that would determine legal parenthood on the basis of individual intentions about procreation and parenting—at least in the context of reproductive technology—would recognize, encourage and reinforce men's choices to nurture children. By adopting a sex-neutral criterion such as intention, the law would partially offset the biological disadvantages men experience in accessing child-nurturing opportunities. The result would parallel recent legal efforts to offset the burdens that childbearing imposes on women who seek equal access to market employment....

Although both sexes are essential to conception, both can try to persuade or coerce the other's procreational behavior, and both share disabilities in effectuating reproductive intentions, major sex differences in access to procreation and parenthood remain. Thus, women bear all the physical risks and burdens of pregnancy and childbirth—a considerable fact given the realities of maternal death, illness and complications from childbirth as well as the accompanying disruptions of work and lifestyle. However, if the genders are compared from the vantage point of an affirmative desire to be a parent, nature gives important advantages to women.

Because men are biologically uninvolved in gestation and birth, they are more dependent on women than women are on them in achieving parenthood. Men do have the advantage of being fertile for more years of the life cycle than women. However, the physiology of procreation gives the mother opportunities to frustrate a father's knowledge and choices about procreation. A woman may hide a pregnancy, physically escaping the man's observation or knowledge during the gestation and birth. She may obscure the timing of conception or assert that other men are more likely the father. Moreover, since the pregnancy occurs within her body, she may try to preserve a pregnancy or to induce a miscarriage.

Despite these natural advantages, women have not generally been inclined to use their procreational dominance to frustrate a man's knowledge about or claim to parenthood. Women may desire emotional intimacy with the father of the child. More importantly, women have historically needed an economically and socially present father for the child. Discrimination in education, employment and domestic roles and responsibilities have kept women's comparatively more immediate access to procreation and parenthood from being an unmitigated benefit. Indeed, the principal historical effect of the natural asymmetry in biological roles has been the greater ability of men to escape the financial and personal burdens of parenthood.

However, recent developments suggest some important changes. The increasing economic, social and legal independence of at least some women gives them greater freedom to exploit their natural procreational advantages. Reciprocally, as some men become more actively interested in parenting, their sex-based disadvantages become more visible and distressing.

The Emerging Version

Modern reproductive technology has greatly enhanced the potential for intention in procreative behavior. Intention conveys the directness, specificity and lack of ambiguity with which voluntary behavior is linked to outcome by purpose. A further element is the presence of options or alternatives; intention connotes choice, or selection among available courses of action. Where behavior is not purposeful or where for one reason or another an individual "has no choice," moral accountability is generally lessened.... New reproductive techniques increase procreative intentionality in both these senses....

Assignment of Parental Status

In the main, the law's assignment of parental status has followed nature. Biology provided definitive identification of the mother of a particular child. Bearing and birthing a child were physically apparent; motherhood was simply a fact. With nature giving authoritative guidance, legal norms had only to reflect and codify the physiologically obvious. The legal status of motherhood, and thus the maternal rights and responsibilities of rearing a child, were readily assigned.

More remote in physical time and space from the gestation and birth of a child, fathers have always been more difficult to identify than mothers. In theory, fathers could be traced through the fact and timing of sexual intercourse with the mother. However, until modern methods of paternity testing were developed, as a practical matter, biological fatherhood has been a matter of inference rather than certainty.

The uncertainty attendant on natural fatherhood has made social values more critical and more obvious in determinations of legal paternity than in the law of maternity. For instance, primogeniture rules in Europe, welfare budgets in contemporary America, and the preferences of putative fathers or other family members as well as a societal preference that children be legitimate have affected whether and how fatherhood was determined. Under some circumstances, men have been able to attain legal fatherhood by acknowledging paternity of a given child. Often, fatherhood has been presumed derivatively on the basis of a man's relationship to a child's mother, particularly where the pair are married.

Paternity-by-presumption rules reflect various societal concerns, but one presumptive purpose has been the codification of empirical inference—the best available method of determining factual biological paternity. Who is the biological father? The most likely candidate is the man having sexual intercourse with the mother. Who is most likely having sexual intercourse with the mother? Her husband. However, what purports to be an inference about biological fact may actually grow out of a normative aspiration and may readily be transformed into a prescriptive command about marriage and family, often without acknowledgement that such a transformation has taken place. The important issue becomes not who is, but who *should* be having sex with the mother: her husband. Thus, the social construct, in fact normative and mutable, draws substantial but disguised legitimacy from the representation that it simply expresses "givens" of nature.

Until recently, the difficulty of proving biological paternity allowed the normative and biological bases of legal presumptions about fatherhood to blur together. And if they did not precisely correlate, in circumstances of uncertainty about biology a preference for legitimacy seemed prudent and permissible. However, modern methods can prove biological paternity to a near certainty. As a result, the law today must *choose* whether to assign legal fatherhood on the basis of biological fact or social values, such as conventional family norms.

In recent years, the Supreme Court has established its preference for conventional nuclear families over biological connection in certain circumstances....

While it is biological certainty that has highlighted policy choices regarding fatherhood, it is biological *uncertainty* that demands judgment regarding motherhood. As noted earlier, the status of motherhood used to be self-evident, but new reproductive methods that can split genetic from gestational components render the legal determination newly problematic.... For now, the point is simply that both for mothers and fathers, biological givens and empirical facts can no longer be assumed to drive the legal assignment of parental status. Once biological justification is undermined, choices must be made....

[M]odern reproductive techniques significantly expand the role of individual intention (purpose and choice). While legal designations of parental status have been legitimated by their presumed reflection of biological fact, modern reproductive developments both expose and intensify the influence of social norms. Given the socially constructed aspects of legal parenthood, increases in procreative intentionality present pressing social and legal issues. How ought the law to react?

Should the law facilitate or inhibit use of the various artificial techniques? How should it respond to the new social and personal alternatives these techniques generate? To what extent ought the law to leave the relevant decisions and arrangements to private ordering? How much and what regulation ought to be imposed? Running through these specific questions is a recurrent meta-question: What are the implications for the law of heightened intentionality in procreative behavior? Ought the law to embrace and institutionalize such intentions, or ought it to ignore or suppress them?

Intention Should Be the Determining Factor

Parenting relationships are among the most significant in life, both to the individuals involved and to the society whose future depends upon its children. While conception may occur quickly and without much deliberation, parenthood competently performed is an unusually important, substantial and long-term activity. Parenting involves such large amounts of time, energy and money that deep commitment to the task seems highly desirable. The needs and dependency of a child are no doubt powerful motivators. Nevertheless, people perform major and responsible tasks better when they feel a desire, exercise a choice, and make a commitment. It is thus preferable for people to be more rather than less purposeful about their procreational and parenting intentions.

Within the context of artificial reproductive techniques, intentions that are voluntarily chosen, deliberate, express and bargained-for ought presumptively to determine legal parenthood.....

Our convictions about the link between biology and quality parenting typically help to anchor and justify legal assignment of parental rights and responsibilities. In part, legal assignment of parenthood based on biology reflects the age-old notion that "blood is thicker than water." Blood ties are usually intensely felt and have extraordinary longevity. Moreover, biology's linkage with committed interpersonal relationship has provided another reason for its use in determining socio-legal parenthood. Sexual relations are one likely index of which relationships among adults are strong enough to provide a desirable context for rearing children. Where the relationship is formalized in conventional marriage, there are additional gains. Entry into legal marriage submits the relationship to normative social control while simultaneously signalling commitment sufficient to ground parenting responsibilities. Thus, marriage has been, among other things, a means of expressing intentions that inferentially extend to parenting.

However, the capacity to separate biological procreation and sexual-relational intimacy means that now, for new reasons, biological co-parenthood need not be tied to the sexual and personal relationships that are often formalized in conventional marriage. Given this potential separation, the question remains what is the appropriate prospective index of good childrearing? Is either biological relatedness or conventional marriage essential?

At the outset, any suggestion that honoring adults' commitments regarding parenthood is antithetical to the interests of children seems wrongheaded. Adults who feel that their needs, concerns and choices have been respected, adults who feel that they are resourceful and efficacious, will likely cope better with the demands of parenthood than parents who are passive or powerless. Moreover, deliberative, articulated and acted-upon intentions regarding child rearing have great importance as indices of desirable parenting behavior. There is a correlation between choosing something and being motivated to do it consistently and well. Where the birth of children is not intended, as is sometimes the case with ordinary coital reproduction, biological connection will not guarantee love or adequate care. By contrast, where children are conceived and born because their parents chose to bring them into being, we at least know that if the law honors those intentions, the children will start life with parents who wanted and prepared for their advent. Of course, intentions can change; plans and promises can be broken. But then, neither biology nor conventional families ever guaranteed permanent or perfect parenting either.

As with biological ties, conventional family forms per se offer no guarantee of good parenting. If they did, the realities of current family constellations in America would already have condemned huge percentages of our children to bad parenting wholly apart from artificial reproductive techniques. Family forms have greatly diversified due to divorce, blended families, single parenting, homosexual commitments and unmarried cohabitation. Many children are now raised in non-conventional settings. Evidence from these sources seems to suggest that familial arrangements based on non-biological ties can be very good settings for children, as long as they provide the physical and emotional nurturance that are the real essentials of healthy child development.

If society were to recognize intention as a basis for claiming parenthood in circumstances of artificial reproductive techniques, intention-based variations in family form would likely be better tolerated and less problematic. Legal recognition itself would alleviate some sources of instability and stigma. Both the number and the types of intention-based arrangements about parenthood would likely multiply. Conventional couples would make greater use of non-conventional techniques, particularly third-party assisted techniques, if they felt more certainty about protection of their expectations and reliance.

Similarly, non-conventional family arrangements would likely increase unless barred by regulation.

Eventually, the heightened intentionality made possible by reproductive technology presses fundamental questions about whether parenthood is necessarily only a one man/one woman proposition. Might there be less than two parents? Or more? Might the gender of parent(s) vary from the biological-socially reinforced standard? Reproductive techniques could be used by single persons of either sex wishing to become parents. They could be employed by various types of "unapproved" couples, for instance gay or lesbian couples, heterosexuals who choose not to marry, or heterosexual couples actually barred from marrying. They could also be used by combinations of more than two persons who wanted to make a shared commitment to rearing a child.

... [T]he distance between where we already are, and where we would need to go to recognize agreements that intentionally negotiate parenthood is considerably smaller than it has been made to appear. The concern that the entire subject matter of parenthood is somehow incapable of deliberation and commitment is reduced to an objection to surrenders of prospective parental status by women rather than men. The premise apparently is that traditional changed circumstances analysis is insufficient to protect women from making these decisions; a total bar is needed. Alternatively, one might argue that it is not gender differences per se that matter. Rather, gender differences are simply a convenient shorthand for differences in the underlying nature of the decision that confronts a prospective father as compared to a prospective mother. Specifically, the argument would be that the physical and emotional connections between a prospective child and a mother up to the time of birth are different from those of a father in ways that make differentiation in the bindingness of their decisions appropriate.... [E]ven if such differences did justify divergent treatment of men's and women's prospective decisions about parental status, one unfortunate cost of such differentiation would be its reinforcement of the sexiest stereotype that women are ruled by unpredictable emotion....

Gendered Spheres of Influence

The *Baby M* decision [in which partial custody of "Baby M" was awarded to her surrogate mother] not only reflected stereotypes of women, it reinforced a division of the world into gendered roles, creating a de facto rule that children are within a realm rightly dominated by women. Doing so was both unnecessary and unwise.

No policy should opt for formal neutrality while ignoring reality—biological or social. No body of rules should systematically disadvantage whole categories of people on the basis of ascribed traits, like sex, that they cannot choose or control, unless doing so is irreducibly necessary. This is one of the most powerful claims not only of basic justice but also of the feminist movement. But neither should policy opt for formal neutrality while ignoring reality—biological or social. A second fundamental justice claim is that those similarly situated should be treated similarly; those differently situated should be treated differently. Men and women have biologically different roles in reproduction. The argument may be offered that the burdens of procreation are not parallel for men and women, so why should the benefits be? Some will feel that since women disproportionately bear the burdens, they should disproportionately receive the benefits to procreation and parenthood. Such a claim has force; but there are compelling counterarguments.

Where sex-based childbearing and childrearing roles disadvantage women's access to dimensions of life that are sought after by both genders, society should act to offset the liability. Thus, in the hotly contested *California Federal Savings & Loan Association v. Guerra (Cal. Fed.)* case, many feminists supported California's statutory requirement that employers guarantee leave and return rights to women interrupting their jobs in order to give birth. Others urged that when granted only to women, such a privilege constitutes special treatment that is constitutionally offensive, prudentially unwise and strategically mistaken. However, the United States Supreme Court, rightly I believe, upheld the challenged statute as necessary to achieve equitable access to gainful employment for both genders.

The obverse of the same debate has been little noted. In *Cal. Fed.*, the issue was access to market employment, long a male domain in which women's responsibility for children has imposed significant disadvantages. By analogy, children have historically been a female domain; men's more remote and limited biological role has disadvantaged their access to having and nurturing children. Granted, men have often been uninterested in nurturing children. Granted also, men have often taken control of aspects of the domain of children that have been of historic concern to them—designation and begetting of heirs, control over economic advantages or assets generated by children, confirmation of male potency, virility, etc. The physical risks, the day to day drudgery, and the responsibility of consistent care have been left to women.

But women's behavior and views are also two-edged. We not only decry the burdens but celebrate the wonder, meaning and joy of children in our lives. Moreover, we, as women, increasingly urge that men should share more equally in the personal, economic and social burdens of childrearing. The rub, of course, is that in the main, they do not yet do so. The goal of equalizing benefits and offsetting burdens, either in employment or in access to and responsibilities for children, is far from realized. Women's angry sense that they get the short end of both sticks can readily be understood. Yet if we mean what we say, and if we seek to make it happen, we should shape rules that lead us toward the future to which we aspire. We should attend to claims that at least some men may actually want what we have said we want them to want: they may genuinely and affirmatively choose to nurture a child. William Stern [the biological father of "Baby M"] may be such a man.

... [We] assume and reinforce the notion that women are appropriately dominant in the realm of children and that men are and will remain secondary because of their biological roles in procreation. There are elements of truth in these assertions, as there are in most stereotypes. But even where there are physiological differences involved, legal intensification of stereotypically gendered spheres is undesirable. It pulls us backward to the sex-limiting and sex-biased roles of the past. If the move toward greater gender freedom and flexibility is to continue, a *Cal. Fed.* analogue should be created in the sphere of children and family life. We need to beckon men to share the burdens and the values of domains where women have predominated. To do this, we must grant more equal access to those realms, creating rules that offset even biological differences and disadvantages....

Summary and Conclusion

Through most of human history, fate—in the guise both of accident and of necessity—has played a large role in procreation. Intention, defined as behavior that is unambiguous in purpose and that selects from among available alternatives, has been a comparatively minor determinant. More recently, the advent of effective birth control and comparatively safe and legal abortion have brought substantially greater personal control over reproductive destiny, albeit control in a negative rather than a positive form.

Modern reproductive technology expands and extends the potential for conscious control and purpose in procreation. Modern reproductive methods have subdivided the previously unitary biological process. That subdivision creates new options, both physiological and social, allowing and sometimes demanding that individuals, and ultimately society itself, make new choices. The new reproductive methods allow broader procreative choice to a number of individuals who previously had little. The most obvious expansion of available options occurs for those who are biologically infertile. Such individuals can now often find processes or persons to replace or substitute for impairments in their own reproductive capacities. In addition, the separation of procreation from sex—the depersonalization of reproduction—allows individuals who have been unable to procreate because of choice or circumstance (single persons, homosexuals) to do so. Still other individuals may undertake technologically-assisted reproduction for any of a wide range of personal reasons having to do with health, employment, preferences about characteristics of offspring, etc.

Whether individuals will be allowed access to the choices that have become technically possible depends on resolution of public debate about the meaning and consequences of the new methods as well as about how the law should accomodate those developments. Objections range from a fear that human control of basic natural processes represents excessive arrogance to anxiety about the depersonalization inherent in subdividing activities of sex, procreation and childrearing that have been historically joined. Particular concern centers on the consequences of reproductive technologies for marriage, parent-child bonds, and the conventional family.

While these concerns are understandable, they are outweighed by countervailing arguments. The capacity to procreate and the opportunity to parent children are profound motivations and deep aspirations of many individuals. The parent-child relationship is central both to the values and to the realities of many people's lives. Obstructing available opportunities to create and shape procreational-parental bonds would be costly as a matter both of social values and of individual fulfillment. Moreover, children are dependent on adults; at least in the main and at the outset, their interests are not likely to run contrary to those of adults who choose to bring them into being. Personal commitment plays a vital role in good parenting. Honoring the plans and expectations of adults who will be responsible for a child's welfare is likely to correlate significantly with positive outcomes for parents and children alike. "Successful families" and "good parenting" depend more on the quality of relatedness and meaning than on any particular family forms or demographic characteristics.

This potential for significant social and personal gains means that basic societal decisions about reproductive technology are mandatory, even if only decisions whether to encourage or discourage the development of those techniques. More importantly, decisions about what legal rules ought to govern the use and consequences of such technologies also now confront us. Essentially, the law has a choice: faced with new reproductive arrangements, it can recognize and facilitate emerging procreative choice and intentions about parenthood. Or it can cling to definitions and frameworks suited to a different biological and social reality, as did the New Jersey Supreme Court in deciding *Baby M.*

The capacity to envision and plan for alternative futures is a crucial and distinctive trait of humanness. The law should embrace and facilitate the opportunities that flow from the more decisive role that intention can now play in procreation. Within the realm of artificial and assisted reproduction, the law should assign parental rights and responsibilities on the basis of bargained-for expectations and induced reliance. The rules governing adoption and artificial insemination already reflect some variation from standard means of attaining parental status. Thus far, however, those factually diverse instances have been assimilated as closely as possible to the traditional scenario provided by biology and endorsed in social convention and law. The continued expansion of modern reproductive techniques, and the opportunities and problems posed by their use, demand a more fundamental reconsideration of how the law assigns parental rights and responsibilities.

Contracts are a major legal tool for projecting intention and choice into the future. Where arrangements involve several persons, where the opportunity for planning and deliberation exists, where reliance is weighty, where expectations are substantial and their validation is personally and socially important— as is true of reproductive agreements—contracts offer a means of arranging and protecting these various interests. If we are to construct legal policies that effectuate intention in assigning legal parenthood, contract law can contribute a set of principles and rules attuned to the problems of private ordering. Some gloss —a body of specialized sub-rules designed for the particular circumstances of reproductive agreements—may well be needed, as has been the case in other transactional contexts. Perhaps special regulation of disclosure and consent procedures is necessary, as in the doctor-patient relationship. Perhaps public policy should require certain screening procedures, or should bar clauses that seek to control rights to abortion. Perhaps some choices or reasons for using reproductive techniques would be barred (e.g. selection of embryos on the basis of sex, eye color, etc.). Individual legislatures or courts may differ; state variation in matters of family policy has been the norm. What is uniformly important, however, is that the principle of private intention be given substantial deference and legal force; the law should not make rules that fundamentally resist the reproductive arrangements that technology now makes possible.

For the foreseeable future, most reproduction will occur in the ordinary way and legal parenthood will likely remain governed by existing rules. However, intentional arrangements that arise out of reproductive technology offer the opportunity for a constructive experiment. In considering such an experiment, it should be borne in mind that existing status-based parental responsibility has hardly been a model of success, particularly as regards divorced or unwed fathers' obligations to children. A narrow experiment with chosen rather than imposed responsibility could hardly come off worse than the dismal realities of abdication and non-compliance that now confront us.

Determining legal parenthood on the basis of intentional agreements also has the potential to create more gender-neutral avenues to parenthood. Parenthood has been determined exclusively on the basis of biology for women, and on the basis of biology augmented and constrained by social and legal convention for men. In both instances, individual intention and commitment regarding parenthood have been obscured. New methodologies provide the opportunity and sometimes the necessity to reconsider old formulas. The *Baby M* decision ignored that opportunity. Under its gender-stereotyped approach, conflicts regarding what effect sex differences should have on access to child-nurturing roles will remain painful, if not intractable. Where, because of reproductive technology choice and explicit reciprocal commitment are the origin of a given child's creation, parental status could instead be assigned on a basis that is accessible to both genders: intention. Such an experiment would be positive and instructive for the future of children and adults alike.

The Neutered Mother

Introduction

A. Definitions

Mother: a female who has borne offspring

Female: of or pertaining to the sex that brings forth young

Neutered: neither masculine nor feminine in gender

Gender: the quality of being male or female

B. Mother as Symbol

I use the term "Neutered Mother" because it represents conflict and contradiction—words in contraposition to each other, incompatible when placed together. The Neutered Mother presents a gendered noun, degendered by the adjective that precedes it—an opposition of meaning that mirrors the conflicts in culture and in law over the significance and potency of the symbol of Mother....

My particular focus in this [selection] will be on those law reform activities which are consistent with the stated position of liberal legal feminists. In their increasingly important role of effecting changes in law and legal institutions, liberal legal feminists have represented women's issues and concerns as though they are due in part to pathology in the traditional institution of motherhood. The result is that their rhetoric surrounding issues of potential law reform constantly reaffirms the notion that Mother must be overcome— refashioned so that the individual woman is left unencumbered. To a great extent the law and legal language have begun to incorporate the liberal legal feminist notion that Mother is an institution which must be reformed—that is, contained and neutralized. In law, this has been accomplished through the transfiguration of the symbolically positive cultural and social components of parenting typically associated with the institution of motherhood into the degendered components of the neutered institution of "parenthood."...

From Martha Albertson Fineman, "The Neutered Mother," *University of Miami Law Review*, vol. 46 (1992). Copyright © 1992 by Martha Albertson Fineman. Reprinted by permission of the publisher and the author. Notes omitted.

A Return to the Law of the Father: Neutering Mother

As a result of the push to gender neutrality, Mother as an explicitly positive symbol with unique connotations and significance in regard to her relationship with her child has been moved out of the text and into the margins of family law discourse. Mother is neutered into Parent and is, at the same time, transformed into "Wife"—a role considered to be more appropriate as it connotes an equal or full partner in the family and extra-family contexts. This emphasis on adult roles and relationships facilitates the tendency to perceive the family as peripheral to the public arena. The focus in that arena is on women as economic actors, a role that requires a degree of independence that is difficult, if not impossible, to reconcile with the demands of "traditional" motherhood. Changes in family law will be justified by the need to refashion Mother, manipulating her to permit the construction of an appropriate egalitarian legal position for women in the market and public sphere.

Furthermore, one consequence of this emphasis has been the alteration of women's relationship to the market. Women and wives as equal partners are expected to work—to be self-sufficient and to assume equal financial responsibility for their children. This is now true at divorce. However, the implications of neutering Mother are not confined to custody questions or to the re-ordering of families that takes place when "private," middle-class families encounter the divorce system. Liberal legal feminist arguments for gender neutrality and family structuring to facilitate market participation have had an impact on "public" family law as well. The way we have refashioned Mother has created significant consequences in areas of law and policymaking outside of the traditional family. It is the neutering of Mother that has paved the way for acceptance of workfare solutions to the persistent poverty of many mother-child families in this country. Requiring single mothers, or any mothers, to engage in market work or to train for work is viewed as compatible and complementary to their status as mothers, not in conflict with it.

The liberal feminist valuing of market work for women has been broadened from its initial conception as an ideal option for middle-class and professional women. The current rhetoric on the appropriate relationship between women and market work establishes it as a universal and *mandatory requirement* for all women, mothers or not. The image of women as independent, economic equals is the mainstay of public and private family policy. The question that arises, of course, is what is the harm in that?

Needless to say, the shift in policy has operated to harm the most disadvantaged and defenseless mothers. The unanticipated byproduct of earlier liberal feminist attempts to achieve economic equality has been that the new images of Mother operate to disadvantage many women encountering the law in the context of nonmarket circumstances. Such women are caretakers, nurturers who live lives of dependency—their child's and their own—which is generated by their roles as Mother. The institutions with which they have to deal, the worlds of work and market, are places in which there are no mothers. Workers are motherless, neither having nor being a mother. The very gendered and

Mothered lives most women live are not accommodated in the liberal legal concept of gender equality.

The boundary between gender-neutral legal discourse and the gendered operation of society cannot be maintained. The significance of Mother as an institution and cultural symbol continues to have a shadowed impact on law; it cannot be erased. Equality rhetoric successfully employed to neuter Mother as a unique legal construct has failed to erase Mother on the societal level, nor has it removed the material manifestations of the institution of Motherhood. The disparity between the experience of Mother and its neutered legal presentation is potentially threatening to the maintenance of the legal system's commitment to gender neutrality. If Mother is and continues to be experienced as different, legal accomodations for Mother will be demanded even within a formally neutral family law system.

Women who are Mothers are not well represented in the political process. It is essential, however, that their perspectives be articulated in the context of law and policy proposals. Yet liberal feminists have been reluctant to make Mother a legislative agenda. An overriding commitment to the equality objective seems to preclude these feminists from conceptualizing and becoming proponents of a gendered analysis of the policy and politics of families in the United States. This is an essentially assimilationist stance which does not challenge existing structures of dominance and control. The liberal legal feminist position on family reforms, which is exemplified in the paradigm of gender neutrality, makes it likely that equality will remain the ideological medium for the construction of legal images—a medium that threatens further destruction of Mother.

Even if a demand for re-examination of the legal implications of the institution of motherhood from a feminist perspective were generated, it is not clear how successful it would be. The nature of law is conservative. It tends to reformulate, not render obsolete, the core tenets of our society, and challenges that are too radical or extreme are typically deflected. In the family context, the basic ideological construct is patriarchy—a decidedly anti-Mother perspective reflecting power relationships in which *pater* consistently trumps *mater* and the law assists in this endeavor.

The Sexual Family

The reflection of the family presented in family law doctrine may be distorted or fragmented, but it constitutes a "reality" and forms the basis for the regulation of actual lives. Because the legally constructed image of the family expresses what is appropriately considered family, it also constitutes the normal and defines the deviant. The designation of some intimate relationships as deviant legitimates state intervention and regulation.

Our continued adherence to patriarchy is inevitable given the tenacity and singularity of our prevalent conception of the family as an institution of horizontal intimacy, based on the romantic sexual affiliation between a man and a woman. The idealized "nuclear family" is a sexual family and its dominance in social and legal thought has restricted real reform and doomed us to recreate patriarchy.

The basic familial connection in our society is the sexual bond. For example, one of the central assumptions underpinning our conceptualization of family is that the entity is dependent upon a heterosexual relationship between a man and a woman. This form of affiliation, romanticized in the glorification of the nuclear family, is central to traditional family law ideology. Politicians as well as religious leaders extol this relationship (if it is sanctified) as the core of the family. While it is true that there is a great deal of emotionally charged rhetoric directed at children, it seems clear that its primary focus is on the traditional family model. Under this rhetoric, children's problems are created, to a large extent by the fact that they are trapped in a deviant family situation.

Historically, in order to qualify as the foundational family relationship, a heterosexual union had to be legally privileged through marriage. There is a great deal of current agitation to eliminate this formality. "Liberals" seek to expand the traditional nuclear family model, urging the recognition of informal heterosexual unions within the definition of family. There are also calls for acceptance and legal legitimation of same-sex relationships in the form of proposed domestic partnership laws.

Even in the context of the proposed liberalized definitions of family, the adult sexual affiliation remains central. The very existence of a sexual relationship is what provides the basis for arguing that these nontraditional unions should be included within the formal legal category of family. The form of argument is by analogy. Nontraditional unions are equated with the paradigmatic relationship of heterosexual marriage.

Formal, legal, heterosexual marriage continues to dominate our imagination when we confront the possibilities of intimacy and family. This domination is evident in the language we use to describe the effect of the end of the relationship through divorce when we speak of the "broken" family. It is also evident in the way we characterize the growth of unwed mother-child units as constituting a threat to the family.

In contrast to the construction of family around a sexual affiliation, a nonsexual construction would not categorize families based on the relationship of men and women (or its adult members). Instead, it might begin with the premise that the basic family unit consists of mother and child. Although this is the family form experienced for significant time periods by many women and children in our society, it has never been accepted as a positive ideological or rhetorical alternative to the sexual family. A woman and her children "alone" are considered an *incomplete*, and thus a deviant unit. They are identified as a source of pathology, the generators of problems such as poverty and crime.

That the relationship between men and women has been at the core of our perception of family is also evident when we see how it has defined other family members. For example, the historic characterization of children as legitimate or illegitimate depended on whether or not their parents were married. The significant reference in defining the status of the child was the nature of its parents' relationship. While such children today are more apt to be labeled "nonmarital," the focus is still the same—the child is defined by the relationship between the parents.

The problem with a notion of family that is culturally and legally dependent upon the formal (or informal) relationship between adults is the inevitable focus on "doing justice" between the adults in public policy and political discussions. Of course, the conclusion that something is just heavily depends upon the articulation of the problem and the context in which any solution is considered. As with all systems of rules, family law cannot help but reflect society's values and choices. When codified as legal standards, the privileging of the sexual tie stands as an eloquent, and potentially coercive, statement about our understanding of the nature of family. Given the contemporary hostility between the sexes and the status of equality as the dominant legal framework for discussions about fairness and justice, the potential negative effects of this codification are apparent. With high divorce rates and the organization of women and men into gendered interest groups when confronted with family issues, we should not be surprised that assets of the family, including children, are considered prizes, providing an arena for competition between women and men when their relationships fail.

In fact, the coalescence of interests along gendered lines is inevitable. The family represents the most gendered of our social institutions and this remains true even after decades of an organized women's movement. While other, non-family transformations have fostered male-female competitiveness, the family is the one area where tensions generated by perceived changes in the position of women seem most clearly visible. Historically, the family was the "private sphere" to which women were assigned in their roles as wife and mother. In recent decades, more and more women have escaped the exclusivity of this assignment and theoretically have more options available now.

To the extent that today's society has developed a system of easy access to divorce and provided some economic security for women, women now can combine private and public roles or reject the imposition of an historically defined role altogether. A woman may choose both work and family or decide to become a mother *without* being a wife. Women can choose to end a marital relationship or never formally establish one, and need not fear that their own or their children's futures in such circumstances will involve total impoverishment and social ostracization. Such changes have not come without costs, however. Some women feel the changes have been expensive for all women while benefiting only a few. Others question whether such changes actually have been advances or whether they operate to further disadvantage many women. In earlier work, I asserted that in our response to changing behavior on the part of women in the evolution of family law, we only reassert, in different forms, the power men implicitly enjoyed within the context of indissolvable marriage and traditional patriarchy.

While Mother has become potentially empowered by these changes, patriarchy has not been displaced. And its beneficiaries (female as well as male) are displeased. Its norm of the male-defined and male-headed family, with heterosexual union at its core, is threatened by the changes that have occurred. Consequently, the desire to contain and undo the reform. Part of the contemporary attack or backlash, against the changes in women's options is found in the neutering of Mother evident in contemporary family law rhetoric.

The Legacy of the Neutered Mother

Consistent with the feminist commitment to gender neutrality, parenthood, like personhood, has become the preferred designation because it encompasses both father and Mother without the idealized distinctions associated with the terms. The desire to have only gender-neutral rules represented an important symbolic component of the legal feminists' battle to demonstrate that there were no relevant differences between the sexes and thus no basis for treating them unequally in law. Certain feminists even anticipated that the rise of these egalitarian expectations in language would have concrete effects on behavior patterns in marriage and divorce situations.

Consistent with the goal of gender neutrality, the legal system had to eliminate any preferences based on a gendered concept of Motherhood. This had to be accomplished for important symbolic reasons, regardless of whether a gendered rule accurately conformed to either intuitive or empirical evidence as to which parent actually was most likely to systematically and continuously invest time and effort into child care.

The law's reluctance to recognize and accommodate the uniqueness of Mothers' role in child rearing conforms to the popular gender-neutral fetish at the expense of considerations for mothers' material and psychological circumstances. Even if the *ultimate* goal is gender neutrality, the immediate imposition of rules embodying such neutrality within the family law context is disingenuous. The effect is detrimental to those who have constructed their lives around gendered rules. In this regard, reformed divorce laws impose the risk of significant emotional as well as economic costs for such Mothers. For example, shifting custody policy creates an increased threat that mothers will potentially lose their children at divorce. To Mother, this risk is too great to contemplate. As a result, many mothers exchange a bargained-down property settlement to avoid a custody contest because they tend, in contrast to fathers, to consider custody a nonnegotiable issue.

Conclusion

As with all symbols about which there is context, some positive components can be extracted from the negative and neutered construction of Mother. Certainly, the power of Mother is conceded in the very recognition that it must be contained. The strands for weaving a feminist legal theory of Mother may even hide in the discourse of patriarchy itself. The question is how to shift contemporary legal discourse, feminist and otherwise, in such a way as to empower Mother. Legal discourse, even in its feminist forms and even in the family law area, continues to be guided by the normative male and confined by concepts such as equality. To those who believe any recognition of differences between men and women will inevitably lead to the designation of an inferior status for women, this is good news. However, for those who believe that acceptance and accommodation of differences are necessary (whether they are viewed as essential and inherent or as socially constructed), the marginalization of Mother in law and in legal theory is cause for concern.

One lesson feminists must learn from the neutered Mother is to be wary of equality. The dominant ideology of equality carries with it a powerful interpretive history which defines and limits the context for change. Liberal legal ideology is rarely compatible with different or "special" treatment. It assumes that the ideal must be equality of circumstances or at least of opportunity. This legal context has made it difficult for reform to take into account the persistent, far-reaching, unequal, and different circumstances that many women experience as a result of Motherhood and the dependency of children.

Equality ideology may resolve some of the problems revealed by focusing on the political and public interaction between men and women. However, this does not mean that it is the inevitable legal context for the entire endeavor of restructuring the legal position of women in the family of in their roles as Mother. Within the family, women are not only wives or partners, but also Mothers, and it is this latter role, in particular, that continues to bear gendered consequences and expectations.

In an earlier work, I argued for the concept of "gendered lives" in order to legitimate differences based on women's perspective. In a world in which gender is more than semantics, feminist legal theory *cannot* be gender-neutral, nor can it have as its goal equality, in the traditional, formal, legal sense of that word. Addressing the material consequences of women's gendered life experiences cannot be accomplished by a system that refuses to recognize gender as a relevant perspective, thereby imposing "neutral" conclusions on women's circumstances. Women's existences are constituted by a variety of experiences —many of them gendered. The potential for reproductive events such as pregnancy, breast feeding, and abortion certainly have an impact on women's constructions of their gendered lives.

This concept of gendered life is my attempt to create a vehicle for arguing that a concept of differences is necessary to remedy harms to women. There are totalizing social and legal constructions that do not conform to our experiences or our needs as mothers. The concept of a gendered experience is an attempt to simultaneously open a space for women's perspective in law, as distinct from men's, while providing the occasion for unity among women over some specifics of their lives. Attention to the force an imposed—and in that sense, "common"—socially constructed concept of neutered motherhood exercises upon aspects of all mothers' lives presents an opportunity for participation by diverse women in resisting that imposition.

Women can coalesce across differences to work together on the project of defining for ourselves the implications and ramifications of this gendered aspect of our lives. Women have an interest in the institution of Mother—how it is understood and given social and legal significance. Therefore, women have a basis for cooperation and empathy across their differences. The experience of struggling with the unreality of the idea of a neutered Mother provides the potential for this cooperation and empathy.

The recognition that women now face an inappropriately neutered concept of Mother reaffirms that the struggle over content and meaning in law is inherently political and that perspectives count. Any focus on perspectives that asserts as a basic premise that there are significant differences between women and men which must be addressed in law is fraught with potential pitfalls. On the other hand, given that male defined and controlled notions of law systematically disadvantage women in a variety of contexts, it seems essential that legal feminists affirm the need for law to respond to what women experience in their gendered lives. Adopting Mother's perspective will, of necessity, call into question the very core of patriarchy and force us to consider how the institution of Motherhood should be defined.

POSTSCRIPT

Should Men and Women Have Equal Parental Rights?

In deciding who the legal parent should be, various pieces are weighed against each other: genetics, gestation, intention, and care. Traditional legal determinations of parental rights rest upon biology for mothers and the creation of a family relationship for fathers. For mothers, gestation is thought to commence the mother's relationship with the child. The maternal role has great social significance. For fathers, the genetic connection does not start the father's relationship with the child or the father role. In society's view, fatherhood is constructed by choice.

The designation of parental rights has become more and more complicated in recent years, challenging traditional definitions of family, motherhood, and fatherhood. Central to this controversy are definitions of motherhood as a unique parental role. Should the laws of parenthood reflect sex-based differences in reproductive roles? How do biological procreative differences affect parental rights claims? Do biological differences undermine equal legal treatment of men and women?

Aspects of legal theory maintain that by definition humans are separate or distinct from one another. Theoretically, this is a way that males and females are treated as equal under the law. But professor of law Robin L. West argues that this is untrue of women. In her opinion, women are fundamentally *connected* to another human life during pregnancy. Furthermore, a pregnant woman and her unborn child comprise a "physical unit" in which the welfare of the mother and child are inseparable. Do women, therefore, have a fundamental difference from men in their connection to other human life? What, if any, are the social effects of women's unique biological connectedness? Does it "naturally" create women's value of intimacy, nurturance, and care?

West observes that there is deep divide among feminists in their perspective on women's potential for biological connection. Both radical and cultural feminists agree that women's potential for physical connection to others is distinctive, making women unique from men. Pregnancy involves many physical effects and consequences and has profound cultural significance. Should we dispute this or celebrate it?

Cultural feminists often celebrate women's uniqueness and believe that it prompts women's relational interests and capacity for care. Radical feminists are known to view women's connection with others as invasive and intrusive. Pregnancy is considered a "physical invasion," limiting behavioral freedom and posing risk of complications and pain.

There has been resistance to claims of women's fundamental biological connection and to the fact of pregnancy (actual and potential) which underlies women's care of and connection to others. The resistance centers on the real and supposed implications of women's capacity for pregnancy. For example, women have faced disadvantages in the workplace and elsewhere that stem from women's capacity to become pregnant.

Some argue that we need to deny or at least minimize the importance of the pregnancy difference. By making men and women more alike or on equal footing, the legal system will be forced to treat men and women similarly. So, for example, in surrogacy cases, the intentions to procreate would take precedence. Supporters of this view believe that contracts established by all parties in the surrogacy arrangements, which set forth the allocations of obligations and entitlements toward the child, should be binding and should override legal traditional presumptions of paternity and maternity.

Others argue that the unique female role in human reproduction creates asymmetrical interests between males and females; the woman's greater investment gives her primacy. Thus, in gestational surrogacy cases, proponents of this view argue that parental rights determination processes in adoption laws should apply. The gestational mother, upon the birth of the child, should have the right to decide whether or not to relinquish her parental rights to the genetic mother. The meaningful contribution of the gestational mother is more than simply employment for a certain biological function. The biological contribution of gestation and childbirth is also a presumption of parental responsibility.

But these maternal determination processes have a much broader impact on others involved in parental rights cases, including father(s), mother(s), and child(ren). Some assert that children's rights have often been overlooked in parental rights cases; the best interests of the child must be given primacy. Reconsider parental rights determination processes in the four cases presented in the Introduction to this issue from the perspective of the children involved. Were the best interests of the children served? Do gender stereotypes of mothers and fathers confound the determination of the best interests of the child?

Suggested Readings

L. B. Andrews, "Beyond Doctrinal Boundaries: A Legal Framework for Surrogate Motherhood," *Virginia Law Review* (November 1995).

M. E. Roberts, "Parent and Child in Conflict: Between Liberty and Responsibility," *Notre Dame Law School* (1996).

M. L. Shanley, "Unwed Fathers' Rights, Adoption, and Sex Equality: Gender-Neutrality and the Perpetuation of Patriarchy," *Columbia Law Review* (January 1995).

ISSUE 15

Can Fathers "Mother"?

YES: Louise B. Silverstein, from "Fathering Is a Feminist Issue," *Psychology of Women Quarterly* (1996)

NO: David Popenoe, from "Parental Androgyny," *Society* (September/October 1993)

ISSUE SUMMARY

YES: Psychologist Louise B. Silverstein asserts that fathers are as capable of nurturing children as mothers and calls for the redefinition of fathering.

NO: Sociologist David Popenoe argues that mothers and fathers should and do play different roles in childrearing.

$\mathbf{F}$or decades there has been active debate about parenting roles and responsibilities. What does it mean to be a responsible parent? Is one sex naturally better at parenting than the other? Are there essential characteristics of fathering versus mothering? Is having parents of two sexes necessary for the well-being of children? Should mothers work or engage in other activities outside the family? Should fathers move beyond the provider or breadwinner role and become more involved in the physical and emotional care of their children? Should fathers emulate mothers' traditional nurturing activities? Or, should fathers uphold their role as masculine role models for their children?

The twentieth century saw significant changes in the American family, including considerable change in the culture of fatherhood. Well over half of mothers are currently in the paid workforce. More than half of all new marriages end in divorce. One-third of all births are to single women. The traditional family ideal in which fathers work and mothers care for children and the household characterizes less than 10 percent of American families with children under the age of 18.

Mothers' increased labor force participation has been a central catalyst of change in the culture of fatherhood. Mothers began to spend less time with children, and fathers began to spend more time. Thus, the cultural interest in fatherhood increased, and it was assumed that fathers were becoming more nurturant. The history of the ideals of fatherhood reveals that fathers have progressed from distant breadwinner to masculine sex-role model to equal coparent.

Despite changes in the *ideals* of fatherhood, some family scholars observe that fathers' behavior has not changed. Rather, it appears that mothers' behavioral change may be responsible for the change in the culture of fatherhood. A recent review of comparisons of fathers' and mothers' involvement with their children (in "intact" two-parent families) reveals a gap: fathers' engagement with their children is about 40 percent that of mothers'; fathers' accessibility is about two-thirds that of mothers. Fathers' lesser involvement is even more characteristic of divorced and never-married families. Nearly 90 percent of all children of divorce live with their mothers. Most single-parent fathers are "occasional" fathers. More than one-third of children in divorced families will not see their fathers at all after the first year of separation. Only 10 percent of children will have contact with fathers 10 years after divorce. Yet at the same time, research has documented the important ways in which fathers influence their children.

There is widespread agreement that fatherhood needs definition. What model(s) of fatherhood will best serve the needs of children and society? Some assert that good parenting is not sex-specific or sex-related. Fathers need to nurture their children, much as women as mothers have done, because nurturance is the cornerstone of good parenting. Nurturance has been strongly associated with mothering, but it is generally agreed that this connection is cultural, not biological.

William Doherty, president of the National Council on Family Relations, poses provocative questions about the reconstruction of fatherhood as nurturing. Is motherhood the model of choice for reconstructing nurturing fathering? Since motherhood is a well-developed nurturing model, do we need to redefine fathering, or can fathering emulate mothering? If nurturing is labeled *mothering,* will men be deterred from nurturant fathering? Does using mothering as a model put men off and make them feel excluded and inadequate? Advocates of nurturant fathering argue that motherhood is the model of choice because it honors and validates women's model of parenting and rejects the gender essentialism that has equated parenting with mothering, limiting women's choices and roles and restricting fathers from parenting.

Others contend that fathers are not mothers; fathers are essential and unique. Many reject a gender-neutral model of parenting, arguing that mothers and fathers have specific roles that are complementary; both parents are essential to meet children's needs. Proponents of this model assert that fatherhood is an essential role for men and pivotal to society. They maintain that fathers offer unique contributions to their children as male role models, thereby privileging their children. Moreover, fathers' unique abilities are necessary for children's successful development.

The following selections advance two models for restructuring parenting. Louise B. Silverstein asserts that fathering must be redefined as nurturing, drawing fathers more actively into caring for their children. In contrast, David Popenoe argues that it is not natural for males to nurture; fathers are unique and essential figures in their children's lives (particularly for their sons).

Louise B. Silverstein

 **YES**

Fathering Is a Feminist Issue

T his [selection] is an effort to inject a feminist voice into the redefinition of fathering, which I see as essential both to the achievement of equality for women, and to the reconstruction of the masculine gender role. Limiting the definition of fathering to the provider role in the family has been central to the problem of male privilege, and thus to the subordination of women within society at large. Similarly, our cultural definition of the fathering role as employment in the *public* world, rather than caretaking in the *personal* world of the family, has been responsible for the inability of most men to be aware of and to articulate their needs for intimacy and emotional connectedness. Thus, redefining fathering to reflect a primary emphasis on nurturing and caretaking, as well as providing, is the next necessary phase in the continuing feminist transformation of patriarchal culture for the benefit of men as well as women.

... [R]edefining fathering as nurturing is central to freeing women from the interlocking inequalities of their public and private roles.... [I]t is important to achieve a balanced view that neither overvalues the importance of fathers, nor defines them as peripheral to family life....

An Historical Perspective

Historically, fathers have been responsible, not only for the economic well-being of their children, but for their religious, moral, and vocational education as well. This was true of both African American and White fathers. When slave fathers were allowed to live with their families, they often cared for children who were the product of the rapes of their wives by their White masters (Pinderhughes, 1989). As farmers and artisans working at home, White and African American fathers interacted closely with their children and trained them in the acquisition of necessary job skills. With the growth of industrialization and the separation of paid work from family life, fathers were forced to spend more and more time away from the family, and their day-to-day involvement in family life declined. The introduction of mandatory public schooling symbolized the demise of fathers as teachers and moral guides for their children.

In the father's absence, mothering became more central in the lives of children than it had been previously. This was true for African American families from the beginning of the middle 1600s (when slavery began) when husbands were sold away from families (hooks, 1981). For White middle class women, this revalidation of motherhood did not occur until the 19th century. Stearns (1991) pointed out that the advice literature of the late 19th and early 20th centuries reflected a reappraisal of the maternal role. Mothers were suddenly considered to have all the necessary virtues for raising children. An ideological position was introduced into popular culture suggesting that women were uniquely suited for child care because of their moral purity and special emotional sensitivity. By 1946, the first edition of Dr. Spock's book devoted only nine pages to the father's role (Hunter College Women's Studies Collective, 1983).

This transformation of parenthood into motherhood in popular culture was echoed in the psychological community with the now famous introduction in 1951 by Bowlby of his maternal deprivation hypothesis (Bowlby, 1951). Bowlby's subsequent expansion of this hypothesis into maternal attachment theory (Bowlby, 1969, 1973) argued that the mother–infant relationship was unique, exclusive, and the most important variable in normal development. Within this cultural context, fathering became reduced almost exclusively to the provider role.

Hewlett (1991) pointed out that this emphasis on the importance of the mother's role has resulted in a lack of data, and therefore, a lack of understanding of the father's role in child development. Nevertheless, Bowlby's theoretical model of the mother–child dyad as the nexus for child development continues to dominate the psychological community, and to generate a preoccupation with both maternal power and mother-blaming. A recent article in a prominent family therapy journal (Kraemer, 1991, p. 378) stated that, among primates, "the male parent has no role after conception."

Barglow, Vaughn, and Molitor (1987, p. 956) pointed out that maternal employment has traditionally been discussed as "maternal absence," while the effects of paternal employment are almost always ignored. Gilbert (1994, p. 545) makes the point that women who are employed in the public world and who parent are referred to as "working mothers," whereas fathers who work outside the home are simply referred to as men. Phares (1992) reported that, in one survey of mental health professionals, 40% felt that mothers should not work outside the home, while 74% believed that mothers' part-time employment was more beneficial to children than full-time employment. One can hardly imagine mental health professionals taking the position that fathers should only engage in paid work part-time.

The Question of Gender Differences in Parenting Behaviors
Despite cultural beliefs to the contrary, research findings have not documented gender differences in competent parenting. In contrast to the hypothesis of a "maternal instinct" among primates that causes females to be more naturally suited than males for caretaking, both animal and social science research suggests that there are no significant differences between males and females in their capacity to nurture. Recent scholarship in the field of primatology (Smuts, 1987; Smuts & Gubernick, 1992; Whitten, 1987) showed that even among non-human primates males and females have the same potential for nurturing. The

extent to which male baboons, gorillas, and chimpanzees, (and, I would argue, human fathers) actively care for infants depends on a complex array of ecological, demographic, and temperamental variables. (See Silverstein [1993] for a detailed review of primate research and its implications for family politics.) Observed differences in parenting behaviors for males and females are thus more accurately conceptualized as cultural constructions, rather than as biological imperatives, even for non-human primates.

Hewlett (1991) pointed out that researchers' biases have skewed the ways in which data about parenting has been collected. He proposed that mother-oriented theories of infant and child development have led cultural anthropologists to design field observations in which families are rarely observed at night. Since early evening is the primary context for father-child interaction, field observers simply have missed the relationships between fathers and their children.

In an attempt to increase our knowledge of father-infant interaction in non-Western cultures, Hewlett (1991) designed a study in which families of the Aka Pygmy tribe of African hunter-gatherers were observed 24 hours a day, in home base and out in the bush. Within this culture, a husband and wife are each responsible for 50% of the family's nutritional requirements. Aka culture is unique in that men's and women's subsistence activities take place in the same geographic locations. They work together on the net hunt and in caterpillar collecting. The husband and wife are within sight of each other 46.5% of daylight hours, and are actively collaborating. Based on these field observations, Hewlett reported that Aka fathers do more infant caregiving than do fathers in any other human society. Forty-seven percent of the father's (24 hr) day is spent either holding the infant, or within arm's reach of the infant (p. 168).

The Aka study demonstrates that there are cultural systems where men can be as active, intimate, and nurturant caregivers as are women. In hunting-gathering cultures where women's contribution to subsistence is equal to or greater than men's contribution, men tend to have higher participation in child care than do men in industrialized societies (Draper, 1975; Hewlett, 1991).

Early in the study of fathering behaviors in Western societies, fathers were observed engaging in more rough and tumble play than did mothers in U.S. families. Given our culture's preoccupation with sex differences, this finding was assumed to reflect a universal, perhaps biological, difference in the way that men and women related to children (Lamb, 1987b). However, this difference has proved to be a methodological artifact. When fathers are studied within a cross-cultural context (Hewlett, 1991; Hwang, 1987), those who have a great deal of contact with their young children are no more likely than mothers to participate in vigorous play. Relying on vigorous play as a way of engaging infants is now thought to be a means of establishing an attachment relationship by caretakers who have less consistent involvement with the child (Hewlett, 1987, 1991, 1992). For example, aunts in Aka Pygmy culture are the caretakers most likely to be observed in vigorous play with infants. If fathers in U.S. culture were to increase their direct interaction with their children, the rough and tumble play characteristic of U.S. fathering behavior would be expected to lessen or disappear.

After reviewing the research on parental caretaking in western cultures, Lamb (1987b) concluded that neither mothers nor fathers are "natural" caretakers. Rather, both parents learn "on the job." Observations of mothers and fathers during the newborn period yield no differences in parenting behaviors. Over time, because mothers spend so much more time with their infants, they become more sensitive than fathers to their infant's cues. Similarly, fathers' lack of direct experience leads them to become increasingly less competent than mothers. This lack of competence generates a corresponding lack of confidence leading in turn to avoidance behavior on the part of fathers. Avoiding opportunities for interaction further reinforces their incompetence relative to mothers. As Hewlett (1987) pointed out, Western cultural expectations lead mothers to embrace caretaking, and fathers to avoid it. Differences become marked over time, but are not irreversible.

When fathers are thrust into the primary parenting role, they become capable of acquiring "mothering" skills. Snowdon and Suomi (1982) studied this phenomenon experimentally by placing a male and a female rhesus monkey together in a cage with an unfamiliar infant. As long as the female was present, she performed 100% of the nurturing and caretaking of the infant. However, the male took over and assumed all of the "mothering" responsibilities as soon as she was removed from the cage. Thus, among some primate species (perhaps including our own), the nurturing potential that is present in males is only expressed in the absence of females....

Gay Fathers

Perhaps the group from whom we have the most to learn about the future of nurturant fathering is gay fathers. These men, like lesbian mothers, struggle with an extreme version of the chilly climate. Because of the homophobia endemic to U.S. society, gay men and lesbians often face hostility from the most basic sources of emotional support: their families of origin, religious institutions, and mental health providers. Homophobia in the community of non-gay parents generates a negative reaction to their homosexuality, and negative attitudes toward parenting by some members of the gay/lesbian community often leave them without social support from non-parenting gay men and lesbians.

Estimates of the number of gay fathers range from 1 to 3 million (Patterson, 1992). This range is broad because both gay and lesbian parents who have children from heterosexual relationships often conceal their sexual orientation for fear of losing child custody and/or visitation privileges. Judicial decision-making in custody litigation and state policy regarding adoption and foster care have been systematically biased against gay and lesbian parents ("Lengthy adoption," 1994). Six states have outlawed adoption by same-sex couples ("Gay Partner," 1995).

Despite these difficulties, the number of gay fathers is increasing. Gay fathers are a diverse group, including men who had children in the context of a heterosexual marriage and subsequently chose to divorce and lead a gay lifestyle, and a more recently emerging group of men who chose to establish an openly gay lifestyle first and then become parents. Within the group of gay men who became parents while married, most choose to divorce, but some men remain with their wives, and either acknowledge their homosexuality or remain closeted. For those who divorce, some become the custodial parent, and others do not. Some acknowledge their gay lifestyle to their children, and others present a facade of heterosexuality. Some men become single fathers, whereas others live in the context of a same-sex love relationship, with their partner fulfilling the role of a stepfather. If the partner also has children, the family becomes a blended family with stepsibling relationships.

Among men who live a gay life before becoming fathers, family configurations also vary. Some choose to become biological fathers through artificial insemination with either lesbian or heterosexual women. Some of these birthing couples cohabit in a variety of family structures, others live separately, but co-parent the child. Some gay men choose to adopt babies, either singly or as part of a gay co-parenting couple. Societal homophobia has made it very difficult for these men to be considered appropriate parents by adoption agencies. In a sample of 16 White gay fathers (Quartironi, Silverstein, & Auerbach, 1995), all of the men had adopted African American or Puerto Rican children, adding an interracial aspect to their families.

Relatively little research exists on gay fathers overall. Most of the studies have been done with divorced gay fathers (see Bozett, 1989; Bozett & Hanson, 1991; Patterson, 1995 for reviews). Research on men who choose to become parents in the context of a preexisting gay identity is only beginning to emerge (McPherson, 1993; Quartironi et al., 1995; Spordone, 1993). Much of the research has been plagued by negative attitudes toward gay men. One concern about gay men as fathers has been that they will encourage their children to become gay. Bozett's (1989) review of the literature found that children of gay men identify themselves as gay in the same percentage (8–15%) as children of heterosexual parents. In contrast to the expectation that gay fathers would foster cross-gender behavior, Harris and Turner (1985/86) found that gay fathers were more likely than lesbian mothers to encourage their children to play with sex-typed toys.

Another concern about both gay fathers and lesbian mothers has been that children in these households are at heightened risk for sexual abuse. This concern does not reflect the reality of the problem, since most sexual abuse is perpetrated by heterosexual men. Patterson's (1992) review of the research found that gay men were no more likely than heterosexual men to abuse their children, whereas Barret and Robinson (1990) in their review of the research found that children living with homosexual parents were at less risk of sexual abuse than children living with heterosexual parents.

Miller (1979) and Bozett (1989) were pioneers in generating research about gay fathering not characterized by hostile and homophobic attitudes. They were concerned with describing the process through which married fathers came to identify themselves as gay men, and then integrated these two identities. This research focused on whether and how these fathers disclosed their sexual orientation to their children.

Other early research on divorced gay fathers compared them to heterosexual divorced fathers and to lesbian mothers. Scallen (1981) compared the parenting styles of gay and heterosexual fathers. Gay fathers were found to be somewhat less traditional in their overall parenting approach than heterosexual fathers, placing less emphasis on the role of provider, and more on nurturance. No differences between the two groups were reported on parental problem-solving or encouragement of autonomy.

Bigner and Jacobsen (1989) found no differences between gay and heterosexual fathers in motivation to become parents, level of involvement with their children, or level of intimacy. These authors did find that gay fathers described themselves as more focused on limit-setting than were the non-gay fathers in their sample. Skeen and Robinson (1985) found no differences between gay and non-gay fathers in perceptions of early childhood and relationships with their own parents.

Only two studies have been reported on gay men who chose to become fathers after establishing a gay lifestyle. McPherson (1993) compared 28 gay and 27 heterosexual couples in terms of division of labor, satisfaction with roles, and general satisfaction with the couple's relationship. He found that the gay couples reported a more equitable distribution of responsibilities, and more satisfaction with their roles than did the heterosexual couples. He speculated that the higher level of satisfaction was due to the fact that the gay fathers could choose whichever role (provider or nurturer) they preferred, whereas in heterosexual couples, these roles were often assigned according to traditional gender role expectations. Not surprisingly, the gay couples also reported more general satisfaction with the couple relationship.

Spordone (1993) compared 78 gay men who had become parents through adoption or surrogacy, with 83 gay men who were not fathers. These two groups were compared on measures of internalized homophobia, self-esteem, and levels of intimacy and autonomy in their relationships with their family of origin. No differences emerged in terms of their relationships with their own families. However, the gay fathers reported higher self-esteem and fewer negative attitudes about homosexuality. Spordone speculated that the experience of parenting positively affected the fathers' sense of self.

In an ongoing qualitative research study of gay fathering couples, a number of themes have emerged (Quartironi et al., 1995). Often, one partner is not motivated to have children, and it may take several years of active lobbying by the motivated partner before his reluctant spouse agrees to become a parent. In all of the couples interviewed so far, the more motivated partner has had a "starter" experience of parenting. Either he was a big brother who had substantial responsibility for younger siblings, or he unexpectedly became a foster parent for the child of a friend or relative. Thus, he had concrete experience of his own competence as a parent.

In contrast to McPherson's (1993) results, not all of the couples in Quartironi et al.'s study report satisfaction with the division of labor and with the relationship as a whole. The men describe an initial sense of euphoria when the baby first arrives, followed by increasing stress on the couple's relationship. Time alone and time for the couple become increasingly difficult to achieve, and their intimate and sexual contact decreases. Most of the couples rebound from the stress, but some continue to struggle, and one couple separated. Like the gay fathers that Spordone (1993) studied, these men report feeling an increase in self-esteem after becoming a parent. Several of the fathers have felt that parenting brought a deepening sense of connection to their own families and to the community at large.

This qualitative research is looking at these men in their own context, that is, a family with two daddies. As the research team has looked and listened to the videotapes of children being raised in an intimate, supportive environment, *without the presence of a mother,* we have been forced to deal with our prejudices. At times we have felt inspired by these men who have had to face tremendous odds to become fathers. At other moments, we have felt, despite ourselves, sad for these motherless children. Getting to know these fathers and listening to them talk about their experience in their own words has exploded our stereotypes about men and the essential importance of mothers. These father/nurturers have been our teachers.

Given our conscious and nonconscious gender ideology, a general lack of governmentally supportive policies, the continuing pay differential between men and women, a chilly climate for nurturant fathering, and direct resistance from some men and some women, what are the prospects that U.S. fathers will significantly increase their involvement with their children in the future? . . .

Transforming the Male Gender Role

Kimmel (1987) pointed out that masculine and feminine are relational social constructions. Since the feminist movement has redefined femininity to include participation in the public world of paid employment, the provider role can no longer remain the mainstay of traditional masculinity. Kimmel maintained that the transformation of masculinity is inevitable. He argued that, although few men now fit the ideal of "the nurturant father," current definitions of masculinity reflect a dynamic tension between the "ambitious breadwinner" and the "compassionate father." This new tension addresses one of the paradoxes of patriarchal society in that although fathers have had enormous economic power over their children, they have remained emotionally isolated from the intimate relationships of family life.

. . . [T]he traditional concepts of "mothering" and "fathering" must be discarded, and the idea of "family" must be dramatically restructured. Our concept of the "normal" family must come to include whatever combination of adults and children choose to live together and care for each other, regardless of their sex, gender, or biological relationship to each other. "Mothering" and "fathering" must both include nurturing and providing economic resources. In addition, the workplace must be reorganized to provide organizational supports to people who are employed *and* bear responsibility for the raising of young children.

Acknowledging and reinforcing men's capacity to nurture would place intimacy and attachment at the center of masculine gender role socialization, in the same way that acknowledging and reinforcing women's capacity to function in the public world of paid employment has begun to find a place for instrumental thinking and active coping skills within the gender socialization of women. I would argue that the experience of nurturing and caring for young children has the power to change the cultural construction of masculinity into something less coercive and oppressive for both women and men. The redefinition of fathering is thus an essential step in the continuing feminist transformation of patriarchal culture.

References

Barglow, P., Vaughn, KB. E., & Molitor, N. (1987). Effects of maternal absence due to employment on the quality of infant–mother attachment in a low-risk sample. *Child Development, 58,* 945–954.

Barret, R. L., & Robinson, B. E. (1990). *Gay fathers.* Lexington, MA: Lexington Books.

Bigner, J. J., & Jacobsen, R. B. (1989). Parenting behaviors of homosexual and heterosexual fathers. *Journal of Homosexuality, 18,* 173–186.

Bowlby, J. (1951). *Maternal care and mental health.* Geneva: World Health Organization.

Bowlby, J. (1969). *Attachment and loss* (Vol. 1). New York: Basic Books.

Bowlby, J. (1973). *Attachment and loss: Separation* (Vol. 2). New York: Basic Books.

Bozett, F. W. (1989). Gay Fathers: A review of the literature. *Journal of Homosexuality, 18,* 137–162.

Bozett, F. W., & Hanson, S. M. H. (1991). Cultural change and the future of fatherhood and families. In F. W. Bozett & S. M. H. Hanson (Eds.), *Fatherhood and families in cultural context. Springer series: Focus on men, Vol. 6* (pp. 263–274). New York: Springer.

Draper, P. (1975). !Kung women: Contrasts in sexual egalitarianism in foraging and sedentary contexts. In R. R. Reiter (Ed.), *Toward an anthropology of women.* London: Monthly Review Press.

Gay partner cannot adopt child. (1995, April 6). *The New York Law Journal,* pp. 1, 27.

Gilbert, L. A. (1994). Reclaiming and returning gender to context: Examples from studies of heterosexual dual-career families. *Psychology of Women Quarterly, 18,* 539–584.

Harris, M. B., & Turner, P. H. (1985/1986). Gay and lesbian parents. *Journal of Homosexuality, 12,* 101–113.

Hewlett, B. S. (1987). Intimate fathers. In M. Lamb (Ed.), *The father's role, cross-cultural perspectives* (pp. 292–330). Hillsdale, NJ: Lawrence Erlbaum.

Hewlett, B. S. (1991). *Intimate fathers.* Ann Arbor, MI: University of Michigan Press.

Hewlett, B. S. (Ed.), (1992). *Father–child relations, cultural and biosocial contexts.* New York: Aldine de Gruyter.

hooks, b. (1981). *Ain't I a woman? African American women and feminism.* Boston, MA: South End Press.

Hunter College Women's Studies Collective. (1983). *Women's realities, women's choices. An introduction to women's studies.* New York: Oxford University Press.

Hwang, C. P. (1987). The changing role of Swedish fathers. In M. Lamb (Ed.), *The father's role: Cross-cultural perspectives* (pp. 115–138). Hillsdale, NJ: Lawrence Erlbaum.

Kimmel, M. (1987). Rethinking "masculinity": New directions for research. In M. S. Kimmel (Ed.), *Changing men: New directions in research on men and masculinity* (pp. 9–24). Newbury Park, CA: Sage.

Kraemer, S. (1991). The origins of fatherhood: An ancient family process. *Family Process, 30,* 377–392.

Lamb, M. (1987b). The emergent American father. In M. Lamb (Ed.), *The father's role: Cross-cultural perspectives* (pp. 3–25). Hillsdale, NJ: Lawrence Erlbaum.

Lengthy adoption battle ends in gay couple's favor. (1994, December 26). *The New York Times,* p. A1.

McPherson, D. (1993). *Gay parenting couples: Parenting arrangements, arrangement satisfaction, and relationship satisfaction.* Unpublished doctoral dissertation, Pacific Graduate School of Psychology, Palo Alto, CA.

Miller, B. (1979). Gay fathers and their children. *Family Coordinator, 28,* 544–552.

Patterson, C. J. (1992). Children of lesbian and gay parents. *Child Development, 63,* 1025–1042.

Patterson, C. J. (1995). Lesbian mothers, gay fathers, and their children. In A. R. D'Augelli & C. J. Patterson (Eds.), *Lesbian, gay and bisexual identities across the lifespan* (pp. 262–290). New York: Oxford University Press.

Phares, V. (1992). Where's Poppa? The relative lack of attention to the role of fathers in child and adolescent psychopathology. *American Psychologist, 47,* 656–664.

Pinderhughes, E. (1989). *Understanding race, ethnicity, and power.* New York: The Free Press.

Quartironi, B., Silverstein, L., & Auerbach, C. (1995). *The new gay fathers: An exploratory study of their experiences, perceptions, and concerns.* Manuscript in preparation, Yeshiva University.

Scallen, R. M. (1981). An investigation of paternal attitudes and behaviors in homosexual and heterosexual fathers. (Doctoral dissertation, California School of Professional Psychology, Los Angeles, 1981). *Dissertation Abstracts International, 42,* 3809-B.

Silverstein, L. B. (1993). Primate research, family politics, and social policy: Transforming "cads" into "dads." *Journal of Family Psychology, 7,* 267–282.

Skeen, P., & Robinson, B. (1985). Gay fathers' and non-gay fathers' relationships with their parents. *Journal of Sex Research, 21,* 86–91.

Smuts, B., (1987). Gender, aggression, and influence. In B. Smuts, D. L. Cheney, R. M. Seyfarth, R. W. Wrangham, & T. T. Struhsaker (Eds.), *Primate societies* (pp. 385–400). Chicago: University of Chicago Press.

Smuts, B. & Gubernick, D. J. (1992). Male-infant relationships in nonhuman primates: Paternal investment or mating effort? In B. S. Hewlett (Ed.), *Father-child relations, cultural and biosocial contexts* (pp. 1–30). New York: Aldine de Gruyter.

Snowdon, C. T., & Suomi, S. J. (1982). Paternal behavior in primates. In H. E. Fitzgerald, J. A. Mullins, and P. Gage (Eds.), *Child nurturance (Vol. 3)* (pp. 63–108). New York: Plenum Press.

Spordone, A. J. (1993). *Gay men choosing fatherhood.* Unpublished doctoral dissertation, The City University of New York.

Stearns, P. (1991). Fatherhood in historical context: The role of social change. In F. W. Bozett & S. M. H. Hanson (Eds.), *Fatherhood and families in cultural context. Springer series: Focus on men, Vol. 6* (pp. 28–51;). New York: Springer.

Whitten, P. L. (1987). Infants and adult males. In B. Smuts, D. L. Cheney, R. M. Seyfarth, R. W. Wrangham, & T. T. Struhsaker (Eds.), *Primate societies* (pp. 343–347). Chicago: University of Chicago Press.

NO ↩

David Popenoe

Parental Androgyny

[T]he real "masculinity crisis" today is... too few fathers. All over America men are abandoning their wives and children and remain apart from family life. The widespread, voluntary father-absence from the American family today is strongly associated with two phenomena: divorce and non-marital births. It is not politically correct these days to say positive things about the 1950s era, but it is a fact that fathers participated more in the lives of their biological children then as a result of high marriage and low death rates, and divorce rates that were not out of bounds. With the startling increase in divorce today, a child's chance of making it to adulthood with a biological father in the home is only about 50 percent. About half of non-custodial divorced fathers drop out of the lives of their children, and, for those who do not, their presence is often minimal. Even more remarkable, the non-marital birth rate has jumped from 5 percent in 1960 to a current 28 percent. In most cases, the father is out of the picture; in many, he could care less, or the mother could care less about him.

These trends toward family decline strongly contribute to the deteriorating well-being of children. The evidence suggests that we may have the first generation of children and youths in our history who are less well off—psychologically, socially, economically, and morally—than their parents were at the same age. While father absence is by no means the sole cause of this deterioration, it is heavily implicated.

About the only contribution that [recent books on men and masculinity] make to this egregious national problem is to put forth the ideal of the "new father." Assuming that men wish to become fathers at all, it is said, fathers should become more like mothers. Men should become more nurturing and share homemaking activities with their working wives, including early infant care, on a fifty-fifty basis. Parental gender roles are entirely learned, we are told, and it is perfectly possible and reasonable "for daddies to become mommies."

The "new man" in the home is an exact parallel to the "new woman" in the workplace, the woman who is able to (and should) do everything in the workplace that men have always done. If women can do everything that men have done in the workplace, why can men not do everything women have done in the home? Indeed, the new father in the home is seen to be absolutely essential if women are to achieve equality in the workplace and still function as mothers.

In addition to widespread absence, the greatest difference between fathers of the present and of preceding generations is that today those fathers who are still present do participate much more in traditional female activities within the home. We have what sociologist Frank F. Furstenberg, Jr., has aptly labeled a "good dad, bad dad" phenomenon. Men who do function as fathers are more nurturing than their own fathers ever were. Some men have fully incorporated the "new father" role, even to the extent of staying home with young children so that their wives can remain in the labor force full time.

The movement in the direction of the new father is certainly strongly to be applauded. The emergence of family- and child-oriented "good" dads—dads who are nurturing and participate equally in the day-to-day lives of their children—is no doubt a positive development. However, implicit in most discussions of the "new father" is the goal of parental androgyny—fathers and mothers playing essentially the same social roles. Social androgyny may be an appropriate goal in the working world, in family life it is not appropriate. Although it is neither possible nor desirable to return to the traditional nuclear family exemplified by *Ozzie and Harriet,* we must take care not to jettison traditional mother-father roles entirely. Unlike the work place, family organization is based on very real, biological differences between men and women. Parental androgyny is not what children need. Neither is it a good basis for a stable, lasting marriage.

The literature is overflowing with statements arguing the case against traditional gender roles, but concerns about androgynous gender roles are seldom heard. My concerns are based on evidence derived from social and biological research into requirements for optimal child development and the biological differences between men and women. And they are shaped by speculation about what is ultimately personally fulfilling for adults, and what men and women "really want" out of marriage.

Child Rearing

No one has spoken more eloquently about the requirements for optimum child development than Urie Bronfenbrenner. Two points in a recent summary of his main findings of the "scientific revolution" in the study of human development bear special significance for the present discussion.

1) In order to develop—intellectually, emotionally, socially, and morally—a child requires participation in progressively more complex reciprocal activity, on a regular basis over an extended period in the child's life, with one or more persons with whom the child develops a strong, mutual, irrational attachment and who is committed to the child's well-being and development, preferably for life.

2) The establishment and maintenance of patterns of progressively more complex interaction and emotional attachment between caregiver and child depend in substantial degree on the availability and involvement of another adult, a third party, who assists, encourages, spells off, gives status to, and expresses admiration and affection for the person caring for and engaging in joint activity with the child.

Here we have not just the "main findings of the scientific revolution," but a confirmation of a relatively traditional division of labor in marriage between husband and wife.

The key element in proposition number one is the "irrational attachment" of the child with at least one caretaker. Empirical support for this proposition has grown enormously in recent years, mostly stemming from the many psychological studies conducted by Mary Ainsworth and others that have upheld attachment theory—the theory that infants have a biosocial need for a strong, enduring, socio-emotional attachment to a caretaker, especially during the first year of life. This is what pioneering attachment theorist John Bowlby has called starting life with "a secure base." Empirical studies have shown that failure to become attached, to have a secure emotional base, can have devastating consequences for the child, and that patterns of attachment developed in infancy and childhood largely stay with the individual in adulthood, affecting one's relationships and sense of well-being....

Yet, why should the primary parent of a young child preferably be the mother and not the father? There is now substantial evidence that fathers can do the job "if they are well-trained and strongly motivated." But it is much harder to train and motivate men than women for childcare. Most dads do not want to be mom, and they do not feel comfortable being mom. To understand why the sexes are not interchangeable in child care, it is necessary to review the biological differences between them.

Biological Differences

Nowhere in the world has there ever been a society known to exist in which men were the primary caretakers of young children. The reason has much to do with the biological nature of males and females....

Across the world's societies, the "natural and comfortable" way most males think, feel, and act is fundamentally different from the way most women think, feel, and act. Not that biology is "determinant" of human behavior; this would be a poorly chosen word. All human behavior represents a combination of biological and sociocultural forces, and it makes little sense, as sociologist Alice Rossi has emphasized, to view them "as separate domains contesting for election as primary causes."

The case can certainly be made, in the interest of equality, that a culture should not accentuate the existing biological differences between the sexes. Cultures differ radically in this respect; consider the difference in gender roles between Arab and Nordic cultures. But an even stronger case should be presented in this time of declining family stability and personal well-being for frank acknowledgment of the very real differences between men and women. Acknowledgment by both sexes of their differences in sexual motives, cognitive styles, and communication patterns, for example, could make for stronger marriages. And recognition that the roles of father and mother are not interchangeable would probably make for better parenting....

While male superiority rests with "things and theorems," female superiority rests with personal relationships. Almost from birth, girls are more interested than boys in people and faces, whereas boys "just seem as happy with an object dangled in front of them." That these differences become accentuated when they reach adolescence strongly suggests that hormones play a decisive role, specifically testosterone in men and estrogen in women....

Not all behavioral differences, however, have a direct effect on family behavior. Most important for family behavior are differences that stem from the dissimilar role of males and females in sexual activity and the reproductive process. The differential "sexual strategies" of men and women have long been noted; in crude, popular terminology, "women give sex to get love, and men give love to get sex." Sex is something that women have and men want, rather than vice versa. Relationships and intimacy are the special province of women.

Sex and Evolution

Probably the most compelling explanation for male-female differences in sexuality and sexual strategies comes from the field of sociobiology. In evolutionary terms, the goal of each individual's life is to perpetuate one's genes through reproduction and maximize the survival of all those with the same genes. Among mammals, the primary reproductive function of males is to inseminate and for females to harbor the growing fetus. Since sperm is common and eggs are rare (both being the prime gene carriers), a different sexual or reproductive strategy is most adaptive for males and females, with males having more incentive to spread their sperm more widely among many females, and females having a strong incentive to bind males to themselves for the long-term care of their offspring.

... As anthropologists Patricia Draper and Henry Harpending have said, male sexual strategies range from the relatively promiscuous and low paternal investment "cad" approach, in which sperm is widely distributed with the hope that more offspring will survive to reproduce, to the "dad" approach, in which a high paternal investment is made in a limited number of offspring. But in every society the biological fathers are identified, if possible, and required to hold some responsibility for their children's upbringing. In fact, compared to other species, human beings are noted for relatively high paternal investment because human offspring have a long period of dependency and require extensive cultural training to survive. The nature of human female sexuality (loss of estrus, for example), too, encourages men to stay around.

Culture, of course, has a major say in which sexual strategies are institutionalized. In industrialized societies high paternal investment is the culturally expected. Monogamy is strongly encouraged in these societies (although "serial monogamy" has become the norm in many nations, especially in the United States), polygamy is outlawed, and male promiscuity is somewhat contained. Because it promotes high paternal investment, monogamy is well suited to modern social conditions.

Whatever sexual strategies are followed, our basic biological nature dictates that society face the problem of how to keep men in the reproductive pair-bond. Sex is rather ill-designed for lasting marriages, especially for males. Margaret Mead is purported to have said that there is no society in the world where men will stay married for very long unless culturally required to do so. This is not to suggest that marriage is not "good" for men, only that their innate biological propensities push them in another direction.

Biologically, male attachment to the mother-child pair is largely through the sexual relationship with the mother. Many anthropologists have noted that motherhood is a biological necessity, while fatherhood is mainly a cultural invention. Because it is not biologically based, a father's attachment to his children must be culturally fostered.

Cross-cultural comparisons show a man is likely to take active care of the children if 1) he is sure they are his; 2) if he is not needed as warrior and hunter; 3) if the mother contributes to food resources; and 4) if male parenting is encouraged by the woman. All these conditions prevail largely in modern societies. Although history is replete with stories of men who have developed very strong attachments to their children, men have almost never been closely involved in childcare in the early stages of life.

Parental Androgyny

Ample evidence suggests that men can make a significant contribution to child-rearing, especially with regard to their sons, and that the lack of a male presence poses a handicap for children. The assistance men give to women in the rearing of children may be more important now than ever before because mothers have become isolated from their traditional support systems. More than in the past, it is crucial now to maintain cultural measures that induce men to take an active interest in their families. It should be recognized, of course, that the parenting of young infants is not a "natural" activity for males. To perform well in that role they require thorough training and experience, plus encouragement from their wives.

Moving too far in the direction of androgynous parenting, however, presents many difficulties both for childrearing and for the marriage relationship. First, while females may not have a "maternal instinct," hormonal changes occur during and after childbirth that strongly motivate a woman to care for her newborn. These hormonal changes are linked, in part, to the woman's capacity to breastfeed. Also, several of the sex differences already noted are directly related to this stage of the reproductive process. "In caring for a non-verbal, fragile infant," sociologist Alice Rossi has noted, "women have a head start in reading an infant's facial expressions, smoothness of body motions, ease in handling a tiny creature with tactile gentleness, and soothing through a high, soft, rhythmic use of the voice."

Men seem better able to perform the parental role after children reach the age of eighteen months. By then children are more verbal and men do not have to rely on a wide range of senses. Yet, even at that age men interact with children in a different way than do women. The father's mode of parenting is clearly not interchangeable with the mother's. Men tend to emphasize "play" over "caretaking," and their play is more likely to involve a "rough-and-tumble" approach.

Reasonably sex-typed parenting in which mothers are "responsive" and fathers are "firm" also seems to have its value. One research review determined that "children of sex-typed parents are somewhat more competent than children of androgynous parents." Social psychologist Willard W. Hartup concluded: "The importance of fathers, then, may be in the degree to which their interactions with their children do not duplicate the mother's and in the degree to which they support maternal caregiving rather than replicate it."

Less widely discussed, certainly much more speculative but probably no less important, are the effects of androgyny on the marriage relationship. Many men, being of a more independent spirit, will simply avoid marrying and having children if they face having to give up their independence and engage in "unnatural" nurturing and caretaking roles. And it is not as if they had few alternatives. The old system was largely based on the marital exchange of sex for love. If a man wanted regular sex (other than with prostitutes) he had to marry. Today, more permissive sexual standards and a huge pool of single and divorced women (to say nothing of married women) provide abundant opportunities for sex outside a permanent attachment. This sociocultural reality may help to explain men's current tendency of delaying marriage, and the growing complaint of women that "men will not commit."

Nevertheless, most men eventually do marry and have children, and when they do they receive enormous personal benefits. The real concern, therefore, is not men's delay of marriage (it is largely to the good), but what happens to the marriage afterwards. If the best thing parents can do for their children is to stay together and have a good marriage, one serious problem with the "new-father" alternative, in which dad tries to become mom, is that such a marriage may not prove very enduring. This is an issue seldom discussed by "new father" proponents. Marriages which follow this alternative, especially those in which a "role-reversal" has taken place, have a high likelihood of breakup.

Why should a marriage in which the husband is doing "just what he thought his wife always wanted" be at high risk? We can only speculate about the answer by looking at the nature of modern marriages. Marriages today are based on two factors: 1) companionship, that is, husband and wife are expected to be close friends; and 2) romantic love based on sexual attraction, a biologically rooted phenomenon which expects husband and wife to be each other's exclusive sexual partners.

The joining of these two principles is not without its problems. For a good companion, you want someone with whom you have a great deal in common. But for a sexual partner, people tend to be attracted to the differences in the other. Therein lies a festering tension that must be resolved if modern marriages are to endure—a couple must have enough in common to remain best friends, but be different enough so that sexual attraction is maintained. In strong marital relationships, differences are viewed as complementary; the relationship is characterized by balanced gender-differentiated behavior and equitable division of labor....

There appear to be sound biological and sociological reasons why some gender differentiation of roles within childrearing families is necessary for the good of society. Gender differentiation is important for child development, and probably important for marital stability. While the fully equal participation of both parents in childrearing is essential, fathers are not the same as mothers, nor should they be. Rather than strive for parental androgyny in the home, and be continuously frustrated, we would do much better to acknowledge, accommodate, and appreciate the very different needs, sexual interests, values, and goals of each sex.

POSTSCRIPT

Can Fathers "Mother"?

Researchers have explored under what conditions optimal father involvement is possible. Some state that the three necessary conditions are: (1) when a father is highly motivated to parent, (2) when a father has adequate parenting skills and receives social support for parenting, and (3) when a father is not undermined by work and other institutional settings. The reconstruction of fathering, whatever the redefinition, has proven to be very difficult, contested by many cultural forces.

Professor of law Nancy Dowd poses this scenario: If the headlines tomorrow indicated that mothers parent less than fathers, nurture their children less than fathers, and frequently abandon their children, there would be outrage and alarm. Yet, the reverse pattern, which has been consistently part of the media landscape in the last decade, has not drawn nearly such a concerned reaction. Why? Dowd suggests that it might have to do with our "weak model of fathering." In her view, we have little understanding of what it means to be a father, so such conduct by fathers does not represent as significant a violation. By comparison, the cultural definition of mothering is clear and rigid. A violation of mothering is considered to be a serious offense. Dowd also suggests that our lack of concern may also stem from our assumption that fathers are not troubled when disconnected from their children.

Men's "job description" as fathers is less clear than expectations of women as mothers. Therefore, fathering is very sensitive to context (including the marital or coparental relationship, children, extended family, and cultural institutions). The role of mother is especially delimiting. Mothers often serve as gatekeepers in the father-child relationship. Father involvement is often contingent on mothers' attitudes toward, expectations of, and support for the father.

Many mothers are ambivalent about active father involvement with their children. The mothering role has been a central feature of adult women's identity, so it is no wonder that some women feel threatened by paternal involvement in their domain, which affects their identity and sense of control. In the absence of social consensus on fathering and counterarguments about the deficits of many fathers, many mothers are restrictive of father involvement. However, some maintain that responsible mothering will have to evolve to include support of the father-child bond.

In addition, with increasing latitude for commitment to and identification with their parental role, men are increasingly confused about how to exercise their roles as fathers. This also makes them sensitive to contextual factors such as others' attitudes and expectations. Worse yet, they frequently encounter disagreement among different individuals and institutions in their surrounding context, further complicating their role choices and enactment. With effort and determination, fathers *can* be decisive in overriding these external pressures, choosing for themselves a fathering identity and working toward developing fathering skills.

Four other contextual forces challenge a redefinition of fathering as nurturing. First, Dowd observed that legal notions of fatherhood disregard nurturing. Adequate fathering is primarily equated with financial responsibility. Even with the recent shift toward gender neutrality in the law, fathers' nurturing is given limited consideration in parental rights cases. Second, concepts of masculinity conflict with nurturant parenting. Nurturant fathers risk condemnation as being "unmanly." How can nurturant fatherhood fit into notions of maleness and masculinity? Third, homophobic attitudes further obstruct nurturant fatherhood. Ironically, active legal debate about sexual orientation and parenting might be influential in reconstructing fatherhood. Is there a model of shared parenting within the gay community?

Finally, nurturing by fathers and mothers has typically functioned in a single-parent model, whether with a two-parent marriage or with parents living in separate households. One parent usually does most, if not all, of the nurturing. Gender neutrality and equality in parenting is undefined. How would you conceptualize a model of shared parenting (taking care not to discriminate against single-parent families)? What would parental equality look like in practice?

Suggested Readings

W. D. Allen and M. Connor, "An African American Perspective on Generative Fathering," in A. J. Hawkins and D. C. Dollahite, eds., *Generative Fathering: Beyond Deficit Perspectives* (Sage Publications, 1997).

D. Blankenhorn, *Fatherless America: Confronting Our Most Urgent Social Problem* (Basic Books, 1995).

S. Coltrane, *Family Man: Fatherhood, Housework, and Gender Equity* (Oxford University Press, 1996).

M. F. DeLuccie, "Mothers: Influential Agents in Father-Child Relations," *Genetic, Social & General Psychology Monographs* (August 1996).

Louise B. Silverstein and Carl F. Auerbach, "Deconstructing the Essential Father," *American Psychologist* (June 1999).

ISSUE 16

Are Welfare Reforms Ineffective Because Welfare Mothers Are Irresponsible and Lazy?

YES: Thomas G. West, from "Poverty and the Welfare State," in Larry P. Arnn and Douglas A. Jeffrey, eds., *Moral Ideas for America* (The Claremont Institute, 1997)

NO: Sarah Drescher, from "Why Welfare Fails: Addressing the Pre-Existing Gender Inequalities Contributing to the Feminization of Poverty," *The Oregon Advocate* (Summer 2000)

ISSUE SUMMARY

YES: Professor of politics Thomas G. West argues that welfare reforms have been unsuccessful because they have worsened "underclass" dependency on government aid; because the underclass lack self-support, sacrifice, and responsibility; and because of deteriorating family values.

NO: Author Sarah Drescher contends that welfare reforms have inadequately addressed gender inequalities and have reinforced sex-segregated work and family roles, thereby worsening the "feminization of poverty."

When I was 19 and pregnant I had heard some of the arguments against welfare. I had heard that "those women" should just go get jobs. And I took this to mean that I could get a job that would support my new family if I put my mind to it. I had worked since I was a little girl, after all. I wasn't terribly worried.

I had a boyfriend, the father of my child. He punched me in the stomach when I told him I was pregnant. I stayed with him. I was sick and pregnant and living in a foreign country and he was the only person I knew. He scared me, but not terribly. He didn't scare me terribly until after my daughter was born. I had to protect her. I had to leave. I moved back in with my parents in California.

I intended to get a job. But even if I could have stayed on living in my parents' house, the wages I could earn as a high school drop-out *would barely pay for the day care. I wanted to spend time with my infant daughter. And I wanted to build a future for us. I applied to college and got in. The financial aid officer told me to go and apply for welfare. . . .*

I had just been taught that welfare was for someone else, for irresponsible mothers, for mothers who had no intention of building a future for their families. I was wrong. . . . I applied for welfare and received a cash grant that paid most of my rent and food stamps that fed my family for nearly six years. Four years of college and two years of graduate school.

By the time I graduated, my daughter was in first grade and I had a resume. . . . I work as an editor and publisher now and have written two books."

— From Ariel Gore, "Welfare Made a Difference: National Campaign"
(http://www.wmadcampaign.org/story09.html)

Stories of individual welfare recipients, such as the story of Ariel Gore above, call welfare recipient stereotypes into question. In fact, it is common for poor women to combine welfare with work or to get welfare benefits between jobs. Many women use welfare to help them get more education—a critical factor in moving out of poverty. Many factors conspire against poor women: they can't find employment; they can't secure high enough pay, particularly if they have children in their care; they are financially penalized if married; and they have to endure public condemnation and discrimination.

Nevertheless, stereotypes of welfare mothers remain rigid and condemning. These stereotypes reflect three dominant perspectives or beliefs about the causes of poverty and wealth: (1) individualism contends that individuals are responsible for their own lot in life. Those who are motivated and work hard will make it. Those who do not make it (i.e., welfare recipients) have only themselves to blame; (2) social-structuralism asserts that due to economic or social imbalances (e.g., in education, marriage and family life, and even welfare programs themselves), opportunities are restricted for some people, overriding individual agency and affecting the likelihood of success; and (3) "culture of poverty," most often associated with African Americans who are thought to have developed a culture—some would say counterculture—of poverty with values, traits, and expectations that have developed from the structural constraints of living in poverty and that may be intergenerationally transmitted.

The following selections provide an interesting juxtaposition of these perspectives. Thomas G. West argues that welfare reforms have been unsuccessful because of deteriorating family values and because they have worsened "underclass" dependency on government aid. He believes that the underclass lacks self-support, sacrifice, and responsibility. Sarah Drescher argues that welfare reforms have inadequately addressed gender inequalities and have reinforced sex-segregated work and family roles, thereby worsening the "feminization of poverty."

287

Thomas G. West  **YES**

Poverty and the Welfare State

Conservatives often criticize excessive government spending and regulation. But liberals leave conservatives tongue-tied when they accuse them of lacking compassion. No word in our political vocabulary—except perhaps racism—can silence critics of the welfare state more quickly and effectively.

Strangely, hardly anyone pauses to consider the easy assumption that it is compassionate to spend money on the poor. Yet we have known for some time that most poor people today have not been helped, but have been positively harmed, by the poverty programs of the 1960s and '70s. Meanwhile, most of these programs are still in place. The numbers of those dependent on them are growing rapidly.

Between 1960 and 1990 government welfare spending increased from about $30 billion (measured in 1990 dollars) to $225 billion per year, an increase of 750 percent. Even during the 1980s, the supposed "decade of greed," federal welfare spending rose almost 50 percent. In California in 1992, a welfare mother of two with a Section 8 housing voucher from the federal Department of Housing and Urban Development had a tax-free equivalent income of $1,817 per month, or $21,804 per year. This is more than twice the after-tax amount she could have earned at a minimum-wage job.

Yet in spite of this generosity, the percentage of poor Americans has hardly budged since 1965. In contrast, before the 1960s, the poverty level had been declining rapidly. According to government figures, almost 35 percent of Americans were poor in 1950. By 1965, that figure had declined to 14 percent, which is about where it has stubbornly remained ever since.

Worse, the nature of poverty has changed. Prior to the 1960s, most poor Americans were poor because their work brought in such a paltry income. After about 1965, there was, in the words of sociologist William Julius Wilson, a "sharp increase in social pathologies in ghetto communities." Poverty became increasingly a problem of a new underclass of able-bodied people who work rarely or not at all. This underclass, unlike the poor of an earlier era, has, says social critic Myron Magnet, "an impoverished intellectual and emotional development that generally imprisons them in failure." Many of them frankly reject the qualities that most Americans admire: self-control, sobriety, hard work, loyalty, courage, fair play, and faith in God. The adult men of the

From Thomas G. West, "Poverty and the Welfare State," in Larry P. Arnn and Douglas A. Jeffrey, eds., *Moral Ideas for America* (The Claremont Institute, 1997). Copyright © 1997 by The Claremont Institute. Reprinted by permission.

underclass rarely marry. Children are brought up by single women or their female relatives. These mothers are often very young, ignorant, and irresponsible. The men in their lives are temporary sexual partners or frightening predators—often both.

Among the black underclass in particular, those who cultivate decent qualities in themselves or their children are sneered at and said to be "acting white." One high school in a poor neighborhood holds its academic awards ceremony at night, without publicity, because when the rest of the students attend, the winners are mocked with jeers and hoots. In the world of the underclass, writes social scientist Charles Murray, "the drug dealer is lionized, the man who mops floors is scorned. The school girl who gets pregnant is envied, the school girl who studies is taunted."

These rejected virtues enabled earlier generations of Americans to rise out of the poverty into which they were born or (if they were immigrants) from which they started out in America. Even today, hard-working and self-disciplined Koreans and others succeed in establishing thriving businesses in the poorest neighborhoods in America, following the path of earlier generations from poverty to modest comfort to the middle class.

Work in low-paying jobs is where many Americans have traditionally learned the basic skills of showing up on time, being pleasant to customers and the boss, and persevering in getting the job done. The underclass regards these jobs as "dead-end" and their pay as "chump change." Ken Auletta quotes a typical underclass male saying, "Man, you go two, three years not working, and hanging around and smoking reefer or drinking, and then you get a job—you can't handle it. You do two, three years of idleness and after the first two, three years of working, you feel people are pushing you. You say, 'I don't want to get up in the morning, get pushed and shoved. I'm gonna get on welfare.' "

Poverty and Welfare, 1776 to 1965

Prior to the new, post-1965 approach, America had the most successful poverty program in history. Two centuries ago most Americans—at least 90 percent—were desperately poor by today's standards. By the 1960s most were middle class. Meanwhile, most of the rest of the world remained as poor in 1965 as they were in 1776. The recipe for America's successful 189-year-long poverty program was simple:

- (1) Establish free markets and opportunity for all who can work.
- (2) Provide strong governmental support for the family and for a morality of self-controlled self-assertion (combining industriousness, self-restraint, and basic decency with the vigilant spirit that says "Don't tread on me").
- (3) Provide support in local communities for the deserving poor: widows, orphans, and the disabled who are unable to work.

Poor people become unpoor when their work is rewarded by income, when they marry and support a family, and when their leaders publicly affirm the dignity of self-support, sacrifice, and responsibility. In the middle ages a serf might have worked hard all his life, but the wealth he produced often went into the hands of a wealthy landowner. In America a man had the right to keep what he earned, and the authorities praised him for doing so.....

Poverty and Welfare After 1965

But it was not until the mid-1960s that welfare was conceived as a right to be demanded of society by anyone in need, regardless of conduct or circumstances. Gone was the earlier worry about welfare creating dependency and therefore subsidizing poverty. Gone was the demand that individuals seeking government support should act in accord with minimal moral standards. Compassion was the watchword. Federal funding provided the cash.

The old system had tried to focus its help on the deserving poor while keeping benefit levels low enough to prevent poverty from being an economically attractive alternative to work. The new system abandoned the distinction between the deserving and undeserving poor, and it raised typical benefit levels above the equivalent of a minimum wage job.

Charles Murray has persuasively explained the perverse incentive structure of the modern welfare state. Generous payments to women with children expand poverty by funding it. "There is no need to invoke the specters of cultural pathologies or inferior upbringing. The choices [of the poor to forego work for welfare] may be seen much more simply, much more naturally, as the behavior of people responding to the reality of the world around them and making the decisions—the legal, approved, and even encouraged decisions—that maximize their quality of life." Robert Rector summarizes the point in this way:

> Current welfare may best be conceptualized as a system which offers each single mother a "paycheck" .... She will continue to receive her "paycheck" as long as she fulfills two conditions: 1) she must not work; and 2) she must not marry an employed male....
>
> Welfare has converted the low-income working husband from a necessary breadwinner into a net financial handicap. It has transformed marriage from an institution designed to protect and nurture children into an institution which financially penalizes nearly all low-income parents who practice it.

Social science research has established with precision that benefit levels are closely correlated with single motherhood. Rector reports:

> In 1979, the National Longitudinal Survey of Youth [NLSY] established a large sample of young women (aged 14 to 19) and then tracked the behavior of these women over the next decade. [NLSY data shows] that a 50 percent increase in the monthly value of AFDC [Aid to Families with Dependent Children] and Food Stamp benefits led to a 43 percent increase in the number of out-of-wedlock births over the study period. [Another study shows that] a 10 percent increase in AFDC benefits in a state will cause a decrease in the marriage rate of all single mothers in the state by 8 percent.

The data also confirm the common-sense view that children raised without fathers are more likely to be spoiled and undisciplined. "[H]olding family income, neighborhood, parental education, and other variables constant, young black men from single-parent homes are twice as likely to commit crimes and end up in jail when compared to young black men raised in low-income families where the father is present."

George Gilder adds an important dimension to this economic analysis. He shows that when government gives women large sums of money, it has the unintended effect of making men feel inferior to their women. Women have a natural superiority to men when it comes to bearing children. To measure up to women as equals, men have always felt the need to be the principal providers in the family. When government support became widely available to unmarried women in the 1960s, "welfare payments usurped the man's role as provider, leaving fatherless families." Welfare destroys the incipient families of the poor by making the struggling male breadwinner superfluous and thereby emasculating him emotionally. His response is predictable. He turns to the super-masculine world of the street: drinking, drugs, male camaraderie, and crime....

Beginning in the '60s, the poor were taught by welfare organizers that welfare is "nothing to be ashamed of." Welfare mothers came to meetings of the National Welfare Rights Organization "with a sense that welfare should be avoided." But "constant repetition of the word rights got through to the women." The result, as one welfare official commented at the time, was "a changing outlook among many poor and the near poor." Within a few years, a much larger proportion of those eligible for welfare chose to take advantage of it. In a similar way, America's elites, who were enthusiastically celebrating the sexual revolution, taught the poor that bearing children outside of marriage was a perfectly acceptable way to live. Those who said otherwise were denounced as puritanical or even racist.

Instead of teaching the virtues of sobriety, self-reliance, and responsible parenthood, America's most influential voices now scoffed at "bourgeois values." "Blaming the victim" and "racism" were the shrill charges leveled against anyone who dared to criticize the teenagers who lightly bore children and then raised them badly without bothering to get married. Far from condemning the able-bodied poor who refused to work or marry, liberals taught the poor to blame "the system." Because of capitalism and racism, the poor were told, they had no control over their fate. They were passive victims, and there was nothing they could do about it. As victims, they had endless rights but no responsibilities....

The dimension of the change appears most obviously in a single disheartening statistic: in 1950, only one-sixth of blacks were born to an unmarried mother; by 1993, over two-thirds of blacks were born illegitimate. In other words, the vast majority of blacks today grow up without fathers, without models of male decency, without the toughness of male discipline, and without the experience and the example of a father's love for a child and for a wife and mother. Out of the nightmare world of impoverished single mothers, undisciplined teenagers, and adult male lawlessness comes the bulk of today's cases of child abuse, drug abuse, and crime.

What Is to Be Done?

In the long run we should aim to restore the welfare policies that prevailed in America prior to the 1960s. The principle of those policies is simple: equal opportunity for all, with government support only for those who are truly unable to provide for themselves.

As a practical matter, in the short run, we should take steps to approximate the older way to the extent politically feasible. First and most important, political and community leaders should again speak candidly about virtue and vice. We know destructive and immoral conduct when we see it. Its carnage is all around us. There is no good reason to refrain politely from pointing out the truth when the lives and souls of the next generation are being trashed so casually every day. America waged its only successful War on Poverty before 1965, when its leaders affirmed the dignity of marriage, work, honesty, self-sufficiency, and individual responsibility. And if a responsible life is a life of dignity, then we must overcome our squeamishness and affirm publicly that an irresponsible life is a life of indignity, of degradation. In Charles Murray's words,

> Let government policy start from the premise that to bring a baby into the world when one is not emotionally or financially equipped to be a parent is not just ill-advised, not just inimical to the long-term interests of the mother; it is profoundly irresponsible. It is wrong.

Second, government must undo the perverse economic incentives that it has created through its misguided, community-destroying generosity. Welfare laws, like all laws, should encourage, and in no way discourage, marriage and work.

Most urgently, we should return to the older and common-sense policy of refusing government support to unmarried women bearing children. This policy led to what Murray calls "a stern self-selection process ... in which the prospects [were] so grim" that single mothers rarely chose "to keep their babies instead of giving them up" for adoption. To keep a fatherless child almost guaranteed a life of physical hardship and social ostracism. Today, true compassion for the well-being of the children as well as the mother demands that government refuse to be a party to single motherhood. Murray rightly remarks that government "cannot and must not intervene in the decision to have a baby." It would be wrong to "give people licenses to have babies" or "take babies away" from unmarried women. But it is also wrong for government to give such women special benefits. They should be eligible only for the same programs, such as unemployment benefits, as everyone else.

For widows and women abandoned by their husbands, some temporary aid is appropriate. However, the aid should be given in such a way as to compel the women to support themselves, or to find men to support them, as quickly as possible. Cash or cash-equivalent benefits—AFDC, food stamps, medical care, housing allowances—should be converted to in-kind provision of basic material needs in institutional settings. Strict rules of civilized conduct should be enforced. Food should be nourishing but plain. In general, wherever welfare is appropriate, it should be made less pleasant, less convenient, and less subject to abuse. There must be a time limit—perhaps as short as three months—for eligibility. Tax credits for babysitting expenses would make it possible for them to work when or before benefits run out.

For those truly unable to provide for themselves due to chronic disease or old age, long-term welfare should be made available only in institutional settings. Small homes or apartment buildings, privately owned and reimbursed by taxpayers, or at least locally administered, would best protect everyone concerned.

Other policy changes not directly related to single motherhood would improve the lives and opportunities of the poor.

For example, a third reform would be a serious response to the crime that poisons poor neighborhoods. The poor deserve, and justice demands, an efficient system of arrest, fair trial (not plea bargains), at least some punishment for every offense, imprisonment for the first serious offense, and escalating punishments for repeat offenders. The juvenile justice system, laughed at by underclass children who breezily commit cold-blooded murders, should be toughened up. The most urgent purpose of government is to protect life, liberty, and property. That purpose is pervasively subverted in every major city in America, where flagrant piracy is a way of life for a substantial minority of the underclass. The law-abiding poor need such protection more than the middle class, who always have the option of moving to a safer neighborhood. . . .

Less obvious than crime, but important for opportunity, are the legal obstacles faced by the ambitious poor. A fourth reform would reduce these obstacles. Since the '60s, regulation and high taxation have made it hard for the poor to enter the market and produce goods and services, and even to find affordable housing. Big companies with well-paid lawyers can cope with the endless red tape of regulation. Businessmen who are just getting started cannot. A federal law exempting all businesses with fewer than 50 employees from most federal and state regulation would be a simple way to start this process. State governments should act in parallel fashion, for instance by setting limits on local zoning laws that prevent the poor from working in their homes and neighborhoods. Housing regulations that require expensive construction methods are known to create homelessness. These should be modified or eliminated wherever possible. Economist Walter Williams has written of other areas for potential reform, for example in arbitrary licensing requirements that exclude blacks and others from driving taxis and practicing other trades.

Fifth, laws strengthening the family are long overdue. The latest social-science research confirms what common sense has always known: broken and single-mother families produce a high proportion of unhappy children, who often grow up to become self-indulgent, abusive, sometimes criminal adults. There should be firm public endorsement of healthy families, consisting of a married father and mother raising their own offspring. So-called alternative family life-styles should be treated with the contempt, or silence, they deserve.

The law can do much to support the family. Parents of children ought to be given tax relief. Because of the dependent exemption, the median family of four in 1948 paid almost no income tax. Today, that family pays almost 24 percent of its income in payroll and income taxes. No-fault divorce ought to be eliminated, and divorce generally ought to be made more difficult. Most controversially, we ought to consider restoring the pre-1900 custom of awarding child custody in divorces to the parent who is in the best position to provide for the children's material needs—usually the father. The full weight of the law could then be lowered on him if he failed to fulfill his legal duty to his children. This last reform would make many a woman and man hesitate before breaking up a family on the basis of a passing fancy or vague feelings of unfulfillment. If women were threatened with losing the children they love, and if men could not look forward to the footloose freedom they might crave, mothers and fathers would be likely to try harder to keep their marriages intact by mutual concessions and affection.

Sixth and last, the scandal of the non-education of the poor in public schools must be repaired. In the immediate term, tax credits for school expenses would instantly enable the poor to send their children to private schools. In the longer term, public schools need radical overhaul, with much higher educational and disciplinary standards. This will only follow from a policy of returning control over schools to local communities. Funding will become available by canceling about three-quarters of administrative positions in public education. This essay has said nothing about government waste, high taxes on the middle class, loose eligibility requirements, welfare cheats, and similar issues. That is because these are not the main problems. Americans are a generous people. They are willing to impose burdensome taxes on themselves if they are convinced that it is for the public good. There is therefore only one way to return to the wisdom, and the effective anti-poverty program, of pre-1965 America. America's leaders must explain clearly that giving things indiscriminately to poor people harms rather than helps them. We need to discover once again—as our Founders knew well—that compassion calls for treating the able-bodied poor as adults with souls rather than as mindless children who will never grow up.

NO ↵

Sarah Drescher

Why Welfare Fails

Why are one in two female-headed families with children and over one quarter of elderly women in the United States living at or below the poverty line? To answer this question, one must explore the causes of poverty that place a disproportionate economic burden on women and contribute to a historic and contemporary phenomenon which has become known as the "feminization of poverty." An examination of empirical studies and present academic commentary demonstrates the presence of preexisting direct and indirect sources of women's economic insecurity. From unpaid domestic labor to the cost of children and gender inequality in economic and social spheres, gender-based economic burdens contribute to the disproportionate number of impoverished females in the US. Ultimately, the policy's inadequacy to address inherent gender inequalities and its reinforcement of sex-segregated roles, contributes to the excessive amount of women in poverty.

It should be noted that data used to support the aforementioned arguments made in this examination are drawn from national poverty rates, family income, per capita income, and the ratio of income-to-needs. Many statistics which trace economic disparities—such as one revealing that one third of black women and one fifth of white women with below-median incomes during marriage are living below the poverty line in the year following marital disruption—are insensitive to income change that remains above or below the poverty threshold and disregards the overall economic fluctuations in living wages.

While recent media accounts have begun to acknowledge this trend, the feminization of poverty has actually been occurring for many decades. State constructed poverty lines have been imposed that are analogous to the methodology proffered by Linda Barrington, Assistant Professor of Economics at Columbia University. She estimates that 12.8 percent of the poor resided in female-headed households in 1939, and that the number rose to 26.3 percent by 1959, and to 51.8 percent by 1979.[1] To understand how these statistics are achieved, and then to determine the direct and indirect causes, one must first understand the process by which the data is obtained. Linda Barrington and Cecilia Conrad explain: "The proportion of poor persons living in female-headed households is a function of the proportion of poor households that are female-headed, which in turn is a function of the number of and poverty rate among

From Sarah Drescher, "Why Welfare Fails: Addressing the Pre-Existing Gender Inequalities Contributing to the Feminization of Poverty," *The Oregon Advocate* (Summer 2000). Copyright © 2000 by *The Oregon Advocate*. Reprinted by permission.

female-headed households, relative to that of male-headed households."[2] Thus, the increase in female-headed households living in poverty cited above can be attributed to the increase in proportion of female-headed households that are poor or the propensity of females to form households relative to males. Sampling the 1940 and 1960 Public Use Microdata Samples (PUMS) of the US population census, one finds an increase in both of the aforementioned.[3] Contributing causes include (1) changes in the demographic composition of female-headed households, (2) a reduction in the minimum level of earnings deemed necessary for a woman to form an independent household, and (3) a shift in the earnings distribution.

Between 1939 and 1959 the home environment changed dramatically. Small houses replaced large farm houses, joint consumption and production in the home became less significant, electrification brought new appliances, and the reduction in time for homemaking produced larger savings in a larger household. However, the shift from extended families to more nuclear families during this time span contributed to a higher incidence of poverty. Barrington and Conrad calculate that the change in the demographic composition of households headed by white women generated an increase in the poverty rate of 7.8 percentage points, while the change by non-white women generated an increase in the poverty rate of 7.9 percentage points. "Clearly, for both whites and nonwhites, the change in the demographic composition of female-headed households contributed to the increasing poverty rate among these households."[4] The choice of living arrangements made by divorced, widowed, and never-married women affects the proportion of female-headed households among the poor. Female-headed households in 1960 had fewer adults and more young children than such households in 1940. This shift in the structure of family has a direct correlation to poverty levels of female-headed households:

> A female-headed family with earnings below the poverty line that is living in a larger male-headed household will not be counted as impoverished if the larger household's income exceeds the poverty line. If the same female-headed family forms an independent household, it will be counted as poor. If a female-headed family with low earnings was more likely to live in a larger male-headed household in 1939 than in 1959, then the poverty rate for female-headed families would have increased between 1939 and 1959.[5]

Conrad and Barrington are quick to point out that social norms could have also played a part in the reduction of threshold earnings. Living with adult children was a greater violation of norms in 1960 than in 1940, thus a shift that could encourage older women to form independent households at a lower earnings level in lieu of living with grown daughters. Additionally, adolescent pregnancy, higher rates of marital disruption, greater male mortality, and severely restricted economic opportunities have affected the household structure.

Whatever the attributing causes, the evidence suggests that among families with the lowest levels of earnings, a greater proportion formed independent households in 1959 than in 1939. This brings one to a closer examination of the female-headed households after the dissolution of marriage and probes one to question what role marriage plays in reducing or increasing economic vulnerability.

Karen Holden and Pamela Smock explain the disproportionate economic cost women pay following marital dissolution in the *Annual Review of Sociology:* "Longitudinal studies of the effects of divorce and widowhood indicate that both types of dissolution have negative and prolonged consequences for women's economic well-being."[6] Adding that this is not the case for men, Holden and Smock explain that marital dissolution often leads to an improved economic situation solely for men. Empirical evidence reveals that men are not only more financially secure compared to women following the dissolution of marriage, but they are situated in a position of greater economic stability compared to the previous economic status of the family as a whole. Unless women remarry, the economic deterioration they experience is likely to be significantly prolonged.

> Women's post-dissolution economic hardship is due to multiple interrelated factors, often only superficially coupled with the marital dissolution event. In particular, the division of labor during marriage, lower wages paid to women both during and after marriage, and the lack of adequate post-dissolution transfers to women imply that unless changes in women's work roles are mirrored by social policy initiatives and men's assumption of equal responsibility for children (both within and out of marriage), economic prospects for previously married women will remain poor.[7]

It is difficult to escape the conclusion that much of the association between marital dissolution and women's economic insecurity lies in the fact that "parenthood's costs are disproportionately borne by women even long after the children leave home."[8] Much of this disproportion can be attributed to the incompatibility of primary parenting and full-time work, the lack of affordable child care and women's disproportionate financial and time responsibility for children after the divorce.

Central to the conditions that cause greater economic insecurity for women are the lower wages paid to women both during marriage and after. In the "Cross-National Comparison of the Gender Gap in Income," Rachel Rosenfeld and Arne Kalleberg provide data which indicate that the greatest income inequality by sex is in the United States and the least in Sweden.[9] US women included in the analysis earn 57% of US men's earnings; Norwegian women, 58%; Swedish women, 64%. These figures, however, include the earnings of those working less than full-time, a more common situation among Scandinavian women. Among those employed at least 35 hours a week, the differences between these countries become sharper: the income for full-time employed women relative to that for full-time employed men is 58% in the United States, 74% in Norway, and 76% in Sweden.

Researchers argue that the primary reason for the gender gap in wages is sex segregation of jobs. Women are in jobs that pay less, and this sex segregation is predominantly lower in corporatist countries than in the dualist countries. The dualist countries, such as the United States and Canada, represent decentralized and non-inclusive employment and family policies, while

Norway and Sweden, representing corporatist countries, reveal greater income equality: "Women in Sweden tended to get greater returns to their job characteristics than men. For them, 'good' jobs are important for getting relatively better pay, while in other countries even good jobs tend to pay women less than men. The indirect effect of family policies on income through their effect on job location is thus an important area for further study."[10]

Women's union membership is more prevalent in these Scandinavian countries than in the US, and the returns from this membership in the Scandinavian countries provides greater income returns to women than men. Canadian women also get larger returns than men from union membership. Additionally, part-time workers in Scandinavia can get various health and other benefits because these are determined by the state rather than the employer. However, in the US, part-time employment usually means few—if any—benefits. This fact alone has serious economic implications on the ability of women in need of work, but also needed in the home. If part-time work isn't recognized in the United States as a means for single mothers to attain economic stability by compensating unpaid labor through benefits and government aid (such as is provided in Scandinavia), then the burden is not being alleviated, but exacerbated.

When examining the evidence, it is hard to ignore the discrepancy between ethnic and social class subgroups. For lower-class blacks and increasingly for poor Mexican-Americans and Puerto Ricans, reproduction occurs outside marriage and a large proportion of marriages end in divorce.[11] For these groups, female-headed households have become more common at both early and later stages of the family life course. Female hardship is becoming a lifelong phenomenon for many minority-group women, necessitating a demographic adaptation. Applying their analysis to the Survey on Aging (SOA), Jaqueline Lowe of the Population Issues Research Center at Pennsylvania State University and Ronald Angel at the University of Texas in Austin suggest:

> In the absence of economically active males, women often adapt by forming multigenerational female-headed households. Although men occasionally contribute economically in these households, for the most part women make up the permanent nuclear unit and must rely on one another for support.[12]

This proposition suggests that the growth in female-headed households among blacks and Hispanics is not a transitory characteristic, and we would expect a high proportion of unmarried older minority women not only to live with family, but to be the head of the household. Additionally, if extended living arrangements substitute institutionalization in the event of poor health and insufficient economic resources, the proportion of black and Hispanic women living with health problems and with family is going to be higher than non-Hispanic white women. Worobey and Angel conclude that the causes of specific living arrangements and of females being heads of household in later life are "unlikely to be due entirely to either health or poverty; instead they are more likely to be a complex response to poverty, with unknown consequences on the health of older women."[13]

The feminization of poverty has been the result of societal changes in the twentieth century. The government must address the inequality of gender, since there is little possibility that society can revert to the family model that existed earlier in the last century. Following the example of Western European countries, particularly Scandinavia, there are measures the government must take to end the impoverishment of women and children, and benefit society as a whole.

The current system of Welfare in the United States fails to address gender inequalities which contribute to the feminization of poverty, ignores the role of the primary caregiver as a labor worthy of compensation, and ultimately denies women of full citizenship benefits because of its ignorance.[14] More recent reforms, including the Personal Responsibilities Act passed under Clinton in 1996, subordinate poor single mothers in a separate system of law, forcing mothers to find economic security outside the home.

Gwendolyn Mink, Professor of Political Science at the University of California, Santa Cruz, argues that poor single mothers have always been judged by welfare policy, and developments in welfare policy have always either enhanced or undermined their rights, security, and ability to care for their children.[15] Single mothers are forced either by law or predicament to choose between children and wages. Mink explains:

> The broad support for disciplinary welfare reform is rooted in the view that mothers' poverty flows from moral failing. Both Democrats and Republicans emphasize the wrongs of mothers—their "unwillingness to work," their failure to marry (or stay married), their irresponsible sexuality and childbearing. Accordingly, the legislative debate about welfare was a contest among moral prescriptions, rather than a conflict between perspectives either on the role and responsibilities of government or on the rights and responsibilities of women.[16]

The Personal Responsibility Act [PRA] is a demonstration of a policy which substitutes a moral prescription for the economic mitigation of poverty. The Act not only ignores poor mothers' vocational freedom provided by the Thirteenth Amendment, which prevents coerced labor, but also endangers poor women's rights to make their own moral decisions about marriage, procreation, and family life. Under the PRA, poor mothers and their children do not have any legally enforceable claim to benefits. The PRA explicitly disclaims an entitlement for individuals in its statement of purposes, and requires states to allocate benefits not on need alone but also on moral conformity.

As Mink explains in her book, *Welfare's End,* there is some truth to the claim that welfare reform affects us all. Single mothers may be the most immediately harmed by the PRA, but the law's invasions of rights and protections affect all women. Congress impairs poor women's reproductive rights by paying states to reduce non-marital births, destroying the constitutional status of reproductive rights fundamental to all women's equality.

> Although the PRA requires disclosure of procreative relations from welfare mothers only, policymakers have proposed requiring mothers to identify biological fathers outside the welfare context[17].... Further, although poor

single mothers are most directly endangered by the elimination of welfare's income entitlement, all mothers surrender equality in gender relations when government withdraws their safety net—their last gap means for economic independence from men.[18]

The initial welfare policies which emerged from the mothers' pension programs of the Progressive Era were based on the concept that welfare was to relieve poor single mothers of the necessity of wage-earning so that they might engage in the full-time care of their children. Today, the welfare policies have shifted in the opposite direction to remove women from the caregiving role inside the home and place them in a wage labor position.[19] Instead of forcing single mothers to choose children or wages, welfare policies must address the problems contributing to the feminization of poverty.

Karen Holden of the Department of Consumer Science and the Robert LaFollette Institute of Public Affairs and Pamela Smock of the Department of Sociology at the University of Wisconsin–Madison provide alternative financial assistance following the dissolution of marriage: "Households with children need continued sharing after marriage in the form of explicit transfers from husband to wife, either through the division of assets, child support payments, or insurance against death."[20] Another viable option is that children should continue to share the standard of living of the higher-income parent—who is usually the nonresidential father.

For households without children, when the husband dies or leaves their spouse alone, the woman should continue to share in the economic prosperity of the missing spouse through insurance against potential earnings lost. Particular emphasis in policy dialogues is thus placed on ensuring adequate child support, whether from the non-custodial parent or through governmentally guaranteed minimum benefit levels.

Part-time workers in the US should be given benefits in a manner similar to that found in other European countries. Part-time working mothers should have health care and government provided child-care so that women are not disadvantaged by being out of the labor force during their child-rearing years, nor do they have to choose full-time employment over their children to afford basic necessities.

The phenomenon of the feminization of poverty is not new. It has its roots in changes in living arrangements prior to 1960. The smaller, nuclear, female-headed families which have evolved from the previous status quo, consisting of larger, male-headed families have significantly impacted the economic status of many women in the United States. Research suggests that policy designed to combat the feminization of poverty cannot ignore the physical constitution of such families and the implications the constitution has upon the economic stability. Moreover, unless changes in female work roles are mirrored by social policy initiatives on several fronts as well as men's assumption of equal responsibility for children (both within and out of marriage), economic prospects for many women and children will continue to be grim.

Notes

1. Barrington, Linda, "At What Cost a Room of Her Own? Factors Contributing to the Feminization of Poverty Among Prime-Age Women." *Journal of Economic History*, Vol. 54, Issue 2, Papers Presented at the Fifty-Third Annual Meeting of the Economic History Association (Jun., 1994), 342–357.

2. Id. at 342

3. Id. at 343

4. Id. at 347

5. Id. at 348

6. Holden, Karen C., and Pamela Smock. "The Economic Costs of Marital Dissolution: Why do Women Bear a Disproportionate Cost?" *Annual Review of Sociology*, Vol. 17, 51–78.

7. Id. at 52

8. Id. at 74

9. Rosenfeld, Rachel, and Arne Kalleberg. "A Cross-National Comparison of the Gender Gap in Income." *American Journal of Sociology*, Vol. 96, Issue 1 (July, 1990), 69–106.

10. Id. at 101

11. Worobey, Jacqueline Lowe, and Ronald Angel. "Poverty and Health: Older Minority Women and the Rise of the Female-Oriented Household," *Journal of Health and Social Behavior*, Vol. 31 (Dec. 1990), 370–383.

12. Id. at 372

13. Id. at 373

14. Mink, Gwendolyn. "Disdained Mothers, Unequal Citizens." Welfare's End. Ithaca: Cornell University Press, 1998.

15. Id. at 9

16. Id. at 5

17. For example, President Clinton's 1994 welfare bill sought the establishment of paternity for all non-marital hospital births.

18. Mink, p. 8

19. Regulating the Poor: The Function of Public Welfare. New York: Random House, 1971. Frances Fox Piven and Richard Cloward explain how this is a technique used to regulate the poor rather than aid them in their book.

20. Holden, Karen, and Pamela Smock. "The Economic Costs of Marital Dissolution: Why Do Women Bear a Disproportionate Cost?" *Annual Review of Sociology*, Vol. 17 (1991), 51–78.

POSTSCRIPT

Are Welfare Reforms Ineffective Because Welfare Mothers Are Irresponsible and Lazy?

A related controversy surrounds the incidence of conception and childbirth while the mother is a welfare recipient (i.e., "subsequent births"). Traditionally, welfare policies grant monetary benefits to families based on the number of children. Thus, the birth of another child would earn the family increased financial support. Critics charge these women with intentionally having additional children so as to increase their financial benefit and view them as irresponsible and promiscuous (though, on average, welfare recipients have fewer children than individuals not on welfare). Critics fear that subsequent births will promote long-term dependency on federal aid. The 1996 federal welfare reform law allows states discretion to adopt strategies for inhibiting subsequent births.

States have adopted a variety of programs that operationalize supposed solutions to the subsequent birth problem. Efforts include family caps on welfare benefits, enhanced family-planning services, directive counseling (telling mothers they should not have another baby and instructing them in how to prevent pregnancy), and financial incentives for young mothers who do not become pregnant. Additional incentives and programs aimed at keeping women from having additional children and keeping young women from having sex include the "Illegitimacy Bonus," which rewards states that reduce their out-of-wedlock birthrate while also reducing abortion rates for all women, not just those on welfare; the Abstinence-Only Standard," which offers financial incentives to states that teach abstinence as the expected or only standard; requiring unmarried mothers under the age of 18 to live with their parents; and enforcing child support by performing paternity tests to identify biological fathers and forcing women to turn in fathers of their children or lose benefits, regardless of the risk of physical or emotional harm to the woman or her children.

Most controversial are family cap provisions, which preclude a welfare recipient from receiving additional case benefits for a child conceived while the recipient parent was on welfare (albeit the child would be eligible for Medicaid coverage and other benefits). The desired outcome of family cap provisions would be fewer out-of-wedlock births.

Supporters of family caps believe that the traditional rule that welfare benefits are determined on the basis of the number of children in a family actually provides a financial incentive to have children while on welfare. Therefore, family caps are implemented to send a message to these women that they should not have more children until they can support them.

Opponents of family caps consider them to be in violation of a mother's right to determine whether or when to have children. Others fear that family caps wil increase welfare families' hardship and increase abortion rates. Interestingly, some evaluation studies of such programs also look for higher abortion rates as an outcome signifying program success. In fact, program evaluation research to date has been underwhelming, resulting frequently in inconclusive or disappointing results.

Another criticism is that efforts at the "rational econometric control" of reproduction are ignorant of the complexities involved in becoming pregnant. Typically, two individuals are involved in a social interaction that is not always volitional and often includes an array of pressures. To what degree can reproduction be controlled by incentive pressures? It is also noteworthy that males' role in fertility are largely ignored in programs aimed at reducing subsequent births.

Welfare legislation and statistics raise serious questions about gender dynamics and differentials. Why are most welfare recipients women? How is the societal construction of "mother" and "father" related to welfare statistics and policies? How is socioeconomic class associated with women's reproductive rights and freedoms?

Suggested Readings

Children's Defense Fund, "Families Struggling to Make It in the Workforce: A Post Welfare Report" (December 2000).

K. Edin, and L. Lein, "Work, Welfare, and Single Mothers' Economic Survival Strategies," *American Sociological Review*, (1997): pp. 363–370.

K. Edin, L. Lein, T. Nelson, and S. Clampet-Lundquist, "Talking With Low-Income Fathers," *Poverty Research News*, 4, (2000).

M. C. Lennon, J. Blome, and K. English, "Depression and Low-Income Women: Challenges for TANF and Welfare-to-Work Policies and Programs," *Research Forum on Children, Families and the New Federalism, National Center for Children in Poverty* (Columbia University, 2001).

M. H. Wijnberg, and S. Weinger, "When Dreams Wither and Resources Fail: The Social-Support Systems of Poor Single Mothers," *Families in Society*, 79, (1998): 212–220.

"X: A Fabulous Child's Story" by Lois Gould

This is a provocative piece of speculative fiction entitled "X: A Fabulous Child's Story" about raising gender-neutral children. This is essential reading for thinking through the possibility of raising children to transcend gender.

http://www.trans-man.org/baby_x.html

The International Journal of Transgenderism

The International Journal of Transgenderism is an online peer-reviewed journal focusing on transgenderism from interdisciplinary and intercultural perspectives. The articles cover a wide variety of aspects and expressions of gender identity. A searchable archive includes numerous informative articles.

http://www.symposion.com/ijt/

Transsexuality

This is a very rich Web site about transsexuality maintained by Jennifer Diane Reitz. Included is discussion of the history and definition of transsexuality, extensive writing on the experience of transsexuality, and frank discussion of the dangers and benefits of "passing" and "coming out" for transsexuals.

http://transsexual.org

Gender, Race, and Ethnicity in Media: Cyberspace

This page is part of a Web site entitled "LINKS to Communication Studies Resources" maintained by The University of Iowa Department of Communication Studies. An extensive list of links (and descriptions) is provided relevant to gender in cyberspace. This is an exceptional resource.

http://www.uiowa.edu/~commstud/resources/
GenderMedia/cyber.html

The Journal of Virtual Environments

The Journal of Virtual Environments, formerly *The Journal of MUD (Multi-User Domain) Research,* is a refereed electronic journal that publishes empirical and theoretical academic research relating to MUDs or making use of MUD environments. Psychological, anthropological, and sociological approaches are featured. Past issues are archived. See Volume 3, Number 2 (July 1998) for an interesting article on character race in MUDs.

http://www.brandeis.edu/pubs/jove/

PART 6

Transcending Gender

*W*hat is the future of gender? Many contemporary scholars remark *that the boundaries of gender have been challenged in recent times and that the future holds promise for the "transcendence" of gender. They foretell movement beyond traditional gender roles to refashioned and more flexible gender motifs or perhaps even to the eradication of gender altogether. What would a gender-transformed or gender-irrelevant future look like and what will enable the attainment of such future visions?*

In this section, new definitions of gender in contemporary and future societies are examined. Are there only two genders (predetermined by the sex binary) or are genders unlimited in form and function, able to be individually and uniquely constructed? In addition, contemporary societal trends are examined as potential catalysts to gender redefinition and transcendence. Can we raise children for whom gender proscriptions are less relevant? How is gender defined in cyberspace? Can alternative virtual *experiences challenge our* real *gender ideologies?*

- Can We Raise "Gender-Neutral" Children?

- Does Transsexualism Solve the Problem of Fixed Definitions of Gender Identity?

- Will the Experimentation With Different Identities in Cyberspace Help Us to Transcend Gender?

ISSUE 17

Can We Raise "Gender-Neutral" Children?

YES: Sandra Lipsitz Bem, from *An Unconventional Family* (Yale University Press, 1998)

NO: Denise A. Segura and Jennifer L. Pierce, from "Chicana/o Family Structure and Gender Personality: Chodorow, Familism, and Psychoanalytic Sociology Revisited," *Signs* (Autumn 1993)

ISSUE SUMMARY

YES: Psychologist Sandra Lipsitz Bem describes the "feminist" child-rearing practices she and Daryl Bem used to raise their two children. Their underlying argument stems from gender schema theory, asserting that gender-neutral child-rearing practices can be effective in developing gender-aschematic thinking in children.

NO: Sociologists Denise A. Segura and Jennifer L. Pierce use sociologist Nancy Chodorow's psychoanalytic theory to understand the acquisition of heterosexual gender identity in Chicana/o families.

Gender identity refers to one's psychological sense of being male or female. Traditional personality theories view gender typing as desirable, a requirement of "normal" development, and even inevitable. Moreover, gender typing is considered to be an endpoint in development. But many scholars ask whether or not gender typing is desirable. Does gender typing or "gender transcendence" predict better individual adjustment and relationship success?

Recently, there is increased momentum toward gender transcendence or moving beyond traditional notions of gender. Advocates argue for the importance of raising "nonsexist," "gender-neutral," or "gender-aschematic" children for prompting social change. Is it possible to raise nonsexist children for whom gender is less relevant to their sense of self?

To address this question, we must explore how gender identity develops. Two theories offer insight into gender identity development and the improbability or possibility of gender transcendence.

The contemporary psychoanalytic theory of sociologist Nancy Chodorow advances that the most important work toward gender identity development and the differentiation of the sexes occurs in the first two years of life. The role of mother or other female caretakers as nurturer creates an early relationship between mother and infant, which permanently marks development.

According to Chodorow's theory, an infant, having no sense of "self," has no concept of distinction between itself and its caretaker (typically the mother) and is thus psychologically merged with the caretaker. A primary task of development is the differentiation of a sense of self distinct from the caretaker, who is the primary love object.

Both boys and girls initially identify with their mother, their primary caretaker. But a mother's awareness of the sex of her children often prompts differential treatment of them. Since mothers and daughters are of the same sex, the mother-daughter relationship is generally closer than the mother-son relationship. In contrast, boys' differentiation of self is more difficult because of their early identification with their mother.

Thus, to develop an identity as masculine, boys have to reject their mother's femininity and develop a different and separate identity. For boys, separation is more complete and even exaggerated, leading boys to repel, denigrate, fear, and mistrust anything feminine.

This early developmental process "locks in" traditional gender roles and attributes. Thus, traditional gender roles (including women's limited opportunities beyond mothering) are reproduced from one generation to the next by the centrality of female caretakers in social arrangements. Transcending gender is very difficult, at best.

In contrast, a cognitive theory, gender schema theory, examines gender identity as constructed by the ways individuals use, organize, and categorize gender-related information in thinking about and solving problems. A schema is a cognitive structure that organizes and orients our perceptions. Gender is a central organizational category in our culture and thus is a primary cognitive schema.

With the development of gender schemata, children become more and more ready to interpret information in terms of gender. Gender schemata contribute to the formation of gender stereotypes or narrowly defined and exaggerated concepts of what is acceptable as masculine and feminine.

Is gender schematic thinking inevitable? Some argue that it is not. We can raise "gender-aschematic children" by limiting the development of gender schemata and substituting alternative schemata.

But gender may not be the only important category of identity. For example, ethnic group membership might be more salient, especially for individuals who are members of ethnic minorities. Thus, culture is another factor in determining the possibility (and desirability) of gender transcendence.

In the following selections, Sandra Lipsitz Bem details her own child-rearing practices and maintains that it is possible to raise "gender-neutral" children by ensuring that they develop gender-aschematic thinking. Denise A. Segura and Jennifer L. Pierce describe Chicana/o family structure within the context of Chodorow's psychoanalytic theory to demonstrate the difficulty of raising children without heterosexual gender identity.

Sandra Lipsitz Bem

 **YES**

Feminist Child-Rearing

Shortly before Emily was born, in 1974, I put an end to our public lecturing on egalitarianism and to interviews about our lives because I didn't want our children to become local celebrities, as we had become. Daryl and I did continue lecturing on egalitarianism in my undergraduate course on gender, however, and within a few years, I developed a second lecture for that course based on our lives, this one on the feminist child-rearing practices we had developed.

Until the 1990s, I rarely gave this lecture outside my class. As early as the mid-1980s, however, I did incorporate parts of it into my scholarly writing, and Daryl also wrote about it in his textbook on introductory psychology. As much as I may have once intended to protect my children's privacy, by the mid-1990s, the story Daryl and I told most often—about what happened to Jeremy the day he wore barrettes to nursery school—had become so well known that a feminist legal scholar used it (with my permission) as both the title and the prologue of a law review article on gender-specific dress requirements in the workplace.

I'll tell the barrettes story a little later. I mention it now only to highlight the fact that, although we were much less public about our feminist child-rearing than about our egalitarianism, here too we quickly transformed our private feminist practice into public feminist discourse. Hence I remember more about how I analyzed my life in public than how I lived my life on a daily basis.

I began thinking about feminist child-rearing in the late 1960s, when I read an influential article by the developmental psychologist Lawrence Kohlberg, in which he suggested that young children are rigidly gender-stereotyped in their thinking and acting not because of the way they are raised but because of their "cognitive-developmental stage." It is not our gender-stereotyped culture, in other words, that convinces our children (and especially our boys) to eschew anything and everything associated with the other sex, including toys, clothes, colors, and even people. No, this idea emerges naturally and inevitably from the child's own immature mind. No need to worry, though. With age and maturity will come a more advanced cognitive-developmental stage and hence a more flexible way of seeing both the self and the world.

"I don't believe this for a second," I thought to myself. It may be difficult to raise a gender-liberated child, but it is surely not impossible. And even the reason it's difficult is not primarily because of any cognitive limitation on the part of the child. It's because the child is situated in a culture that distinguishes ubiquitously on the basis of sex from the moment of birth. Given that social reality, moreover, it ought to be possible for even young children to be gender-liberated if we can inoculate them early enough and effectively enough against the culture. . . .

How are children to be protected against the culture's sex-and-gender system? I always describe inoculating our own children in two distinct phases.

During the first phase, our goal was to enable Emily and Jeremy to learn about both male-female difference and the body without simultaneously learning any cultural stereotypes about males and females or any cultural stigmas about the body. Put somewhat differently, our goal was to retard their gender education while simultaneously advancing their sex education.

To retard their gender education, Daryl and I did everything we could for as long as we could to eliminate any and all correlations between a person's sex and other aspects of life. For example, we took turns cooking the meals, driving the car, bathing the baby, and so on, so that our own parental example would not teach a correlation between sex and behavior. This was easy for us because we already had such well-developed habits of egalitarian turn-taking. In addition, we tried to arrange for both our children to have traditionally male and traditionally female experiences—including, for example, playing with both dolls and trucks, wearing both pink and blue clothing, and having both male and female playmates. This turned out to be easy, too, perhaps because of our kids' temperaments. Insofar as possible, we also arranged for them to see nontraditional gender models outside the home.

I remember telling my class I was so determined to expose our children to nontraditional models that when Emily was very young, I drove her past a particular construction site every day because a female construction worker was a member of the crew there. I never let on that it was always the same site and the same woman we were seeing because I wanted there to be a time in her life when Emily didn't even think of such women as unusual. More important, we never allowed there to be a time in our children's lives when they didn't know that some people had partners of their own sex and other people had partners of the other sex. This was both extremely easy and extremely important in our family because so many of our closest relatives were either lesbians or gay men. . . .

Another way we retarded our children's gender education was to monitor—even to censor—books and television. I had no qualms about limiting television to three hours a week because, in addition to being filled with gender stereotypes, it also kills children's brain cells (metaphorically speaking) by addicting them (again, metaphorically speaking) to a state of passivity. Books, in contrast, I hated even the thought of monitoring because I love books and wanted our children to love them, too. The problem is that if young children are allowed to sample freely from the world of children's literature, they will almost certainly be indoctrinated with the idea that girls and boys are not only different from each other but, even worse, that boys are more important. What else can one conclude, after all, when there are approximately ten boys in these stories for every girl and almost a hundred "boy" animals for every "girl" animal? (I'm not exaggerating.) Or when the few females who are in these books almost always stay indoors and at home—no matter what their age or species—while the males go outdoors and have adventures. Or, perhaps worst of all, when the females are so unable to affect their own environments that when good things happen to them, those things just fall out of the sky, whereas when good things happen to males, their own efforts have usually played a part in making them occur.

Not only did we censor books with traditional messages like these. For a time, we restricted our children's access even to feminist books like *William's Doll*. After all, for a child who doesn't yet know about the American cultural taboo with respect to boys and dolls, even a book that argues that it's all right for boys to have dolls is teaching a gender stereotype in the very process of trying to counter it.

To compensate for all this censorship, I worked hard to locate as many books as I could that were free of gender stereotypes. Ironically, this may have been easier in the 1970s than it is today because of the many small feminist collectives that specialized in producing such books then. And although I have no artistic talent, I was handy with my whiteout and magic markers, which I used liberally to transform one main character after another from male to female by changing the character's name, by changing the pronouns, and even by drawing long hair (and, if age-appropriate, the outline of breasts) onto the character's picture. Nor did I limit my doctoring to the main characters. I frequently changed even background characters who appeared in the illustrations from male to female because, if I didn't, the main character would be living in a world disproportionately populated by males.

The only time I remember this getting me into trouble was when I bought my children a Curious George book and decided to change the tall man in a yellow hat into a tall woman in a yellow hat. Never having heard of Curious George, I didn't know it was a series, and I also didn't know how very, very often the tall man would reappear. So, after making him a woman in the first book, I let her revert to a man in the rest of the books, thereby giving our children their first encounter with an implicit sex-change operation. They, bless their gender-liberated hearts, never seemed to notice.

When reading books aloud to our children, we also chose our pronouns carefully in order not to imply that all characters not wearing a dress or a pink hair ribbon must necessarily be male: "And what is this little piggy doing? Why, he or she seems to be building a bridge." Jeremy, in particular, seemed to hear this pronoun phrase as a single word because, for many years, he used the he-or-she form exclusively in almost all third-person contexts. If I asked Jeremy to tell me what Emily or Dad or some character in a book was doing, Jeremy would typically say that "heorshe" was doing whatever he or she was doing. I had thus unwittingly introduced a gender-nonspecific (but not neuter) third-person pronoun into the English language.

So much for retarding our children's gender education. To advance their sex education, we taught them about the body as early as we could. That is, we provided a clear and unambiguous bodily definition of what sex is. A boy, we said again and again, is someone with a penis and testicles; a girl is someone with a vagina, a clitoris, and a uterus; and whether you're a boy or a girl, a man or a woman, shouldn't matter unless and until you want to make a baby. Consistent with this premise, I also refused to provide a simple answer when the kids asked me in the supermarket or the park or wherever whether someone was a boy or a girl, a man or a lady. Instead I said (quietly, so as not to draw attention to myself) that I couldn't really tell without seeing under the person's clothes. When this answer began to be unsatisfactory, I complicated things a bit by conceding, for example, that since the person was wearing a dress, we might guess that he or she was a girl because, in this country, girls are the ones who more often wear dresses. As always, however, I concluded that one cannot know for certain without seeing under the person's clothes.

I was not the only person my children talked to, of course, and they were not dummies, so eventually they came to understand that I was playing a kind of game with them, and then we began to play the game together. One time I remember in particular, Emily brought me a magazine with a male face on the cover and teasingly said to me, "Look, Mom, it's a boy head." Knowing it was a game, I immediately started laughing and said to her, "What do you mean it's a boy head? I don't see any penis on that head. How can it be a boy head if it doesn't have a penis?" Then she started laughing too. But even if everyone treated these interactions playfully, the game had a serious subtext: an important distinction must be made between an attribute that is merely correlated with sex and an attribute that is definitional of sex. Attributes that are merely correlated with sex, like clothing and hairstyle, don't really matter; only your genitalia define you as male or female.

Both the liberation that can come from having a narrow bodily definition of sex and the imprisonment that can come from not having such a definition are strikingly illustrated by what happened to Jeremy on the day he decided to wear barrettes to nursery school. When Jeremy came to me that morning and asked me to put barrettes in his hair, the first thought that came into my mind was: "Hmmm. I wonder if Jeremy knows that barrettes are 'just for girls.'" The next thought was the script I imagined the good liberal parent would now begin to read from. "Jeremy," this good liberal script would say, "you're certainly welcome to wear these barrettes to nursery school if you want to. It's fine with me. But there's something I need to tell you to help you make your decision. Even though our family thinks boys and girls should be able to do anything they want as long as it doesn't hurt anybody or break anything, a lot of other people still have the old-fashioned idea that some things are just for girls and other things are just for boys, and (can you believe it?!) barrettes are actually one of the things these people think of as just for girls. Now just because that's what some people think about barrettes doesn't mean you shouldn't wear them. But you probably should know ahead of time that if you do wear them, you might get teased a bit."

I myself said none of this, however, because I had vowed long before, never, in the domain of sex and gender, to be the carrier of the culture to my children. So with barrettes in his hair, off Jeremy went to nursery school.

When Jeremy came home that day, I was dying to find out what, if anything, had happened, but I didn't want to ask because I didn't want to make a big deal of it. I waited and waited for Jeremy to bring it up spontaneously. But he never did, not that day, not the next day, not for a long time. Then I forgot about it until one of his teachers asked me at a parent-teacher get-together if Jeremy had ever described what happened on the day he wore barrettes to nursery school. Several times that day, another little boy had asserted that Jeremy must be a girl, not a boy, because "only girls wear barrettes." After repeatedly insisting that "Wearing barrettes doesn't matter; I have a penis and testicles," Jeremy finally pulled down his pants to make his point more convincingly. The other boy was not impressed. He simply said, "Everybody has a penis; only girls wear barrettes."

But I didn't try to "teach the body" only to provide our children with a stereotype-free definition of male and female. I also tried to teach the body as a stigma-free foundation for sexuality....

By advancing our children's sex education and retarding their gender education, Daryl and I enabled them to learn their earliest lessons about sex and sexual difference without simultaneously learning the many cultural stereotypes and stigmas that typically accompany these lessons. But how were we to keep them from sliding over to the enemy side, so to speak, as they gradually began to hear the voice of the dominant culture? How, in other words, to keep them from forsaking these early lessons when they later began to realize, as they inevitably would, that their parents' beliefs about sex and sexual difference were different from those of most other people? This question brings me to the second phase of the children's inoculation process.

During this second phase, our overarching goal was to make our children skeptical of whatever conventional cultural messages about sex and gender they might be exposed to, whether from television, from books, from movies, from other people, or from anywhere else. More specifically, our goal was to provide them with the kind of critical feminist lens or framework that would predispose them to "read" the culture's conventional messages in an unconventional way. How did we go about trying to provide them with such a framework? In retrospect, four things we did seem particularly important.

The first thing we did—though I'm not sure we understood its relevance to our feminist goals when we did it—was to emphasize the theme of difference and diversity long before it was relevant to sex and gender. "Why are some of our friends not allowed to play in the nude, but we are?" our children would ask when they were young. "Why do other families say grace before meals but we don't? Why can cousin so-and-so drink Pepsi with dinner but we have to drink milk?" To these questions and dozens like them, our answer was always the same: Different people believe different things, and because they believe different things, they make up different rules for their children.

Few of these early diversity conversations focused on sex or gender. Nevertheless, they provided our kids with the underlying premise that different—and even contradictory—beliefs are the rule rather than the exception in a pluralistic society. This premise served as an excellent foundation for what we would later say about difference and diversity when our conversations turned to sex and gender, as they did when the kids started asking questions like: Why is some boy in Emily's nursery-school class not allowed to dress up in a princess costume for Halloween? Or, why is some girl in Jeremy's kindergarten class not allowed to sleep overnight in Jeremy's bedroom?

The second thing we did was to provide Emily and Jeremy with a non-gendered way of reframing the many conventional messages about male-female difference that they began to hear when they were three or four or five years old. These messages came in many variations, but they all boiled down to the same idea: Boys and girls are different from each other in innumerable ways, as are women and men. We always responded with a script something like the following: Yes, it's true, some girls don't like to play baseball. But you know what? Other girls like to play baseball a lot (including, for example, your Aunt Bev and Melissa who lives across the street), and some boys don't like to play baseball at all (including your dad and Melissa's brother Billy). As soon as our children began to mouth the conventional cultural stereotypes about male-female difference, we extended our earlier discussions of difference and diversity by telling them that it's not males and females who are different from each other. It's people who are different from each other.

The third thing we did was to help them to understand that all cultural messages about sex and gender (indeed, all cultural messages about everything) are created, whether now or in the distant past, by particular human beings with particular beliefs and biases. The appropriate stance to take toward such messages is thus not to assume that they are either true or relevant to your own personal life but to assume instead that they merely convey information about the beliefs and biases of their creators.

Perhaps the most obvious example of my trying to teach this stance occurred when I sat down to read to Emily from her first book of fairy tales. An older relative had given her this book when she was four years old, and although I knew it would expose her to many gender stereotypes she had never seen before, I didn't want to hold back from reading it because I thought that would indirectly and inappropriately be a criticism of the gift-giver. Besides, I thought Emily would probably enjoy the fairy tales immensely, just as I had when I was a child. Once again the challenge was how to get her own "reading" of the fairy tales to subvert the culture's messages about males and females rather than support them.

I gave Emily a little feminist lecture before I started to read. "The fairy tales in this book," I said, "are wonderfully exciting, and I think you'll like them a lot, but you need to understand before we read them that they were written a *long looooong* time ago by people who had some very peculiar ideas about girls and boys. In particular, the people who wrote these fairy tales seemed to think that the only thing that matters about girls is whether they're beautiful or not beautiful, and the other thing they seem to think about girls is that they are the kind of people who always get themselves into trouble and then need to be saved by boys, who—according to these fairy-tale writers anyway—are naturally brave and smart. Now, I haven't read these particular fairy tales yet, but I did read a lot of other fairy tales when I was little, and I'm willing to bet that if you listen really carefully, you'll hear lots and lots of stories where a brave, wise boy rescues a beautiful girl, but what you won't ever hear is even one story where a brave, wise girl rescues a beautiful boy.""

Emily loved the fairy tales, just as I thought she would, but after each one, she giggled with glee about how I had been right. "There's another one, Mom," she would say. "Aren't the people who made up these stories silly?"

Several years ago, a feminist colleague of mine was lamenting a question her preschool daughter had asked after watching *Mr. Rogers' Neighborhood* on television. "Why are kings royaler than queens?" her daughter had wanted to know. The question had troubled my colleague because she couldn't figure out how to use her daughter's question as a springboard for a feminist lesson. I knew immediately what I would say, but then I began to wonder what my kids would say, so I asked them (they were then maybe eleven and fourteen), and they both said basically the same thing: "Your friend should tell her daughter to think about who writes the script for *Mr. Rogers' Neighborhood.* If King Friday is more royal than Queen Sarah, it's not because kings *are* more royal than queens. It's because Mr. Rogers *thinks* kings are more royal than queens."

All this talk about difference and diversity is fine as far as it goes, but from a feminist perspective, not all beliefs and biases are equally valid. At some point, we also needed to convey to our children that the view of women and men represented by fairy tales, by the mass media, and by sexist and homophobic people of all ages everywhere is not only different or even "old-fashioned." It is plain and simply wrong. Accordingly, the fourth thing we did to provide our children with a critical feminist framework was to teach them about sexism and homophobia.

I distinctly remember how I introduced the concept of sexism to Emily because she immediately custom-fit my lesson to her own needs. I'm not sure why I chose the particular moment I did. Probably Emily had been quoting some classmate at nursery school who said that either Emily or some other girl couldn't do this activity or that because of her sex. Whatever the catalyst, I then read Emily a children's book I had been saving for just this occasion. The book was *Girls Can Be Anything,* by Norma Klein. The main characters are two kindergartners named Marina and Adam. Marina and Adam love to pretend that they are grown-up workers in a grown-up work environment. One day they're flying an airplane, another day they're staffing a hospital, a third day they're running a country. The plot has a certain redundancy. Both Marina and Adam want to pilot the airplane, but Adam says "girls can't be pilots... they have to be stewardesses"; both Marina and Adam want to be doctors, but Adam says "girls are always nurses"; and so on. I think you get the message. Luckily, Marina not only has feminist parents. She also has an abundance of extremely accomplished female relatives. Thus, when she complains to her parents at dinner about whatever sexist stereotype Adam asserted that day, her parents not only reply that of course girls can be pilots or doctors. They also remind her that one or another of her aunts is either a famous jet pilot who just logged her millionth mile (see her picture on the front page of the *New York Times*) or a famous heart surgeon who just performed her millionth heart transplant. I'm exaggerating a bit, but not much.

After we read this book together, Emily, then age four, spontaneously began to call anyone who said anything the least bit gender-stereotyped an "Adam Sobel," in the most contemptuous voice she could muster. Clearly Adam Sobelness (also known as sexism) was a concept she was ready for.

Chicana/o Family Structure and Gender Personality: Chodorow, Familism, and Psychoanalytic Sociology Revisited

Chicana/o Family Structure and Gender Personality

Chicanas and Chicanos come to maturity as members of a racial and ethnic minority in a social and historical context in which their political, economic, and cultural uniqueness is constantly undermined, denigrated, and violated. Since the annexation of northern Mexico by the United States in 1848, Chicanas and Chicanos have experienced second-class citizenship both politically and economically. Chicanas and Chicanos have faced discrimination in employment, education, and political participation. They have been and continue to be concentrated among the poor and the working class in the United States (Barrera 1979; Rochin and Castillo 1991). Furthermore, Chicanas and Chicanos maintain and affirm a distinct culture that emphasizes familism, *compadrazgo* [extended family ties], and a collectivist orientation that is devalued by the dominant culture's emphasis on individualism....

Much... research emphasizes the heterogeneity among Chicana/o families by immigrant status, urban/rural residence, household size, acculturation, and class status. Such empirical research also establishes important commonalities. In 1990, nearly 90 percent of Chicana/o families reported income below $50,000 to maintain families significantly larger, on the average, than the societal "norm" (4.03 persons in Chicana/o families compared with 3.12 persons in white families) (U.S. Bureau of the Census 1992, table 1). Half of all Chicana/o families in 1990 were maintained by $23,240 or less for a family of four while 25 percent lived below the poverty level ($13,359 for a family of four) (U.S. Bureau of the Census 1991a, 18, 25). In contrast, 8.1 percent of European-American families and 29.3 percent of black families lived below the poverty rate in 1990 (U.S. Bureau of the Census 1991b, 15). These figures indicate that Chicana/o families are primarily working class and often among the working poor; they provide a key socioeconomic context to the analysis of this community.

Bolstered by empirical data, revisionist researchers often examine features commonly associated with both working-class and middle-class Chicana/o families, including familism (beliefs and behaviors associated with family solidarity), *compadrazgo* (extended family via godparents), *confianza* (a system of trust and intimacy), high Spanish language loyalty, a gender-specific division of labor, and high fertility. But most such research has focused on working-class families; the degree to which these traits vary by class has not been sufficiently explored. In view of the limited research on middle-class Chicana/o families, we limit our discussion to working-class families and caution that our analysis may be less relevant as income levels rise. Some evidence exists, however, that middle-class Chicana/o families display surprisingly high loyalty to the Spanish language and place a high premium on familism (Keefe and Padilla 1987); our analysis thus may resonate within this more privileged sector of the Chicana/o community.

Revisionist researchers typically analyze characteristics attributed to Chicana/o families within the context of Chicanas' and Chicanos' historically suppressed social, economic, and political opportunities, their historical clustering within certain geographic areas (the southwestern United States), and their limited political clout (Saragoza 1983; Baca Zinn and Eitzen 1987). This broader social context is important to an analysis of mothering and the reproduction of gendered personalities in Chicana/o families; this context helps to shape and define the unique constellation of features that characterize Chicana/o families. We begin by describing this constellation, which includes features such as familism, *compadrazgo,* and nonexclusive mothering. Then, by extending [Nancy] Chodorow's more recent argument (1989) about social specificity and mothering, we explore the psychological consequences this particular social context poses for the development of gender personality among Chicanas and Chicanos. We argue that in Chicana/o families the blending of gender identity and ethnic identity creates forms of masculine and feminine personality distinct from that of the European-American middle class.

The Constellation of Features in Chicana/o Families

Contemporary sociologists consider familism to be a primary characteristic of Chicana/o families (Griswold del Castillo 1984, 146). Maxine Baca Zinn observes that familism is observable in four ways: by macrocharacteristics such as large family size (demographic familism); by the presence of multigenerational households or extended households (structural familism); by the high value placed on family unity and solidarity (normative familism); and by the high level of interaction between family and kin networks (behavioral familism) (Baca Zinn 1982/83, 226–27).

Compadrazgo, another prominent feature of Chicana/o families and one associated with behavioral familism, refers to two sets of relationships with godparents who become "fictive" kin: *padrinos* and *ahiados* (godparents and their godchildren) and *compadres* (godparents and parents who become co-parents) (Falicov 1982). *Compadrazgo* relationships with godparents create connections between families, thereby enlarging Chicana/o family ties. According to Richard Griswold del Castillo, "godparents [are] required for the celebration of major religious occasions in a person's life: baptism, first communion and marriage" (1984, 42). At these times, godparents enter "into special religious, social and economic relationships with the godchild as well as the parents of the child." They act as co-parents, "providing discipline and emotional and financial support when needed." As *compadres,* they are expected to become the closest friends of the parents and members of the extended family (1984, 40–44). While *compadrazgo* is principally a feature of Roman Catholic Chicana/o families, non-Catholic Chicanas and Chicanos who go through baptism and marriage rituals may also gain *compadres....*

The continuing high fertility rate of Chicanas, for example, enhances their opportunities to acquire *compadres* and to affirm close connections to extended family members. In 1988, Hispanic women had an estimated fertility rate of 94 births per 1,000 women between the ages of 18 and 44, compared with European-American women's 67.5 births per 1,000 women (U.S. Bureau of the Census 1988). High fertility, thus, is one mechanism that reinforces the significance of familism and *compadrazgo* in Chicana/o communities. While *compadrazgo* may be changing, especially in its economic functions, Williams observes it remains an important resource for emotional support and cultural affirmation (Williams 1990, 138, 140).

Extended households and extensive family networks are other important features associated with Chicana/o familism. In their study on extended households or structural familism among whites, blacks, and Hispanics, Marta Tienda and Ronald Angel (1982) found that low-income Chicanas who headed families were more likely than European-Americans to live in households composed of several generations of kin. Charles Mindel (1980) compared European-American, African-American, and Mexican-American families and found that Mexican-Americans had the largest and most socially active extended family networks in several local geographic areas. This study and others emphasize the extensive interaction (behavioral familism) across kinship systems (fictive and real) in Chicana/o families (Horowitz 1983; Zavella 1987).

Behavioral familism reinforces what Zavella terms "the cultural principle of *confianza*" or the belief that "only certain people outside the immediate family are to be trusted with private information" (1987, 28). Mirandé suggests that the mistrust of outsiders to Chicana/o kin networks has developed historically "in response to the oppressive conditions of internal colonialism" (1985, 163). "Trust" that resides solely within Chicana/o families serves as an important strategy for cultural survival and resistance in the face of racism and other forms of domination by creating ties within and across kin networks (Bott 1971; Caulfield 1974). Extensive interaction across kin networks also enhances the opportunities for relatives other than the mother to become involved in child rearing and providing child care as well as emotional support. In times of crisis, members of the extended family provide physical and affective care for children and emotional and economic support for the parents (Sotomayor 1971; Keefe 1979; Wagner and Schaffer 1980).

Among Chicanas, mothering and paid employment are not mutually exclusive. In 1990, Chicanas' labor force participation rate was 50.6 percent while that of Chicanos was 79.6 percent (U.S. Bureau of the Census 1991a, table 2). Several researchers have observed that employed Chicanas and Chicanos rely on female kin for child care instead of on institutional arrangements (Zavella 1987; Segura 1988). A recent study of Chicana/o and European-American families in the Sunbelt region confirms this finding, but with a twist: Chicano fathers actively parent and care for their children more than Anglo fathers (Lamphere, Zavella, and Gonzalez 1993, chap. 6). The conditions under which this occurs are quite specific: female kin are not available, and men's work schedules allow them to assume child-care duties. It is possible that the higher participation of some Chicano men doing child care reflects their relatively higher representation in shift work (compared with Anglo men). On the other hand, it may also reflect a different cultural orientation. The greater willingness of Chicano fathers to engage in expanded parenting flows from their commitment to their families and familism and lack of *confianza* for nonfamily caretakers. While these parenting and child-care strategies used by Chicanas and Chicanos may not be exclusively cultural, but may also be economic strategies of a low-income group—shared to some extent by other disadvantaged groups—they are nevertheless important to consider in analyzing the reproduction of gender personality.

The practice of nonexclusive mothering, in particular, has critical implications for the development of feminine and masculine personalities in Chicana/o families. Multiple mother figures among Chicanas and Chicanos have been reported in numerous accounts. Griswold del Castillo (1984) discusses the important role of godmothers and godfathers in Chicana/o communities. Closeness between Chicanas and their grandmothers is described by many social narrators, including Diane Neumaier (1990), Lorna Dee Cervantes (1980), and Tey Diana Rebolledo (1983). Lisa Hernandez describes the critical grandmother-mother-daughter triad as a "process of transformation" integral to Chicana self-affirmation and empowerment (1988). That is, Chicanas want to affirm themselves "as Chicanas," women with a unique racial and ethnic history, language, and ways of relating to one another through close interaction with women in the kin networks.

Chicanas, Ethnicity, and Gender Identity

Like European-American women, Chicanas are more likely to identify with their daughters than with their sons. Daughters, in turn, identify with their mothers' female role. Because a Chicana's activity as a mother revolves around family and home, Viktor Gecas (1973) argues that these constitute a major arena for the daughter's definition of self. This psychological identification is framed within Chicanas' cultural practices and beliefs. For example, José Límon (1980) discusses the socializing function of a commonly played folk game, La Vieja Inés, which emphasizes Chicana-appropriate mothering roles. This game is usually played by girls and has two major roles: the prized role of *la mamá* and the stigmatized role of *la vieja Inés*. Other child players do not have names, for part of the game is for *la mamá* to assign them name of colors. If *la vieja Inés* can guess the color name of a child, a chase ensues, which ends with a capture by *la vieja Inés* or the safe return to *la mamá* (home). Límon notes that *la mamá* is often selected for her proven proficiency in assigning color names that have successfully eluded the previous guesses of *Inés*. He argues that this game is a "symbolic learning experience" in which Chicanas "learn" and "practice" how "to take responsibility for children by naming them and speaking for them against the world beyond this known kin group" (1980, 92).

Other important differences exist between European-American women and Chicanas. In many poor Chicana/o families, infants often sleep with parents until they are weaned (Johnson 1980). And the larger the family, the more likely young Chicana/o children are to sleep with their parents or with one another. While this theme is not well researched in academic accounts of Chicana/o family life, it shows up in many literary works (Anaya 1972; Elasser, MacKenzie, and Tixier Y Vigil 1980). Chicanas and Chicanos also exhibit a high degree of residential stability by remaining in or close to their community of origin for many years, or several generations (Keefe and Padilla 1987). Moreover, unmarried Chicanas and Chicanos tend to live with their families of origin until they get married. Interaction with primary kin, particularly the mother, intensifies once childbearing begins.

Because many Chicana/o families do not practice exclusive mothering, daughters often have several female attachment figures responsible for the teaching of gender-related cultural behaviors. Chicanas are sometimes as close, if not closer, to grandmothers or godmothers as they are to their own mothers. Marlene Zepeda's research (1979) indicates that grandmothers are important role models for young Chicanas, particularly with respect to culturally specific skills (speaking Spanish, cooking traditional foods, celebrating Mexican holidays), and that they form particularly strong ties to their daughters' children as opposed to the children of their sons.

Norma Alarcón (1985) also discusses the closeness of grandmother/ granddaughter relationships, particularly regarding culturally gendered role expectations. Grandmothers, by virtue of their age and long relationship with the family, are honored by others in the kin network. The grandmother/ granddaughter relationship is less tense than that of mothers and daughters. Mothers are directly responsible for teaching their daughters how to be Chicanas knowledgeable in cultural traditions and behaviors that signal their gender and ethnicity. Their transmission of a culture overlaid with patriarchal prerogatives can be hotly contested by their daughters, situated generationally in a different social and historical setting. Grandmothers stand one step away from the mother/daughter identity process; they offer granddaughters love and support without dramatically altering cultural messages.

A Chicana may experience herself, thus, not only as an extension of her mother but also of her grandmother. Depending on the extent of behavioral familism, a Chicana may also see herself in relation to her godmother and/or an aunt. Extending Chodorow's theory here suggests that, unlike European-American girls, Chicanas may not develop an inner psychic "triangular object relational constellation" of daughter/mother/father but, rather, a multi-object relational configuration of daughter/mother/aunt/grandmother/godmother/father. To recreate this internal psychic world as an adult, having children may be even more important to Chicanas than to European-American women, and maintaining relationships with other women in the *compadrazgo* system may be particularly crucial for Chicanas to fulfill their relational needs.

Furthermore, for the majority of Chicanas who are working-class, mothers and mothering are enveloped and cast in particular cultural representations, imagery, and symbols (Mirandé and Enríquez 1979; Melville 1980; Baca Zinn 1982). In Chicana/o literature and art and in Catholicism, women, particularly mothers, are represented as essentially sacred and holy. Chicanas are held accountable to *la madre*'s self-sacrificing and pure nature in the image of *La Virgen de Guadalupe* (the Catholic patroness of Mexico whose portrait graces many Mexican immigrant and Chicana/o houses and churches in the Southwest). *La Virgen* as both cultural and religious representation of the good mother frames this gendered/ethnic sense of self. Chicana/o culture identifies several images of "bad" women and mothers, including *La Llorona* (the weeping woman), to dramatically describe the evil fate in store for women who deviate from the norm of the "good" mother. *La Llorona* killed her children and committed suicide. She wanders for eternity, a condemned ghost, in search of her lost children. Both images, *La Virgen* and *La Llorona,* frame a cultural context for mothers and mothering in Chicana/o communities.

Mario García's historical research (1980) on Chicanas highlights women's responsibility to transmit Chicana/o–Mexican cultural values as well as to care for the family unit. Baca Zinn (1975, 1979) argues that Chicana/o families tend to be mother-centered, with women responsible for the majority of household and child-rearing decisions and tasks. These responsibilities form a complementary sphere to the work of men done for the family. Women's mothering occurs in a patriarchal context and is not a direct challenge to male providers but, rather, an assertion of her culturally gendered role. That is, among Chicanas and Chicanos, women's work in the home is often articulated as part of "doing Chicana" (Segura 1992), a claim legitimized by a shared sense of the Chicana/o culture as under assault by outside social pressures (Baca Zinn 1975, 1982; Segura 1992). The sense that a woman's mothering is part of her Chicana identity is bolstered by interaction across kin networks and the larger ethnic community that can result in Chicanas feeling more strongly motivated to mother than European-American middle-class women whose kinship ties are more dispersed. When Chicanas contest traditional patterns they can become caught between their desire for personal empowerment and their politically charged responsibility for cultural maintenance. Thus, the need or motivation to continue traditional patterns may be more complex for Chicanas inasmuch as it is one potential site for reinforcing Chicana/o culture and ethnicity (Segura 1992; Pesquera 1993).

Chicanos, Ethnicity, and Gender Identity

The psychological consequences the Chicana/o family constellation poses differs for the young Chicano. His early relationship with the mother differs from that of the young Chicana. Although he too may be mothered by more than one primary female caretaker, his maleness means that his female nurturers do not identify with him in the way they identify with their daughters. In *Hunger of Memory: The Education of Richard Rodriguez,* Rodriguez writes that from the time he was a little boy, his mother would "repeat the old Mexican dictum [to him] that men should be *feo, fuerte y formal*" (1982, 128). Roughly translated, this means rugged, strong, and steady, a man of responsibility and a good provider for the family. The process Rodriguez describes is found in other writings by Chicanos on "becoming masculine" (e.g., Villarreal 1959; Galarza 1971; Acosta 1972). Moreover, Gecas's (1973) research finds that young Chicanos are more likely than their sisters to identify with their fathers and with their potential male occupational roles. In sum, the Chicano boy must learn his gender identity as being not female—or not mother, not grandmother, and not godmother. Extending Chodorow's theoretical formulation, this suggests that the young Chicano must repress his identification and attachment with many women—not just one—and, at the same time, strive to achieve a masculine gender identification with his father and many other men.

Chicanos' personality development is in some ways similar to that of European-American men. Brooks Brennis and Samuel Roll (1975), for example, found that Chicanos tended to organize their internal psychic world around a highly visible, demarcated self that was seen as robust, randomly active, and engaged in contentious interactions with unfamiliar others. Chicanos' repression of several female objects instead of one, however, suggests that they may develop masculine identity differently than do European-American men. Divergent possibilities exist: nonexclusive mothering may make Chicanos more responsive to women—or conversely it may make them more disdainful. The presence of several female caretakers may actually ameliorate male contempt for women because the Chicano child is not completely dependent on any one woman. The opposing view is that nonexclusive mothering makes it much harder for the young Chicano boy than for his European-American counterpart to achieve a masculine identification because the energy involved in repressing feminine identification is greater—a difficulty exacerbated by the disadvantaged structural position of Chicanos. Baca Zinn (1979), for example, argues that machismo may be one response to the structural obstacles Chicano men face in achieving masculinity in a social world that has historically denied them equal participation. In Chodorow's model, boys' repression of their early identification with their mothers engenders a highly ambivalent stance toward women. With more women caring for the Chicano boy, the ambivalence could be greater, suggesting that Chicanos might be even more likely than European-American men to experience strong feelings of longing and disdain for women.

This scenario directly implicates machismo, the politically loaded notion that Chicanos are in some sense more dominating or macho than European-American men. Much of the early pejorative literature on Mexican national character employed psychoanalytic concepts to depict machismo as a problematic psychological component of Mexican men (Bermúdez 1955; Díaz-Guerrero 1955; Gilbert 1959). In a 1959 study based on interviews with nine Mexican men, G. M. Gilbert concluded there was "a pronounced tendency to either severely constricted affect or morbid-depressed-hypochondriacal types of response among older males... this may be indicative of increasing importance and 'castration anxiety' as the males fail in the lifelong struggle to live up to the demands of machismo" (1959). Other early researchers constructed an image cast in the discourse of the "normative" wherein diverse Chicana/o families became the "Chicano family" ruled by "macho-dominated," authoritarian males demanding complete deference, respect, and obedience from wives and children (Humphrey 1944; Jones 1948; Peñalosa 1968).

From the vantage point of the 1990s, the findings of these early and influential studies read like ludicrous stereotypes rather than as valid descriptions of Chicana/o culture and people. As Baca Zinn, Mirandé, and others have concluded, however, the machismo stereotype contains a grain of truth. The most recent research on Chicana/o families confirms patriarchal privilege structurally, ideologically, and interpersonally (Zavella 1987; Williams 1990). Patriarchy within Chicana/o families does not constitute a culturally unique pathology (or machismo). In Baca Zinn's review of the social science literature on Chicana/o families, she argues that male domination/female subordination transcends any one cultural group. Indeed, the central tenet of feminist theorizing about the family is that the family is not simply a "haven in a heartless world" (Lasch 1977) but the "locus of struggle" and the source of psychological oppression of women (Hartmann 1981; Thorne and Yalom 1982). In this respect, Chicana/o families struggle over the meanings of gender and mothering in the same way that European-American working-class families do. Chicanas and Chicanos are unique, however, insofar as they simultaneously invoke and perceive themselves as reinforcing a distinct Chicana/o and Mexican culture.

Chicanos invoke "family" and "community" in ways that suggest a cultural and political overlap in masculine identity. Accounts of high-achieving Chicanos reveal considerable overlap between their desire to "help the community" and their wish to attain individual excellence. Themes of individual and group identity, family, and community responsibilities inform the autobiographies of prominent Chicanos such as activist-scholar Ernesto Galarza's *Barrio Boy* (1971), Chicano movement leader Rodolfo "Corky" Gonzales's *Yo Soy Joaquín* (1972), and Fred Ross's biography of labor leader César Chávez (1989). Chicano literary critic Ramón Saldívar analyzes what he terms the "themes of transformation and identity" in *Barrio Boy*, asserting that "the motifs of transformation and identity which might have been offered in terms of the individual, are transferred instead to the entire community within which the individuals exist, by which they are created, and which they in turn dialectically transform" (1990, 164). This suggests Chicanos are more likely to affirm their gender identity as masculine by pursuing their interests and affiliations in the immediate ethnic community. For example, Zavella (1989) suggests that Chicano political activists during the turbulent 1960s and 1970s established organizations to reconstruct *familia* and *carnalismo* (Chicano brotherhood).

This blending of gender identity with community also occurs with Chicanas. Writer Helena María Viramontes writes, "I want to do justice to their voices. I want to tell these women, in my own gentle way that I will fight for them, that they provide me with my own sense of humanity" (1990, 292). Similarly, in a personal account of her graduate school experiences, sociologist Gloria Cuádraz characterizes the importance of doing well in school as part of the larger struggle of her community rather than the more individualistic frame of her Anglo counterparts (Cuádraz and Pierce 1993). In a related vein, discussions of Chicana muralists highlight how their works typically express "both personal and collective expression" (Mesa-Baines 1990). Other accounts stress that Chicana political activism (e.g., running for school board, joining the Mothers of East Los Angeles, labor union organizing) is often spurred by Chicanas' desire to better the opportunities for their families and their communities (Pardo 1990; Segura and Pesquera 1992). The ideological commitment in Chicana/o communities to the intertwined notions of *familia* and community is emphasized in recent research on Chicano political activism and political consciousness. What this research suggests is that in the particular constellation of Chicana/o families the development of gender identity and group or ethnic identity are closely intertwined. Chicana mothers do not raise their children to be "independent" or "individualistic," as European-American mothers do (Anderson and Evans 1976). Instead Chicana/o mothers encourage their children to think and act communally—for the good of the family and the community (Ramírez and Castañeda 1974; Trueba and Delgado-Gaitan 1985). This, as well as the constellation of features associated with Chicana/o family structure —working-class status, large family size, familism, *compadrazgo,* nonexclusive mothering—helps explain why Chicanas and Chicanos often realize their interests, skills, and desires in the community and *la familia* instead of the larger public domain. Much of the current research on Chicana feminism highlights the "collective" orientation of Chicanas' struggles against oppression based on gender, race, ethnicity, and class—a struggle distinct from mainstream liberal feminism's focus on gender inequality and individual rights.

Our analysis shows the applicability of Chodorow's theoretical account of gender development to Chicana/o families. The crucial role of women emphasized by Chodorow is evident in Chicana/o families, but as a part of a unique constellation of features that together bear on the acquisition of gender identity and the related development of group identity. In particular, the psychological meaning of other women within the kin network must be taken into account.

References

Acosta, Oscar Zeta. 1972. *The Autobiography of a Brown Buffalo.* San Francisco: Straight Arrow.

Alarcón, Norma. 1985. "What Kind of Lover Have You Made Me, Mother? Toward a Theory of Chicanas' Feminism and Cultural Identity through Poetry." In *Women of Color Perspectives on Feminism and Identity,* ed. Audrey T. McClusky. Occasional Papers Series 1. Bloomington: University of Indiana Women's Studies Program.

Anaya, Rudolfo A. 1972. *Bless Me, Ultima.* Berkeley: Tonatiuh International.

Anderson, James, and Francis B. Evans. 1976. "Family Socialization and Educational Achievement in Two Cultures: Mexican-American and Anglo-American." *Sociometry* 39:209–22.

Baca Zinn, Maxine. 1975. "Chicanas: Power and Control in the Domestic Sphere." *De Colores: Journal of Emerging Raza Philosophies* 2:19–31.

———. 1979. "Chicano Family Research: Conceptual Distortions and Alternative Directions." *Journal of Ethnic Studies* 7:59–71.

———. 1982. "Chicano Men and Masculinity." *Journal of Ethnic Studies* 10:29–44.

———. 1982/83. "Familism among Chicanos: A Theoretical Review." *Humboldt Journal of Social Relations* 10:224–38.

Baca Zinn, Maxine, and Stanley D. Eitzen. 1987. *Diversity in American Families.* New York: Harper & Row.

Barrera, Mario. 1979. *Race and Class in the Southwest: A Theory of Racial Inequality.* Notre Dame, Ind.: University of Notre Dame Press.

Bermúdez, María. 1955. *La Vida del Mexicano.* Mexico City: Antigua Liberia Robredo.

Bott, Elizabeth. 1971. *Family and Social Networks.* 2d ed. New York: Free Press.

Brennis, Brooks, and Samuel Roll. 1975. "Ego Modalities in Manifest Dreams of Male and Female Chicanos." *Psychiatry* 38:172–85.

Caulfield, Mina Davis. 1974. "Imperialism, the Family and Cultures of Resistance." *Socialist Revolution* 2:67–85.

Cervantes, Lorna Dee. 1980. "Beneath the Shadow of the Freeway." In her *Emplumada,* 11–14. Pittsburgh: University of Pittsburgh Press.

Chodorow, Nancy. 1989. *Feminism and Psychoanalytic Theory.* New Haven, Conn.: Yale University Press.

Cuadráz, Gloria, and Jennifer Pierce. 1993. "From Scholarship Girls to Scholarship Women: Race, Class and Gender in Graduate Education." Paper presented at the National Association for Ethnic Studies conference, Salt Lake City, Utah, March 6.

Diaz-Guerrero, Rogelio. 1955. "Neurosis and the Mexican Family Structure." *American Journal of Psychiatry* 112 (December): 411–17.

Elasser, Nan, Kyle MacKenzie, and Yvonne Tixier Y Vigil. 1980. *Las Mujeres: Conversations from a Hispanic Community.* Old Westbury, N.Y.: Feminist Press.

Falicov, Celia Jaes. 1982. "Mexican Families." In *Ethnicity and Family Therapy,* ed. Monica McGoldrick, John K. Pearce, and Joseph Giordano, 134–63. New York: Guilford Press.

Galarza, Ernesto. 1971. *Barrio Boy.* Notre Dame, Ind.: University of Notre Dame Press.

García, Mario T. 1980. "The Chicana in American History: The Mexican Women of El Paso, 1880–1920—a Case Study." *Pacific Historical Review* 49:315–37.

Gecas, Viktor. 1973. "Self-Conceptions of Migrant Settled Mexican Americans." *Social Science Quarterly* 54(3):579–95.

Gilbert, G. M. 1959. "Sex Differences in Mental Health in a Mexican Village." *International Journal of Psychiatry* 3 (Winter): 208–13.

Gonzales, Rodolfo. 1972. *I Am Joaquín, Yo Soy Joaquín.* New York: Bantam.

Griswold del Castillo, Richard. 1984. *La Familia: Chicano Families in the Urban Southwest.* Notre Dame, Ind.: University of Notre Dame Press.

Hartmann, Heidi. 1981. "The Family as the Locus of Gender, Class, and Political Struggle: The Example of Housework." *Signs: Journal of Women in Culture and Society* 6(3):366–94.

Hernandez, Lisa. 1988. "Canas." In *Palabras Chicanas,* ed. Lisa Hernandez and Tina Benitez, 47–49. Berkeley: University of California, Berkeley, Mujeres in March Press.

Horowitz, Ruth. 1983. *Honor and the American Dream: Culture and Identity in a Chicano Community.* New Brunswick, N.J.: Rutgers University Press.

Humphrey, Norman D. 1944. "The Changing Structure of Detroit Mexican Families: An Index of Acculturation." *American Sociological Review* 9 (December): 622–26.

Johnson, Carmen Acosta. 1980. "Breast-feeding and Social Class Mobility: The Case of Mexican Migrant Mothers in Houston, Texas." In *Twice a Minority: Mexican American Women,* ed. Margarita B. Melville, 66–82. St. Louis: Mosby.

Jones, Robert. 1948. "Ethnic Family Patterns: The Mexican-American Family in the U.S." *American Journal of Sociology* 53 (May): 450–52.

Keefe, Susan E. 1979. "Urbanization, Acculturation and Extended Family Ties: Mexican Americans in Cities." *American Ethnologist* 6:349–45.

Keefe, Susan E., and Amado M. Padilla. 1987. *Chicano Ethnicity.* Albuquerque: University of New Mexico Press.

Lamphere, Louise, Patricia Zavella, and Felipe Gonzales, with Peter B. Evans. 1993. *Sunbelt Working Mothers: Reconciling Family and Factory.* Ithaca, N.Y.: Cornell University Press.

Lasch, Christopher. 1977. *Haven in a Heartless World.* New York: Basic.

Límon, José E. 1980. " 'La Vieja Inés,' a Mexican Folk Game: A Research Note." In *Twice a Minority: Mexican American Women,* ed. Margarita B. Melville, 88–94. St. Louis: Mosby.

Melville, Margarita B. 1980. "Introduction" and "Matresence." In *Twice a Minority: Mexican-American Women,* ed. Margarita B. Melville, 1–16. St. Louis: Mosby.

Mesa-Baines, Amalia. 1990. "Quest for Identity: Profile of Two Chicana Muralists: Based on Interviews with Judith F. Baca and Patricia Rodriguez." In *Signs from the Heart: California Chicano Murals,* ed. Eva Sperling Cockroft and Holly Barnet Sanchez, 69–82. Venice, Calif.: Social and Public Art Resource Center.

Mindel, Charles H. 1980. "Extended Familism among Urban Mexican Americans, Anglos, and Blacks." *Hispanic Journal of Behavioral Sciences* 2:21–34.

Mirandé, Alfredo. 1985. *The Chicano Experience: An Alternative Perspective.* Notre Dame, Ind.: University of Notre Dame Press.

Neumaier, Diane. 1990. "Judy Baca: Our People Are the Internal Exiles." In *Making Face, Making Soul—Haciendo Caras,* ed. Gloria Anzaldúa, 256–70. San Francisco: Aunt Lute Foundation.

Pardo, Mary. 1990. "Mexican American Women Grassroots Community Activists (Mothers of East Los Angeles)." *Frontiers: A Journal of Women's Studies* 11(1):1–7.

Peñalosa, Fernando. 1968."Mexican-American Family Roles." *Journal of Marriage and the Family* 30(4):680–88.

Pesquera, Beatríz M. 1993. " 'It Gave Me Confianza': Work Commitment and Identity." *Aztlán: Journal of Chicano Studies Research,* in press.

Ramírez, Manuel, III, and Alfredo Castañeda. 1974. *Cultural Democracy, Bicognitive Development, and Education.* New York: Academic Press.

Rebolledo, Tey Diana. 1983. "Abuelitas: Mythology and Integration in Chicano Literature." *Revista Chicano-Riquena* 11(3–4):148–58.

Rochin, Refugio I., and Monica D. Castillo. 1991. "Immigration, *Colonía* Formation and Latino Poor in Rural California: Evolving Immigration." Working Paper no. 91-38. University of California, Davis, Department of Agricultural Economics.

Rodriguez, Richard. 1982. *Hunger of Memory: The Education of Richard Rodriguez.* New York: Bantam.

Ross, Fred. 1989. *Conquering Goliath: Cesar Chavez and the Beginning.* Keene, Calif.: United Farm Workers.

Saldívar, Ramón. 1990. "Ideologies of the Self: Chicano Autobiography.: In his *Chicano Narrative: The Dialectics of Difference,* 154–70. Madison: University of Wisconsin Press.

Saragoza, Alex M. 1983. "The Conceptualization of the History of the Chicano Family." In *The State of Chicano Research on Family, Labor, and Migration: Proceedings of the First Stanford Symposium on Chicano Research and Public Policy,* ed. Armando Valdez, Alberto Camarillo, and Tomas Almaguer, 11–38. Stanford, Calif.: Stanford Center for Chicano Research.

Segura, Denise A. 1988. "Familism and Employment among Chicanas and Mexican Immigrant Women." In *Mexicanas at Work in the United States,* ed. Margarita B. Melville, 24–32. Houston: University of Houston, Mexican-American Studies.

———. 1992. "Chicanas in White Collar Jobs: 'You Have to Prove Yourself More.'" *Sociological Perspectives* 35:163–82.

Segura, Denise A., and Beatríz M. Pesquera. 1992. Beyond Indifference and Antipathy: The Chicana Feminist Movement and Chicana Feminist Discourse." *Aztlán: Journal of Chicano Studies Research* 19(2):69–88.

Sotomayor, Marta. 1971. "Mexican-American Interaction with Social Systems." In *La Causa Chicana: The Movement for Justice,* ed. Margaret M. Manfold, 148–60. New York: Family Service Association of America.

Thorne, Barrie, and Marilyn Yalom. 1982. *Rethinking the Family: Some Feminist Questions.* New York: Longman Press.

Tienda, Marta, and Ronald Angel. 1982. "Headship and Household Composition among Blacks, Hispanics and Other Whites." *Social Forces* 61:508–31.

Trueba, Henry T., and Concha Delgado-Gaitan. 1985. "Specialization of Mexican Children for Cooperation and Competition: Sharing and Copying." *Journal of Educational Equity and Leadership* 5:189–204.

U.S. Bureau of the Census. 1988. "Fertility of American Women." *Current Population Reports,* Series P-20 (June). Washington, D.C.: Government Printing Office.

———. 1991a. "The Hispanic Population in the United States: March 1990." *Current Population Reports,* Series P-20, no. 449 (May). Washington, D.C.: Government Printing Office.

———. 1991b. "Poverty in the United States: 1990.": *Current Population Reports,* Series P-60, no. 175. Washington, D.C.: Government Printing Office.

———. 1992. "Household and Family Characteristics: March 1991." *Current Population Reports,* Series P-20, no. 458 (February). Washington, D.C.: Government Printing Office.

Villarreal, José Antonio. 1959. *Pocho.* New York: Doubleday.

Viramontes, Helene María. 1990. "Nopalitos: The Making of Fiction." In *Making Faces, Making Soul –Haciendo Caras: Creative and Critical Perspectives by Women of Color,* ed. Gloria Anzaldúa, 291–94. San Francisco: Aunt Lute Foundation.

Wagner, Roland M., and Diane M. Schaffer. 1980. "Social Networks and Survival Strategies: An Exploratory Study of Mexican-American, Black and Anglo Female Family Heads in San Jose, California." In *Twice a Minority: Mexican American Women,* ed. Margarita B. Melville, 173–90. St. Louis: Mosby.

Williams, Norma. 1990. *The Mexican American Family: Tradition and Change.* New York: General Hall.

Zavella, Patricia. 1987. *Women's Work and Chicano Families: Cannery Workers of the Santa Clara Valley.* Ithaca, N.Y.: Cornell University Press.

Zepeda, Marlene. 1979. "Las Abuelitas." *Agenda* 6 (November/December): 10–13.

POSTSCRIPT

Can We Raise "Gender-Neutral" Children?

Scholars caution that achieving gender transcendence is highly unlikely in contemporary American society, primarily because of the rarity of support for challenging traditional gender norms. What triggers personal motivation to work toward raising nonsexist children? What kind of family environment is necessary for transcending gender?

What kind of societal or cultural context is necessary for raising children who can transcend gender? Gender identity development theories such as Chodorow's have been criticized for being "culture bound" and thus limited in generalizability across ethnicity and social class. European American middle-class family structure has been the focus of theorizing. How do cultural differences among Americans affect the possibility of raising nonsexist children?

Varying cultural frameworks are believed by some to have a differential impact on gender structures and dynamics. The two major cultural patterns are individualism and collectivism. In individualistic cultures, individual goals come before group goals. The emphasis in individualism is on individuals' rights, personal autonomy, self-realization, personal uniqueness, self-expression, and individual initiative. Individual attributes define personal identity. European American middle-class families (such as the Bems) are usually individualistic. In contrast, in collectivistic cultures, group goals come before individual goals. The emphasis in collectivism is on group loyalty, interdependence, group decision making, interconnectedness, and mutual caring. Personal identity is defined by group membership. The Chicana/o culture described by Segura and Pierce is collectivistic.

Is gender transcendence more likely to be realized in individualistic or collectivistic cultures?

Suggested Readings

C. Beal, *Boys and Girls: The Development of Gender Roles* (McGraw-Hill, 1994).

C. Etaugh and M. B. Liss, "Home, School, and Playroom: Training Grounds for Adult Gender Roles," *Sex Roles* (1992).

B. Fagot and M. D. Leinbach, "Gender Knowledge in Egalitarian and Traditional Families," *Sex Roles* (April 1995).

S. M. Okin, "Change the Family; Change the World," *Utne Reader* (March/April 1990).

ISSUE 18

Does Transsexualism Solve the Problem of Fixed Definitions of Gender Identity?

YES: Jennifer Diane Reitz, from "Entombment: Being the Dysphoria Story of Jennifer Diane Reitz," http://transsexual.org/mystory.html (December 29, 1998)

NO: Richard Ekins and Dave King, from "Blending Genders: Contributions to the Emerging Field of Transgender Studies," *The International Journal of Transgenderism* (July–September 1997)

ISSUE SUMMARY

YES: Author and artist Jennifer Diane Reitz describes her plight in becoming a postoperative transsexual woman. Her poignant story documents the role of sex and gender in her experience of transsexualism.

NO: Transgender scholars Richard Ekins and Dave King discuss the limitations of the medical categories of transvestism, transsexualism, and gender dysphoria and promote a process of blending gender and even of living "beyond gender" altogether.

The Western "gender system" is constructed in a hierarchical and interconnected fashion whereby we believe that sex (male/female) causes gender (masculine/feminine), which causes desire (heterosexual desire for the "opposite sex"). Individuals are fit into these narrow binaries; any deviation is often deemed pathological. Many contemporary gender scholars view this conceptualization of the Western gender system as problematic. Can we and should we transcend this binary notion of two separate genders? Can gender be defined without reference to sex? How do we learn to tolerate—even enjoy—gender as fluid and unstable?

An early effort to bridge the gender binary was the concept of *androgyny*. Androgyny is defined as a combination or even balance of masculine and feminine attributes developed according to individual nature, preferences, and needs. Androgyny is thought to give individuals greater behavioral flexibility and adaptability, making them better equipped to deal with a variety of life experiences. But critics argue that androgyny is still reliant on, and therefore further reifies, the gender binary of masculine and feminine. Furthermore, it undermines the possibility of separating behavior from gender. For example, being assertive is not necessarily being masculine.

Another vantage point on "gender beyond the margins" has been the study of transvestism, gender dysphoria, and transsexuality. *Transvestism* is the desire to change sex through a cross-dressing fetish. *Gender dysphoria* defines the desire to change sex as pathological. *Transsexuality* is defined as gender identification with the opposite sex, creating a desire to change sex through hormonal and surgical sex reassignment. Transsexual individuals have been described as feeling that they are in the "wrong body." Contemporary theorists observe that all three phenomena reinforce a binary, oppositional mode of gender identification. Transsexuals, for example, transform from one pole of the sex/gender binary to the other. In fact, gender artifacts and symbols (e.g., dress and mannerisms) are used to emphasize the "sex endstate" of the transition. Importantly, transsexuals, by nature, may not fit so neatly into the sex/gender binary, but transsexualism has been culturally constructed within this limited gender lens, thereby profoundly influencing the experiences of many transsexuals.

Contemporary scholars argue that we must eliminate or deconstruct the gender dichotomy and reconstruct unlimited unique gender identities, or better yet, give freedom to individuals to develop their own unique identities (gendered or not). Some say that it is meaningless to talk about an individual in terms of one group identity (e.g., female) because identities contain so many elements and are constantly reinvented. Thus, gender is viewed as multidimensional and contextual rather than dichotomous. Moreover, contemporary theorists argue that gender is not fixed in our biology or culture but rather is a matter of individual expression; gender is something we *do*, not something we *have*. Some argue that we *perform* gender. Our gender performances are fluid and flexible, changing over time and across different contexts. Thus, there are unlimited expressions of gender, free from proscribed linkages between sex, gender, and desire.

Finally, the concept of "gender blending" has been used to reflect the ways in which individuals combine and harmonize established components of gender to the point where gender practically becomes meaningless.

Androgyny, transsexuality, transgenderism, and gender blending all reflect attempts to challenge the sex/gender binary. Richard Ekins and Dave King observe that some approaches involve "transferring" from one preexisting gender category to the other (either temporarily or permanently) while others involve "transcending" or living beyond gender altogether. Have they succeeded in deconstructing the sex/gender binary?

In the following selections, Jennifer Diane Reitz presents a profound personal account of a transsexual individual experiencing the transition from male to female, outlining her effort to assume the gender identity that is correct for her. Ekins and King introduce the concept of gender blending to demonstrate that transsexualism is not necessary to solve the problem of fixed gender identity. To what degree is the sex/gender binary reflected and/or deconstructed in these experiences?

331

 **YES**

Entombment

My earliest memory of my gender plight occurred somewhere just prior to entering kindergarten, and I can make no claim to knowing my exact age, but I reason that it must have been near the age of five or so.

I was playing in the living room of my mother's house... with my many stuffed animals, among them my favorite, Lilly the Leopard, a largish bespotted doll who was my best friend. I had made a little house of blankets and was setting about taking care of my little family in miniature. My father was sitting, possibly reading, behind me. Through the kitchen archway came my mother to announce that 'You boys should get ready for dinner now' and in that frozen moment, something occurred in my young consciousness.

My dad was certainly a boy, as were many of the children I had known, and my mom was a girl, as were the children I preferred to play with, but it offended me somehow to be included with my dad in being called a boy. I knew I did not act like boys did, and that is what bothered me most. Boys were mean, they hit, they shouted, they liked to bang things together, and when they were big, like my dad, they were very mean and often full of punishment, as well as scary. I was not that. I knew that I was like my mom, that I was like the girls I played with. I did not like being called a name that I felt was icky. I told my mother this.

I do not exactly remember what occurred after this declaration, but I do know that it frightened and hurt me somehow. Perhaps they were appalled, perhaps my father yelled at me, which would be an expected behavior, as would a spot of hitting me, but whatever it was, it definitely traumatized me. Thus was my earliest conscious knowledge of my gender dysphoria revealed to me.

Kindergarten afforded my next accessible memory of conflict over my gender. Early in the morning, the teacher asked the class to line up, boys on one side and girls on the other, for some sort of game. I stood with the girls, of course. When this caused the predictable problem, I threw quite a tantrum, and the teacher, at a loss, had me stand in the venetian-slatted closet until 'She said so'. I stood there, crying, seeing the classroom through thin wooden slats, for most of the day. I believe I was only let out at lunchtime....

I found that the increasing conflict occurring over my true gender versus my physical sex was becoming very painful. How I stood, how I sat, how I spoke and the mannerisms of my expression, all became terrible issues to my parents, my teachers, and very much to other children. Even the fact that I always sat down to urinate became a problem, as did my love of colorful and frilly clothing. Soon I danced and sang no more. I feared the constant teasing and embarrassment that resulted from my every action or commentary. I was afraid to laugh lest I be teased for how it sounded, I was fearful of description, for it necessitated holding my hands behind me carefully, deliberately, lest I be chastised for waving them about. I confined my emotions, and forcibly contained my happy exuberance or my tear filled joys or sadness.

I became ingrained with absolute terror at the thought of being called a 'fag' or a 'queer'. I was inculcated with narrow attitudes and seemingly infinite self loathing. To be considered a 'sissy', especially because I knew I was one, was unbearable. It became standard for me to cringe in embarrassment at the merest mention of such terrible words. I was shriveled and blasted by hatred and intolerance. Nothing imaginable could be worse than anyone knowing what I really was.

A strange thing occurred to my mind, born of this absolute terror of discovery and self loathing. I was too psychologically broken to face admitting my gender identity to even myself, and it was a basic impossibility to ignore it. This paradox created a mental division between my inner truth and the outer lie I felt hopelessly forced to perform. My mind split, and I increasingly lived two separate mental states, one aware of my gender problem, the other all but ignorant of the reason for it's endless suffering....

The most disturbing time that I ever told anyone prior to my transition was around the age of 17. For a brief week, I somehow became conscious of my suppressed identity. I remembered my life, always a dim fog to me otherwise, and understood what I was. The terrible split in my mind had mostly healed. I am not sure what precipitated this event, but I believe that it was a brief television bit about transsexuality....

By high school, I had begun to learn how to avoid some of the constant abuse. No longer were groups of disturbed boys trying to flush my head down the toilet (as happened in Yermo, California) or taking turns kicking me in the stomach to get me to stand up and fight, or holding me down and urinating on me for being a disgusting 'girly faggot' (as happened in Europe, Oregon). Doubtless this was partly due to the general effect of growing older, but also I had begun a campaign of careful selective adaptation. I studied boys. I drew how they walked and moved, I practiced their actions and tried to mimic them. I increasingly suppressed my natural behavior in favor of an affected one that attempted to match those of the sex I was perceived as. It was horrible, but at least it was less fraught with violence....

I grew ever more suicidal. Every day it was harder to face being alive, and I could not bear to gaze into the mirror to see my mutating, increasingly masculine face, nor to suffer the chorus of screaming questions when I did so. I could not bear to look at or deal with my body, and in every way I felt living, yet dead. I felt already and hopelessly entombed, buried undead inside a crypt of misery, and the horrific filth of my own flesh. I could not understand why my body was so revolting to me, just as I could not bear to let myself know why I was suffering. Then one night, at age 21, everything changed. . . .

I knew what I had to do, I had to find doctors to fix my problems, to give me hormones and surgery. . . .

The doctor was Alfred Auerbach, and as I would find out, he had a long experience with transsexuals. An associate of both Harry Benjamin and Wardell Pomeroy, he was one of the most recognizable figures in the treatment of trans-sexuality—not that I understood that at the time. Dr. Pomeroy, the co-author of the *Kinsey Report,* became my second, required doctor necessary to obtain permission for surgery. Soon I had a hormone doctor as well, and I was on hormones in a few weeks. . . .

Thus was the beginning of my two year transition.

With circumstances more or less stabilized, I could devote my energies to the process of transition itself. Once or twice a week, for the first three or four months, I would go to somebody, either Dr. Auerbach, or Dr. Pomeroy, or to see my hormone doctor, Dr. Garfield, or to get a psychiatric evaluation. . . .

Nature's biochemical magic began to work, to correct the tragic mistake of my birth. Within a few weeks I noticed a definite alteration of my mood and my perception. My sex drive faded, and I was increasingly in balance. For the first time since that long ago acne treatment [taking female hormones at age 14 to clear up acne], I once again knew that same faery contentment and angelic peace. Everything seemed brighter, colors seemed sharper, and all of my senses seemed new and awake. I realized, by comparison, what it was to think clearly, to feel alive inside.

The longer I was affected by estrogen, the better I felt. It was like settling into a warm, comfortable bath, with a happy rubber duck, and sweet smelling soaps. I began to cherish being alive, and enjoyed each new day, filled not only with inner contentment, but also expectant joy. I felt filled with light.

I observed my body. Within two months, I noticed the first physical changes. It began with my hands. Glancing down while I made sandwiches, I realized that my hands were different. Examining them carefully, I saw that the skin had become softer, smoother, and that the texture was finer on the backs of my hands. The wrinkles on my knuckles were smoothing, and the overall shape of my fingers seemed less bony and angular. The skin on the back of my hands became my barometer of change, and throughout my transition, I was fascinated with such a clear indicator of my progress. By five months, the few hairs on my hands had vanished, and my skin was very soft. By a year, my hands were utterly those of a woman, in texture, shape, and the very feel of the skin. . . .

The half-way of sex, to be both and neither, is a special sort of hell. Neither definably male nor definably female, yet somehow both, is a disturbing state to many people, at some fundamental level. It is certainly the worst part of transi-tion. I found acceptance most easily from heterosexual women at the time, the majority of my coworkers. Straight men, like the majority of the construction workers who I had to pass by on my way to work each day, enjoyed mocking and swearing at me. But oddly, or so I thought, was the abuse I suffered at the hands of gay folk. I erroneously believed that gay folk, themselves oppressed and the object of bigotry, would be supportive of me if anyone would. But I found only scorn and ridicule, and even outright disgust, in most of the gay community. Gay men looked upon me in a kind of horror, presumably because I represented their worst nightmare, the destruction of what they prized and held most dear, maleness. Lesbians seemed to see me as some strange kind of threat, a danger and an invasion, and acted with almost paranoid revulsion. It quite shocked me that the oppressed could so easily turn upon their own kind, for the transsexual certainly counts as equally Queer, in the sum scheme of things, and in the collective oppressions of society.

... Eventually, it came time for me to enter the required 'Real Life Test' which is mandatory to win approval to have surgery. The principle of the Real Life Test is simple, and sensible. Surgery will not change anything, except to the person having it, for no one can tell what anyone really has in their pants, or under their skirt. Surgery is good for only one thing: correcting an absolute discomfort with the genitalia. What matters truly in regards to gender is not what sex one is between the legs, but how one is accepted and treated. It is true that I suffered terribly with the pain of feeling deformed and having the wrong organs. I certainly would not have been able to endure this suffering indefinitely. It was a serious issue. But what I wanted most was to be able to be myself. I needed to be accepted utterly, able to act in an unaffected and honest way, to no longer be despised for my expression of my identity.

To pass the 'Real Life Test' a transsexual must live, work, and prove that they can survive completely and utterly within the gender presentation they seek, for at least one year. Some doctors require the period to be two—or more —years. I was fortunate, I had only to prove myself for one year.

The 'Real Life Test' is a dangerous time for transsexuals, because if they are 'caught', discovered in some fashion, they can be the target of great abuse. Although whether or not one has the correct sex organs does not matter day to day, it can become an enormous issue if one is forcibly Outed. The transsexual who is found out about, and who is known to have opposite organs, may be arrested or become the target of harassment or violence by those who find out. Using the restroom becomes a lesson in worry, and the workplace can become a hell pit of damnation.

The Test is also a time of great insecurity... the very first months of dressing and being entirely in the preferred social context is a time fraught with concern over every little detail. The ultimate goal is to be able to 'Pass', to be totally accepted as the person one is. But, without a lifetime of preparation and training of how to act and be, this forces the transsexual to essentially and instantly become what takes other human beings a lifetime to master. Details such as social graces, appropriate behaviors in given contexts, and the very basics of growing up as a given sex have to be perfected overnight. Worst of all, a lifetime of self suppression and affectation of behavior must be given up as quickly as possible. The transsexual, to succeed, must overcome all of this, in a matter of months, sometimes days, often without the benefit of a family, friends, or even a decent understanding of what is expected....

I was, of course, petrified. I was sure that I still looked horridly masculine, and was certain that if I dared to wear clothing that was obviously female, I would be instantly attacked and beaten to death for it. I worried about my voice, my hands, my chin, and my behavior. I was certain that all I would ever be was a hideous, laughable freak, the sport of all and a matter of disgust. The closest I came to wearing womanly clothing was to dress in what I imagined was an androgynous manner, but to be honest, it was really more toward the masculine. The clothes I had always worn were like a safety blanket, and the more drab the better. I felt like I could become invisible in such garb.

The fact was that I had become so female in appearance that my clothing was an anomaly now, and became a source of curiosity to the folks I interacted with. My natural behavior and appearance was not by any means 'butch', indeed quite the opposite, yet I dressed like a man. This did not fit any of the conventions of society at the time, gay or straight. I also did not yet pass perfectly, so any anomalies only made me stand out more.

[My young ward] Robin saw this and tried for weeks to get me to finally start living full time as a woman. I was terrified to make the leap from being a laughable whatsit to something defined. I was afraid I would fail. As long as I did not try any further, I could always have the hope that someday I would succeed. I was terrified to have that hope crushed. I also had the foolish idea that I could retreat into being male if it got too horrible. It was far too late for that. . . .

I had years of shame and bigotry ingrained in me, however, and while it was wonderful for others to be flamboyantly themselves, it was anathema for me to permit myself that freedom. Deep down I lived in terror of being found out, of being called a 'faggot', a 'queer', a 'sissy' . . . a 'transsexual'. Now out of male drag and into female clothes, living full time as woman, I was not out of condemnations for myself, nor out of fears of punishment for the crime of being a woman.

This shame and fear would haunt me in far too gradually lessening degree, right until the present day. It took some five years after my surgery to get to the point that I no longer felt constantly paranoid about whether I 'Passed' for female, and the reason for the creation of this site is to assist me in finally crushing my own internalized shame. I have never dared to wear lipstick, or makeup. I fear to wear dresses, and stick to jumpsuits and prim pantsuits. My vile parents, and the cruel attacks of children and adults when I was growing up, indoctrinated me well. Such concepts, such narrow and hateful bigotry, are poison to the self, intellectual and emotional cancer, and they destroy the soul.

It is my dear hope to finally overcome them. . . .

Just a few months after the end of my first year of transition, everything was nicely on course. I had begun my 'Real Life Test' in preparation for earning the right to have surgery. Hormones had resculpted my body, and calmed my mind. Speech therapy had taught me how to possess a natural and acceptable voice. I had passed the many psychological tests and I had performed the great medical dog and pony show required of the transsexual. . . .

When I was first facing transition, I had only one book, Jan Morris's *'Conundrum'*, and a few snatches of televised information as my entire basis for understanding my plight. I just assumed that I would become a heterosexual woman out the other side, a proper Suzy Homemaker with husband and adopted baby. This was certainly what my doctors seemed to desire me to be, and I dearly wanted to please my doctors, because they held my very life in their hands. I was willing to do anything, be anything, to earn my passage to womanhood. I had little concept of even what that meant exactly, only that that was clearly my goal.

Certainly nothing would stop me in my quest. Not even the truth. My first, early, evaluations by a psychologist indicated that I had a "masculine oriented mentation", and would not be a safe candidate for surgery. I was "penile fixated". This was news to me. So I had hit the books at my college library, to find out how on earth such a conclusion could possibly be reached. What [I] learned shocked me. The tests I had been given, the Rorschack Ink Blot Test, as well as other visual tests involving pictures of people and scenes, were not grounded in any rational science. In fact, they are essentially arbitrary, culturally based catalogs of expected interpretations, based on a laughable model of what it means to be female or male of mind.

For instance, if one sees in a random inkblot suitably feminine images, such as flowers and cooking pots, then one is judged female. If one sees cars and planes, then one is judged a boy. It is that silly. In my first evaluations, I saw what was relevant to my life. I played fantasy games, so I saw dragons and griffins. I read science fiction all of my life almost exclusively, so I saw starships and galaxies. I studied science, so I saw cells and DNA. Guess what? According to respectable psychology, none of these things could possibly interest a woman. Only men should care about, and envision such things. Women should only see domestic subjects, or matters relating to child care.

To say this angered me alone would be to ignore the vast disillusionment and disgust I felt. I resolved that no idiotic psudoscience would determine my survival. I studied the same textbooks that my psychologist used.

My next evaluations uniformly portrayed me as the ideal of blessed womanhood. I saw butterflies and daffodils. I saw train tunnels and doughnut holes. I saw diapers and teapots. And the most telling part is that my psychologist ate it up with a spoon. Of course all of that useless, degrading therapy I endured to meet the standards of care must have helped me to grow into a successful female psychology. How wonderful was the science of psychotherapy. Back pats all around, and a hug for our exemplary case study.

. . . In one meeting I gained a wondrous new view. I could be free. I did not have to swap one limited role for another, equally limited role. I could actually be whatever I wanted, and still be a woman. I really did not want to be Suzy Homemaker. I could love who I chose. I could love women. I really did not like men, for they were the constant source of all of my misery for my entire life. Males were the ones who beat on me, called me names, degraded me, bullied me, hurt me. Woman were nice. Females were like me. I did not hurt people.

I realized I could still love women, and be a woman. I could do this and still get my surgery . . . provided I continued to lie even more to my doctors of course. I was prepared to do this. Gladly. . . .

In time I was admitted. The . . . offices . . . seemed like a clinic in a barely demilitarized zone. . . . I was weighed and measured. I was interviewed briefly.

Dr. Biber asked me if this was what I really wanted to do. He took "Before" pictures of my naked body....

He told me to take a taxi to the hospital outside town, and what I should have ready. He took the rest of my money for the surgery....

Mount San Rafael was shining white with tall arches and polished marble. It was beautiful, gargantuan, and utterly out of place in the crumbling, decaying little town.... It is a monument to the determination and financial resolve of over 15,000 transsexuals....

In the early morning I was awakened for my sedatives. I was cleaned and shaved, disinfected and prepped. A whirlwind of activity ensued. I was wheeled into the operating theatre....

[My hospital roommate] Charlotte was congratulating me, as best as she could, for she was little better than I. The sun was setting. I was informed about my pain options, and was told not to move about, for I was bolted into a frame of sorts. Dr. Biber eventually came to see me. He removed my dressings and I got my first look at my new organs.

Frankenstein stitchwork ran across swollen hunks of bloody meat. Purplish swelling and raw gory hamburger was penetrated by plastic tubes and a strange metal loop that came out of my flesh and went back beneath it. For all the world it looked like clothes hanger wire. The wire loop was attached to an armature that lifted it. I truly was a monster now.

"Looks great! I think you'll do fine!" pronounced Dr. Biber, obviously suddenly struck blind. "You call for the nurse if you have any problems, OK?". I made a mental note of that invaluable information. I sank back exhausted from the Olympic effort of craning my neck. I thanked my doctor very much, and even managed to get in my prepared joke "Did you get it all?". He half-heartedly laughed. I did not know at the time that it is probably the standard of all transsexual post-operative jests.

Time came and went, as did consciousness. By the next morning, I was awake, jovial, and constantly in pain. Pain like that almost transcends perception. It almost becomes background noise, because it is difficult to fully appreciate the true depth and rich complexity of it. It is sublimely horrendous. Medication does help, but even with pain killers there is no escape from the constant news that a large Nerve Faction has decided to violently overthrow the current regime for mismanagement of affairs....

Nearing day five, it was time to get me off the catheter, and to remove the wire and stent. The funny wire loop that impaled me just around my pubic bone was unhooked from the armature. Two nurses came in with a serious pair of pliers and a wire cutter. They informed me this might feel a little funny.

They cut the thick wire, with some effort. It made a loud metallic twang, and felt like nothing I ever hope to remember, even for a moment. They then clamped the pliers onto one end of the severed clothes-hanger wire loop. Together, both nurses muscled the wire out of my abdomen. One end dived into me as the other was pulled straight up. I could feel it running like a metal snake around and under my pubic bone. After several million years of this, the wire came free from my body in a slippery, bursting, pop....

In the 16 years that has followed, my life has just improved.... There are so many adventures beyond this point, such incredible stories to tell. Hundreds of pages worth. But the point of them all would be to show that after surgery, there is life. Transition is a wonderment, but it is not a goal. Transition is a means to an end, a way to find the beginning.

This then, at this point, was the beginning of my life. I was entombed. Resurrected, I began my life for the first time. This has been the story of how I came to be born. At last I was myself, at last my body fit my identity.

I have never regretted my transition. It is truly a blessing to have the correct flesh to wear. Not a night goes by that I do not hug my bosom or touch in wonder my delicate labia before I fall asleep, and say a silent prayer of thanks . . . for the utter relief that I feel. I have been freed from the prison of the wrong life in the wrong body, and there is everything good about it.

Oh, but it is wonderful to be myself.

Oh, but it is wonderful!

Jennifer Diane Reitz 1998

Richard Ekins and Dave King   ◄ NO

Blending Genders: Contributions to the Emerging Field of Transgender Studies

Prior to the categorization and medicalization of sexual 'perversions' in the latter half of the nineteenth century, gender blending could be written about in terms of simple descriptions of enjoyable experience and preferred behavior (Farrer, 1987, 1994). Medicalization, however, brought with it new 'conditions' and the emergence of new identities. Increasingly, gender blending experiences and behaviors were made sense of in terms of the categories of 'science', most notably those of the 'transvestite' and the 'transsexual'....

In the past and this is probably still true for most, the actions and emotions involved in gender blending have initially been confusing and often distressing. Adopting an identity which makes sense of things—'finding oneself' as it is sometimes put—can therefore be immensely liberating. As April Ashley put it 'You cannot imagine the comfort in knowing that one is something, and not merely monstrous' (Fallowell and Ashley, 1982: 76). Those who we interviewed in the late 1970s and 1980s and into the 90s did not doubt the existence of a special group of people characterized by a condition to which the terms transvestite and transsexual had some reference, despite doubts about their own or others 'correct' identity and despite some controversy over the central characteristics of the conditions. There were a number of aspects to this claimed identity or condition.

Firstly, it was endowed with a reality and a centrality which was denied to other aspects of their existence which by contrast, would be described as 'not real', 'an act' or peripheral to the 'real self'. In many cases, this real self was also a purely private self or one which only a small number of others were aware of. In some cases the private 'real' self had become harmonized with public identity through 'changing sex'.

Secondly, transvestism and transsexualism were seen as pervasive aspects of self. They were described as a part of the actor's nature of which they were 'always' aware. In some cases, this pervasiveness also extended to actual effects on the person's life style, for example influencing choice of job or house, spending patterns and, of course, in the case of some transsexuals, resulting in an almost total change of life style and public identity.

From Richard Ekins and Dave King, "Blending Genders: Contributions to the Emerging Field of Transgender Studies," *The International Journal of Transgenderism*, vol. 1, no. 1 (July–September 1997). Copyright © 1997 by Symposion Publishing. Reprinted by permission of Symposion Publishing and the authors. Some text and references omitted.

A third aspect of this state of being, perhaps readily inferred from the foregoing, is the assumption of its permanence. Although some recalled believing at some time in the past that it was or could be temporary, perhaps conceptualizing it as something which they would 'grow out of' or which could be removed by therapy of some kind, at the time they were interviewed, they were convinced that transvestism or transsexualism had been and would be always a central feature of their existence.

Finally, as an inherent and integral part of their nature, transvestism or transsexualism was seen as something over which they had no control. Whether childhood experiences or biological anomalies were cited as the cause, the emergence of their natures was not seen to be dependent on their own volition and neither could it be effectively or permanently brought under their own control. Most informants reported periods of fighting 'it' without any lasting success.

Their identities also contained a strand which related to conventional gender identities. So male transvestites might talk of expressing their feminine self and male to female transsexuals might see their quest for surgery as bringing their bodies into line with their gender identity as women. Transvestite and transsexual identities only made/make sense in relation to the conventional gender dichotomy.

These identities were/are also hidden identities. The male transsexual and the male transvestite in public seek to pass as women—not to be read as a transsexual or transvestite.

In contrast, the transgender identity breaks down the gender dichotomy by mixing and matching its characteristics in any combination. It is also a more open identity in that transgenderists are perceived as neither male nor female.

Pushed further, the idea of permanent, core identities and the idea of gender itself disappear. The emphasis today, at least in some parts of the literature, is on transience, fluidity and performance. In Kate Bornstein's *Gender Outlaw,* she talks about 'the ability to freely and knowingly become one or many of a limitless number of genders for any length of time, at any rate of change. Gender fluidity recognizes no borders or rules of gender.' 'A fluid identity', she continues, 'is one way to solve problems with boundaries. As a person's identity keeps shifting, so do individual borders and boundaries. It's hard to cross a boundary that keeps moving' (1994: 52 quoted by Whittle, 1996). In this writing, however, the experiences and behaviors are made sense of in terms of the deconstructions of postmodernist cultural theory rather than from the standpoint of the experiences of cross-dressers and sex-changers themselves. In consequence, these writings have yet to make a substantial impact on the subjective experience of the vast majority of gender blenders. In that gender fluidity recognizes no borders or 'laws' of gender, the claim is to live 'outside of gender' (Whittle, 1996; see also Devor, 1987): as 'gender outlaws'. Whether this can be sustained remains to be seen.

The Social Organization of Gender Blending

Under certain conditions, subcultures or communities develop around shared spheres of activity. When that sphere of activity is considered deviant and is thus both unexpected and without moral sanction, there are additional pressures towards subcultural or communal formations. When an activity is deviant, engaging in its carries additional problems such as those concerning access, secrecy and guilt. A subculture can thus be seen to provide solutions to some of these problems. Deviant activities, to varying degrees, provoke a hostile response from others. Such condemnation can further contribute to the emergence of subcultural forms by reinforcing, alienating and segregating deviant groups (Plummer, 1975).

The men who wrote to various publications about their experiences of wearing female clothing in the later years of last century and the early years of this (see Farrer, 1987; 1994), appear, in the main, to have pursued their activities in isolation from other men who were similarly engaged. There is some evidence that around this time a number of informal networks of cross-dressers were emerging, but it was not until the 1960s that these became more formalized and extensive (King, 1993; chapter five). The male femalers who provided the material on which Richard Ekins' analysis (1993) is based had available a wide range of organizations and settings in which to pursue their activities along with others in similar situations. By contrast, there has been little available to the 'female maler' who has often been forced to carve a small niche in the world of the male femaler. This is reflected in the literature which is almost exclusively concerned with male femalers. In that literature we can discern two types of community.

The first type of community covers a range of small communities which seem to be centrally concerned with doing rather than being, with celebrating and enjoying the artistic possibilities and the pleasures of cross-dressing and its associated sexual and other activities. In some cases such communities may be occupational ones concerned with, for example, prostitution (Perkins, 1983), or female impersonation (Newton, 1979). Some may be geographically located in those areas associated with deviant sexuality which are to be found in most large cities—Soho in London, Kings Cross in Sydney, the Tenderloin in San Francisco.

The members of these communities are full time 'outsiders', living out their gender 'deviance' in 'deviant' ways—stripping, engaging in prostitution, performing as female impersonators in bars and night clubs (Driscoll, 1971; Kando, 1973). They may also be involved in drug use or petty theft. This type of community is not consciously organized as such although particular aspects of it will obviously require organization of some kind. It depends primarily on face to face contact and is not literate in the sense that its members are concerned more with enjoyment, expression or practice than analysis or remote communication. The 'outpourings' of such a culture are in the form and language of art—for example, the photograph and the novel.

The second type of community is... not delineated by a geographical area and its members are not full time 'outsiders'. They come together because they feel they share a common problem, one which is often hidden from the members of the other social worlds within which the major part of their lives is lived. If and when their lives do become organized around their gender deviance, this happens still within 'respectable' worlds, not the 'underworld' of prostitution or stripping. This community is more centrally concerned with individual being or identity. It has been consciously engineered in relation to the terms supplied by modern medicine. It is a literate community since one of its central characteristics is the production of written accounts of its aims, its policies and its activities. It does not depend on face to face contact (although this does, of course, take place) since membership depends not on doing but on identity. It is possible to live in remote parts, never meet another member, yet to feel a part of a community to which one is linked by the written word. Such a community is thus less locally based than the first type and its potential membership much larger. It forms a national and even international network of those who identify with the terms transvestite or transsexual.

During the 1990s, but with roots reaching back earlier, some changes have taken place. The two types of community mentioned above continue, but currently commentators have drawn attention to a number of changes.

Firstly, the emergence of a greater diversity of transgendered people not conforming simply to the transvestite/transsexual patterns and associations created to cater for them. As Whittle puts it 'there is now a plethora of groups catering for a significant level of diversity in cross-gendered behavior' (1996; see also Bolin, 1994).

Secondly, at the same time as there is an acknowledgment of diversity, there also appears to be developing a greater sense of unity. So writers now comment on the 'transgender community' and this is sometimes seen to extend into the gay community (see Mackenzie, 1994; Whittle, 1996).

Thirdly, the greater visibility of transgendered people as a permanent status or 'third sex'. Formerly, the transsexual ideal was to disappear into the other gender and to be known simply as a man or a woman. Transvestites typically pursued their activities in solitude or in safe, private venues (Bolin, 1994; MacKenzie, 1994).

Fourthly, the greater involvement of transgenderists in gender and sexual politics both in a practical and a theoretical sense. This has become possible as a result of the changes detailed above and also as a result of the changing view of the political significance of transgenderism (Bolin, 1994; MacKenzie, 1994). . . .

The history of medical intervention in this area stretches over little more than a hundred years. This history discloses much controversy over the nature of 'transvestism' and 'transsexualism' and particularly over the appropriate methods of dealing with the latter. Since the late 1940s, when the endocrinological and surgical means to 'change sex' began to be more widely employed, transsexualism has dominated the literature with some practitioners advocating physical or psychological methods directed at the removal of the transsexual's 'pathological' wishes and desires, and others being willing to facilitate a 'change of sex' in what are regarded as appropriate cases. Both approaches can be regarded as seeking to restore harmony in a situation of discord. Both are, in different ways (and this is also true of the patients who seek out the practitioners of these approaches), seeking to ensure that identity, social status and biology 'match'. The end result is that the binary structure of gender is maintained.

The dominant medical position is that transsexualism is a 'given' disorder which has been discovered. Several critics from outside the profession and some within it have argued, in contrast, that transsexualism has been invented. The medical conception of transsexualism is, it is claimed, an illusion, a fabrication whose explanation must therefore be sought in terms other than the putative 'thing' itself. Once conjured up, legitimated and disseminated, this illusion has real social consequences through the actions of members of the medical profession, 'transsexuals' themselves and other members of society, all of whom have been seduced into believing in it. The invention of transsexualism is said to serve the interests of men and patriarchal society (Raymond, 1980) [depending] on whose account you read. Whilst we certainly would not deny the need for a critical/skeptical stance towards medical or any other categories, we have argued elsewhere (King, 1987; 1993) that the arguments of Raymond, Billings and Urban and others are flawed and do not accord with empirical reality.

In what ways has medical practice changed during the 1980s and into the 90s? What transsexuals wanted, in the past, was to slip invisibly into the other gender—to assimilate. Transvestites wanted to be 'cured' if they came to the idea, they wanted to be able to cross-dress without being seen to do so; to remain in private settings or to pass in public. With regard to transsexuals, medicine either helped them to cross over completely or remain where they were. Much the same was true with regard to the medical approach to intersexual conditions, patients had to be one or the other, they could not remain in between (Fausto-Sterling, 1993). Fausto-Sterling suggests that maybe we should accept what she calls sexual multiplicity instead of shoehorning people into one or other of the two available sexes. We know of at least one group of intersexual people who are now campaigning for just that (The Intersex Society of North America). Something similar seems to be occurring in the transgender field too. Bolin (1994), for example, argues that one factor which facilitated the emergence of a transgender category was what she calls the 'widespread closure of university-affiliated gender clinics in the 1980s.' Such clinics, in selecting patients for sex reassignment surgery, had enforced the segregation of transvestites and transsexuals and the latters' conformity to conventional sex/gender dichotomies. The reduction of such clinics, as she argues, left a smaller number of non university-affiliated, 'client-centered' clinics which contributed to 'greater flexibility in the expression of gender identities' (p. 463).

This apparent shift in power may perhaps be reflected in Bockting and Coleman's use of the term gender dysphoric client rather than patient. Such clients they claim 'often have a more ambiguous gender identity and are more ambivalent about a gender role transition than they initially admit' (1992a: 143). Their treatment program allows their clients, they say to 'discover and express their unique identity' (1992a: 143) and 'allows for individuals to identify as neither man nor woman, but as someone whose identity transcends the culturally sanctioned dichotomy' (1992a: 144)....

In addition to encouraging positive attitudes towards transsexualism and changing sex, Billings and Urban (1982), Birrell and Cole (1990) and Raymond (1980) argue that one of the wider consequences of the media dissemination of current conceptions of and responses to gender dysphoria is, by affirming the link between sex and gender, a reinforcement of an oppressive gender system. In a similar vein, Garber (1992) argues, with regard to the discussion of the motives of Billy Tipton, that 'such normalization reinstates the binary (male/female)' and 'recuperates social and sexual norms' (Garber, 1992: 69).

It is not possible to disagree: behind all the various press, television and radio reports of cross-dressing and sex-changing and informing all the novels, films and stage plays which deal with these themes, there is a necessary backdrop—a system of two gender categories, based on sex and distinguished by 'appropriate' dress, mannerisms and many other characteristics. The 'self-evidence' of this system is what gives the media content any point at all. Only on this basis can the producer and consumer make sense of it. However, this is true of all media content and not only that fraction which is concerned with gender blending in some way....

By the end of the 1970s, transsexualism was seen by some writers to have increasing political significance. Raymond (1980; 1994) is the best known exponent of these views. She argues that transsexuals are among the victims of patriarchal society and its definitions of masculinity and femininity. By creating transsexualism and treating it by means of sex change, the political and social sources of the transsexuals' suffering are obscured. Instead it is conceptualized as an individual problem for which an individual solution is devised. By means of this illegitimate medicalization, then, the 'real' problem remains unaddressed. Medicalization also serves to 'domesticate the revolutionary potential of transsexuals' who are 'deprived of an alternative framework in which to view the problem'. (p. 124)

Raymond also sees other reasons for the creation of transsexualism and sex change surgery. She places these alongside 'other male interventionist technologies such as cloning, test-tube fertilization, and sex selection' as an 'attempt to wrest from women, the power inherent in female biology' (p. xvi) or 'an attempt to replace biological women' (ibid., p. 140). She also sees 'gender identity clinics' where transsexuals are 'treated' as prototypical 'sex-role control centers' (p. 136). Thus transsexualism is not merely another example of the pervasive effects of patriarchal attitudes—it actually constitutes an attack on women. 'Transsexualism constitutes a sociopolitical program that is undercutting the movement to eradicate sex role stereotyping and oppression in this culture' (p. 5). Views such as this were sometimes used, for many years, to legitimate violence towards transsexuals and effectively silence the production of any dissenting views within the academy.

In contrast, crossing the gender border is now seen by some as subversive, transgressive. Recently Garber (1992: 17), for example, has argued that 'transvestism is a space of possibility structuring and confounding culture: the disruptive element that intervenes, not just a category crisis of male and female, but a crisis of category itself'. Similarly, Anne Bolin (1994: 485) argues that the transgenderist 'harbors great potential to deactivate gender or to create in the future the possibility of "supernumerary" genders as social categories no longer based on biology'. This is because of its 'decoupling of physiological sex, gender identity and sexuality' (1994: 483).

Conclusion

Gender blending is not a static phenomenon which remains unchanged as we look at it from different perspectives. At times, the perspectives we use can have a major impact on its nature as many writers have argued the medical gaze has had. Moreover, as a social and cultural practice, it changes as a result of other dynamics. Over the past ten to fifteen years, gender blending has become more complex and diverse. It has also been subjected to some reassessments and new interpretations of its political significance. For some, the issue of transsexualism has been largely superseded by debates over transgenderism or what has been called 'sexuality's newest cutting edge' (Raymond, 1994: xxv). In particular, gender blending has achieved a position of prominence in a number of recent contributions to cultural studies and in what has come to be known as queer theory. This, according to Segal (1994: 188) 'seeks to transcend and erode the central binary divisions of male/female, heterosexual/homosexual in the construction of modern sexualities'.

Once this move is made, however, the tension in the umbrella term 'gender blending' becomes apparent. As Plummer (1996) points out: ' "Gender blending" ... might imply that a core gender exists that can be mixed, merged and matched'. On the other hand, it might refer to those ' "blenders" who transcend, transgress and threaten', with a view to living 'beyond gender'. In each of the areas we have considered, we have traced a shift from the former to the latter.

References

Billings DB, Urban T. The Socio-medical Construction of Transsexualism: An Interpretation and Critique. Social Problems 1982;29(3):266–82.

Birrell S, Cole CL. Double Fault: Renee Richards and the Construction and Naturalization of Difference. Sociology of Sport Journal 1990;7(1):1–21.

Bockting WO, Coleman E. A Comprehensive Approach to the Treatment of Gender Dysphoria. In: Bockting WO, Coleman E., eds. Gender Dysphoria: Interdisciplinary Approaches in Clinical Management. New York: Haworth Press, 1992.

Bolin A. Transcending and Transgendering: Male-To-Female Transsexuals, Dichotomy and Diversity. In: Herdt G, ed. Third Sex, Third Gender: Beyond Sexual Dimorphism in Culture And History. New York: Zone Books, 1994.

Bornstein K. Gender Outlaw: On Men, Women and the Rest of Us. London: Routledge, 1994.

Devor H. Gender Blending Females: Women and Sometimes Men. American Behavioral Scientists 1987;31(1):12–40.

Driscoll JP. Transsexuals. Transaction 1971 March/April: 28–37 66 68.

Ekins R. On Male Femaling: A Grounded Theory Approach to Cross-Dressing and Sex-Changing. Sociological Review 1993;41(1):1–29.

Fallowell D, Ashley A. April Ashley's Odyssey. London: Jonathan Cape, 1982.

Farrer P. Men in Petticoats. Liverpool: Karn Publications, 1987.

Farrer P. Borrowed Plumes: Letters from Edwardian Newspapers on Male Cross-Dressing. Liverpool: Karn Publications, 1994.

Fausto-Sterling A. The Five Sexes: Why Male and Female Are Not Enough. Sciences 1993;33(2):20–5.

Garber M. Vested Interests: Cross-Dressing and Cultural Anxiety. New York: Routledge, 1991.

Kando T. Sex Change: The Achievement of Gender Identity among Feminished Transsexuals. Springfield, Illinois: Charles C. Thomas, 1973.

King D. Social Constructionism and Medical Knowledge: the Case of Transsexualism. Sociology of Health and Illness 1987;9(1):351–77.

King D. The Transvestite and the Transsexual. Public Categories and Private Identities. Aldershot: Avebury, 1993.

MacKenzie GO. Transgender Nation. Bowling Green, Ohio: Bowling Green University Popular Press, 1994.

Newton E. Mother Camp: Female Impersonators in America. 2nd ed. Chicago: University of Chicago Press, 1979.

Perkins R. The Drag Queen Scene: Transsexuals in King's Cross. Hemel Hempstead: Allen and Unwin, 1983.

Plummer K. Sexual Stigma. London: Routledge and Kegan Paul, 1975.

Plummer K. Foreword: Genders in Question. In: Ekins R, King D, eds. Blending Genders: Social Aspects of Cross-dressing and Sex-changing. London: Routledge, 1996: xiii-vii.

Raymond JG. The Transsexual Empire. London: The Women's Press, 1980.

Raymond J. The Transsexual Empire. Second ed. New York: The Teachers Press, 1994.

Segal L. Straight Sex: The Politics of Pleasure. London: Virago, 1994.

Whittle S. Gender F—ing Or F—ing Gender?? Current Cultural Contributions to Theories of Gender Blending. In: Ekins R, King D, eds. Blending Genders: Social Aspects of Cross-Dressing and Sex-Changing. London: Routledge, 1996.

POSTSCRIPT

Does Transsexualism Solve the Problem of Fixed Definitions of Gender Identity?

Transgendered individuals are often treated as "gender outlaws" in modern society. They are seen as pathological and problematic, threatening to "natural" gender categories. Leslie Feinberg reminds us in *Transgender Warriors: Making History From Joan of Arc to Dennis Rodman* (Beacon Press, 1996) that historically, in many societies, gender outlaws were accepted and even honored. But in other sociohistorical contexts, they were also persecuted and rejected. Some scholars argue that twentieth-century America was a most narrow and constricted time in the history of gender.

Transgender individuals may "pass" as males or females for legal, economic, or safety reasons. United States law typically excludes transsexual and transgendered individuals from protection against such infractions as sexual harassment and sex discrimination because they are neither male nor female, the two sexes recognized by the law. This creates legal *and* economic problems, seemingly necessitating "passing" as either male or female.

There is a growing "transgender movement" fighting for the rights of transgendered individuals, including legal protection. Many advocates argue that passing as one sex or the other is neither useful nor authentic if an individual is really both male and female. Thus, there is growing encouragement and support for the free expression of transgenderism among the transgender community. This political backdrop is important for understanding many of the historical and contemporary experiences of transsexuality and the degree to which they have kept the sex/gender binary alive.

Traditionally, the determination of eligibility of gender reassignment surgery has been regulated by the Harry Benjamin International Gender Dysphoria Association. Their standards of care specify requirements for approval for hormone therapy and sexual reassignment surgery, including written consent of a certified therapist and the successful completion of living full-time in the desired gender for at least a year. Riddled throughout this process are "gender criteria" used to determine the appropriateness of the individual to the sex of choice. The goal goes beyond constructing anatomically intelligible females or males to the construction of appropriately gendered women and men. In this way, contemporary theorist Sandy Stone argues that the physical "fact" of sex is confused with the "performative character" of gender.

Many transsexuals whose primary goals include assimilating into the new gender internalize such treatment goals. Stone explains, "The highest purpose of the transsexual is to erase h/erself, to fade into the 'normal' population as soon as possible.... What is gained is acceptability in society. What is lost is the ability to authentically represent the complexities and ambiguities of lived experience." Stone argues that this is a personally expensive and disempowering process. Part of the process is constructing a plausible history that fits existing gender constructs, in other words, "passing" to live successfully in the chosen gender and passing as an accepted "natural" member of that gender.

But in transsexuals' erased histories exist rich stories, which are disruptive to accepted notions of gender. Part of the challenge is changing the language used to describe gendered individuality. We have only known how to speak about experiences through existing constructs of gender. Gender variance creates dissonance with traditional gender constructs. Rather than retreat from such dissonance and fit individual experiences within the traditional gender boundaries, contemporary scholars argue that we must take advantage of the dissonance by reconstituting gender in unexpected ways.

The proliferation of gender alternatives is seen by many as a mechanism for increasing the rights and safety of transgendered individuals. But along with alternative gender performances come attempts to label them. Should we create more labels to describe the many performances of gender variance? Current descriptors include: gender resistant, gender reversal, gender mobility, gender migration, gender crossing, gender transient, gender fluidity, whole gendered, gender creative, gender bending, gender blending, male femaling, female maling, pansexual, etc. What are the risks of labeling? Will the proliferation of expressions and labels subvert or reinforce conventional gender constructs? If the goal is to become more fully human and individually free, can we achieve it by becoming "freely gendered," or must we eradicate gender altogether? Can gender as we know it be eradicated?

Suggested Readings

A. Bolin, "Transcending and Transgendering: Male-to-Female Transsexuals, Dichotomy and Diversity," in G. Herdt, ed., *Third Sex, Third Gender: Beyond Sexual Dimorphism in Culture and History* (Zone Books, 1994).

K. Bornstein, *Gender Outlaw: On Men, Women and the Rest of Us* (Routledge, 1994).

B. Bullough, V. L. Bullough, and J. Elias, eds., *Gender Blending* (Prometheus Books, 1997).

R. Ekins and D. King, eds., *Blending Genders: Social Aspects of Cross-Dressing and Sex-Changing* (Routledge, 1996).

L. Feinberg, *Transgender Warriors: Making History From Joan of Arc to Dennis Rodman* (Beacon Press, 1996).

R. Wichins, *Read My Lips: Sexual Subversion and the End of Gender* (Firebrand Books, 1997).

Will the Experimentation With Different Identities in Cyberspace Help Us to Transcend Gender?

YES: Sherry Turkle, from "Who Am We?" *Wired* (January 1996)

NO: Lori Kendall, from "MUDder? I Hardly Know 'Er! Adventures of a Feminist MUDder," in Lynn Cherny and Elizabeth Reba Weise, eds., *Wired Women: Gender and New Realities in Cyberspace* (Seal Press, 1996)

ISSUE SUMMARY

YES: Sherry Turkle, a professor in MIT's Program in Science, Technology, and Society, explores "virtual genderswapping" in Multi-User Domains (MUDs), showing that they allow individuals to try out new identities and potentially to redefine their many selves.

NO: Assistant professor of sociology Lori Kendall concludes from her experience on MUDs that gender stereotypes and expectations are even more constraining in cyberspace than in face-to-face socializing.

W e are swiftly entering a virtual age, where some say interactions through electronic media will be more common than physical contact. Our primary social contexts will likely be virtual communities or networks of personal relationships in cyberspace. In cyberspace, people are interconnected but physically separated.

In computer-mediated communication, two of the most powerful gender cues—voice and physical appearance—are unavailable. Thus, many of the nonverbal aspects of gendered interaction are absent. Remaining gender cues are unreliable in predicting a user's sex. As a result, we must speculate about sex and gender or proceed without this knowledge. How important is it to know sex and gender when interacting with others?

There are different types of virtual communities, including bulletin boards, list server groups, and multi-user domains (MUDS), which are used for a wide variety of educational, recreational, business-related, and social purposes. Some virtual communities involve individuals writing and responding at different times. In contrast, other virtual communities enable individuals to simultaneously interact with one another in cyberspace. In some virtual communities, users represent their "real" selves; other domains expressly require the creation of new "virtual" identities.

In MUDs, multiple users simultaneously login and have "real time" conversations with others in the virtual community. Together, they build a fantasy world in cyberspace. A user, whose identity is unknown to other users, may enact any role he or she wants to, sometimes by designing or selecting a different identity. Users choose a name and describe chosen attributes such as sex, age, race, sexual desires, and even mood—using *emoticons* like ":)" or ":(" Some users deliberately choose sex-neutral names. In general, users try to guard their private or "real" identity. Anonymity is important to the magic of MUDs.

Gender swapping (creating a virtual identity of the opposite sex) appears to be a common practice. In the real-world population, the most common MUDers (participants in MUDs) are male college students. Research also shows that men are more likely to gender swap than women. Why would a man take on a female identity? How does one determine the sex of a MUDer? When a *real* man pretends to be a *virtual* woman, what information does he use to construct his virtual identity? What impact does this role-playing have on him after several months or even years of *virtual* experience?

Sherry Turkle sees the Internet as a social laboratory for experimenting with self-construction and reconstruction. What is the relationship between "virtual identities" and our "core" or "whole" identity? Is there such a thing as unity of self, or do we have fluid, multiplicative identities? In Turkle's book *Life on the Screen. Identity in the Age of the Internet* (Simon & Schuster, 1995), she explores whether by creating a virtual self different from one's real self, we are devastated by the gap between the selves or enriched by complementary identity elements. Can virtual identities help us gain self-awareness and confidence, learn new interpersonal skills, expand our ideologies, or change our *real* selves?

More specifically, can virtual identities in which we choose a different sex and different gender characteristics provide us with experience and insight that will prompt a reconstruction of our "real" gender identity? Ultimately, with more and more widespread virtual experimentation, will cyberspace be the vehicle by which sexism is abated? Will virtual gender experimentation contribute to the diversification of gender beyond the sex/gender binary?

The following selections present two views on the power of MUD interaction for affecting gender identity change. Turkle is optimistic about the power of virtual interaction for *real-life* identity change and asserts that experimentation in cyberspace can help us to transcend gender. Lori Kendall expresses her skepticism and states that gender roles and expectations are present in cyberspace. Gender identity, real and virtual, influences one's MUD experiences.

Sherry Turkle

Who Am We?

[T]he Internet links millions of people in new spaces that are changing the way we think and the way we form our communities.... [W]e are moving from "a modernist culture of calculation toward a postmodernist culture of simulation." ... [L]ife on the screen permits us to "project ourselves into our own dramas, dramas in which we are producer, director, and star.... Computer screens are the new location for our fantasies, both erotic and intellectual. We are using life on computer screens to become comfortable with new ways of thinking about evolution, relationships, sexuality, politics, and identity." ...

As players participate [in a game of social virtual reality called Multi-User Dungeons (MUDs)], they become authors not only of text but of themselves, constructing new selves through social interaction. Since one participates in MUDs by sending text to a computer that houses the MUD's program and database, MUD selves are constituted in interaction with the machine. Take it away and the MUD selves cease to exist: "Part of me, a very important part of me, only exists inside PernMUD," says one player....

The anonymity of MUDs gives people the chance to express multiple and often unexplored aspects of the self, to play with their identity and to try out new ones. MUDs make possible the creation of an identity so fluid and multiple that it strains the limits of the notion. Identity, after all, refers to the sameness between two qualities, in this case between a person and his or her persona. But in MUDs, one can be many.

A 21-year-old college senior defends his violent characters as "something in me; but quite frankly I'd rather rape on MUDs where no harm is done." A 26-year-old clerical worker says, "I'm not one thing, I'm many things. Each part gets to be more fully expressed in MUDs than in the real world. So even though I play more than one self on MUDs, I feel more like 'myself' when I'm MUDding." In real life, this woman sees her world as too narrow to allow her to manifest certain aspects of the person she feels herself to be. Creating screen personae is thus an opportunity for self-expression, leading to her feeling more like her true self when decked out in an array of virtual masks.

MUDs imply difference, multiplicity, heterogeneity, and fragmentation. Such an experience of identity contradicts the Latin root of the word, idem, meaning "the same." But this contradiction increasingly defines the conditions of our lives beyond the virtual world. MUDs thus become objects-to-think-with for thinking about postmodern selves. Indeed, the unfolding of all MUD action takes place in a resolutely postmodern context. There are parallel narratives in the different rooms of a MUD. The cultures of Tolkien, Gibson, and Madonna coexist and interact. Since MUDs are authored by their players, thousands of people in all, often hundreds at a time, are all logged on from different places; the solitary author is displaced and distributed. Traditional ideas about identity have been tied to a notion of authenticity that such virtual experiences actively subvert. When each player can create many characters in many games, the self is not only decentered but multiplied without limit.

As a new social experience, MUDs pose many psychological questions: If a persona in a role-playing game drops defenses that the player in real life has been unable to abandon, what effect does this have? What if a persona enjoys success in some area (say, flirting) that the player has not been able to achieve? Slippages often occur in places where persona and self merge, where the multiple personae join to comprise what the individual thinks of as his or her authentic self.

Doug is a Midwestern college junior. He plays four characters distributed across three different MUDs. One is a seductive woman. One is a macho, cowboy type whose self-description stresses that he is a "Marlboros rolled in the T-shirt sleeve kind of guy." The third is a rabbit of unspecified gender who wanders its MUD introducing people to each other, a character he calls Carrot. Doug says, "Carrot is so low key that people let it be around while they are having private conversations. So I think of Carrot as my passive, voycuristic character." Doug's fourth character is one that he plays only on a MUD in which all the characters are furry animals. "I'd rather not even talk about that character because my anonymity there is very important to me," Doug says. "Let's just say that on FurryMUDs I feel like a sexual tourist." Doug talks about playing his characters in windows and says that using windows has made it possible for him to "turn pieces of my mind on and off.

"I split my mind.... I can see myself as being two or three or more. And I just turn on one part of my mind and then another when I go from window to window. I'm in some kind of argument in one window and trying to come on to a girl in a MUD in another, and another window might be running a spreadsheet program or some other technical thing for school.... And then I'll get a real-time message that flashes on the screen as soon as it is sent from another system user, and I guess that's RL [real life]. RL is just one more window, and it's not usually my best one."

Play has always been an important aspect of our individual efforts to build identity. The psychoanalyst Erik Erikson called play a "toy situation" that allows us to "reveal and commit" ourselves "in its unreality." While MUDs are not the only "places" on the Internet in which to play with identity, they provide an unparalleled opportunity for such play. On a MUD one actually gets to build character and environment and then to live within the toy situation. A MUD can become a context for discovering who one is and wishes to be. In this way, the games are laboratories for the construction of identity.

Stewart, a 23-year-old physics graduate student, uses MUDs to have experiences he can't imagine for himself in RL. His intense online involvements engaged key issues in his life but ultimately failed to help him reach successful resolutions.

Stewart's real life revolves around laboratory work and his plans for a future in science. His only friend is his roommate, another physics student whom he describes as even more reclusive than himself. For Stewart, this circumscribed, almost monastic student life does not represent a radical departure from what has gone before. He has had heart trouble since he was a child; one small rebellion, a ski trip when he was a college freshman, put him in the hospital for a week. He has lived life within a small compass.

Stewart is logged on to one MUD or another for at least 40 hours a week. It seems misleading to call what he does there playing. He spends his time constructing a life that is more expansive than the one he lives in physical reality. Stewart, who has traveled very little and has never been to Europe, explains with delight that his favorite MUD, although played in English, is physically located on a computer in Germany and has many European players.

On the German MUD, Stewart shaped a character named Achilles, but he asks his MUD friends to call him Stewart as much as possible. He wants to feel that his real self exists somewhere between Stewart and Achilles. He wants to feel that his MUD life is part of his real life. Stewart insists that he does not role play, but that MUDs simply allow him to be a better version of himself.

On the MUD, Stewart creates a living environment suitable for his ideal self. His university dormitory is modest, but the room he has built for Achilles on the MUD is elegant and heavily influenced by Ralph Lauren advertising. He has named it "the home beneath the silver moon." There are books, a roaring fire, cognac, a cherry mantel "covered with pictures of Achilles's friends from around the world.

"You look up . . . and through the immense skylight you see a breathtaking view of the night sky. The moon is always full over Achilles's home, and its light fills the room with a warm glow."

Beyond expanding his social world, MUDs have brought Stewart the only romance and intimacy he has ever known. At a social event in virtual space, a "wedding" of two regular players on a German-based MUD I call Gargoyle, Achilles met Winterlight, a character played by one of the three female players on that MUD. Stewart, who has known little success in dating and romantic relationships, was able to charm this desirable player.

On their first virtual date, Achilles took Winterlight to an Italian restaurant close to Stewart's dorm. He had often fantasized being there with a woman. Stewart used a combination of MUD commands to simulate a romantic evening —picking Winterlight up at the airport in a limousine, driving her to a hotel room so that she could shower, and then taking her to the restaurant and ordering veal for her.

This dinner date led to others during which Achilles was tender and romantic, chivalrous and poetic. The intimacy Achilles experienced during his courtship of Winterlight is unknown to Stewart in other contexts. "She's a very, she's a good friend. I found out a lot of things, from things about physiology to the color of nail polish she wears." Finally, Achilles asked for Winterlight's hand. When she accepted, they had a formal engagement ceremony on the MUD.

At the engagement, Winterlight gave Achilles a rose she had worn in her hair; Achilles gave her 1,000 paper stars.

Although Stewart participated in this ceremony alone in his room with his computer and modem, a group of European players actually traveled to Germany, site of Gargoyle's host computer, and got together for food and champagne. Many of the 25 guests at the German celebration brought gifts and dressed specially for the occasion. Stewart felt as though he were throwing a party. This was the first time that he had ever entertained, and he was proud of his success. In real life, Stewart felt constrained by his health problems, his shyness and social isolation, and his narrow economic straits. In the Gargoyle MUD, he bypassed these obstacles, at least temporarily.

The psychological effects of life on the screen can be complicated: a safe place is not all that is needed for personal change. Stewart came to MUDding with serious problems, and for Stewart, playing on MUDs led to a net drop in self-esteem. MUDs did help Stewart talk about his troubles while they were still emotionally relevant; nevertheless, he is emphatic that MUDding has ultimately made him feel worse about himself. MUDding did not alter Stewart's sense of himself as withdrawn, unappealing, and flawed.

While Stewart has tried hard to make his MUD self, the "better" Achilles self, part of his real life, he says he has failed. He says, "I'm not social. I don't like parties. I can't talk to people about my problems." The integration of the social Achilles, who can talk about his troubles, and the asocial Stewart, who can only cope by putting them out of mind, has not occurred. From Stewart's point of view, MUDs have stripped away some of his defenses but have given him nothing in return. In fact, MUDs make Stewart feel vulnerable in a new way. Although he hoped that MUDs would cure him, it is MUDs that now make him feel sick. He feels addicted to MUDs: "When you feel you're stagnating and you feel there's nothing going on in your life and you're stuck in a rut, it's very easy to be on there for a very large amount of time."

Stewart cannot learn from his character Achilles's experience and social success because they are too different from the things of which he believes himself capable. Despite his efforts to turn Achilles into Stewart, Stewart has split off his strengths and sees them as possible only for Achilles in the MUD. It is only Achilles who can create the magic and win the girl. In making this split between himself and the achievements of his screen persona, Stewart does not give himself credit for the positive steps he has taken in real life. Like an unsuccessful psychotherapy, MUDding has not helped Stewart bring these good experiences inside himself or integrate them into his self-image.

Relationships during adolescence are usually bounded by a mutual understanding that they involve limited commitment. Virtual space is well suited to such relationships; its natural limitations keep things within bounds. As in Thomas Mann's *The Magic Mountain,* which takes place in the isolation of a sanatorium, relationships become intense very quickly because the participants feel isolated in a remote and unfamiliar world with its own rules. MUDs, like other electronic meeting places, can breed a kind of easy intimacy. In a first phase, MUD players feel the excitement of a rapidly deepening relationship and the sense that time itself is speeding up. "The MUD quickens things. It quickens things so much," says one player. "You know, you don't think about it when you're doing it, but you meet somebody on the MUD, and within a week you feel like you've been friends forever."

In a second phase, players commonly try to take things from the virtual to the real and are usually disappointed.

Gender-swapping on MUDs is not a small part of the game action. By some estimates, Habitat, a Japanese MUD, has 1.5 million users. Habitat is a MUD operated for profit. Among the registered members of Habitat, there is a ratio of four real-life men to each real-life woman. But inside the MUD the ratio is only three male characters to one female character. In other words, a significant number of players, many tens of thousands of them, are virtually cross-dressing.

What is virtual gender-swapping all about? Some of those who do it claim that it is not particularly significant. "When I play a woman I don't really take it too seriously," said 20-year-old Andrei. "I do it to improve the ratio of women to men. It's just a game." On one level, virtual gender-swapping is easier than doing it in real life. For a man to present himself as female in a chat room, on an IRC channel, or in a MUD, only requires writing a description. For a man to play a woman on the streets of an American city, he would have to shave various parts of his body; wear makeup, perhaps a wig, a dress, and high heels; perhaps change his voice, walk, and mannerisms. He would have some anxiety about passing, and there might be even more anxiety about not passing, which would pose a risk of violence and possibly arrest. So more men are willing to give virtual cross-dressing a try. But once they are online as female, they soon find that maintaining this fiction is difficult. To pass as a woman for any length of time requires understanding how gender inflects speech, manner, the interpretation of experience. Women attempting to pass as men face the same kind of challenge.

Virtual cross-dressing is not as simple as Andrei suggests. Not only can it be technically challenging, it can be psychologically complicated. Taking a virtual role may involve you in ongoing relationships. You may discover things about yourself that you never knew before.

Case, a 34-year-old industrial designer who is happily married to a co-worker, is currently MUDding as a female character. In response to my question, "Has MUDding ever caused you any emotional pain?" he says, "Yes, but also the kind of learning that comes from hard times.

"I'm having pain in my playing now. Mairead, the woman I'm playing in MedievalMUSH, is having an interesting relationship with a fellow. Mairead is a lawyer, and the high cost of law school has to be paid for by a corporation or a noble house. She fell in love with a nobleman who paid for her law school. [Case slips into referring to Mairead in the first person.] Now he wants to marry me although I'm a commoner. I finally said yes. I try to talk to him about the fact that I'm essentially his property. I'm a commoner... I've grown up with it, that's the way life is. He wants to deny the situation. He says, 'Oh no, no, no.... We'll pick you up, set you on your feet, the whole world is open to you.'

But every time I behave like I'm now going to be a countess some day . . . as in, 'And I never liked this wallpaper anyway,' I get pushed down. The relationship is pull up, push down. It's an incredibly psychologically damaging thing to do to a person. And the very thing that he liked about her that she was independent, strong, said what was on her mind, it is all being bled out of her."

Case looks at me with a wry smile and sighs, "A woman's life." He continues: "I see her [Mairead] heading for a major psychological problem. What we have is a dysfunctional relationship. But even though it's very painful and stressful, it's very interesting to watch myself cope with this problem. How am I going to dig my persona's self out of this mess? Because I don't want to go on like this. I want to get out of it. . . . You can see that playing this woman lets me see what I have in my psychological repertoire, what is hard and what is easy for me. And I can also see how some of the things that work when you're a man just backfire when you're a woman."

Case further illustrates the complexity of gender swapping as a vehicle for self-reflection. Case describes his RL persona as a nice guy, a "Jimmy Stewart type like my father." He says that in general he likes his father and he likes himself, but he feels he pays a price for his low-key ways. In particular, he feels at a loss when it comes to confrontation, both at home and in business dealings. Case likes MUDding as a female because it makes it easier for him to be aggressive and confrontational. Case plays several online "Katharine Hepburn types," strong, dynamic, "out there" women who remind him of his mother, "who says exactly what's on her mind and is a take-no-prisoners sort."

For Case, if you are assertive as a man, it is coded as "being a bastard." If you are assertive as a woman, it is coded as "modern and together."

Some women who play male characters desire invisibility or permission to be more outspoken or aggressive. "I was born in the South and taught that girls didn't speak up to disagree with men," says Zoe, a 34-year-old woman who plays male and female characters on four MUDs.

"We would sit at dinner and my father would talk and my mother would agree. I thought my father was a god. Once or twice I did disagree with him. I remember one time in particular when I was 10, and he looked at me and said, 'Well, well, well, if this little flower grows too many more thorns, she will never catch a man.' "

Zoe credits MUDs with enabling her to reach a state of mind where she is better able to speak up for herself in her marriage ("to say what's on my mind before things get all blown out of proportion") and to handle her job as the financial officer for a small biotechnology firm.

"I played a MUD man for two years. First I did it because I wanted the feeling of an equal playing field in terms of authority, and the only way I could think of to get it was to play a man. But after a while, I got very absorbed by MUDding. I became a wizard on a pretty simple MUD. I called myself Ulysses and got involved in the system and realized that as a man I could be firm and people would think I was a great wizard. As a woman, drawing the line and standing firm has always made me feel like a bitch and, actually, I feel that people saw me as one, too. As a man I was liberated from all that. I learned from my mistakes. I got better at being firm but not rigid. I practiced, safe from criticism."

Zoe's perceptions of her gender trouble are almost the opposite of Case's. While Case sees aggressiveness as acceptable only for women, Zoe sees it as acceptable only for men. These stories share a notion that a virtual gender swap gave people greater emotional range in the real. Zoe says: "I got really good at playing a man, so good that whoever was on the system would accept me as a man and talk to me as a man. So, other guys talked to Ulysses guy to guy. It was very validating. All those years I was paranoid about how men talked about women. Or I thought I was paranoid. Then I got a chance to be a guy and I saw that I wasn't paranoid at all."

... [O]nce we take virtuality seriously as a way of life, we need a new language for talking about the simplest things. Each individual must ask: What is the nature of my relationships? What are the limits of my responsibility? And even more basic: Who and what am I? What is the connection between my physical and virtual bodies? And is it different in different cyberspaces? These questions are equally central for thinking about community. What is the nature of our social ties? What kind of accountability do we have for our actions in real life and in cyberspace? What kind of society or societies are we creating, both on and off the screen?

When people adopt an online persona they cross a boundary into highly charged territory. Some feel an uncomfortable sense of fragmentation, some a sense of relief. Some sense the possibilities for self-discovery, even self-transformation. Serena, a 26-year-old graduate student in history, says, "When I log on to a new MUD and I create a character and know I have to start typing my description, I always feel a sense of panic. Like I could find out something I don't want to know." Arlie, a 20-year-old undergraduate, says, "I am always very self-conscious when I create a new character. Usually, I end up creating someone I wouldn't want my parents to know about.... But that someone is part of me."

... People can get lost in virtual worlds. Some are tempted to think of life in cyberspace as insignificant, as escape or meaningless diversion. It is not. Our experiences there are serious play. We belittle them at our risk. We must understand the dynamics of virtual experience both to foresee who might be in danger and to put these experiences to best use. Without a deep understanding of the many selves that we express in the virtual, we cannot use our experiences there to enrich the real. If we cultivate our awareness of what stands behind our screen personae, we are more likely to succeed in using virtual experience for personal transformation.

NO ⬅

Lori Kendall

*Mud*der? I Hardly Know 'Er!
Adventures of a Feminist *Mud*der

How meaningful is gender online? On most current online forums, all communication is through text. Theoretically, people can name themselves and describe themselves however they choose. Does this ability to hide identifying characteristics "level the playing field," creating new opportunities for equality among male and female participants? Does gender identity become more fluid under these circumstances? Those were some of the questions I had a year ago when I started researching MUDs, which are online, text-based interactive forums. . . .

Being Female on a MUD

Far fewer women than men participate on MUDs, although the exact ratios vary from MUD to MUD. As in other areas of the Internet, participation by women is probably increasing, but newly arriving women encounter a social environment and behavioral norms formed largely by men. In some cases, these norms may be disturbing enough to discourage further participation by women. As one MUDder explains:[1]

> Women get treated differently from men. It's not that they get more slack or anything, but they get chased out differently. Part of it is that most women tend not to talk immediately, just by normal socialization. Guys are much more likely to mouth off early. But women often get turned off by less nasty hazing than men.

On the various Usenet newsgroups and email lists devoted to discussions of MUDs, MUD participants mainly worry about the effects of sexual harassment on women participants. The following stories are typical:

> I recently (last week) showed a female friend how to MUD. . . .
> We were sitting side-by side in a comp. lab during her 1st session.. and although she used a more or less male name. She marked her sex as female. The male character who soon found it his mission to pamper her in the game was very nice to her. All

seemd well, and I went back to writing something in emacs on my screen.

After about 15 minutes (and 30.. maybe 40 newbie questions from my friend ;) This guy in the game started making advances on her..

A female friend of mine lagged out on one MUSH and another player took advantage of the situation and "posed" himself as raping her. When she unlagged, the person in question was gone and she was left with the equivalent of an obscene phone call on her screen.[2]

Generally my reaction was to foofoo that there was any problem except that I recently was able to get my wife interested in mudding. I could NOT believe what she had to put up with just to play. I got very angry at what seemed like a bunch of children trying out 'social' commands that they wouldnt ever do in public. It went far beyond role-playing.

Although it's unclear how prevalent this type of harassment is, it's only the extreme end of a range of behaviors directed at female characters (who, it should be kept in mind, may or may not be operated by female participants). Participants running female characters may find themselves the focus of constant sexual interest and innuendo.

MUD participants also describe other forms of differential treatment, especially overly helpful treatment of female characters:

Beryl whispers "the main area you notice it is when newbies log on. a female newbie will be given more breaks & more attention, even (especially?) by women"

In this situation, gender becomes almost a stance of relationship to the MUD—a way to designate one's desired treatment, rather than a statement of identity. Thus, some men portray female characters because they are dissatisfied with the "neutral" reactions they get when portraying male characters:

Amnesia whispers " 'Oblivious' was my male persona briefly, but it was less fun"
You whisper "less fun? how so?" to Amnesia.
Amnesia whispers "hard to say.Perhaps less attention is paid male characters."
You whisper "hmmm. I've heard that from other people as well." to Amnesia.

Others specifically portray female characters for the sexual adventure of engaging in TinySex with other male characters.[3] This led one participant to comment:

I think the rule should be: If you are a homophobe, don't have tinysex cuz that cute broad might be a guy in real life. If you aren't bothered by this, have fun.

Meanwhile, many women portray male characters to avoid the very behaviors these men are courting.

> Amnesia stares at CH. "Oh, no, you don't actually admit to being female on line, do you?"
> Amnesia notes that she didn't mean to imply that CH was not a female, but rather that anyone who really is female canonically ought to pretend to be male

It is true that any woman who doesn't like the way she is treated when she logs on as a female character can change her identity to a male or neutral representation. However, this solution leaves intact a status quo in which being female, especially if you are new, means being hit on. Many MUDders, male and female, see this as a problem and are working to change it.

But differences in treatment of male and female characters are only part of the story. Even on MUDs where everybody is treated more or less the same, norms of behavior, as well as topics of discussion, contain gendered meanings and expectations.... [F]or instance, performances of swaggering masculinity by anonymous guests are accompanied by intimations of homosexuality used as put-downs....

In the... example below, friendship between two male participants is expressed through a joking negotiation for the possession of female sexual objects. This conversation took place in a public room in which women participants were also present:

> henri says "[Mender], if we meet a couple of supermodels in NYC, the rule is: you take the brunette, I take the blonde"
>
> Mender says "what if they are both blonde?"
>
> henri says "you take the shorter one"
>
> Mender says "hsm"
>
> henri says "you are shorter than me after all"
>
> Mender says "OK"
>
> fnord says "what if you meet a short blonde and a tall brunette?"
>
> Mender says "trouble"
>
> henri says "hair color overrides height"
>
> henri says "domehead and I used to use the blonde/brunette system when scoping babes (from afar) at basketball games" ...

Are You Male or Female?

Choosing a gender-neutral or male character may free a female participant from fears of direct harassment or overeager sexual interest, but regardless of the gender of her character, a female participant observing the types of conversations previously related is continually reminded of the male-dominated environment in which she moves. Furthermore, choosing one gender or another does nothing to change the expectations attached to particular gender identifications.

In theory, choosing a neutral gender designation would mean escaping the dualism of male and female gender expectations. (After all, in our face-to-face interactions, we don't meet many people we would designate as gender-neutral, and therefore we don't have a clearly assigned role for such persons.) In fact, it would appear that a significant number of MUDders use neutral designations just for this purpose. GammaMOO, for instance, has the following choices: neuter, male, female, either, Spivak, splat, plural, egotistical, royal, and 2nd. "Neuter" designates the character with the pronoun *it*. "Either" uses the *s/he* and *him/her* convention. "Spivak" uses a set of gender-neutral pronouns such as *e* and *em*. "Splat," similarly, uses **e* and *h**. As might be expected, "plural" uses *they* and *them*, "egotistical" uses *I* and *me*, "royal" uses *we* and *us* and "2nd" uses *you*.

As of October 17, 1994, out of 8,541 total characters on GammaMOO, 23 percent (1,991) were neuter, and only 2.5 percent (216) were anything else, other than male or female. Significantly, only 21 percent (1,770) of GammaMOO's characters were designated as female. Thus, male characters outnumber all others put together, and more people choose some form of neutral designation than choose female. But almost all the gender-neutral characters I have met were guest characters who had not yet set their gender designation, so it is unclear to me how well this strategy works. My guess is not very well, for the very reason that we *do* expect everyone to be either male or female. No one encountering someone using the pronoun *e* is likely to believe that this expresses their "true" gender, and is thus likely to treat the character's gender designation as a mere mask. Some may respect this desire to "hide" gender, but others probably will not.

Consider, for instance, that at least in areas where guests or other anonymous characters are common, the question "are you male or female?" is frequent enough to have acquired joke status among experienced MUD participants.

> Copper_Guest says, "Infrared, Are you male or female?"
>
> Infrared_Guest says, "male"
>
> Copper_Guest says, "Cool! Lets chat. So, you're from Austin, right?"
>
> Infrared_Guest says, "copper are male or female"
>
> Copper_Guest says, "I am most definitely female."
>
> Yellow_Guest [to Copper_Guest]: *most definitely*?
>
> Copper_Guest says, "Just wanted to stress the fact, since you can't see me and all..."

Furthermore, since everyone knows that character gender need not reflect the face-to-face gender of the participant, setting one's gender doesn't make one immune to the "male or female" question.

> Previous asks, "are you really female or is that just your char?"
>
> achina [to Previous]: that question kind of surprises me. Why do you want to know?
>
> Previous smiles at you.
>
> Previous says, "just checking"
>
> Previous says, "best to catch these things early.. people here tend to switch sexes almost as often as clothing"
>
> achina is female in real life.
>
> Previous says, "good :)"
>
> achina still isn't sure why you need to know my RL gender, though.
>
> Previous says, "I don't like being switched genders on, so I make sure early on so I don't inadvertently use the wrong social mores with anyone"

Some experience a later change in gender as a deep betrayal, particularly if they considered the relationship to be intimate. One MUD participant said:

> Back when I viewed MUDS as a REAL reality, I fell in love with a female character.... But anyways turned out "she" was a he. Since then my personal policy is to NEVER get involved with anyone on a mud in a deep personal way.

As these examples demonstrate, choosing a gender, even a neutral gender, doesn't free people from standard gender expectations. Such expectations also affect how participants are able to enact the gender identities they do choose. Consider, for instance, ... Amnesia, the female character of a male participant. I had a long conversation with Amnesia about his/her portrayal of a woman character, some of which I've excerpted here:

> You whisper "so I'm curious—if everyone knows you're not female, why still the female pronouns? Continuity?" to Amnesia.
>
> Amnesia whispers " 'Amnesia' is a woman, and always has been. Amnesia was (is) my 'ideal woman', and so is more caricaturial than any real woman can be. I think that means her femininity shows through easier via text."
>
> You whisper "your 'ideal woman' is caricaturially female?" to Amnesia.
>
> Amnesia whispers "no, I mean that I have no real experience in being a woman, so can only draw a crude image with a broad brush when I'm acting."

Amnesia's belief that one can portray a female character well only if one has been a woman reflects a cultural belief that women and men are substantially different from each other. Yet, by playing into these beliefs Amnesia was in fact quite successful. According to both Amnesia and other participants on BlueSky, Amnesia successfully masqueraded as female for over a year and only had to give up the guise when he met several other MUDders in person. Note especially that Amnesia's "jeune femme fatale" description, a weird juxtaposition of Lolita-esque pornography and Dungeons and Dragons-type iconography, seems not to have impinged on his ability to be convincingly female, despite its clear references to male-oriented literature.

Amnesia's successful masquerade thus probably relies in part on the wishful thinking of the predominantly male MUD participants. But it also depends upon the wider cultural beliefs that certain behaviors are feminine and certain behaviors masculine. This puts all MUD participants in the position of "masquerading" as their chosen gender, regardless of their "real life" gender identity. Everyone is in "drag" on MUDs; being more or less female has no relationship to one's gender identity off-line, as Amnesia and I discussed:

> Amnesia whispers "when I was full-out a woman, the differential was unbelievable and measurable."

> You whisper "but you know, I haven't really noticed [being treated different]. 'Course, I haven't been on here as a male, but comparing myself to other people, it doesn't really seem to me that I get more attention. Heh. Maybe if I was male, I'd get *no* attention." to Amnesia.

> Amnesia whispers "you don't 'act female' in the traditional sense, as far as I've seen."

> You whisper "ah. I suppose that's true. So maybe it's not females that get more attention, per se. Am I less a woman than Amnesia?;)" to Amnesia.

To a certain extent, this is not significantly different from face-to-face interactions. We are all expected to perform certain roles and meet particular gender expectations in all of our social interactions. However, both subcultural norms and technical limitations of MUD communication can limit gender performance on MUDs to stereotypical caricatures. Conversations move quickly, and one's presence in the conversation is apparent only when one continues to speak. In the limited bandwidth of text, typed conversation is the only means of communicating gender identity, and communicating it in a complex or nuanced way can be very difficult.

Given that the stereotypical characteristics attributed to men are more valued than those attributed to women, it is not surprising that the limitations inherent in online gender portrayal work out a bit better for men than for women. As indicated above, I've made no special effort to portray myself as specifically female, merely designating my gender and including information indicating that I am female in my character description. This has worked acceptably for me, perhaps partly because my known role as researcher has deflected attention from my gender and partly because I'm not particularly "feminine" in my face-to-face interactions and therefore do not attempt to portray this type of personality online. But other women I've met have indicated that attempting to "just be themselves" online produces less than desirable results.

Several female BlueSky participants feel that their lack of computer knowledge in particular affects the type of identity they are able to enact. One infrequent female participant said she wasn't interested in all the "tech talk" that occurred on BlueSky, and that "they all consider me a bimbo here." Another more frequent participant, Sparkle, said:

> In the bar [on BlueSky], I most likely seem more flakey than I am, but that's mostly because they don't talk about things I know anything about. All I can do is crack jokes and laugh when I read something that's funny to me.... For the longest time, I was too scared to talk to anyone on here, I just hung out in the bar and laughed—which is why people think I am a ditz

Masculinity similarly becomes a mask to be performed, but even extremes of "masculine" behavior such as obnoxiousness and bullying are less likely to reflect negatively on the performer than similarly extreme forms of "feminine" behavior such as coquetry or flattery. This is particularly true because, in the interwoven subcultures that make up the MUD social environment, intelligence is highly valued and attributed more often to males. Textual obnoxiousness can at least sometimes be read as the incisive application of a keen wit, whereas demureness or other feminine virtues are likely to come across as merely dumb. Sparkle's shyness and laughter earn her the reputation of stupidity (reported to me by several other BlueSky MUDders), while even the most notorious of bullies on BlueSky are credited with high intelligence and even appreciated for their humor value.

Conclusion

I don't present these examples of MUD behavior as typical—there are hundreds of MUDs on the net, and I spend time on only a few. What I've tried to show are some of the ways in which gender gets enacted online. What's important, I think, is that the social context on any given MUD significantly limits what kinds of identities can be enacted there. You can set whatever gender designation you want and describe yourself as you will, but if no one believes your presentation, it won't be effective. If no one likes the way you present yourself, or thinks you're dumb because you present yourself in a stereotypically feminine way, that too will be limiting. In this way, online socializing is little different from face-to-face socializing. Social expectations shape who we can be.

The stereotypes of masculine and feminine identity found on MUDs aren't new. Nor is the higher value placed on the "masculine" characteristics of intelligence and aggressiveness. But the greater male presence online and the limitations of this form of textual communication create a context in which these stereotypes are relied upon to a greater degree. So the answer to the question with which I began my research is that gender, in fact, has a great deal of meaning online. Although individuals can choose their gender representation, that does not seem to be creating a context in which gender is more fluid. Rather, gender identities themselves become even more rigidly understood. The ability to change one's gender identity online does not necessarily result in an understanding that gender identity is always a mask, always something merely performed. Rather, there can be an increased focus on the "true" identities behind the masks. Further, what I've found is that the standard expectations of masculinity and feminity are still being attached to these identities.

... [T]he appearance of more women on MUDs, and online generally, is likely to help only if both women and men make specific efforts to counter the types of stereotypical understandings I have identified. Ultimately, I think the situation on MUDs, and online generally, is more a symptom of wider social problems than a cause in itself. The status of women, and understandings about gender, need to be addressed societywide.

Notes

1. I have changed the names of all the MUDs and MUD characters mentioned in the essay. All quotations cited in this essay were gathered from logs of my participation on several MUDs, from postings to Usenet newsgroups relating to MUDs, and from an email list also relating to MUDs. All are quoted verbatim.

2. "Lag" refers to a delay between the typing of commands and the execution. A MUSH is a type of MUD program.

3. " 'TinySex' is the act of performing MUD actions to imitate having sex with another character, usually consensually." From "Frequently Asked Questions: Basic Information About MUDs and MUDding," a document regularly posted to the Usenet newsgroup, *rec.games.mud.misc.*

POSTSCRIPT

Will the Experimentation With Different Identities in Cyberspace Help Us to Transcend Gender?

A profound test of whether or not events and circumstances in the virtual worlds of cyberspace are "real" and transformative of identity occurred in 1993 on a MOO (MUD Object Oriented) called LambdaMOO.

LambdaMOO is a "social MUD." One day a character named Mr. Bungle used his voodoo doll (a controversial subprogram that allows players to attribute actions to other characters that their players did not actually write) to force another room occupant, legba, to perform sexual acts on him.

In a statement to an in-MOO mailing list, legba emotionally called for Mr. Bungle's recrimination for a breech of civility. These were real emotions in a virtual world. But, in real life, there was no physical interaction, no assault, no rape. This created controversy about the definition of this virtual community and its political structure. Is rape illegal in this virtual world as it is in the real world?

The uniqueness of cyberspace culture is that computer commands are not just communicative. Should virtual rape be taken seriously? If virtual rape is "real" and there is no physical damage, then should "real rape" include sex crimes of the mind? Many gender-related assumptions were made during this event. What if a female user created Mr. Bungle? What if male users created some of the virtual victims? Would this change the virtual characters' and real users' interpretations and outcomes of the events? In general, did these events in cyberspace challenge or reinforce conventional gender roles and attitudes?

Suggested Readings

L. Cherney, "Gender Differences in Text-Based Virtual Reality," http://lucien.berkeley.edu/MOO/GenderMOO.ps (December 1996).

A. Escobar, "Welcome to Cyberia," *Journal of Current Anthropology* (1994).

E. Reid, "Cultural Formations in Text-Based Virtual Realities," http://www.ludd.luth.se/mud/aber/articles/cult-form.thesis.html (January 1994).

A. Stone, "Will the Real Body Please Stand Up? Boundary Stories About Virtual Cultures," in M. Benedikt ed., *Cyberspace: First Steps* (MIT Press, 1992).

Contributors to This Volume

EDITOR

ELIZABETH L. PAUL is an associate professor of psychology and an affiliate of the Women's and Gender Studies Program at the College of New Jersey in Ewing, New Jersey. Her research focuses on relational challenges of late adolescence and young adulthood, particularly as they impact and are impacted by the college transition. She also studies how gender delimits personal relationship development and experience. Her writings have appeared in *Adolescence, Journal of College Student Development,* and *Journal of Counseling and Development,* as well as edited volumes on women's lives. Starting in the year 2000 Dr. Paul is coeditor with Dr. Juda Bennett of *Transformations: A Resource for Curriculum Transformation and Scholarship,* the journal of the New Jersey Project. She received her Ph.D. in personality psychology at Boston University.

STAFF

Theodore Knight   List Manager
David Brackley   Senior Developmental Editor
Juliana Gribbins   Developmental Editor
Rose Gleich   Administrative Assistant
Brenda S. Filley   Director of Production/Design
Juliana Arbo   Typesetting Supervisor
Diane Barker   Proofreader
Richard Tietjen   Publishing Systems Manager
Larry Killian   Copier Coordinator

AUTHORS

MARYANN BAENNINGER is associate professor of psychology at the College of New Jersey. Her research interests include spatial and visual perception throughout the lifespan and the role of experience in developing cognitive abilities.

SANDRA LIPSITZ BEM is professor of psychology and women's studies at Cornell University. Her research interests focus on the social construction of gender and sexuality. In 1995 she was selected as an "Eminent Woman in Psychology" by the divisions of General Psychology and the History of Psychology of the American Psychological Association. She is the author of the award-winning book *The Lenses of Gender* (Yale University Press, 1993).

DAVID M. BUSS is professor of psychology at the University of Texas at Austin. His research interests include the evolutionary psychology of human mating strategies; conflict between the sexes; prestige, status, and reputation; jealousy; and social relationships, including coalitions and dyadic friendships. He has published numerous articles and books, including most recently *The Evolution of Desire: Strategies of Human Mating* (Basic Books, 1994) and coedited with Neil M. Malamuth, *Sex, Power, Conflict* (Oxford University Press, 1996).

MARIAN COHEN is a senior social worker and behavioral science educator at the Department of Family Medicine of the University of Michigan Medical School.

MARY CRAWFORD is professor of psychology and director of Women's Studies at the University of Connecticut. Her research interests include gender and communication, feminist research methods, and gender and cognition. She is coauthor, with Rhoda Unger, of *Women and Gender: A Feminist Psychology* (McGraw-Hill, 1996). She is the author of *Talking Difference: On Gender and Language* (Sage Publications, 1995).

ATHENA DEVLIN is an author who writes on gender issues.

MILTON DIAMOND is professor of anatomy and reproductive biology and director of the Pacific Center for Sex and Society at the University of Hawaii in Honolulu.

SARAH DRESCHER is on the staff of the *Oregon Advocate* and a member of the University of Oregon Future Lawyers Association.

ALICE H. EAGLY is professor of psychology at Northwestern University. She has published widely and influentially on the psychology of gender, including research on gender and social influence, leadership and management potential, aggression, physical attractiveness, altruism, and stereotypes. Her recent work focuses on the impact of gender on participation in leadership roles. She has received several awards, including the Donald Campbell Award for Distinguished Contribution to Social Psychology and a Citation as Distinguished Leader for Women in Psychology.

RICHARD EKINS is professor of psychology and communication at the University of Ulster in Londonderry, U.K. He is coeditor, with Dave King, of

Blending Genders: Social Aspects of Cross-Dressing and Sex Changing (Routledge, 1996). He is the author of *Male Femaling: A Grounded Theory Approach to Cross-Dressing and Sex-Changing* (Routledge, 1997).

MARY ELLSBERG is a research fellow at the Preventative Medicine Department of the Nicaraguan National University and an advisor to international agencies such as the World Health Organization. She has published numerous articles based on her research on domestic violence in Nicaragua.

EQUAL EMPLOYMENT ADVISORY COUNCIL (EEAC) is a nonprofit association made up of more than 315 major companies that are committed to the principle of equal employment opportunity. Founded in 1976, the EEAC provides a wide variety of services and benefits to its member companies, some of which also are available to nonmembers.

A. E. EYLER is clinical associate professor of family medicine at the University of Michigan Medical School. He is a fellow of the American Academy of Family Physicians.

ANNE FAUSTO-STERLING is professor of medical science at J. Walter Wilson Laboratories and professor of women's studies at Brown University. She is the author of *Myths of Gender: Biological Theories About Women and Men,* 2d ed. (Basic Books, 1992) and *Sexing the Body: Gender Politics and the Construction of Sexuality* (Basic Books, 1999).

MARTHA ALBERTSON FINEMAN is Maurice T. Moore Professor of Law at the Columbia University School of Law. Her research and teaching interests are in civil procedure, decision making, family law, children and the law, feminism and legal theory-critical theory, and families and poverty. She is the author of *The Neutered Mother, The Sexual Family and Other Twentieth Century Tragedies* (Routledge, 1995).

MEGAN GOTTEMOELLER helped to establish the Latino Health Outreach Project, a community mobilization and health education project located in New Orleans. She has worked in health education projects both in Latin America and in the United States.

BERNICE L. HAUSMAN is associate professor of English at Virginia Tech University. She is the author of *Changing Sex: Transsexualism, Technology, and the Idea of Gender* (Duke, 1995).

LORI HEISE is a long-time advocate of women's health. She is codirector of the Center for Health and Gender Equity (CHANGE) and her research interests include sexuality, women and HIV, and gender-based abuse.

STANLIE M. JAMES is associate professor of Afro-American studies and women's studies and director of the Women's Studies Research Center at the University of Wisconsin, Madison. He is coeditor, with Abena P.A. Busia, of *Theorizing Black Feminisms: The Visionary Pragmatism of Black Women* (Routledge, 1993).

LORI KENDALL is assistant professor of sociology at Purchase College of the State University of New York. Her research interests include computer-mediated communication; feminist theory; intersections of race, class, and gender; popular culture; and sociology of technology.

MICHAEL KIMMEL is professor of sociology at the State University of New York at Stony Brook. He has received international recognition for his work on men and masculinity. Kimmel's numerous books include *The Gendered Society* (Oxford University Press, 2000), *The Politics of Manhood* (Temple University Press, 1996), and *Manhood in America: A Cultural History* (Free Press, 1996).

DOREEN KIMURA is professor emeritus of psychology at the University of Western Ontario in London, Ontario. Specializing in psychobiology and clinical neuropsychology, her research interests focus on neural and hormonal mechanisms in cognitive function. She is a fellow of the Royal Society of Canada and received the 1992 John Dewan Award for outstanding research from the Ontario Mental Health Foundation. She recently authored *Sex and Cognition* (MIT Press, 1999).

DAVE KING is Lecturer of Sociology at the University of Liverpool in England. His research spans the broad areas of crime, deviance, and medicine. He is particularly interested in sexual crime/deviance and medical forms of social control. His previous research has dealt mainly with homosexuality, transvestism, and transsexualism. He is coeditor, with Richard Ekins, of *Blending Genders: Social Aspects of Cross-Dressing and Sex Changing* (Routledge, 1996).

LORETTA M. KOPELMAN is a professor in and chair of the Department of Medical Humanities in the School of Medicine at East Carolina University in Greenville, North Carolina. She is coeditor, with John C. Moskop, of *Children and Health Care: Moral and Social Issues* (Kluwer Academic Publishers, 1989).

LANCET is a general medical journal that publishes contributions that advance or illuminate medical science or its practice or that educate or entertain the journal's readers. Editorials are written in-house by the journal's editorial-writing team and signed simply "The Lancet."

BERNICE LOTT is professor emeritus of psychology at the University of Rhode Island. She is the author of numerous theoretical and empirical articles, chapters, and books on issues relevant to women and to interpersonal attraction. Her latest books are *The Social Psychology of Interpersonal Discrimination* (Guilford Publications, 1995), coedited with Diane Maluso, and *Combating Sexual Harassment in Higher Education* (National Education Association, 1995), coedited with Mary Ellen Reilly.

CATHERINE A. MacKINNON has received a J.D. from Yale Law School and a Ph.D. in political science from Yale University. Professor of Law at the University of Michigan at Ann Arbor, she also practices law and consults nationally and internationally. Her fields of concentration include constitutional law, in particular sex equality; and political theory, in particular feminism and Marxism. She is the author of numerous articles and books, including *Toward a Feminist Theory of the State* (Harvard University Press, 1989).

JOHN B. McDEVITT is director of research at the Margaret S. Mahler Psychiatric Research Foundation. He is also training and supervising analyst in adult and child analysis at the New York Psychoanalytic Institute.

NORA NEWCOMBE is professor of psychology at Temple University. Her research interests include early childhood memory, the development of spatial cognition, and individual differences in spatial ability. She is editor in chief of the *Journal of Experimental Psychology*.

JENNIFER L. PIERCE is associate professor of sociology at the University of Minnesota. Her research interests include gender, feminist theory, race relations, the sociology of work and occupations, sociological theory, qualitative methods, and the sociology of emotions. She is the author of *Gender Trials: Emotional Lives in Contemporary Law Firms* (University of California Press, 1995).

DAVID POPENOE is associate dean for social and behavioral sciences and professor of sociology. He lectures on family and community life and social change in advanced societies. His most recent book is *Life Without Father: Compelling New Evidence That Fatherhood and Marriage Are Indispensable for the Good of Children and Society* (Free Press, 1999).

ALVIN POUSSAINT is clinical professor of psychiatry and faculty associate dean for student affairs at Harvard Medical School. He is the director of the Media Center of the Judge Baker Children's Center in Boston and national director of the Lee Salk Center at KidsPeace. He is a highly regarded expert on children, race relations in America, and the dynamics of prejudice. He is coauthor, with Amy Alexander, of *Lay My Burden Down: Unraveling Suicide and the Mental Health Crisis Among African Americans* (Beacon Press, 2000).

JENNIFER DIANE REITZ is an artist and game designer. She has authored an extensive Web site on transsexuality located at http://transsexual.org.

WILL ROSCOE is a trained anthropologist and historian. He is a research associate at the Center for Education and Research in Sexuality at San Francisco State University. His research and writing focus on the study of alternative genders across the world and in Western history. He has written numerous books, including *The Zuni Man-Woman* (University of New Mexico Press, 1992). His most recent book is *Changing Ones: Third and Fourth Genders in Native North America* (St. Martins Press, 1998).

DENISE A. SEGURA is associate professor of sociology at the University of California at Santa Barbara. Her research interests include gender, feminist studies, Chicano studies, race relations, and work.

MARJORIE MAGUIRE SHULTZ is professor of law at the University of California at Berkeley. She is a member of the advisory committee for the National Institute of Health's Office of Research on Women's Health. She serves on the board of The Foundation for Genetic Medicine and is on the scientific editorial board of the *Journal of Gender-Specific Medicine*.

H. KEITH SIGMUNDSON is affiliated with the Department of Psychiatric Services at the Ministry of Health in Victoria, British Columbia.

LOUISE B. SILVERSTEIN is associate professor at the Ferkauf Graduate School of Psychology at Yeshiva University and a family therapist in private practice in New York City. She is cofounder of the Yeshiva Fatherhood Project, a qualitative research study of fathering from a multicultural perspective.

SHERRY TURKLE is professor of the sociology of science at the Program in Science, Technology, and Society of the Massachusetts Institute of Technology. Her most recent research is on the psychology of computer-mediated communication on the Internet. She is the author of *Life on the Screen: Identity in the Age of the Internet* (Simon & Schuster, 1995).

J. RICHARD UDRY is Kenan Professor of maternal and child health and sociology at the Carolina Population Center of the University of North Carolina at Chapel Hill. The main theme of his research interest is the integration of biological and sociological models of human behavior. His current externally funded research projects include Biosocial Models of Adolescent Behavior, which integrates biological and sociological models explaining the development of sexual and other behaviors that begin in adolescence.

GAIL VINES is a writer for *New Scientist.* She is the author of *Raging Hormones: Do They Rule Our Lives?* (Virago Press, 1993) in which she examines the political and social environment that induces science (and followers of science) to look at hormones for explanations of the essence of "femaleness" and "maleness."

REBECCA WALKER is a feminist lecturer, writer, and contributing editor to *Ms.* magazine. She is cofounder of Third Wave, a national multicultural membership organization devoted to facilitating and initiating young women's leadership and activism. Her writing addresses issues such as reproductive freedom, domestic violence, and sexuality. Walker edited the book *To Be Real: Telling the Truth and Changing the Face of Feminism* (Anchor Books, 1995) and coedited, with Ophira Edut, *Adios, Barbie: Young Women Write About Body Image and Identity* (Seal Press, 1998).

THOMAS G. WEST is director and senior fellow of the Claremont Institute and professor of politics at the University of Dallas. He is the author of *Vindicating the Founders: Race, Sex, Class, and Justice in the Origins of America* (Rowman & Littlefield, 1997) which won the 2000 Bagehot Council's Paolucci Book Award for the best book on American history or politics.

KATHERINE K. WILSON is affiliated with The Gender Identity Center of Colorado, Inc., a nonprofit corporation organized in 1978 to provide support to those people who cross-dress, are transsexual, or are experiencing gender identity confusion. The Gender Identity Center of Colorado, Inc. is also an informational and educational resource to the community at large.

PHILIP YANCEY serves as editor-at-large for *Christianity Today* magazine. He has authored numerous books, including *The Jesus I Never Knew* (Zondervan Publishing House, 1995) and *What's So Amazing About Grace?* (Zondervan Publishing House, 1997).

Index